FIGHTS OF OUR LIVES

ELECTIONS, LEADERSHIP, AND THE MAKING OF CANADA

FIGHTS

OF OUR LIVES

ELECTIONS, LEADERSHIP, AND THE MAKING OF CANADA

JOHN DUFFY

IMAGE RESEARCH BY OTHERWISE EDITIONS
DESIGN AND ORIGINAL GRAPHICS BY KNICKERBOCKER DESIGN

HarperCollins*Publishers*Ltd

AN OTHERWISE EDITION

FIGHTS OF OUR LIVES
Text Copyright © 2002 by John Duffy

Original visual graphics, design, and compilation Copyright © 2002 Otherwise Inc.

For information, address:

HARPERCOLLINS PUBLISHERS LTD.
55 Avenue Road, Suite 2900
Toronto, Ontario, Canada M5R 3L2.
www.harpercanada.com

HARPERCOLLINS books may be purchased for educational, business, or sales promotional use.

For information, please write:

Special Markets Department
HARPERCOLLINS CANADA,
55 Avenue Road, Suite 2900
Toronto, Ontario, Canada M5R 3L2.

First edition

ISBN 0-00-200089-X (hardcover)
ISBN 0-00-639150-8 (paperback)

Canadian Cataloguing in Publication Data

Duffy, John, 1963–
Fights of our lives

Includes index
ISBN 0-00-200089-X

1. Elections–Canada–History.
1. Title.
JL193.D78 2002   324.971   C2002-900003-3

RRD 9 8 7 6 5 4 3 2 1
Printed and bound in England

Produced by
OTHERWISE EDITIONS
356A Queen Street West, Suite 300
Toronto, Ontario, M5V 2A2

To my father and the memory of my mother

"It is not enough to be good;
   we must send good out into the world."

CONTENTS

INTRODUCTION

ELECTIONS MATTER.

This statement shouldn't be controversial, but it is. Academics, journalists, and political dissenters of various stripes have worked very hard for many years to convince voters in democracies that elections are inconsequential or, even worse, rigged, so that this or that social group maintains dominance no matter what happens at the polls.

I don't buy it. If any of these fantasies were true, my work in Canadian party politics for almost twenty-five years would have been a lot easier. Voters are unpredictable. It's hard to come up with policies that meet their needs. It's murder to try to push these ideas through the vortex of information and opinion that is modern public discourse. Finally, everything that can go wrong in a complex human system like politics usually does. I work in politics and government because they bubble with meaning and purpose – and the chance to make that positive difference presents itself most profoundly in elections. This idea, that elections are important – the most important piece of our political process – was the genesis of *Fights of Our Lives*.

The most significant elections since Confederation have changed our country in profound and lasting ways, marking important steps in our progress from a federation of agrarian colonies to a dynamic, sophisticated nation. As I came to know our political past, five elections emerged as the ones to watch (historians don't like keeping lists, but most of the rest of us do). When I chose to write a book about these great political contests, I asked myself: Just what was it that made them so special? Why did they engage me as a political strategist, amateur historian, and involved citizen? In the end I concluded that each of them shares certain crucial characteristics. Or to put it another way, each of them meets the criteria for a great election.

The first of these criteria is a good fight that could go either way between strong competitors. We've experienced many of these contests in the 130-plus years since Confederation.

The second criterion is that the election must resolve some nation-shaking question. A controversial tax measure or some soon-to-be-forgotten scandal doesn't qualify; conscription or the Constitution does. Only eleven of the thirty-seven national elections between 1867 and 2000 have centred on such critical issues: 1891 on free trade; 1896 on the Manitoba Schools Question; 1911 on free trade again; 1917 on conscription; 1926 on the monarchy; 1945 on the welfare state; 1957 on one-party rule; 1963 on foreign policy; 1979 and 1980 on the central government's power; and 1988 on free trade once again. These are the elections that have really mattered; they prove that voting day means more than some inconsequential shuffling of the government benches in the House of Commons.

Finally, a great election has to represent a milestone in the development of our political process, in the way we reach our electoral decisions. The broad form of our system has remained the same since Confederation – British-style parliamentary democracy – but within that, the system has been profoundly transformed. There's a world of difference between electoral politics in Confederation's first fifty years, in which the vast majority of voters simply turned out for their ethnic and religious tribes in one canvass after another, and modern campaigns like that of 1988, when huge chunks of the electorate switched their voting intentions once or even twice during a seven-week campaign.

The evolution of national politics has happened incrementally, sometimes one election at a time, alongside the broader changes in Canadian society. Essentially the evolution took place in three stages. First came the politics of the post-Confederation era, dominated by two massive, labour-intensive party organizations exerting significant control over large blocks of ethnically and religiously motivated voters. After the Great War (1914–18) and its confused aftermath, a second system emerged, mainly under the Liberals, featuring a more stripped-down party organization, with regional ministers holding much of the power, and an increasing emphasis on the leader as a means of attracting the growing numbers of swing voters. The third system, which began with a bang in 1957, shoved the parties into the background in favour of a much more direct relationship between large masses of volatile voters and the figure of the national leader. Under the third system, moreover, voters have begun to play a very direct role in deciding policy issues, to the point where, in 1988's free trade campaign, voters threatened to submerge the election itself in a referendum-like vote on the trade deal. The direction of this evolution has been clear: a long-term trend towards greater democracy – and great elections have marked key moments in this evolutionary story.

There we have it: my three criteria of electoral greatness. Each of the five elections featured in this book saw a great fight over a pivotal issue and yielded a nation-altering result, while also advancing the evolution of our system. These fights of our lives have made our country what it is today.

These criteria are the common qualities of the five elections that most seized my attention. They're what makes an election (I've treated back-to-back elections, which really constitute a single, two-part campaign, as one extended contest) stand out as a great one. Laurier's first win in 1896 was a hard-fought affair with a basic issue, French–English relations, at stake. It also saved the tottering political system of the time, which threatened to take down Confederation if it collapsed. The next big shootout came in the double-header of 1925–26, when Mackenzie King turned a constitutional crisis in the House of Commons into an act of nation building on the campaign trail, while simultaneously ushering in the second era of national politics. That system lasted until the Diefenbaker uprising of 1957–58, which is probably my favourite campaign – even though my party (the Liberals) lost – and certainly meets all three criteria. The Clark–Trudeau battle of 1979–80 was significant on all levels: a see-saw struggle with big issues at stake that marked some key shifts in the evolution of our politics. As for the fifth and final election featured here – 1988 – I worked in that campaign and, like everyone who was there, I knew it was going to be a great one even before the starting gun. The intensity of Mulroney's and Turner's performances and the importance of the free trade issue combined with a fascinating result – a majority of anti–free trade votes but a majority of pro–free trade Tory MPs – that showed both the extent of the democratization of our politics and its limits. Elections don't get any better than that.

But you can't fully appreciate these five nation-shaping electoral contests without understanding the elections that came before them and the events that shaped their eras. That's why each of the main chapters in *Fights of Our Lives* follows a description of earlier fights I call "warm-ups." I'm using the term loosely. The elections of 1917 or 1945 weren't really warm-ups, but rather full-fledged battles in which serious issues were at stake. Taken together, however, the elections in each "warm-up" section set the scene for the great election that follows.

Viewed as a continuum, these five elections tell a fascinating story: how Canadians voted themselves a country. If we were to design the best possible Canada we could fashion out of a bunch of just-federated British possessions in the northern half of this continent, we'd make sure the French and English could work together in the government, chart a steady progress from colony to nation, make sure no one party assumed the will and gained the means to trample democracy, establish some sort of common citizenship with an emphasis on human rights, and make sure the country was plugged directly into the emerging global economy. And these are the decisions Canadian voters have made in the five great campaigns.

I have tried to bring to this book the sense of how a campaign looks from the perspective of someone who's inside it. Historians tend to describe how elections illuminate certain key historical themes. For us political types, certain historical themes illuminate how to win an election. In our terms, elections are about deploying major policies or themes and key leadership qualities to build a coalition of often-disparate supporters. We use the policies that jibe with our parties' traditions and outlooks to bring voters into the polling station asking the right questions and coming up with the right answers, questions they can answer only by voting our way.

But policy isn't everything. In fact, blindly peddling a policy outlook can be disastrous. In 1891, for example, a seventy-five-year-old Sir John A. Macdonald headed a tired government that was reeling under defections, scandals, and the death of key figures to face an election against the Liberal Party under its new leader, fifty-year-old Wilfrid Laurier. The Liberals were crying for direction – any direction that differed from the government's, so Laurier steered the party firmly towards free trade. Liberals liked free trade and they liked the Americans. Many Liberals had favoured annexation by the southern neighbour in the Confederation debates. Now Laurier allowed his anti-tariff hawks to package the party's proposal as "commercial union" with the United States. This bold, clear, and forthright position certainly got the party troops excited. Then the old pro who was still prime minister began exacting the price. Macdonald called an election for March 5, 1891, and hammered the Liberals with ringing denunciations of disloyalty to Great Britain. Instead of attacking the Liberal policy, he attacked their patriotism. Macdonald's flag-waving was enough to reverse the Tories' sagging fortunes in Ontario and the Maritimes. He won a come-from-behind victory.

In so doing, Macdonald was manipulating the fundamental fact of Canadian politics to his electoral advantage, what today we might call a "hot button." The hot button connects, in Macdonald's day as in our own, to the fact of our country's divided heritage – the distinguishing element of Canada's history. Every country has a core political fact that all successful national politicians must master. British politics is still shaped by the power of the centuries-old class system. A US senator once said that no matter what an American politician seems to be talking about, he's really talking about race. And regardless of what Canadian politicians are saying, they are always referring to region – an expanded, late-twentieth-century term for the traditional clash of the French and English "races" and their religions.

Canada was founded by regional leaders who cobbled together a union of four existing and highly disparate colonies. Sir John A. Macdonald made the brokering of regional forces by national parties the stuff of nation building. In the roughly fifty years between Confederation and the First World War, it was the racial and religious aspect of our regionalism that mattered; the struggle between English Protestants and French Catholics dominated national politics. Over time, as religious bigotry faded, we came to call it "the language question." When the West came into its own in the 1970s with money and power and a century's worth of alienation under its belt, we started lumping Quebec's and the West's concerns together as "regionalism," with a tip of the hat to Atlantic Canada's unique story and docket of problems. (Ontarians are only now beginning to understand their regionhood, as globalization reveals the province's true position in the world.) Whatever we call this set of facts and tensions and wherever we see it, it's really the same dynamic in national politics: the particular tendencies of the country's geographic parts, as distinct from the things we all share regardless of where in the country we live. "Canada," said no less a political authority than William Lyon Mackenzie King, our longest-serving prime minister, "is a country with too much geography and not enough history." That's still true sixty years after the master said it.

This is not to suggest that region is the only thing that Canadian politics is about. Like the United States and every European country, we have a conventional left-centre-right spectrum. We have populists and elites, family-values evangelicals and urban secular humanists. We can and do mix and match, with different politicians, parties, and factions to reflect each of these views. Sometimes our politics is about these kinds of things – normal issues like the tariff or welfare or the rights of parliament. But that little flag of region is always waving somewhere, sometimes off in the background, but usually way out front. In trying to figure out how our national elections were won and lost, we run inevitably into the regional facts of life. Policy and leadership are the tools that Canadian politicians use to shape coalitions out of regional clay.

Our most successful prime ministers have always struck a balance between regional realities and national dreams. A leader like Sir Robert Borden was mostly a regional operator, who could piece together election wins but couldn't bring the whole country together. His polar opposite was John Diefenbaker, who subordinated every practical consideration to his broadly inclusive "Vision." Macdonald and Mackenzie King got the balance just about perfect, while Laurier, Trudeau, and Mulroney made impressive attempts at building an enduring edifice on the slippery rocks of our divided nationhood. *Fights of Our Lives* illuminates these achievements by focusing on the point of maximum uncertainty – the unpredictable electoral contests that gave their dreams a chance to become realities.

It's one thing to recognize that region is the key to understanding Canada's electoral politics; it's another to convert this understanding into success at the polls. When you look closely at our most successful leaders – the ones who somehow find a way to get elected and re-elected – you see them using certain fundamental electoral strategies over and over again. These strategies can be reduced to three essential approaches, which I've highlighted by imagining them as part of a Canadian political "playbook," a handbook of Canadian electoral success. To make the plays easy to remember, I've given them names: the Quebec Bridge, the Double Tribal Whipsaw, and the Populist Rush. Either alone or in combination they lay bare the underlying dynamics of every federal electoral victory. The Quebec Bridge was improvised out of the chaos of post-Confederation politics by Canada's first great politician, Sir John A. Macdonald, who won election after election by making sure his most reliable regional bloc, the province of Quebec, was properly cared for. After alienating Quebec by hanging Louis Riel in 1885, Macdonald also improvised the second basic play, the Double Tribal Whipsaw, and, in the election of 1891, he played the extremist ends of French and English Canada against the moderate middle, gathering just enough on each side to squeak back into power. Variations of these two basic plays accounted for pretty much all the successful election strategy until 1957, the year John Diefenbaker invented the Populist Rush. In its purest form, it's the only Canadian political play that ignores region – or, rather, unites all regions around a single idea. Since Diefenbaker's day our successful political teams have been running variations of these three plays, to the point where they are perhaps doing more to stifle national politics than to keep it generating new dynamics for the benefit of the country.

My intention in this book has been to portray the big picture: how our leaders' decisions are made within the constraints of our electoral system and in the context of the choices made by voters. Elections matter, and the voters confront their leaders face to face because, as the hours tick down to voting time, the final decision rests with the electorate. *Fights of Our Lives* tells the story of how a sovereign people have exercised this power to build a country that is worthy of them and their dreams.

FROM CREATION TO CRISIS

THE ELECTIONS OF
1867 / 1872 / 1874 / 1878 / 1882 / 1887 / 1891

A GREAT FIGHT NEEDS STRONG and roughly equal antagonists. But in the first years following Confederation there was only one true party on the national scene, the one led by Prime Minister John A. Macdonald. With each succeeding election, however, a national two-party system gradually emerged out of the patchwork of pre-Confederation combinations. The pivotal moment in this evolution came in 1874, when the newly formed Liberal Party handed Macdonald his one and only electoral defeat. For a time thereafter, it seemed that Canada was on the way to a healthy, functioning system along British and American lines, with conservatives and liberals arguing about development strategies, trade policies, and agrarian issues. By the time Edward Blake assumed the Liberal leadership in 1880, he captained a more or less cohesive national party with the real potential of defeating the Tories. But no sooner had this two-party structure emerged than it began to crack, as one issue after another began splitting the parties internally by pitting Catholic against Protestant, French against English, Quebec against the other provinces. By the early 1890s Canada seemed to be descending back into the political chaos from which it had so hopefully emerged less than thirty years before. Lord Durham's gloomy 1839 depiction of Canadian politics as "a struggle not of principles but of races" appeared to be a prophecy of the young nation's impending collapse.

Canada's first national general election, held in the country's 179 ridings during August and September of 1867, was at best a ratification of a *fait accompli*, if not an outright rubber stamp of the interparliamentary deal that brought four of the colonies of British North America together into Confederation. The 1867 campaign would be barely recognizable to a modern voter. There was no federal election authority, so each province conducted its vote according to its own rules. In each riding, voting took place at a different point within a six-week period, with the government in each province getting to choose the most advantageous sequence. Safe government constituencies voted early in the election timetable, giving the party in power momentum as the election progressed. Moreover, in each constituency, voting generally took place over a two-day period, with the first day's returns published before the second day of voting began. In 1867 each riding's federal and provincial vote took place simultaneously, and candidates could stand for both the federal and provincial parliaments. Voting was conducted "openly" – that is, in public – with enumerated electors signing their names to the candidate of their choice.

With the country itself only a few weeks old there was no time for the varied groupings of politicians from the four new provinces to choose leaders, develop platforms, or agree on messages. As a result, Canada's first election saw voters choose many of the same men who had represented them under the previous structure. During the campaign, Macdonald, who everyone assumed would gain the confidence of the new House of Commons and emerge as prime minister, explicitly attacked the idea of party voting. Only in Nova Scotia did the partisan spirit dominate, as a ferocious backlash against Confederation elected Joseph Howe and his multipartisan gaggle of "repealists" to eighteen of the province's nineteen seats. Howe led his band of determined opponents of the new federation – in effect, Canada's first separatist party – as one of many opposition "parties" in the House of Commons.

Once in Ottawa, Macdonald quickly formed a government, mainly drawing from his pre-1867 coalition of Ontario's Tories and Quebec's governing elites. During this first term in power, he relentlessly used the patronage and policy-making powers of the new national government to bind to this core all the like-minded politicians and their followers he could get in the two Maritime provinces. Thus was born Canada's first political party, Macdonald's Liberal-Conservatives.

The opposition was far less cohesive. While Ontario's Reformers, or "Grits," certainly shared with Quebec's progressive *rouges* a suspicion of the established

CONFEDERATION
The Dominion of Canada –
made up of Quebec,
Ontario, New Brunswick,
and Nova Scotia – comes
into existence. John A.
Macdonald *(left)* is sworn in
as Canada's first prime minister. Macdonald had been
the leader of the move-
ment to unite Britain's North
American possessions, a
goal that had taken years
of negotiations. He would
be elected as PM six times
before his death in 1891.
John A. didn't just invent
Confederation, he practically
invented Canadian politics.
Our first PM created the first
national party, the first lasting French–English coalition,
and two of the three basic
strategies for winning a
national election that
are still in use to this day.
Macdonald never really had a
worthy opponent, however –
Wilfrid Laurier was young
and green when the old
chieftain dispatched him in
his last campaign – so never
got to fight a great election.

BETRAYED FOR 80 cents, A HEAD VOTE FOR JONES AND POWER NORTHUP, COCHRAN AND BALCAM DEFENDERS OF THE PEOPLES RIGHTS

VICTORIA.

September 20, 1867
CONSERVATIVES WIN FIRST
GENERAL ELECTION
Although anti-Confederation posters like this one appear throughout disgruntled Nova Scotia, Macdonald's Tories win Canada's first election.

July 1870
MANITOBA BECOMES
A PROVINCE
Manitoba joins Confederation to become Canada's fifth province. *(Above)* The Red River.

July 1871
BC ENTERS CONFEDERATION
Canada's sixth province is created, under the condition that the federal government will build a railroad to the Pacific Ocean. *(Above)* A bird's-eye-view map of Victoria in 1879.

social and political elites, their anti-Catholic and often anti-Quebec outlook ruled out effective cooperation among the two groups. Similarly, few deals could be made with Nova Scotia's anti-confederationists, who wanted to get better terms of entry for their province or exit the new country altogether. The opposition didn't even have a leader; the provinces' respective organizations preferred to campaign and manoeuvre in parliament on their own.

During his first five years in national power, Macdonald's loose following hardened into a disciplined party to which he attracted new adherents. By the mid-1870s it would largely drop the "Liberal" adjective and be known simply as the Conservative Party, although some Tory candidates would run under the old label as late as 1911. In January 1869, for example, he lured repealist leader Joseph Howe across the floor with the offer of a cabinet position. In 1872's late-summer election, the Liberal-Conservatives were sustained by the electorate, with losses in Quebec and Ontario partially offset by the supportive voters of the two new provinces admitted in 1870 and 1871, Manitoba and British Columbia. During the campaign, Macdonald rolled out for the first time his program of a protective tar-

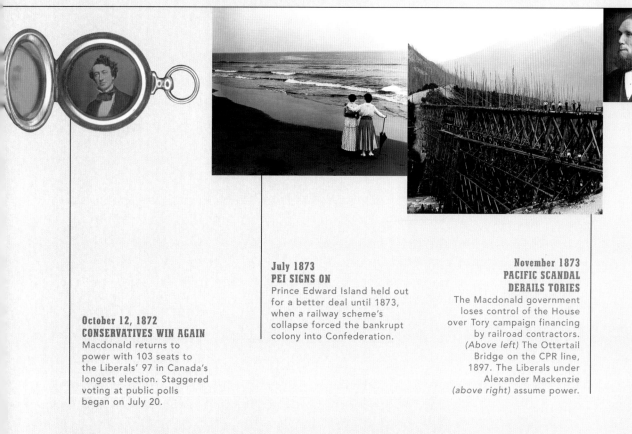

October 12, 1872
CONSERVATIVES WIN AGAIN
Macdonald returns to
power with 103 seats to
the Liberals' 97 in Canada's
longest election. Staggered
voting at public polls
began on July 20.

July 1873
PEI SIGNS ON
Prince Edward Island held out
for a better deal until 1873,
when a railway scheme's
collapse forced the bankrupt
colony into Confederation.

November 1873
PACIFIC SCANDAL
DERAILS TORIES
The Macdonald government
loses control of the House
over Tory campaign financing
by railroad contractors.
(Above left) The Ottertail
Bridge on the CPR line,
1897. The Liberals under
Alexander Mackenzie
(above right) assume power.

iff for manufactured goods, an at-first modest adjustment that he called the "National Policy."

Macdonald's rising political machine was held together not only by government resources but also by private support. His dream of a coast-to-coast railway had harnessed to his party a powerful stable of businessmen, most notably the one to whom he had awarded the railway-building monopoly, Sir Hugh Allan of Montreal. The support was mutual; Allan's Canadian Pacific Railway financed the Liberal-Conservative Party on a vast scale, single-handedly providing the Quebec organization of Macdonald's partner, George-Étienne Cartier, with $3.5 million (in today's dollars) and Macdonald himself with $1.2 million for Ontario. But all this political glue soon proved troublesomely sticky. When the story of this unprecedented combination of money and political favour broke after the election in the fall of 1873, Macdonald's caucus and cabinet melted away in the political firestorm. On November 5, facing certain defeat in the House, our first prime minister resigned and the governor general, the Earl of Dufferin, called upon the opposition to form a government.

But the opposition remained fragmented, lacking even a parliamentary leader. After a brief scramble, the Ontario and Quebec caucuses decided they could all live with Alexander Mackenzie of Lambton County, Ontario, a stonecutter by trade and a dour moralizer. The central Canadian power brokers invited colleagues from the Maritimes to get behind Mackenzie or be frozen out. Once in power, and following victory in Canada's first single-day election held on January 22, 1874, Mackenzie the anti-politician set about undoing the ways of Macdonald and his gang of thieves. He abolished the practice of cross-sitting; no longer could a member simultaneously hold a seat at the federal and the provincial levels. He extended the franchise to men of modest means, introduced the "Australian," or secret, ballot, made election results subject to judicial review, established a supreme court, and appointed good reformers to root out corruption in the federal departments.

Mackenzie made an industrious reformer but a bad prime minister, quite incapable of welding his followers into a cohesive political force. Within his government, "Clear Grits" from the pre-Confederation era battled with both the new Liberals of Ontario, who wanted a rapprochement with their province's Irish Catholics, and with Quebec in general, and the rising *rouge* group who were from Quebec (the progressive political grouping opposed to the church-dominated *bleus*, the party of the conservative, established elites that had allied itself with Macdonald's Tories). To make matters worse, the financial panic of 1873 touched off a major economic depression, which in turn cut immigration from Europe and triggered a wave of emigration from Canada to the United States.

Macdonald lay low as his party re-formed around him and an increasingly desperate electorate began returning to him and to the National Policy. On July 1, 1876, the leader of the opposition spoke before the Liberal-Conservatives of Uxbridge at the first political picnic in Canadian history. Within a year, even grumpy Alexander Mackenzie had gotten into the picnic act, as both leaders devoted increasing time to this newfangled form of campaigning in the crucial battleground of Ontario. At the next election on September 17, 1878, Macdonald was returned to office with a massive 67 per cent of parliament's seats. As the 1870s ended, the sequence of Conservative downfall, redemption, and restoration, followed by Liberal accession, disillusion, and banishment, confirmed the emergence of a two-party system in national politics.

January 22, 1874
MACKENZIE WINS CLEAN CAMPAIGN

A many-headed monster, or hydra, representing the evil of politics – bribery, perjury, calumny, intrigue – threatens to consume the nation. This is how the *Canadian Illustrated News* depicted the failure of party politics that led to the Pacific Scandal and other ills. The antidote? A vote in the general election for Alexander Mackenzie's Liberals, who swept to victory, winning 133 seats to the Tories' 73. From the moment Mackenzie succeeded Macdonald as prime minister, he promised sound and scandal-free government. As proof of his commitment, he immediately did away with staggered elections, making the 1874 campaign the first in which all ballots were cast on the same day. Other reforms followed swiftly.

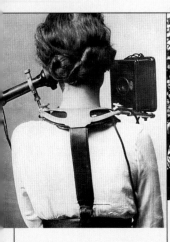

THE POLITICAL BRIAREUS.
THE VERSATILE CANDIDATE MAKING HIMSELF ALL THINGS TO ALL MEN.

August 1876
CANADA STARTS
MAKING CALLS
Alexander Graham Bell
makes the first telephone
call between buildings
when he rings up his Uncle
David in Brantford. *(Above)*
A Bell telephone operator
in 1880 wearing a 6.5-
pound headset.

September 1877
BLACKFOOT SIGN TREATY 7
The Blackfoot under Chief
Crowfoot sign Treaty 7,
the last one of major nine-
teenth-century treaties,
ceding to Canada all the
lands from the Cypress
Hills to the Rocky
Mountains. *(Above)* Chief
Crowfoot *(centre)* with
other chiefs on a visit to
Ottawa in 1886.

September 17, 1878
MACDONALD RETURNS TO POWER
"The Versatile Candidate Making Himself All Things
to All Men," from the *Canadian Illustrated News.*
The Tories win 137 seats to 69 for the Liberals.

Alexander Mackenzie limped out of the leadership in 1880. The opposition caucus chose as his successor Edward Blake, a brilliant, upright Toronto lawyer. Blake understood many of the new requirements of party politics. He worked hard at accommodating his Quebec wing. He also continued the outreach to Catholics, taking his cue from Oliver Mowat's moderate provincial Liberal government of Ontario. He hammered out consensus within the caucus on contentious issues and sought to reconcile them with public opinion. He moderated the Liberals' opposition to the National Policy, recognizing that, because its 1878 restoration had coincided with economic recovery, it was too popular to fight head on. When it came to the business end of politics, however, he emulated the ineffectiveness of his predecessor, failing to win any business support and thus having no money to help bind his loose following together. Canada's liberals naturally began to gravitate towards the provincial level, where better leadership gave them a taste of power. Canada's tradition of balancing a dominant federal party against dominant provincial ones was taking shape.

Prime Minister Macdonald stormed into the new decade with an aggressive restart of the railroad project, a blatant gerrymandering of Ontario's ridings to iso-

April 1881
POPULATION PASSES 4 MILLION
Canada's population had
grown relatively slowly
since 1867, when it stood
at 3.5 million.

June 20, 1882
TORIES WIN EASILY
Cautious new Liberal
leader Edward Blake
backs away from the
Grits' controversial free
trade policy – but to no
avail. Macdonald's
Conservatives win re-
election, tallying 139
seats to the Liberals' 71.

March 1879
ENTER THE NATIONAL POLICY
Macdonald hikes tariffs to protect
Canadian industry. (Above) A later Tory
election poster contrasts the National
Policy with free trade.

late opposition voters, and the appointment of two tough new Quebec lieutenants, J.-A. Chapleau and Hector Langevin. (George-Étienne Cartier had died in 1873.) On June 20, 1882, the *bleu* team delivered its biggest majority ever, part of a national effort that yielded another two-to-one majority in the House.

But in 1885 the recurrence of violence in the North-West Territories – in an area now part of Saskatchewan – set in motion the English–French dynamics that, within a decade, would take the country to the brink of political collapse. Louis Riel's second rebellion was easily put down, but his hanging caused a traumatic and last-ing split along racial and religious lines that played havoc with the parties' delicate coalitions. Seventeen mostly Catholic Conservatives voted with the opposition to commute Riel's death sentence, while twenty-three Protestant Liberals sided with the government. Macdonald's refusal to show mercy infuriated Quebec, which led to the formation of a nationalist provincial party under hitherto-liberal Honoré Mercier and the defeat at his hands of a provincial Tory government in Quebec City. Ontario struck back in October 1886 as a grassroots and press campaign against government-funded French and Catholic schooling broke out, driven by the sense that Quebec had "dictated" national policy in the Riel affair.

November 1885
CPR COMPLETED
Financier Donald Smith drives the ceremonial last spike of the Canadian Pacific Railway at Craigellachie, BC, fulfilling the national dream – and keeping Macdonald's promise to British Columbia.

January 1885
STANDARD TIME ADOPTED
Following the International Prime Meridian Conference in Washington, DC, nations around the world adopt standard time, which is still in use. *(Above)* An entry from CPR chief engineer Sandford Fleming's notebook showing the division of the world into twenty-four time zones.

November 1885
RIEL HANGED
Louis Riel *(centre)* is executed for treason in a Regina jail. His second rebellion had been finally defeated at Batoche in May.

June 1886
TASCHEREAU MADE CARDINAL
Archbishop of Quebec Elzéar-Alexandre Taschereau becomes Canada's first Catholic cardinal.

Macdonald called an election for February 1887, hoping to anchor his inter-racial coalition before it was swamped by the rising racial tensions. All things considered, Quebec held up well, but the *bleu* seat-count did fall from 51 to 33. The rest of the country stayed solid for Macdonald, and Edward Blake resigned as Liberal leader. The Liberal caucus chose young Wilfrid Laurier of Quebec as Blake's successor, mainly for lack of any stronger candidate. The party he inherited was dispirited by yet another defeat, but could cheer itself with its new-found majority in Quebec and the hope that a new leader would wrest that vital province away from Macdonald for good.

John A. Macdonald – indeed, the party system as a whole – appeared to have withstood the gravest of political earthquakes, yet within a few months of his re-election the rift between French and English began widening once again. In early 1888 the Mercier government in Quebec legislated restoration of certain Crown lands to the Jesuit order, from which they had been seized following the conquest of 1760. Several Ontario Tory MPs, led by the fierce, brilliant Protestant militant D'Alton McCarthy, broke with Macdonald on his refusal to override Mercier's bill (a

March 1890
MANITOBA PASSES SCHOOLS ACT
The Manitoba Schools Act passes, folding the province's Catholic, francophone schools (like the one above) into the English, Protestant-dominated public system.

June 1887
LAURIER BECOMES LIBERAL LEADER
The forty-five-year-old Wilfrid Laurier becomes Liberal Party leader, and the party's first from Quebec. He replaces Edward Blake.

June 1889
MCCARTHY FIGHTS JESUIT ESTATES ACT
D'Alton McCarthy forms the Equal Rights Association to oppose Quebec's Jesuits' Estates Act, which compensated the Catholic order for lands seized in 1773.

February 22, 1887
MACDONALD WINS FIFTH TERM
At age seventy-two, Macdonald survives Quebec's post-Riel backlash and defeats Blake's Liberals by 123 seats to 92.

power granted to Ottawa under the terms of the British North America Act). The demands of McCarthy's newly formed Equal Rights Association included the subjugation of the French language in Canada and the abolition of the French and Métis Catholic minority's separate school system in the troubled province of Manitoba. In 1890 the new Manitoba government rode the wave McCarthy had stirred up and abolished its Catholic schools, setting the Manitoba Schools Question on its long rise to the top of the fragile country's agenda.

From Ottawa, Macdonald watched the rising tides of racial militance threaten to engulf his core political strategy of bridging the interests of English and French Canada. His political worries worsened later, in 1890, when the shady administration of government contracts by his Quebec lieutenant, Langevin, erupted into a major scandal. But just when it seemed that the Old Chieftain was finally cornered, Laurier and the Liberals handed him a lifeline when they resolved to fight the next election on their policy of "unrestricted reciprocity" with the United States. This aggressive approach to tariff reduction seemed to the Liberals not only a sound means of reinvigorating an economy once again plunged into cyclical depression, but an effective way of uniting an opposition caucus threatened by the same racial and religious strife that was rending the Conservatives.

Macdonald saw before him an unexpected and timely opportunity to turn the spotlight away from his decaying government and onto his opponent's proposal. He transformed the election called for March 5, 1891, into a two-month attack on Laurier's loyalties, arguing that unrestricted reciprocity was "commercial union" and tantamount to "annexation" by the United States. Macdonald played both of the country's militant extremes against the middle, hammering the Liberals as traitors in English Canada while enlisting his church allies in Quebec to trash Laurier as an anticlerical *rouge* out to destroy Quebec's Catholic character. It worked. The Tories managed to hang on to their majority despite losses in Ontario and Quebec.

The 1891 election was not the first to turn on the trade issue, and certainly not the last. The perennial Canadian question of which way we orient ourselves (to Britain? the US? or beyond?) is with us to this day, even after the issue was supposedly settled in the free trade election of 1988. Yet for all the undeniable importance of the trade issue in 1891 and at other times, its mere presence in that year's election campaign was not enough to make for a great election. While the issue was great and the fight a close match, the election never really touched on the evolution of the system itself. Democracy was not enhanced, the system underwent no evolutionary changes, and the parties' coalitions did not shift all that much. While the nation had grown from roughly 3.5 million people in 1867 to about 5 million in 1891, its politics had remained essentially the same. Campaign '91 was a run-of-the-mill post-Confederation election with a great issue in it, but no more. Beneath the surface debate on free trade, the more fundamental widening of the racial rift continued to pose a growing threat, not only to Macdonald's party but to the very idea that both French and English could participate in national government.

The wily old magician Macdonald had turned the trick again, but it was to be his last. Three months after the election victory, he was dead and his party more divided than ever. Now the transformation of the two great parties' coalitions began in earnest. As his successors struggled to preserve the interracial combination Macdonald had built, the Manitoba Schools Question – begun in 1890 – loomed ever larger, threatening to splinter not only the Tories but the Liberals as well and to leave the young dominion ungovernable. The stage was set for Canada's first great election fight.

THE OLD FLAG,
THE OLD POLICY,
THE OLD LEADER.

Toronto Litho Co.

March 5, 1891
MACDONALD'S LAST HURRAH
In what would turn out to be Sir John A. Macdonald's last election, his party takes 123 seats to the Liberals' 92. Under new leader Wilfrid Laurier, the Liberals campaigned on a policy of free trade with the United States. The Conservative campaign focused on their aging chieftain, with the rallying cry "The Old Flag, The Old Policy, The Old Leader." The seventy-six-year-old Macdonald would pass away a mere three months after the election, having led his party to a majority six times and having won four elections in a row – both records that have never been surpassed. The Tories' 1891 campaign poster is a Canadian political icon that still resonates. In it the three key tools of federal victory are spelled out: appealing policies, strong leadership, and the racial/regional appeal encoded in the British flag, which is used to contrast the loyalist Sir John with that suspiciously French Laurier fellow.

TO THE BRINK

JUNE 23
1896

WILFRID LAURIER

VS.

JOHN ABBOTT

JOHN THOMPSON

MACKENZIE BOWELL

CHARLES TUPPER

It is the evening of August 22, 1894. Under the wooden rafters of Toronto's Union Station, a private passenger car is coupled to the Canadian Pacific Railway's *Atlantic Express*. The opulent sleeper "Saskatchewan" has been loaned by the railway's boss, Sir William Van Horne, to a distinguished passenger. Wilfrid Laurier, the leader of the opposition and of the Liberal Party of Canada, is setting out on a journey that will take him to the far west of the country for seventy days of flesh pressing, luncheons, rallies, and speeches – a full-scale campaign-style tour.

Laurier's big send-off had taken place earlier that afternoon in Brampton, when five thousand citizens turned out at the lacrosse grounds to hear him give an address. Normally, the Liberal leader summers at his home in Arthabaska (part of modern Victoriaville, Quebec), but not this year. Instead, he is about to embark on the grandest political pilgrimage of his career.

The tour's basic purpose is to introduce Laurier to the West, a crucial step in the Liberals' plans for the forthcoming election, expected sometime in 1895. The time has come for him to meet the crowds, scatter his rhetorical stardust on the prairie soil, and bring to the local Liberal organizations the vigour and motivation that only a leader's tour can do. There will be no time during the forty to sixty days of the campaign itself for a two-month junket through the empty plains and mountain passes. The summer of 1894 is the last opportunity for the young leader to show himself to the West.

Most of us think of election campaigns as the period from the call to election day. Politicos, however – a century ago as today – define the whole affair more broadly, with a pre-writ campaign leading up to the issuance, or "dropping," of a writ of election, and then a writ-period campaign until voting day. In our day the pre-writ and writ-period campaigns are equally important. A century ago the writ period was little more than a brute organizational effort that came at the end of an elaborate and more critical pre-writ battle. Laurier's western tour marked the beginning of the Liberals' pre-writ campaign for the

Nation, government, and railroad: each working to conjure the other. Laurier's borrowed sleeper car – his home for two months during his western swing of 1894 – was even dreamier than this one, which belonged to the Canadian Northern Railway that Laurier would establish as PM.

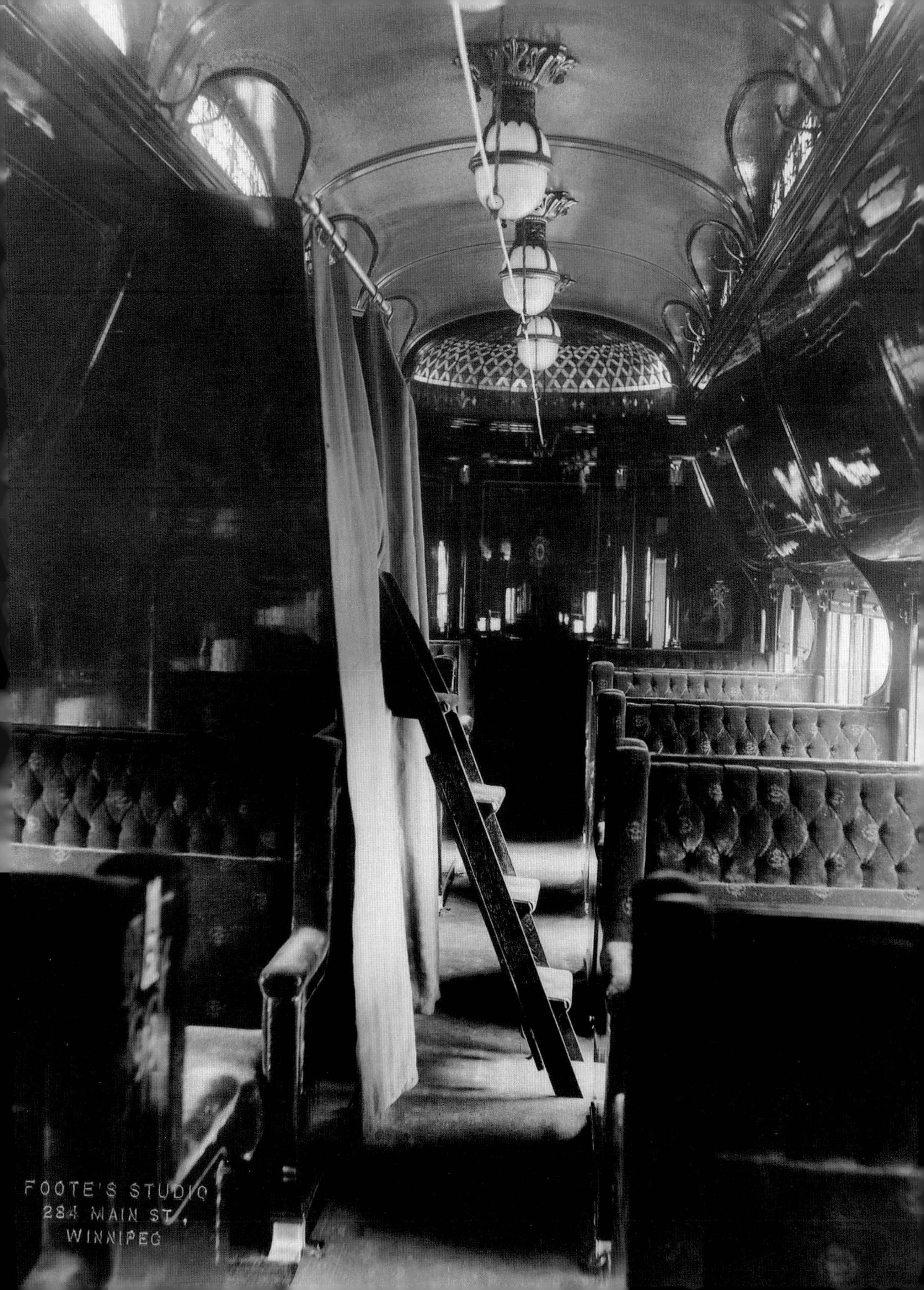
FOOTE'S STUDIO
284 MAIN ST,
WINNIPEG

coming election – a great election that, more than any other in half a century, would be decided by a single issue played out in the lengthy pre-writ run-up to the campaign proper.

It took time not only for Laurier to get to know the region and its players but also for the region to get used to the idea of Laurier as leader. Western Liberals had to be convinced that Laurier wasn't some weird Frenchman who took his orders from the pope, as the Tories were saying. During the trip, westerners would meet the real Laurier, who spoke the King's English better than the king and extolled English liberties better than the English. If Laurier's trip in the late summer of 1894 had been a modern campaign commercial, its tag line would have read "Wilfrid Laurier: A Frenchman you can trust."

Laurier's western foray was about what today's political operatives would call "pre-writ leader positioning" – the pre-election reinforcement of certain positive attributes of their man against the inevitable negative portrayal the

enemy would push during the campaign. Laurier and his team had learned about leader positioning the hard way in the midst of the 1891 election, when the Conservatives, under an ailing Sir John A. Macdonald, had smeared the largely unknown Liberal leader as a disloyal, almost treasonous puppet of the Americans. This negative campaigning had saved the Tories in 1891. But now in 1894, after nearly thirty years of almost continuous rule, the edifice of Tory power was crumbling. The first blow was the death of its architect and master operator, Macdonald, soon after his final election victory. The second was the emergence of a dispute over religious education, the Manitoba Schools Question, which jeopardized the ability of Macdonald's successors to maintain a stable government based on an electoral coalition of French Catholics and English Protestants. Unfortunately for Laurier, the Schools Question threatened the unity of the Liberals as well. Both parties desperately needed to stick together for the election ahead and for the challenge of governing thereafter. Thus, as he headed west, Laurier knew that he fought two opponents: the party of Macdonald's heirs (if it could stay united) and the even more formidable spectre of a hung parliament. A stalemate would result if neither party held together and instead fell prey to fanatical splitters and religious independents in the House of Commons.

The possibility of an ungovernable parliament in which neither party could form a stable government was a standing feature of late nineteenth-century Canadian politics. It had happened before. From 1841 to 1867 Ontario and Quebec had dwelt in miserable coexistence as a single British possession called

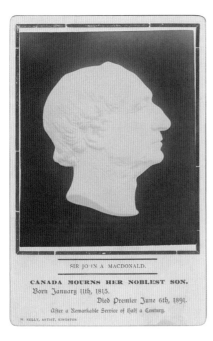

SIR JOHN A. MACDONALD.

CANADA MOURNS HER NOBLEST SON.
Born January 11th, 1815.
Died Premier June 6th, 1891.
After a Remarkable Service of Half a Century.

H. KELLY, ARTIST, KINGSTON.

Cashing in. One of numerous mementoes of Macdonald's passing. Modern equivalents include the magazine special editions published when Pierre Trudeau died.

A FRENCHMAN YOU CAN TRUST

If Laurier, the first French Canadian national leader, hadn't been a passionate believer in all things British, it would have been politically necessary for him to become one. After losing the 1891 campaign over both his Frenchness and his pro-American policies, the Liberal leader relentlessly pitched himself as a super-Brit.

"TWO NATIONS WARRING IN THE BOSOM OF A SINGLE STATE"

the Province of Canada. John A. Macdonald and his associate, George-Étienne Cartier, struggled to hold their bi-racial conservative coalition government together. The alternative group of reformers, led by Ontario's George Brown and Quebec's A.-A. Dorion, was unable to form a government that lasted more than a few months. This deadlock had led directly to Confederation: the wholesale restructuring into a federal union of Quebec, Ontario, and the two Maritime colonies of New Brunswick and Nova Scotia. Now in the 1890s the Manitoba Schools Question once again raised the spectre of deadlock. This time it might break the union of 1867.

The Schools Question posed such a deadly threat because, in nineteenth-century Canada, the basic fact of politics was parties, and the

basic fact of the parties was religion. Both the Tories and the Grits had strong bases in Protestant Ontario and the Maritimes, but neither could form a government without support in French, Catholic Quebec. When the Protestant-dominated government of Manitoba had closed the province's Catholic French schools, in 1890, the ensuing debate had split the country along ethnic and religious lines, threatening the delicate balance of the races within the two parties. In both parties the Manitoba Schools Question inevitably pitted the country's two main religious denominations and racial groups against each other. What if neither party could get its ethnic and religious factions working together? What if neither party could push a program through the House without defections and the loss of a

Lord Durham's 1839 description of Canada held true long after Confederation. Regular displays of religious/racial power echoed the underlying political dynamic. This early twentieth-century Toronto Orange Lodge parade (opposite) is a typical expression of Protestant muscle in arch-Loyalist Ontario. The 1910 nuncio's visit to the Winnipeg suburb of St. Boniface (above) served to remind local, French-speaking Catholics where part of their allegiance lay.

vote of confidence? What if the issues were too tough and the leaders not talented enough for either party to form a successful government?

In the dominion's early years every serious politician was haunted by the fear that the new structure would crack apart as had its predecessor. "Canada" at the time was little more than a federal government (and, after 1886, a railroad). If the federal structure cracked, the country itself could easily disintegrate into its seven provincial parts. And, after that, who knows how expansionist America and over-extended Great Britain would have disposed of a prostrate gaggle of defederating North American colonies? We cannot know what the map would have eventually looked like, but "One Dominion, from sea to shining sea" would have gone down as one of history's mirages.

Canada in the 1890s was a combustible cloud of political, religious, regional, ideological, and jurisdictional vapours. The Manitoba Schools Question was a bright-blue spark. If it blew the two parties to bits, it would probably blow up Confederation as well. The stakes could not have been higher.

Along with Wilfrid Laurier and his wife, Zoë, seven other distinguished passengers boarded the train in Toronto that late August evening. They included the key Liberal power-brokers William Mulock, MP for North York since 1882; Niagara MP William Gibson; MP James Sutherland from the "clear Grit" farm country of southwestern Ontario; Anglo-Quebec backroomer Sydney Fisher;

Philippe-Auguste Choquette, *député* for the South Shore county of Montmagny; Charles Hyman, Liberal Party treasurer from London; and Duncan Cameron Fraser from Nova Scotia. The balance of region, race, and religion aboard the plush passenger car was far more delicate than that of the train's bumpy suspension. Quebec, Ontario, the Maritimes, and the West were all represented. Wives excluded, however, only Laurier and the aging, ineffectual Choquette were French Catholics. Joseph-Israël Tarte, Laurier's controversial Quebec right-hand man, had been noticeably and angrily left behind. The face presented by the Liberal Party to western Canada would be resolutely English and Protestant by a ratio of three to one.

This careful representation of religious affiliation was the key to the Liberal road show. These men represented voting blocs that were infinitely more solid than today's fluid mass of voters. They weren't just the messengers; they were the message. The salient characteristic of nineteenth-century elections was that few voters changed their minds during the campaign. They didn't change their minds much between campaigns either. During the nineteenth century the largest single vote swing from one election to the next was 8 per cent; most of the time it was more like 2.5 per cent. Today, swings of 9 per cent are the norm, and up to 20 per cent of voters can switch sides in the middle of a campaign. Joe and Joan Modern Voter make their voting decision during the campaign – there's no point fretting about politics until you have to. Modern voters flick on the national news for a few nights, glance at the newspapers, watch a few commercials, find out who's ahead in the polls … and decide. The decision is about leadership: Who is the man or woman who can best lead the country? Everything else – which party to support, which candidate to vote for locally – falls out of that basic question.

The nineteenth-century elector thought differently about voting. Instead of putting the leader first, he – and they were all men – voted for the party. A lousy leader was no excuse for switching sides. After all, a man's identity lay in family, church, neighbourhood, and party. Attempts to organize the party system around the clash of ideas were, therefore, only partially successful. By the 1890s in English Canada the Conservatives had become the party of most English and Scots Protestants; the Liberals, that of the Catholic Irish and groups of Low Church Anglicans, Methodists, and Baptists. As they had for generations, Quebec's francophone Catholics divided between the conservative *bleus*, who were generally pro-church, and the anti-clerical, liberal *rouges*, yet all kept a sharp eye out for which party could best protect Quebec's minority interests in the anglophone sea. In a primarily rural country, with most voters staying more or less in place and with few cities blending their ethnic and cultural traditions, these lines stayed clear-cut, generation after generation. In this context, political contests were about muscle: the party that dragged more of its semi-inert tribal voters out to the polls in the key swing ridings won the election.

This heavy hauling required a big machine, much like the train – or perhaps the railway company itself – that was carrying the Liberal dog-and-pony show through the boreal forests of Ontario in late August 1894. The two parties were set up like most big nineteenth-century enterprises: high-overhead, labour-intensive operations, with dozens of layers of management between the faceless gangs on the factory floor and the fellow in the mansion on the hill. Beneath the leader stood, in roughly descending order, the cabinet, the backbenchers, the major financial supporters and their employees, the party newspapers and their staffs, the lawyers receiving government work, the contractors building the untendered public works projects, the riding clubs with their paid organizers, the individual patronage recipients from senators on down to postmen, and finally the volunteers – mostly young men beginning their long climb up the system. This massive corps of middle managers was sustained by government patronage jobs or paid by the parties as local organizers. Today, there's almost nothing and nobody between the folks on the ground and the guy on TV. Sure, there's a "party," but it's more like a lean, fully outsourced, just-in-time services provider than the industrial behemoths of a hundred years ago. As a result, the centre of political action today lies in the relationship between the voters and the leader. A small, nimble crew of pollsters, strategic advisers, and advertising pros manages this relationship. Most of the leader's time is spent preparing for and making appearances, such as Question Period, press conferences, and lunchtime speeches that will pump out The Message to the vast universe of fickle voters. A century ago the leaders were remote figures, holed up in Ottawa, meeting face to face almost exclusively with fellow MPs and churning out endless letters to party operatives across the country. In the 1890s, stroking the middle management was the centre of the action.

The MPs and the local operatives mattered because their enthusiasm and support meant everything. If they were motivated and optimistic, with wind in their sails and money in their pockets, they would recruit the workers and haul the voters to the polls with great efficiency. If they felt otherwise, these functions would be neglected and the riding lost. Leadership wasn't about hi-tech persuasion as it is today; it was a high-touch business of keeping the chieftains, the provincial parties, and the caucus holding much the same position on the

great issues of the day. All this meeting, letter writing, and backslapping took time. And it all went on before an election was called. Once the writ came down from the governor general to set an election campaign formally in motion, the leader could do little more than get on a train and attend rallies of people who had already decided to support him.

Higher up in the system, it became harder to make everyone happy. The man at the top had to keep together an array of bosses who represented very antagonistic groups. Getting all the Methodists and Anglicans in, say, Orangeville to stop fighting over temperance and to vote together on election day was one thing. It took real talent to get that MP for the Protestants of Orangeville to cooperate with the *député* of a bunch of French Catholics in Trois-Rivières. But that's what it meant to run the country – to "keep Scottish Presbyterians and French Canadians in the same party," as the great economic historian Harold Innis astutely said. If the leader started choosing sides between Mr. Orangeville and M. Trois-Rivières, someone would get mad. And in the nineteenth century angry MPs didn't just mean trouble at election time; they meant caucus revolts, leadership coups, and collapsing governments.

In the period 1867–1917, known to political historians as the Great Party era, keeping the party machine together was everything. Nowadays, the worst thing about a squabbling party is that it *looks* bad. It gets those fickle voters thinking: If the leader can't run his own team, how can he run the country? In the nineteenth century a squabbling party *was* bad. A disunited cabinet could replace its leader. (Leadership conventions didn't occur until 1919, and leadership review by party members not until the 1960s.) A disunited caucus could force a government's fall. A disunited party machine could throw an election. In the 1890s two disunited parties would likely have spelled

NAME: Wilfrid Laurier

PARTY: Liberal

ROLE: Opposition leader since 1887, defeated in 1891 election. French, Catholic Quebecker. Anglophile. Free-trader.

the end of Canada. Most electors would probably have gone about their voting business in their usual ways, but if a few militants here and there split away from their parties and gave just enough votes to certain splinter candidates, these wild-card members would hold the balance of power in the House and the whole party-government-country house of cards might start to collapse from the top down.

Travelling in his compartment in the "Saskatchewan," sitting in amiable silence with his wife of twenty-six years or simply watching the dark, endless Ontario forest roll by, Wilfrid Laurier had plenty of time to think about his young country's delicate political health. The fifty-two-year-old native of St-Lin, north of Trois-Rivières, was entering his twenty-fourth year of elected politics, his seventeenth as a federal MP, and his eighth as federal Liberal leader. He had gained the leadership by default, chosen on the resignation of his unsuccessful predecessor, Edward Blake, by a reluctant caucus that could find no better candidate. His first national campaign in 1891 had been a disaster. Laurier had run on a clear policy proposition – "commercial union" with the United States – only to be bested by Sir John A. Macdonald, who twisted the election into a fight to preserve the nation's British character. The French, Catholic, pro-American Laurier didn't stand a chance; it was a cruel lesson from a hard master in the realities of national politics.

Laurier came by his ideological clarity honestly. Since his days as a rebellious student at the classical college at L'Assomption in the

1850s, he had made the pursuit of liberty his political compass. He skipped classes and masses to hear local orators sing the praises of liberal ideas such as universal male voting, free trade, and the separation of church and state. At McGill University's faculty of law, he became acquainted with such giants of the Anglo-American liberal tradition as John Milton, Sir William Blackstone, Thomas Macaulay, and Abraham Lincoln. Over the years he kept up his light church attendance and his deepening acquaintance with liberal thought until he knew the ideas as his own.

Liberals behaving badly. This 1891 pro-Tory cartoon shows traitor/free-trader Laurier and his front-bench crew plotting the American annexation of Canada.

Laurier's attraction to liberalism was easy to understand. To him and his fellow-believers it stood for "progress"– the nineteenth century's watchword – which meant industrial development, technology, liberty, new ideas, and a better life for all. In the 1850s there were two kinds of countries: liberal societies like Britain, France, and the United States, and all the others, backward places mired in ignorance, tyranny, and poverty. Laurier knew which kind of place he wanted Quebec to be. And he saw a liberal, democratic, federal Canadian state as the vehicle that would carry Quebec into the light.

This liberalism put Laurier in the middle of an intense ideological struggle over the role of the Catholic Church, which stood in staunch opposition to liberalism and all it entailed. The issue of the church's role pervaded Quebec politics at mid-century. On one side were the conservative, pro-church *bleu* "ultramontanes" (their name taken from French compatriots who deferred in politics to the pope "over the mountains"). Ultramontanism was more than a political tendency; it was an international current of thought, a comprehensive approach to faith and to politics. "Let each say in his heart," wrote Bishop Bourget, Montreal's great ultramontane prelate, "I hear my curé, my curé hears the bishop, the bishop hears the Pope, and the Pope hears our Lord Jesus Christ."

Laurier was on the other side of this "Holy War," firmly aligned with the *rouges*, Quebec's liberals. If the *bleus* were the heirs to the province's authoritarian, conservative, and clerical traditions, the *rouges* carried the equally proud banner of Quebec's democratic, modernizing, and secular tendencies. The *rouges* were hell-raisers. When electors asked the *curés* about their Catholic duty in elections, he priests usually answered: "Le ciel est bleu et l'enfer est rouge." This association of the *rouges* with hell had deep roots. In the rebellions of 1837 their grandfathers had stood with the rebel Joseph Papineau against the crown and the church. In the Confederation debates their fathers under A.-A. Dorion had fought for the rights of the provinces in the new dominion while the bishops backed Macdonald to the hilt. Overseas, in the Paris Commune uprising of 1871, workers waving red banners had executed royalist priests.

The intellectual duel between *rouge* and *bleu* underpinned Quebec politics. The *bleus* controlled the government in Quebec City for twenty-five of the thirty years following

Confederation, while the *rouges* formed an angry opposition. In Laurier's first incarnation as a provincial politician from 1871 to 1877, it had been easy to push his *rouge* ideology. He continued to argue his uncomplicated, optimistic beliefs even as he jumped into the federal arena. "You will see together," he said, campaigning in a federal by-election in 1878, "those who are attracted to all that is ancient and you will see together those who are always disposed to reform … For my part, I am a liberal. I am one of those who think that always and everywhere in human things there are abuses to be reformed, new horizons to be opened up, and new forces to be developed."

Once Laurier entered national politics (a logical move for a bilingual anglophile *Canadien* at a time when the dominion government was far more powerful than those of the provinces), things got more complicated. The

BLEU AND ROUGE
WHICH SIDE ARE YOU ON?

The hundred-year duel between liberal "progress" and conservative "order" was fought intensely in Quebec on several fronts. The struggle echoed the larger political battles of the old country, France, which originated in the French Revolution of 1789.

BLEU	ROUGE
CHURCH	STATE
ROYALISM	REVOLUTION
RELIGION	LAW
NAPOLEON III	PARIS COMMUNE
CHURCH TEACHINGS	VOLTAIRE
DORION	CARTIER
CROWN	PAPINEAU
ROME	LONDON, NEW YORK

The 1885 North-West rebellion led by Louis Riel (here seen defending himself in a Regina courtroom) was crushed by Prime Minister Sir John A. Macdonald, the Canadian Militia, and the Mounties (who issued medals like the one below to commemorate the event). But even as the Mounties buried Riel's coffin *(bottom left)*, his ghost struck back at his Tory "assassins" when Macdonald's support in Quebec rapidly sank.

THE LAST LAUGH

SEATS BEFORE
Quebec party standings from the 1882 election
TORY 51
LIBERAL 13

SEATS AFTER
Quebec party standings from the 1887 election
TORY 33
LIBERAL 32

BOXER AMMUNITION
FOR 577 BORE
SNIDER RIFLES
1867

NORTH WEST 1885 CANADA

THE MARTYR

LOUIS DAVID RIEL.

SIR ALEX. CAMPBELL.
HON. A.W. McLELAN.
HON. THOS. WHITE.
SIR JOHN A. McDONALD.
HON. JOHN COSTIGAN.
HON. MACKENZIE BOWELL.
HON. G.E. FOSTER.
HON. J.H. POPE.
HON. T. CARLING.
HON. J.S.D. THOMPSON.
SIR HECTOR LANGEVIN.
SIR A.P. CARON.
HON. J.A. CHAPLEAU.

AND HIS ASSASSINS.

ideological battle between conservative and liberal – which was going on all over the Western world – was inevitably bound up in Quebec with the question of *la survivance*. The minute anyone started thinking federally, a clash of liberal *rouge* values and conservative *bleu* ideas would turn into a question of how French, Catholic Quebec could survive and flourish on an English, Protestant continent. The *bleus* believed that survival would come from a strong church protecting Quebec's identity. They believed that Quebec should deal with *les anglais* as a united, Catholic collectivity. Under federal *bleu* leaders like the renowned George-Étienne Cartier, a united Quebec could determine the government in Ottawa and enlist that government in the defence of its French, Catholic soul. After Confederation, Quebec delivered between half and three-quarters of her seats to Macdonald's Tories and usually provided up to half the government's caucus. With a head start like that at election time, Macdonald could afford split decisions in Ontario, the Maritimes, and the West. In return, Sir John let the *bleu* leadership and the church run things at home. It was a sweet deal all around, unless you were a *rouge*, stigmatized as both a heretic and traitor.

As Laurier matured in federal politics, he struggled to break the *bleus'* monopoly on patriotism, Catholicism, and national reconciliation. Laurier moved into this territory not only out of a desire to win votes, but also from the deep conviction that, for Quebec, a close association with English Canada and its institutions was the surest means of joining the elite club of successful liberal societies. This link posed certain challenges, however: not only did Laurier have to convince French Catholics that liberalism did not mean dissolving into an English Protestant stew but, once he became a federal party leader, it became necessary as well to persuade English Protestants that he

wasn't some French agent of the pope. It was a cruel paradox. In English Canada the Tories flayed Laurier for being too French and too Catholic; in Quebec they flogged him for being not French and not Catholic enough. The intellectual man of ideas was easily nailed to the political cross of race and religion. Welcome to the big leagues, Monsieur.

As Wilfrid Laurier's train pulled out of Sault Ste. Marie on August 27, with another successful local rally behind him, the leader could reflect on all he'd learned since 1891. He had tuned the presentation of his ideas to the key of race, carefully emphasizing the fundamentally British character of his liberal beliefs. He now played the role of pluperfect Brit with aplomb and sincerity – Laurier truly believed that British parliamentarianism was the highest form of government, and it showed. Back home in Quebec, he let others do the church bashing and watched with anticipation the slow erosion of *bleu* power.

While Laurier was growing more adept at national politics, the inexorable forces of time and change were loosening the Conservative grip on Quebec. Macdonald's 1885 hanging of Louis Riel had damaged the *bleus* severely and permanently. Later, internal quarrels broke out between hard-line ultramontanes, called *castors*, and moderates who continued, confusingly, to call themselves *bleus*. From Confederation until Riel's death, the Tories had won, on average, forty-three of Quebec's sixty-five seats. In the first election after Riel's hanging, the number sank to thirty-three; in 1891 it went down to twenty-eight. In Ontario the contest between Conservative and Liberal had grown more competitive as well, such that the province was evenly split by 1891. The Tories' only salvation lay in an ongoing majority position in the Maritimes, along with Macdonald's wins in the new and growing West: eight of eleven in 1882; fourteen of

CORRALLING THE WEST

French Canada's leaders initially hoped to build on the region's small French-Indian-Métis prairie society, but their hopes were swamped first by immigration from Ontario and the US, then by the defeat and execution of Riel. In this new west – English, Protestant, expansionary – Conservatives and Liberals would vie for dominance, seeking to corral the rising region into their existing coalitions.

NAME: Thomas Greenway

PARTY: Liberal

ROLE: Premier of Manitoba since 1887. Protestant. Free-trader, provincial rights enthusiast. Passes anti-Catholic schools bill in 1890.

NAME: Clifford Sifton

PARTY: Liberal

ROLE: Attorney general of Manitoba from 1891. Protestant. Political boss of Manitoba, newspaper owner, key Laurier man.

fifteen in the election five years later; and the same lopsided number again in 1891.

After 1891 Laurier restlessly scanned the regions for a potential breakthrough. To his eye, the path to power ran through Ontario to the West. He dreamed of harnessing to Quebec's emerging *rouge* majority the strength of Sir Oliver Mowat's enduring Ontario Liberal government, to construct "a party built on Lower Canada and on the Party of Mowat in Ontario." After thirty years of Tory rule in Ottawa, provincial governments had naturally become the powerhouses of Canadian Liberalism: solid, muscular organizations like Mowat's, the Nova Scotia administration of W.S. Fielding, and Manitoba's new Liberal dynasty, led by Premier Thomas Greenway but masterminded by the owner of the *Winnipeg Free Press*, provincial attorney general Clifford Sifton. Even if redistribution would give the West only 17 of the Commons' 213 seats, every bit helped. And in the long run, seeds planted in the expanding West were sure one day to yield a bumper crop.

The *Atlantic Express* rounded the Lakehead while August slipped away. As the train turned straight towards the sunset, a new Canada beckoned Laurier: a wide-open land of free-trading farmers, drawn from all over Europe and America and working together to build a new society. Sure, there was conflict, but out here the politics of ideas predominated: liberal versus conservative, free trade versus protectionism, farmer versus manufacturer, little guys versus big interests – a politics familiar to Laurier from his fights in the academy and in the Quebec legislature. For Laurier, the West held out the great hope that the politics of the future would be a principled battle between the liberal progress he called "the charm of novelty" and the conservative "charm of habit" – not the stale, frustrating

politics of race and religion that bedevilled the old Canada that now lay far behind.

At 2 a.m. on Saturday, September 1, the "Saskatchewan" was unhitched from the *Atlantic Express* to lie for the night in a siding at Rat Portage, Ontario (fortunately renamed Kenora in 1905). At 10 that morning all was in readiness. The entourage was led through a tour of Rat Portage's main attractions (a new dam, a flour mill, a mine, and a steamer ride on the *Lake of the Woods*). At 8 that night a thousand citizens crowded into the town's curling rink, passing through an arch illuminated by two hundred electric lights spelling out "Laurier." First William Gibson, then William Mulock, then a local English Protestant and a local French Catholic gave warm-up speeches. When Laurier finally spoke he uttered a liberal cry for a new politics of ideas in place of the Tories' racial appeals coded as affirmations of loyalty. "When Tory interests are on top, we hear of loyalty … We want to have free trade, but are called disloyal … What is going to make this country, is it a crying for loyalty, or is it the buying of the goods on our shelves?"

Two days later in Winnipeg the big show began. From noon on, a crowd of hundreds mobbed the railway station to greet the incoming train. "The ninetieth [regiment] band blew forth its stirring welcome; there was tremendous cheering as the Liberal leader and the gentlemen accompanying him were seen on the platform and steps of the car, and then the band played 'God Save the Queen.'" The welcome was even more tumultuous than its Liberal organizers had hoped. "The party made their way to the ladies' waiting room, where it was intended to have a little informal reception, but it was at once seen that any attempt at introduction and hand shaking would consume an hour and be attended with great difficulties; so it was thought best to ask Mr. Laurier to make a short speech of a minute or two in length." Laurier said a few brief words before rolling off in triumph to an official reception.

It was here in Winnipeg that Laurier's plans for victory, and for a new politics of ideas, would be put to the real test. In 1894, as it does today, the city at the confluence of the Red and the Assiniboine rivers represented the symbolic mid-point in Canada. Winnipeg was not only the place where East and West met; its location just above the headwaters of the Mississippi made it an ideal funnelling spot through which the riches of Canada could be poured south towards the markets in the burgeoning Midwest. Manitoba stood at the intersection of Canada's two economic pathways: the nationalist east–west reach and the continentalist north–south pull. The rail yards in Winnipeg's North End neatly symbolized the economic questions facing the country, a new politics of issues and ideas, of class and economic interests, and, by extension, a new Canada free of racial and religious discord. But the city's racial composition, with a 7 per cent Franco-Manitoban minority concentrated on the east side of the Red River in St. Boniface, symbolized the enduring legacy of the old Canada's divided heritage. And in St. Boniface's parish halls and modest wooden houses, the French Catholic minority brooded on a terrible injustice: the closing of the Catholic school system four years before by the English Protestant majority. Which

For a little logging town like Rat Portage *(opposite top)*, a VIP visit was a chance to show off – hence the archway's lumber-industry theme. But the real show was Laurier himself, who spoke *(opposite)* from a platform groaning with symbols of empire, nation, and racial reconciliation.

WINNIPEG
THE BATTLE LINES

Winnipeg in 1894 was a frontier city profoundly divided: between the working class in the North End around the CP rail yards zone (Canada's first multicultural neighbourhood), and the commercial and professional South and Central districts. In classic Canadian fashion Winnipeg was also divided linguistically by the Red River, which hived off francophone, Catholic St. Boniface from the rest of the city. Laurier tried to address each of these constituencies by appealing to its desire for progress, however defined.

Laurier offered the city's Anglo commercial class free trade: markets for the products that paid their bills.

To francophones, Laurier offered himself: a Catholic Quebecker with a genuine shot at the country's top job.

Laurier offered the city's industrial workers a vague commitment to social reform and "progress."

Winnipeg did Laurier wish to address? The city divided by the railway or the one divided by the river? Issues such as economics and class, or questions of religion and race? Laurier's intellectual preferences dovetailed nicely with the strong advice of his senior Manitoba advisers: duck the Manitoba Schools Question and stay on trade.

That night the real pre-writ campaign took off. Six thousand onlookers – an impressive portion of Winnipeg's forty thousand residents – packed Brydon's Skating Rink to double its capacity. They were jammed into aisles, onto window ledges, and even hung from rafters, "where the advantage of a good view and easy hearing compensated for the discomforts of the position." Laurier looked out over a sea of people and placards with such slogans as "Tariff for revenue only!" and "No class legislation." He spoke of "the rights of the masses" and claimed for the Liberal tradition "the good Saxon word, freedom; freedom in every sense of the term, freedom of speech, freedom of action, freedom in religious life and civil life, and last but not least, freedom in commercial life." This introduction took him to the heart of his speech, a passionate case for free trade. "Manitoba is a young giant manacled. The limbs of Manitoba are bound to the ground, but if they were set free [by an end to Macdonald's protectionist National Policy] and the shackles removed, [the province] would go forward with leaps and bounds to a period of unprecedented prosperity." As the rink shook with cheers, Laurier smiled. So what if free trade had dragged him down in the last election? This was Manitoba, and word of his speech would trickle back slowly to the East. More important, this was what his audience had come to hear. Above all, this was what politics should be about: freedom versus slavery, producers versus manufacturers, Liberal continentalism versus the

THE DISPOSSESSED

Laurier could feel the pain of the French-speaking people of Manitoba, but he was coming to realize there was nothing he could do about it.

The coming of the railroad ended the Métis buffalo-hunting economy, forcing many to abandon their traditional way of life.

Riel's defeated general Gabriel Dumont stands by his tent after the capture of Batoche, which ended the North-West Rebellion.

Manitoba's government moved on Catholics in 1890, merging schools (like this one in St. Léon) into the public system.

Tory National Policy, and enlightened progress versus the dead hand of tradition. It sure beat the hell out of talking religion, especially when your opponents were saying you were secretly on the pope's payroll.

It wasn't until the next morning, September 4, that the old demons caught up with the Liberal leader, forcing him to face what politics in Victorian Canada was really about. An impromptu drawing-room reception for all comers at the mansion of his host, Augustin Richard, occasioned a visit from the leading Catholic citizens of the town. They had come to discuss the Schools Question.

On February 12, 1890, the Liberal government of Manitoba had introduced two bills that effectively abolished Manitoba's existing system of separate schools by collapsing the Catholic system of the French-speaking minority into the public, Protestant-dominated one. The move went straight to the heart of the delicate, twenty-year-old structure of the Dominion of Canada – one that had been built carefully in 1867 around the country's racial and religious fault-lines. Confederation could be acceptable only if the provinces, Quebec in particular, maintained their distinct ethnic and religious characteristics. Provincial control of education was key. Yet the new country would have dignity and worth only if the rights of minority populations in every province could be protected. Two protections had been written into the British North America Act of 1867: explicit constitutional guarantees of minority education rights and the federal government's powers of reservation, disallowance, and remediation that enabled Ottawa to override certain types of objectionable provincial legislation. Manitoba's new laws virtually dared the federal government to invoke these controversial override provisions. It seemed as though a bomb had been placed in the midst of the growing and shifting latticework of federal and provincial rights and powers.

In Quebec the effect had been most pronounced. Manitoba's French and Métis Catholics were historical orphans, made so by the ruin of the Métis buffalo hunting economy and the failure of the Riel rebellion in 1885. French Quebec had rooted for the rebels and then exploded when Riel was hanged.

NAME: Honoré Mercier

PARTY: Parti National

ROLE: Quebec premier 1887–91. Catholic. Blends soft *rouges* and nationalist *bleus* into Quebec-rights party after Riel's death.

Party lines had seemed instantly to dissolve. The *bleu* organ, *La Presse*, had thundered: "Henceforward there are no more Conservatives nor Liberals … There are PATRIOTS AND TRAITORS." On Sunday, November 22, 1885, forty thousand people had gathered at Montreal's Champs de Mars to mourn Riel and to burn effigies of Macdonald and his Quebec ministers. They also had come to listen to Honoré Mercier, a provincial Liberal whose call to unite the threatened nation triggered a political earthquake: the founding of Quebec's first nationalist party. Two years later, Mercier's party would go on to form the government in Quebec City.

The lions of English Canada had roared back. Referring to Quebeckers' "arrogant attempts to dictate clemency for a convicted rebel," the *Toronto Mail* bellowed in 1885, "Let us solemnly assure them again that rather than submit to such a yoke, Ontario would smash Confederation into its original fragments, preferring that the dream of a united Canada should be shattered forever." Thus, the Manitoba Schools legislation, coming only

five years after the execution of Riel, seemed at once a death-knell for the province's remaining francophone community and a portent of doom for Catholic minorities in the remaining provinces. It appeared designed to pulverize the dominion.

The Manitoba francophone minority, led by its archbishop, Alexandre Taché, had cast about for a higher power to give it back its schools. The Liberals looked unpromising: their *rouge* wing had no particular love for religious education, and the entire party was staunchly opposed to federal intrusion into areas of provincial jurisdiction such as education. The Conservatives under Sir John A. Macdonald were more attractive. The House of Macdonald was home to the Quebec clergy and its *bleu* allies in the secular world. Yet the bishops were not optimistic that Macdonald would go far to protect the Catholics of Manitoba. Archbishop Louis-François Laflèche of Trois-Rivières, one of Quebec's most influential clerics, wrote to Taché: "I have no more confidence than I must in our *Canadien* ministers in Ottawa and their Chief, Sir J. But what I believe is that you would be even more badly treated if the Liberals took power federally."

A shrewd man, Laflèche: he was right to fear the Liberals but also to doubt the Tories' resolve. The essence of Macdonald's party had been the encouragement of moderation and compromise among the bulk of the caucus and the cabinet. But his death following the victory in 1891 robbed the Tory coalition of its master operator just when he was needed most.

It was in the cockpit of the Tory caucus that the nation-wrecking potential of the Schools Question first began to be truly felt. Amid the growing concern over Manitoba, the constituency of religious and ethnic moderation within the Tory machine was hammered from both sides even as it cast about for a successor to Sir John A. In the Ontario delega-

tion the brashly pro-British and Protestant
D'Alton McCarthy and Clark Wallace, grand
master of the ultra-Protestant Orange Order
for British North America, raged against moderate candidates like Sir John Thompson, a
Methodist convert to Catholicism (or "pervert"
in the charming Protestant phrase of the time).
The Quebec wing tottered under the aging and
scandal-tainted Hector Langevin, with *castors*
and *bleus* at each other's throats. Individual
leadership aspirations were afoot as well. Such
a pit of militancy, mistrust, and ambition
was the Tory caucus that the only successor
to Macdonald on whom they could all agree in
June 1891 was John Abbott, their elderly leader
in the Senate. Abbott's most memorable contribution to the Canadian quote book would be
"I hate politics."

NAME: D'Alton McCarthy

PARTY: Conservative

ROLE: Key militant Anglo
Protestant backbench
MP in Tory governments
from 1870 on.

The Abbott government played for time,
dumping the Manitoba Schools Question onto
the Supreme Court of Canada, which ruled
against Manitoba in October 1891. Manitoba
promptly appealed to the highest authority, the
Judicial Committee of the Privy Council in
London, which ruled in July 1892 that the
legislation was constitutional. Still refusing
to face the issue, the federal government early
in 1893 began tossing to the Canadian courts
the question of whether it could lawfully over-
rule the Manitoba government, hoping to be
told it could not. Time and again the courts
ruled the matter political; time and again the
politicians worked up new avenues of appeal. In
Winnipeg in the summer of 1894, as Laurier sat

in the airless room facing the imploring questions of his Manitoba brethren, the court game
was still going on. All that had really changed
was that Abbott had resigned and John Thompson
had become prime minister in December 1892.

While the Tories played for time, Laurier
also stalled, calling for more facts and further
investigations. As opposition leader, there had
been no need for him to act, and he had no
strategic interest in raising a racial and religious issue to the top of the political agenda.
The issue had divided the Liberals almost as
badly as the Conservatives. With luck, the
whole wretched matter would be over with
by the time the election rolled around.

That morning on September 4 the little
delegation of Manitoba Catholics grilled an
uncomfortable Liberal leader for about an
hour, answering his calls for facts with more
facts, his pleas for compromise with evidence
of their own willingness to make concessions.
In the end Laurier escaped the meeting without making any binding commitments or
unduly offending his co-religionists – who,
after all, could not have been expecting
much from him anyway.

To have toured Manitoba with no Schools
Question splatter stains on him was no mean
feat. That night the Liberal pre-writ campaign
got back on track towards its key strategic goal
– making Anglos comfortable with Wilfrid.
Speaking in the packed town hall in St. Boniface, Laurier passed over the schools matter as
quickly as possible and spent a good deal of

NAME: John Abbott

PARTY: Conservative

ROLE: Prime minister,
1891–92. Quebec Protestant,
senator, Macdonald's successor. Fails to handle party
religious divisions. Quits
for health reasons.

NAME: John Thompson

PARTY: Conservative

ROLE: Prime minister, 1892–94. Former Nova Scotia premier. Catholic convert from Methodism. Tries to balance party religious divisions.

time locating his liberal credentials in the British Isles. He defined himself as "a Liberal of the school of Daniel O'Connell, Gladstone and others." Nice messaging, to use a 1990s term. There's Daniel O'Connell, the great liberator of the Irish Catholic peasantry in the 1830s, who never raised a hand against the authority of the British Crown – a stirring but safe appeal to the Irish Catholic Liberals of Winnipeg. And William Gladstone, Britain's "Great Commoner" prime minister, moderate Liberal, and the epitome of reform over revolution – nice to the Irish, too. Great stuff.

As Laurier and his wife boarded the "Saskatchewan" and settled down for the overnight run to Regina, the leader could rest more easily. Federal remediation? Provincial rights? Why, Saskatchewan wasn't even a province yet. In 1896 Regina was the capital of something called the North-West Territories, a sea of grass stretching from the Arctic Ocean to the US border and from Manitoba to the passes of the Rockies.

On the morning of September 5 the Laurier road show rolled into Regina. That afternoon he addressed a crowd at the local curling arena. He was in the clear now, hammering on his favoured subjects: trade, liberty, and prosperity for the West. Later he joined 113 prominent citizens for a non-partisan banquet, at which, the *Regina Standard* reported, "a happy departure was made from the time-honoured but exceedingly doubtful custom of a lengthened programme of speeches."

So went the trip's remainder – a sprint to the coast, with a few whistle stops ending in Port Moody, BC, on September 8. Laurier spent his week there touring around the Lower Mainland and eastern Vancouver Island, delivering much the same message from place to place: economic development through free trade, liberty, and justice, combined with the subtle assertion that he wasn't some dangerous Frenchman out to impose Catholicism on English Canada. On the 8th in the Fraser Valley town of Mission, a local journalist reported that Laurier departed from his usual text to explain that, "accompanying him on his trip was a gentleman, an Englishman, Mr. Fisher, ex-MP for Brome county, Que., and a Protestant, who would bear him out in every statement he made concerning the tolerant manner in which the people of Quebec treated each other. (Applause.) He felt that many were labouring under a misapprehension in reference to this matter." The long road back took him to meetings and rallies in Edmonton on October 20, Calgary two days later, and an impressive number of smaller communities throughout the prairies before he returned at last to Montreal on October 29.

As his train rolled homeward through the brilliance of autumn, Wilfrid Laurier could take considerable satisfaction in what he had accomplished. He had generated pre-campaign momentum in a part of the country whose seats could go either way at election time. He had successfully positioned himself as a moderate British economic liberal, raised the trade issue in that part of the country where it was least likely to provoke a loyalist backlash, and vigorously stoked the Liberal machine. Above all, as he gazed out from the thin line of the railway, Laurier had witnessed his country of the future, the world that lay beyond the politics of race and religion. As November began, he rested at home in Arthabaska before returning

ALL ABOARD:1894
LAURIER REACHES OUT TO THE WEST

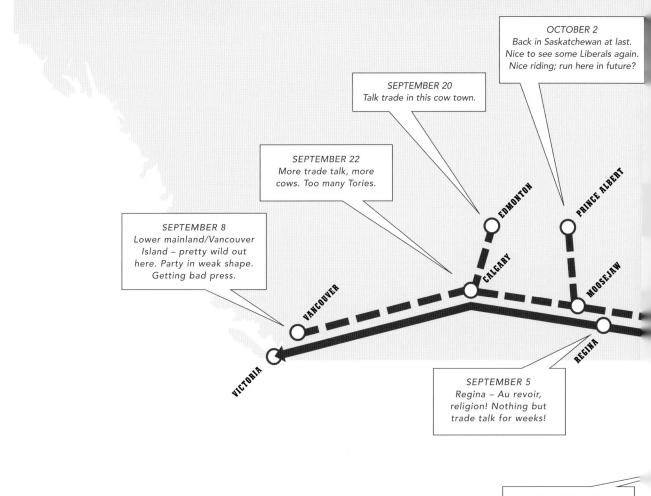

OCTOBER 2
Back in Saskatchewan at last.
Nice to see some Liberals again.
Nice riding; run here in future?

SEPTEMBER 20
Talk trade in this cow town.

SEPTEMBER 22
More trade talk, more
cows. Too many Tories.

SEPTEMBER 8
Lower mainland/Vancouver
Island – pretty wild out
here. Party in weak shape.
Getting bad press.

SEPTEMBER 5
Regina – Au revoir,
religion! Nothing but
trade talk for weeks!

MID-OCTOBER
Sneak back through
US – no events.
Get home fast.

EDMONTON

PRINCE ALBERT

CALGARY

MOOSEJAW

VANCOUVER

REGINA

VICTORIA

In the late nineteenth century a federal leader couldn't possibly tour the whole country during a sixty-day writ period. Everyone understood that the western swing – the tour's toughest haul – should be gotten out of the way before the election was called. Laurier's goal in his 1894 trip west was to forge a diverse English Canadian coalition, including Ontario's genteel bourgeoisie (second and third from *left*) and the free-trading, resource-extracting frontiersmen of the prairies and British Columbia (*far left* and *opposite page*). His gospel of free trade promised prosperity to each town he visited, but as far west as Winnipeg, Old Canada dogged him at every whistle stop.

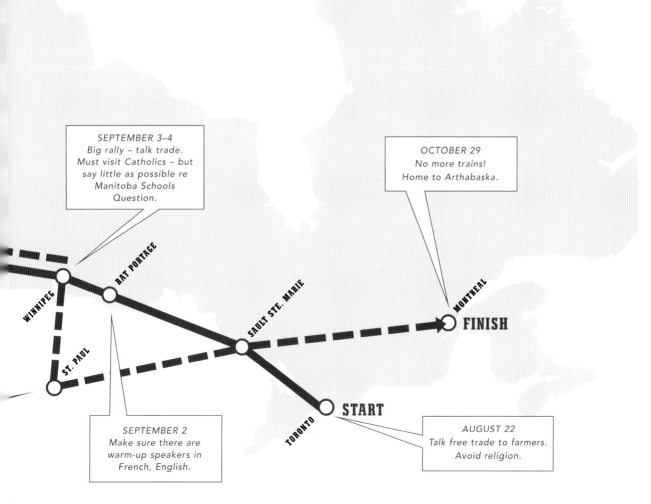

SEPTEMBER 3–4
Big rally – talk trade.
Must visit Catholics – but say little as possible re Manitoba Schools Question.

OCTOBER 29
No more trains!
Home to Arthabaska.

SEPTEMBER 2
Make sure there are warm-up speakers in French, English.

AUGUST 22
Talk free trade to farmers.
Avoid religion.

WINNIPEG

RAT PORTAGE

ST. PAUL

SAULT STE. MARIE

MONTREAL
FINISH

TORONTO
START

to the capital city and its ancient battles.

Perched on a cliff, overlooking the white waters of the Ottawa River dividing Ontario and Quebec, the twenty-seven-year-old Parliament Buildings neatly reflected the precarious position of John Thompson's Conservative government. In the fall of 1894 it was halfway through its fourth year, yet the Manitoba Schools Question with which it had wrestled since the 1891 election was no closer to resolution. For the Tories there could be no worthwhile pre-writ campaigning until this deadly crisis was solved. In the green House of Commons chamber the government benches and the lobby behind them seethed with division and intrigue. Thompson's continuing attempts to push the schools issue off to the courts seemed destined to fail, as the judiciary kept closing the legal avenues down which it might be shunted. The court route aside, the government had three options. The first was most unattractive: accept Manitoba's *fait accompli* and manage the political fallout in Quebec as best it could. The only two real alternatives to this course entailed direct action by the dominion government, either through the cabinet "disallowing" the province's legislation or through parliament enacting a "remedial" bill. Disallowance was out of the question: it was not only a profoundly obnoxious weapon in the eyes of the provinces but a series of judicial decisions had sharply circumscribed its effectiveness. That left remediation by parliament.

There were two problems with remediation. It would offend all the Protestants who thought closing Manitoba's Catholic schools was a dandy idea, and it might not even be doable. The real possibility existed that a remedial bill would split the Tory caucus, causing enough English Protestants to vote against the government to defeat the bill and cause it to fall. Today, such a scenario would be next to impossible for a government with a majority. Our federal government implements its policies on the strength of its majority, relying on a system of party discipline that is among the most rigid in the democratic world. Members vote their party line or face expulsion from the caucus, making Canadian prime ministers virtually unassailable between elections. (They can be dethroned only at party conventions, which meet too infrequently to exert much discipline. More than half of John Diefenbaker's cabinet banded together to dump him in 1962, for example, but he simply told them all to go to hell and carried right on governing badly.)

The system one hundred years ago put much less power in the prime minister's hands. In the 1890s our parliament had not yet evolved away from its British roots. To this day British MPs enjoy considerable leverage in shaping policy and maintaining the leader in power. If enough government members get angry enough, they can vote with the opposition and force an election. This threat keeps the leadership honest, forcing it to maintain the support of the caucus for its program and its continued hold on power. The cockpit of this system is the cabinet. Cabinet building in Britain involves appointing the leaders of the party's various factions, cliques, and intellectual ten-

Macdonald's high-Anglican gothic-revival parliament soars above the Ottawa River and the prosaic realities of the logging emplacements and barge canal below.

dencies to the inner circle. By co-opting these leaders, the executive can function and the legislative program of the government can be implemented with some comfort that the whole structure won't collapse the next time the House votes. At the same time, this system can become a sport for the bloodthirsty if the heads of the factions, cliques, and tendencies resign from cabinet and threaten to leave the government caucus with their followers. If the rebels are strong enough, a prime minister has no choice but to step down. (These cabinet mutinies can come suddenly and with little outside warning. A 1990 cabinet uprising deposed Margaret Thatcher in a matter of days, although to outside observers she seemed securely in command. So it was in 1890s Canada.)

NAME: Sir Charles Tupper

PARTY: Conservative

ROLE: Prime minister, 1896, former premier of Nova Scotia, "Minister of Everything" for Macdonald, frustrated heir apparent. Protestant. Ambassador to UK.

As Prime Minister Thompson weighed his options, the potential for a government-threatening mutiny based on religious sentiment loomed foremost in his mind, followed closely by the threat of a leadership revolt. Thompson's Catholicism made him vulnerable, and a major rival loomed in the person of Sir Charles Tupper, who many felt had been unfairly passed over in the voting that led to the selection first of Abbott and then of Thompson. A living legend, Tupper had been premier of Nova Scotia at Confederation and a key player in Canada's foundation. A mainstay of the Macdonald ministries, serving in such critical portfolios as Railways and Finance, he had, since 1884, represented the dominion's interests with distinction as Canada's high commissioner

in London. Even at the age of seventy-three and 3,300 miles away in London, the still-ambitious Tupper posed a threat. His son, Charles Hibbert Tupper, lurked in the cabinet as minister of justice, always looking to strike on his father's behalf.

We'll never know if Thompson could have navigated a remedial bill through these rapids of ambition, bigotry, and dissent. In November 1894 he left for London to be invested formally in the Queen's Privy Council. Soon after his return to Canada his government's last judicial appeal would have been exhausted. But on December 12 word reached Ottawa that he had died while visiting Her Majesty Queen Victoria at Windsor Castle. Once again the Tory cabinet erupted in a brawl for the top prize. Supporters of Tupper sprang into action, but what we'd now call an "Anybody But Tupper" movement reared up to thwart him. However, this gang of pygmies could not choose a leader from among themselves. "Here we are," said one minister, "twelve of us and every one as bad or as good as the other – Jack as good as his master." In the end the prize was awarded on seniority. On December 29, 1894, the governor general sent for Mackenzie Bowell, who had served as an MP, then a senator, for an unbroken twenty-seven years.

Bowell's selection demonstrated how thoroughly dysfunctional the Tory Party had become. As a Belleville-based former grand master of the arch-Protestant Orange Lodge for all of British North America, Bowell was actually a decent choice for pushing through a remedial bill; no one would ever suspect him of pandering to papists. Moreover, he was prepared to swallow his religious bigotry in the name of the constitution and to preserve the Tory Party. But Bowell was weak and indecisive. He presided over a cabinet by now so badly riven that keeping it in one piece would have taxed a better man to the limit. Leading this group into a battle for remediation was far beyond Bowell's capacities. Moreover, as a senator, he couldn't take a seat in the House of Commons and was forced to marshal his troops from a perch behind the Speaker's chair underneath the gallery.

The year 1895 opened with the expectation of high parliamentary drama. Four years having elapsed since the last campaign, an election was expected. The time had come for the Tories to set aside personality politics and for the Liberals to move beyond positioning their leader. The year 1895 would be the year of the Schools Question, in which its divisive force would be fully felt. The pre-writ period was entering its critical phase; whichever party held together would enter the election far ahead of the one that didn't. And if neither could cohere, parliamentary, electoral, and even constitutional chaos would result.

The Judicial Committee of the Privy Council in London, the Tories' court of last resort, spoke in January, clearly reaffirming parliament's legal ability to remediate and sealing off the government's final avenue of easy escape. Only two possible courses now remained open to Bowell: remediate or do nothing to address the situation. The prime minister and his divided cabinet spent weeks working to split the difference between these two irreducible options. On March 19, 1895, the government issued an ultimatum commanding Manitoba's government to reopen the Catholic

schools or face federal remediation. Two days later, worried that the tone of the ultimatum was too strong, Bowell back-pedalled with a clarification emphasizing his hope for Manitoba's acquiescence to the threat of federal remediation. All this deliberation meant delay, killing the chance of a spring election. On March 21, the day the clarification was issued, the younger Tupper, who believed that the government needed a fresh mandate before remediating the Manitoba legislation, resigned in fury. (The opportunity to sabotage Bowell and pave the way for his father's return cannot have been far from his mind.) Bowell thought Tupper had gone mad. To call an election now, "while the political heather was ablaze throughout the whole country, would be a piece of political folly inexcusable in any public man."

This high-level brawl over strategy opens a fascinating window into the politics of the day. The Schools Question clearly topped the national agenda: it couldn't be buried during a campaign. The key calculation was not how remediation would play among voters – Protestants would tend to want to keep the schools in Manitoba shut, and Catholics would want them reopened – but how it would play within each party. The governing Tories sought the course less likely to explode their party machine before voting day: either fight an election campaign on the mere threat of remediation or fight one after remediation had passed, hoping the furor would die down before their mandate expired.

Bowell chose the latter course, gambling that he had enough time, skill, and luck to find a solution that would keep the Conservative machine in one piece. But he made the wrong call in two ways: he overestimated his chances at finding a result that would satisfy the Tories' various factions and he failed to understand the cost of moving slowly and cautiously. A caucus that contained both ferocious anti-Catholics

NAME: Mackenzie Bowell

PARTY: Conservative

ROLE: Prime minister, 1894–96. Senator, Ontario Protestant, journeyman-minister for Macdonald. Succeeds Thompson on basis of seniority, not smarts.

like D'Alton McCarthy and Clarke Wallace and ultramontane *castors* like Auguste Angers was unlikely to rally around any one position. Dragging the matter out only deepened the disillusionment within the party while extending the grace period during which Laurier could continue to duck the issue. Bowell thereby allowed the Liberal machine to hold together while his own was falling apart. His folly was to play for time when time was not on his side.

A week after his "sort-of" ultimatum on remediation, the prime minister staged a wobbly recovery by hauling his justice minister back into cabinet. But the impression created by his and the younger Tupper's backs-and-forths was one of vacillation and weakness. According to a well-placed civil servant: "Then followed days which I never recall without a blush, days of a weak and incompetent administration by a Cabinet presided over by a man whose sudden and unlooked for elevation had visibly turned his head, a ministry without unity or cohesion of any kind."

Over on the Liberal side of the still-recessed House the opposition observed with considerable glee the government's floundering attempts to close with the issue. "They are in the den of the lions!" giggled Joseph-Israël Tarte. Tarte's opinions carried a lot of weight with Laurier. He represented the kind of disgruntled moderate *bleu* Laurier needed to attract from the Tories to swing a big majority in Quebec. He had served as editor-in-chief of the *bleu* newspaper *Le Canadien*, but he had

IN THE LIONS' DEN
Then, as now, politicians spoke in metaphors. Liberal Israël Tarte's gleeful description of Bowell's ghastly predicament drew from the biblical story of Daniel.

NAME: Israël Tarte

PARTY: Liberal

ROLE: Laurier's chief fixer in Quebec. Former *bleu* organizer; still pro-church. Determined to bring Tory organizational chops to Liberal campaign in Quebec.

been cornered in a series of vicious factional struggles within the Quebec Tory machine and had staved off bankruptcy – and the extinguishing of his political career – only by jumping fences and joining the Liberals in 1890. Like some anti-hero in a frock-coat film noir, he had assured himself a warm welcome by bringing with him a black bag of documents that touched off the celebrated Langevin scandal which nearly cost the Tories the 1891 election. Laurier welcomed his old friend and newfound ally into the Liberal fold, and Tarte was duly elected as an independent MP in an 1893 by-election. He soon became Laurier's eyes, ears, and organizational mainspring in Quebec.

Along with most French Catholics, Tarte thought remediation was necessary to protect his race and religion. Some of the Liberals' Ontario key players agreed – Irish Catholic leaders such as Toronto lawyer Frank Anglin and even the occasional high-minded Protestant such as once-and-future minister David Mills. But ranged against these men was the Protestant majority of Ontario and Maritime members as well as the provincial parties. The provincial machines had a lot more clout among the federal Liberals than their counterparts had with the Conservatives; they had at their disposal immense resources of patronage and pork barrelling unavailable to Laurier. Unsurprisingly, then, the Liberals were generally the party of provincial rights, a matter very much at stake in the schools issue. Liberal premiers like Oliver Mowat and W.S. Fielding, and the lynchpin of Liberalism in Manitoba, Clifford

Sifton, held firm for the provinces' prerogative to handle education as they wished.

Once the London judiciary forced the issue back into the lap of Canada's parliament, the Liberals' internal divisions burst into the open. That winter Grit newspapers – Catholic and Protestant – launched editorial salvoes against each other. Laurier even considered resigning, on the logic that a French Catholic could never unite the party or sell a position to the country. He was also plagued by his intense sense of justice, which made it difficult for him to treat the situation of the Manitoba Catholics as a purely political calculation.

There was also the eternal question of *la survivance*, unavoidable for any *Canadien*. If the provinces were left to pick on their minorities, would the country's English majority not eventually turn on Quebec? Was the demand of hard-line nationalists like Mercier – for Quebec to turn inwards, erecting high

NAME: David Mills

PARTY: Liberal

ROLE: MP for Bothwell, Ontario. Key frontbencher. Protestant, yet pro-remediation.

protective walls – the only solution? Laurier instinctively opposed this approach. Not only was he a federal politician inclined towards the idea of Quebec playing on the national stage but he had long believed that the organization of national politics around the racial and religious divides would ultimately be fatal to both French and English. As far back as 1877 Laurier had attacked the ultramontanes on this point, saying: "You wish … to organize all the Catholics into one party without other bond, without other basis, than a common religion. Have you not reflected that by that very fact you will organize the Protestant population as a single party, and then, instead of the peace and harmony now prevailing between the different elements of the Canadian people, you throw open the door to war, a war of religion, the most terrible of all wars?"

Reflecting on the schools issue, Laurier saw that a French, Catholic leader pushing for remediation would only contribute to the polarization of national politics along the axis of race and religion. He would set back by years the cause of a progressive politics based on principle. Yet how could he sell out his brothers on the Red River? For a time that winter he wondered if the best solution was to remove himself from the play, allowing room for an English Protestant. Laurier had run out of time for dither and delay. To stay on as leader meant having to choose.

NAME: John Willison

PARTY: Liberal

ROLE: Editor of the *Globe* since 1890. Key Laurier adviser and party operator. Protestant. Anti-remedialist. Provincial rightser.

As the spring parliamentary session approached, Laurier cast about for advice from the most trusted, thoughtful people he knew. In a key private exchange of letters with the Toronto *Globe*'s powerful Liberal editor-in-chief, John Willison, Laurier posed his questions of justice for the Manitobans. Willison replied that the heart of the matter was not the Manitoba minority; its fate was sealed regardless of what Ottawa did. "I doubt very much if in any conceivable case federal interference in a province could be effective." The real issue was whether Ottawa would seek to override the rights of the provinces, and how far it would go to enforce its will. "If Mr. Greenway resists Dominion legislation," Willison wrote, "it will be an ill day for the country when the attempt was made to exercise federal power in that province."

For Willison, the nub of the problem was enforcement. Ottawa could pass remedial legislation, but if Manitoba defied the federal command there would be no choice but to send in the North-West Mounted Police. Confederation had barely survived the suppression of the Riel Rebellion, which, whatever its rights and wrongs, was a patently unlawful uprising. Ottawa's physical coercion of a legitimate, democratically elected provincial government would be an unworkable nightmare. If a Tory government tried forcible remediation, a potentially violent federal–provincial confrontation would ensue. A Liberal government, committed to provincial rights, wouldn't even get that far without cracking up and falling from power. Either way, Canada would sunder. And so would die not only the dream-country of all who sought dominion under Britain over annexation by the United States but also Laurier's vision of a broad horizon for the French in Canada and their hope of becoming a truly modern, liberal society. That spring Laurier agonized over the prospect of sacrificing the French of Manitoba for what he saw as the greater good. He knew that many men of goodwill would disagree with him and that the bishops would again anathematize him. In the end he decided to follow his dream of a nation from coast to coast, whatever the cost. He would stay on, sell out the Franco-Manitobans, and cover the move as best he could.

As for the electoral fallout among the country's Catholics, Tarte judged it manageable. He thought that the Quebec bishops' shrillness on the schools issue masked their

LAURIER'S CHOICE, 1895

A ☐   **SUPPORT REMEDIATION** (put rights first). Requires federal muscle to enforce Catholic rights. Will cause Protestant backlash. Equals religious wars as bad as France's *(below)*.

B ☐   **OPPOSE REMEDIATION** (put Confederation first). Equals sell-out of Manitoba Catholics (like this native man, *below*). Avoid religious war, but be damned to eternal hellfire?

waning power. As a French Canadian with a real shot at becoming prime minister, Laurier could carry Quebec despite vehement ecclesiastical opposition. Tarte also believed that, outside Quebec, the Liberals could keep the party united on the strength of their alliances with robust provincial machines (bolstered by their provincial-rights positioning on the Schools Question) and farmers' continued support for free trade. In sum, the national interest, the party's provincial rights orientation, and the Liberals' direct electoral prospects all pointed Laurier towards the same official position. The Grits would oppose the federal initiative in the provinces' name, but they would make no promises on the fate of the minority itself beyond vague suggestions of Liberal-to-Liberal compromise.

And so, on April 18, Laurier led his troops back into the House for the new session. They expected that the government's next move would be remediation, followed by dissolution at the end of June. That would pave the way for a fall 1895 election.

Instead, the weeks ticked by without action. Finally on June 19, 1895, Manitoba replied to Ottawa's March ultimatum with a flat no. Once Bowell's bluff was called, he buckled, announcing on July 6 that there would be no remedial legislation during the session. The prime minister was postponing the election until the last possible date, the spring of 1896. To cover this disorderly retreat, Bowell made a ridiculous show of offering Manitoba a chance to reconsider its answer, promising that if no satisfactory reply was received, a new session would be called no later than January 2, 1896, during which

remedial legislation would finally be passed.

Bowell's latest humiliating stall provoked more outrage. On July 9 all three of his French Catholic ministers resigned – the *bleus* Joseph Caron and Joseph Ouimet and the *castor* Auguste Angers – leaving a gaping hole in his fourteen-man cabinet. All three had faced intense pressure from the Catholic Church, had lobbied ferociously for the introduction of a remedial bill, and now had to make good on previous threats of resignation. The next day, however, Caron and Ouimet recanted, leaving only Angers in huffy exile. When the two *bleus* returned to their benches on July 10, they were greeted with howls of Liberal derision: "The cats have come back – the cats have come back." The government staggered into summer recess on July 22.

Mackenzie Bowell spent the summer soothing his cabinet. In the early fall he undertook his own western tour. But where Laurier had triumphed a year before, the Tory prime minister met indifferent crowds. A defiant Premier Greenway refused to reconsider his rejection of the federal ultimatum. Nationwide, the Tories finally began mounting their pre-writ effort against Laurier, branding as rank cowardice his ducking of the issue, in contrast to their resolute plans for action. The Conservatives sought to shame Laurier and his team into facing the costly choices that events had thrust upon them. Laurier knew that if he showed weakness or hesitation in defending his position, Liberals everywhere would sense that the issue had not been settled internally, the knives would be unsheathed, and the party would head towards the campaign in disarray. He had to

The walk to power. Israël Tarte, the Tory defector, and his new boss, Wilfrid Laurier, march up Parliament Hill from the Langevin Block (background *right*), named for Macdonald's Quebec lieutenant and Tarte's old boss. Times change.

LAURIER'S BRILLIANT STRADDLE

THE SUBSTANCE

Laurier's "Sunny Ways" pledge (see Aesop fable *above*) stated in folksy terms the choice he had made: cheerfully sell out Manitoba's Catholics through friendly negotiation with province.

THE STYLE

Lest anyone think Mr. Laurier a cowardly politician, he evoked the great Duke of Wellington (immortalized in paint by Thomas Jones Barker *above*), whose 1810 defensive manoeuvres at Torres Vedras in Portugal humbled Napoleon's army. Rule Britannia!

In October 1895 the Liberal leader rolled out his new approach to the Manitoba Schools issue, which threatened to tear the country apart. Laurier understood both the style and the substance of politics, and he made sure that his audiences knew he had covered both bases with his new strategy.

ensure that everyone knew his position was final, definitive – and a strong enough platform on which to fight an election.

Laurier spent the late summer in Quebec, interrupting his vacation with a speaking tour on which he made reassuring noises about looking after the Franco-Manitobans but refused to be specific. Not until October 8, with the crops in and the voters more likely to pay attention, did he enter Ontario to set out his position. He chose the setting for the tour's kick-off brilliantly. Morrisburg, Ontario, was situated in the Upper St. Lawrence valley near the Ontario–Quebec border, providing a nice symbolism of the closeness of the two founding nations. More important, it lay in the heart of a major area of settlement for thousands of Loyalists immediately following the American Revolutionary War. The Loyalist myth was central to English Canada's psyche: the idea that honourable British-American patriots had sacrificed homes and livelihoods to journey into exile rather than submit to a rebellious republic. In choosing Morrisburg, Laurier was replaying his standard British-liberal routine and giving it a symbolism that voters could understand: Laurier the Loyalist; trade without treason in commerce; peace without popery on schools.

Under overcast skies and amid blustery fall winds off the wide river, a crowd of four thousand gathered at the town's agricultural grounds to hear the Liberal leader. Seizing on the weather, Laurier recalled Aesop's fable of the man with the coat, accosted by the blustering wind and the warm sun. Which of those two elements had been able to make the man remove his coat? "Well, sir," said the Liberal leader, "the government are very windy. They have blown and raged and threatened, but the more they have threatened and raged and blown the more that man Greenway has stuck to his coat. If it were in my power, I would try the sunny way." A memorable phrase, "sunny ways" – a peppy slogan

with which all Liberals could face the voters. "What's the Liberal policy on schools?" "Sunny ways." "What does that mean?" "Meaningful federal–provincial negotiations, you got a problem with that?" Smile, move on. Beautiful.

Laurier's carefully crafted fable was no mere gag. "Sunny ways" was what a modern politician would privately call a "process answer" – refusing to come down for or against a proposal and instead describing the means by which the decision will be made. It is a classic politician's substitute for taking a stand. After five years of trying to evade the Manitoba Schools Question, Laurier was now making a big public show of asking Canadians to do the same thing by shunting the matter off into some ill-defined process with no particular outcome required. He needed to put the festering Schools Question into a little box where it couldn't hurt the Liberal Party and would do minimal damage to the country. He knew his audience, and sensed that voters in all parts of the country wanted an end to this fiendishly complex and ominous issue that the government swore could wreck the young country.

But even if "sunny ways" responded to the voters' desire to move on, it remained to be seen whether it was a position their representatives in the Liberal caucus could live with. Was the process answer a strong enough position for the party to rally around? The answer to this second question came when Laurier defended his policy. "I am not responsible for that [Manitoba Schools] question, but I do not want to shirk it; I want to give you my views, but remember that war has to be waged in a certain way. When the Duke of Wellington was in Portugal, as those of you will remember who have read that part of the history of England, he withdrew at one time within the lines of Torres Vedras, and there for months he remained, watching the movements of the enemy … Gentlemen, I am within the lines of Torres Vedras. I will get out of them when it suits me and not before."

The crowd exploded with applause and appreciative laughter. In a province where every town had its Wellington Street, here was Laurier, a francophone Catholic Quebecker whose loyalty had been successfully questioned in an election just four years earlier, showing a daunting command of English history and public admiration for its greatest general, the man who had humbled the French emperor Napoleon. He might just as well have handed out General Wolfe lapel pins. The Torres Vedras metaphor showed his unimpeachable pro-British tendencies, and, by invoking the Iron Duke, Laurier reworked an awkward straddle as a brave and noble stand. In comparing himself to the legendary Wellington and stylishly shrugging off the tortuous issue that was tearing the Tories apart, Laurier depicted himself as a leader head and shoulders above the vacillating Tory prime minister. If the public was tiring of the Manitoba Schools Question, as Laurier hoped, there was a market for his blithe, Aesopian wisdom – but only if he could marry it to the manly leadership of the Iron Duke. "Sunny ways" spoke to his specific policy approach, but his echoes of Wellington answered the yearnings of a country that had been essentially leaderless since Macdonald's passing. More important, it signalled to Liberals in caucus and out in the ridings that the man at the top was fully in command, not for turning, and above all, a winner.

"Sunny ways" and "Torres Vedras" were the equivalent of party television commercials in our day. Laurier would repeat them in fifty-two venues in Ontario alone that fall, often more than once in an hour-long speech. He retailed these buzzwords throughout Ontario for two months, and they were amplified and distributed through the Liberal press. In the process Wilfrid Laurier was transforming him-

self into Sir John A. Macdonald's political heir: the strong leader, the passionate Brit, the man of conciliation and unity between the races. Yet for all his bravado, he realized that Confederation still hung in the balance. Out on the road, he wrote to a colleague that the Schools Question may still "break the Opposition or break the government."

By early September Mackenzie Bowell had returned from the West to Ottawa and to a caucus and cabinet preparing to move against him. A month later his colleagues pushed him into inviting Sir Charles Tupper back from London, ostensibly to discuss plans for a North Atlantic steamship service. The aging giant eagerly accepted, and Bowell readied for the worst.

On December 12, the eve of Tupper's return, two straws blew in on the wind. First, Clark Wallace, the customs controller (a non-cabinet office) and ultra-Orange Ontario MP, resigned his post in anger over the approaching remedial legislation. The last of Bowell's key Orangemen had now departed from his front bench. But good news for the prime minister came as well: a government by-election triumph in the rural riding of Ontario North, followed swiftly by three more heavy defeats for the Liberals in by-elections. Laurier's coalition may have been holding together in parliament, but it looked to be in trouble out in the ridings.

The by-election results carried other, less encouraging messages to the Tories. *Castor* candidates who promised full remediation had won the Quebec ridings. But in Ontario one riding had been won by a hard-line anti-remedialist Tory, and the other by a former Tory breakaway follower of arch-Protestant D'Alton McCarthy. Voters seemed to be dragging the Tory Party in opposite directions.

The Tories were executing a dangerous but standard move from the early Canadian political playbook, a whipsaw designed to cut the tribal ends of both English and French Canada away

PLAYBOOK I

Most successful national campaigns are based on one of three timeless strategies. These have never been written down in the way that, for example, the timeless strategies for winning at any sport or game are consolidated into playbooks. But the political game, like any other, has standard plays that the pros learn and use. If a Canadian political playbook really existed, its first entry would be the play I've named the Double Tribal Whipsaw. As the diagram shows, this play means whipsawing: using extreme French and English positions to cut moderates such as Laurier to pieces. In 1896 PMs Bowel, then Tupper, tried and failed to use this play that Macdonald had invented in the 1890s.

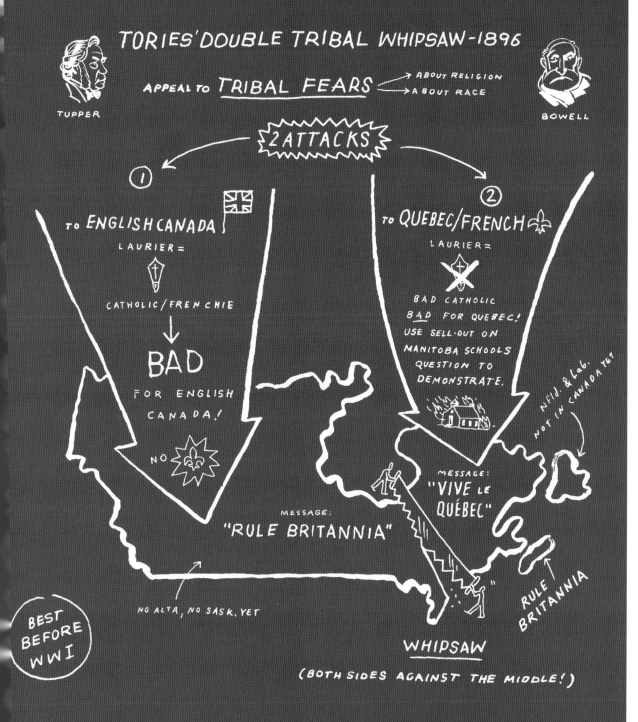

TORIES' DOUBLE TRIBAL WHIPSAW - 1896

TUPPER

BOWELL

APPEAL TO **TRIBAL FEARS** → ABOUT RELIGION
→ ABOUT RACE

2 ATTACKS

① TO ENGLISH CANADA
LAURIER =
CATHOLIC / FRENCHIE
↓
BAD
FOR ENGLISH CANADA!
NO ⚜

MESSAGE:
"RULE BRITANNIA"

② TO QUEBEC / FRENCH
LAURIER =
✕
BAD CATHOLIC
BAD FOR QUEBEC!
USE SELL-OUT ON MANITOBA SCHOOLS QUESTION TO DEMONSTRATE.

NFld. & Lab. NOT IN CANADA YET

MESSAGE:
"VIVE LE QUÉBEC"

RULE BRITANNIA

NO ALTA, NO SASK. YET

BEST BEFORE WWI

WHIPSAW
(BOTH SIDES AGAINST THE MIDDLE!)

from any moderate middle. This Double Tribal Whipsaw strategy had been used successfully by Macdonald in 1891 and appeared in the by-elections to be working again. But while marketing tribal extremism might be a good way to win by-elections, it made it extremely difficult to keep a government united, since the Tory cabinet would inevitably be composed of those representing one tribal extreme or another. The Tory formula for electoral success seemed sure to make governing impossible once the Manitoba issue came to a head; and the Liberal formula for governing might well prevent that party from winning an election in the first place. The spectre of an ungovernable country loomed ever larger as the ultimate showdown year of 1896 approached.

On December 21, 1895, Manitoba's final rejection of the ultimatum was transmitted to Ottawa. On January 2, 1896, the MPs arrived in Ottawa for what each man knew would be a par-liamentary endgame leading to an election. In the Speech from the Throne the government at last irrevocably pledged remedial legislation in the coming session. Two days later seven of Bowell's ministers, all of them English Protestants, resigned en masse, using as their pretext Bowell's failure to plug the vacancy left by Angers's defection, but clearly setting the stage for the prime minister to be toppled. Tupper, now back on the scene and the obvious beneficiary of the revolt, made it known through his son that, as prime minister, he would carry through the gov-ernment's pledge to pass remedial legislation – thus advertising himself as the pro-remediation replacement for Bowell.

But the governor general, Lord Aberdeen, despised Tupper as a reactionary and an adul-terer. Twice Bowell went to Rideau Hall with his resignation in hand; twice he was told by Lord Aberdeen to try again to stop Tupper. Meanwhile, the Commons was in an uproar, with the Tories moving for recesses and

adjournments and the Liberals determined to keep the government's feet to the fire. On January 7, following a condemnation of Bowell's leadership in the House by one of the cabinet bolters, the prime minister emerged from his dugout behind the Speaker and began shaking hands with the leading Liberal MPs, saying that it was "such a comfort to shake hands with honest men, after having been

NAME: Alphonse Desjardins

PARTY: Conservative

ROLE: Senator. Stopgap minister in Bowell shuffle. Pro-church *castor*. Alienates moderate Quebec Tories.

in company with traitors for months."

To fill the cabinet slots left by the walkout, Bowell worked the telegraph lines to summon backbenchers, prominent citizens – anyone he could. In one of the most comic episodes in Canadian political history, the resigned minis-ters waylaid Bowell's reinforcements at the old Ottawa railway station beside the canal. As the arriving politicians emerged from the station into the frozen January air, they encountered a phalanx of ex-ministers holding up picket signs. The mutineers succeeded in persuading many of Bowell's new men to refuse the prime minister's offers. Alcohol may have been a factor, and rumours flew of bagfuls of CPR money. On January 9 a defeated Bowell shuffled back to Government House and, for the third time, Lord Aberdeen refused his request to resign. Laurier was told to ready himself for the call to form a government.

Then on January 11, to everyone's surprise, Mackenzie Bowell reappeared at Government House with a re-formed ministry. The Quebec hole had been plugged by one

Alphonse Desjardins, a Quebec senator, who
had been proposed directly by Père Albert
Lacombe, the celebrated Catholic missionary
to the North-West and now passionately working the levers of the Tory Party to defend the
Catholics of Manitoba. Lacombe was just one of
many prominent Catholic churchmen battling to
keep the government afloat and, with it, the
hope of remedial legislation. "If you are
beaten in presenting frankly and loyally before
the House the [remedial] law," he wrote to
Langevin on December 31, "in the general elections we will return you to power." This direct,
blanket assurance of political intervention by the
church was unprecedented in national politics.

For the time being Senator Desjardins
would serve as a down payment on further
church support. Quebec seemed stabilized for
the Tories. Along with Desjardins, there was
another (arguably) new face: the mutton-
chopped visage of Sir Charles Tupper, sworn
in as secretary of state and facing a by-election
in Cape Breton scheduled for February 4.
Frustrated by their inability to get a Tupper
government past the governor general, six of
the bolters had returned, happy enough to
have their man at last in cabinet. Only
Tupper Junior stayed out, the prospect of two
Tuppers in cabinet being unpalatable to all.

When this re-treaded cabinet wobbled
into the House on January 15, Liberal warhorse
Richard Cartwright delivered a characteristically elegant put-down. "We are here," he said,
"in the presence of the Ottawa Low Comedy
Troupe, and should be grateful for the amuse-
ment they have afforded us. What we have been
listening to, after all, has really been a series of
rehearsals. We had number one rehearsal ...

The Old Lion. Sir Charles Tupper, in the uniform of a
Knight Grand Cross of the Order of St. Michael and
St. George, or "GCMG" (often parodied as "God
Calls Me God"). Tupper wouldn't have minded. His
forty years near the top of the nation's political food
chain only made him hungrier for the kill.

when three members of the cabinet went out and two came back. Then we had what I may call a full-dress rehearsal when seven members went out and practically seven came back. Now, these honourable gentlemen being nearly letter-perfect, we can have the rest of the performance, which will not be long delayed, when all of them go out and none come back."

On February 4 Tupper won his by-election and immediately assumed the role of leader of the government in the House of Commons. Bowell remained prime minister in name but effective power within the Tory government passed from him to the senior Tupper, the man responsible for holding the Commons caucus together to get the remedial bill through. After a month spent drafting the legislation, the new Tory supremo was ready. The climactic final act began on the afternoon of March 3, 1896, when the secretary of state moved second reading of Bill 58, the Remedial Act (Manitoba).

Now that the Tories had run out of stalling time, their last hope lay in making the Liberals share the agony of decision. Even at seventy-four, Tupper cut a commanding figure, his rock jaw and fierce eyes still visible under the sagging flesh. For almost twenty years he had served in Macdonald's cabinets, earning his reputation as the master's right-hand man. Since the old man's death he had languished in London. Now at last he stood where destiny had intended, the heir of Macdonald, leading the fractious Tory clans into battle against the common foe.

Tupper began his address in a tone of solemn statesmanship, laying on the line the grave threat to Canada posed by the Manitoba Schools issue. His bill "afforded the means of removing that antagonism of race and religion

Laurier was a superb orator whose long, exquisitely cadenced sentences still hit the key points hard. If he paused to quote from an outside source, it was only to gather words before cranking up the music again.

which has been found to act so fatally in reference to the interests of Canada." He went further, invoking the high principles of equality and rights: "It is a question of the Constitution of the country – that all the rights guaranteed under it will be sacredly guarded. Within this wide Dominion you have got over forty-one per cent of the population Roman Catholics. Are we to leave rankling in the minds of over forty-one per cent of the people of this Dominion the sentiment that a Roman Catholic cannot obtain the same just consideration that he would if he were a Protestant?" Tupper's point was simple: rights come first. His fine words were chosen mainly to shame his own Protestant Tory colleagues into supporting the bill, to show his own party that he could make the case for remediation forcefully and that he could split the Liberals with the force of his logic.

All eyes fell on the member for Québec-Est as he rose to reply to Tupper in his florid yet rhythmic and muscular English. "Mr. Speaker," Laurier began, "if in a debate of such moment it were not out of place for me to make a personal reference to myself – a reference which, however, may perhaps be justified, not so much on account of the feelings which may not unnaturally be attributed to me, being of the race and creed of which I am, but still more in consideration of the great responsibility which has been placed on my shoulders by the too kind regard of the friends by whom I am surrounded here – I would say that, in the course of my parliamentary career, during which it has been my duty on more than one occasion to take part in the discussion of those dangerous questions which too often have come before the parliament of Canada, never did I rise, sir, with a greater sense of security; never did I feel so strong in the consciousness of right, as I do now, at this anxious moment when, in the name of the constitution so outrageously misinterpreted by the

government, in the name of peace and harmony in this land; when in the name of the minority which this bill seeks or pretends to help, in the name of this young nation on which so many hopes are centred, I rise to ask this parliament not to proceed any further with this bill."

Laurier's counter to Tupper was simple: Canada's preservation comes first, not rights. But his statement was much more than a theoretical riposte. In one interminable sentence, Laurier had managed to dodge bravely, duck gloriously, and cover his brow with laurels and his backside in plate armour. In parliamentary terms, he had moved "the hoist" – a six-month suspension of debate on a bill and the most drastic procedural motion in the House of Commons rule book. Normally, moving the hoist carried the strong risk of a backlash against those obstructing the nation's business. In this instance, however, suspending the interminable debate on Manitoba Schools was totally "on-message," as a strategist might put it today, because the hoist was Laurier's process answer hardened into concrete action. What should we do about Manitoba Schools? Ummmm … try Sunny Ways. When will you do that? Later – so let's hoist the damned thing right now! Moreover, this rarely used parliamentary tactic made for a dramatic effect on the morale of Laurier's colleagues; it showed that the general of Torres Vedras was mounting a stout defence and was still firmly in command. And, to the broader, extra-parliamentary audience, Laurier had managed to give the appearance of firmly rejecting the bill while maintaining his options for explaining why. To Catholics he could still argue that the bill only "pretends to help," implying that he would go further. To Protestants he could point to the bald fact of his motion "not to proceed." All the while he kept faith with his core audience of provincial-rights advocates, "in the name of the constitution so outrageously misinterpreted by the government." If the Grits could carry the motion, or obstruct passage in some other way for just a few weeks, they would go into an election unified behind a leader who now appeared rather dashing compared with the blundering Tories. In one stroke Laurier had frustrated Tupper's attempt to break up the Liberals' unity.

And the opposition leader had only begun to speak. He went on to reveal a private communication to him from Father Lacombe, the previous January, in which the priest had confirmed his promise to the Tories with a threat that, "if the [Tory] government … is beaten and overthrown while keeping firm to the end of the struggle, I inform you, with regret, that the episcopacy, like one man, united with the clergy, will rise to support

NAME: Oliver Mowat

PARTY: Liberal

ROLE: Premier of Ontario since 1872. Heads nation's most powerful Liberal machine. Fierce provincial rightser.

those who may have fallen in defending us. Please pardon the frankness which leads me to speak thus." "Not many weeks ago," said Laurier in the House, "I was told from high quarters in the Church to which I belong that unless I supported the School Bill … I would incur the hostility of a great and powerful body."

In his March 3 speech, Laurier put in motion the Liberal strategy to frustrate the Double Tribal Whipsaw play of the Conservatives. The Tories would try to rally Catholic Quebec against him? Bring them on; the fact that he was a *Canadien* on the brink of the

prime ministership would cover a multitude of sins. Besides, how many more Quebec supporters would he gain by making nice with the church? Would anyone buy a pro-church turnabout from an old *rouge*? And even if they did, would it be worth the cost? Any attempt to embrace the bishops would spell doom in English Canada, where Laurier's race and religion had done him in before. By taking on the church, Laurier had, in fact, armoured himself against the inevitable Tory onslaught in English Canada. If the bishops hadn't attacked him, he probably would have found some excuse to attack the bishops.

"Laurier has burned his ships …" wrote Alphonse LaRivière, a Manitoba Catholic Conservative MP, to Archbishop Langevin, one of the leading episcopal power brokers pushing for remediation, "and his speech has been a veritable revolt against clerical authority." The revolt was furthered by the hoist attempt. That afternoon LaRivière told no less a Protestant than D'Alton McCarthy that "Laurier has stolen your motion." The Liberals would use their anti-remedial record, with the hoist motion as its leading example, to counter a reprise of the Tory attacks on Laurier as too French and too Catholic. If the remedial bill hadn't existed, it would have been necessary for Laurier to invent it. In these moves, Laurier was working towards the opposing play to the Double Tribal Whipsaw, one I'll call the Quebec Bridge: deflate Anglo bigotry by downplaying racially divisive issues, while quietly keeping Quebec convinced that its interests will be looked after. This play had been the essence of Macdonald's first two decades in power, until Riel and the ensuing French–English militancy had forced him to improvise the trickier Double Tribal Whipsaw. The greatest virtue of the Quebec Bridge was that it was easy to keep the message straight. While Tupper had to sell

★ PROVEN EXPERIENCE

★ HANDLES CATHOLICS

★ A REAL MACHINE

THE LAURIER-MOWAT TICKET

Laurier's alliance with Mowat offered everything he needed, yet the Ontario premier extracted a surprisingly modest price, insisting only on a safe senatorial seat and a sound provincial-rights policy.

his colleagues on moderation in parliament, then turn around and tell them to go sell militant Catholicism and militant Protestantism in their ridings, Laurier had one simple story to tell any audience: sunny ways.

Of course, sunny ways meant provincial rights too. Laurier's gathering strength brought him closer than ever to closing on the most important federal–provincial deal of all: drawing Sir Oliver Mowat out from his Ontario redoubt onto the federal field of battle as a Liberal candidate. Mowat would be the anchor of a provincial-rights dream-team for the election. Premier Fielding of Nova Scotia had signed up before Christmas. By March, Manitoba's Clifford Sifton was almost in, as was Premier Andrew Blair of New Brunswick. But Mowat could bring more to the team than these three men combined. In Ontario he controlled the country's strongest, most successful Liberal machine. Mowat also had great symbolic value as the country's foremost

proponent of provincial rights. Lastly, he had earned a national reputation for the handling of his own schools question in the 1880s, successfully containing a wave of English militancy that, like Manitoba's, had threatened to drown Ontario's separate schools. Mowat had been able to maintain Ontario's 1863 Separate Schools Act in the face of Protestant pressure by shrewdly reducing church control of the Catholic schools. Mowat's mere name on the dream-team would be enough to convince Ontario and Quebec Catholics that Laurier would find a fair solution in Manitoba.

Well before Laurier moved the hoist, his emissaries had offered Mowat everything the federal leader had to give: a lifetime annuity to ease any financial concerns; a Senate seat to protect Mowat from adverse electoral winds; a senior cabinet post of the premier's choosing; and seats, maybe even in cabinet, for any of Mowat's colleagues who might come with him. After his March 3 hoist speech, Laurier intensified his pitch to Mowat with an apparent offer to hand over the Liberal leadership. "It would be a pleasure," Laurier wrote on April 20, "for me to make any sacrifice in order to induce Sir Oliver to enter federal politics … I would most gladly make way for Sir Oliver." No doubt Mowat understood that Laurier meant the gesture as a supreme form of flattery, not as a genuine offer to make way for the Ontario premier.

With Laurier's hoist motion now attached to Bill 58 in the form of a proposed amendment, the parliamentary battle moved swiftly to its climax, with both parties well aware that the clock was ticking towards the mandatory April 26 dissolution date. The Tories' goal was to drive the Remedial Bill through second reading debate, then into committee, and finally back for third reading and final House passage before dissolution. The Grits wanted to deny the Tories this success, and also hoped to avoid having to vote yea or nay on the final bill.

For the next two-and-a-half weeks both sides of the House engaged in an epic parliamentary struggle as the bill moved through second reading debate. With dissolution only weeks away, the Tories needed to ram it through if they were to keep to their strategy of going to the people after the bill was passed. The Liberals had merely to stall. To create enough time to exhaust the Liberals' delaying tactics, Tupper put the House on twenty-four-hour duty; there was one hour of rest for dinner and the occasional half-day to allow clean-up crews to remove the debris. Within days, the House of Commons came to resemble a seedy Gents' Club whose members had neglected to go home. MPs slept in their offices, straightening their ties each morning and slapping on cologne in lieu of a bath. The stink of unwashed bodies blended with the smell of whiskey, as party whips on both sides pulled

out all the stops to keep their troops motivated, then merely entertained, and finally too dulled to do anything but endure.

Yet the second reading debate was more than just a parliamentary circus. Some of the finest speeches in the young dominion's history were delivered in that reeking chamber. Choices were made and minds were changed on both sides. The votes came at 6 a.m. on March 20, after an all-nighter that capped the long debate since Tupper had introduced his bill. In the first vote Laurier's hoist amendment was defeated, 115 to 91, with seven Liberals, mainly hard-line Catholics from Ontario and Quebec, voting against the amendment and eighteen Conservatives, mostly anti-remedialist Protestants from Ontario, voting with the opposition. Laurier's approach did not attract any moderates, but it drew more Protestant hard-liners from the Tories than it repelled Catholic hard-liners in his own ranks. In the vote later that day on the bill itself, although three more Ontario Tories sided with the Liberals, it passed through second reading by a vote of 112 to 94. Tupper's bill was halfway home.

Ahead loomed the agony of clause-by-clause examination, debate, and voting in the House Standing Committee on Justice, then the formality of third reading. The exhausted House rose for a few days' rest while one last vain attempt was made to work out a compromise between the federal and the Manitoba governments. Then, on March 31, with parliament's legal life set to expire in just twenty-seven days, committee debate on the bill began.

The Grits hoped to talk Bill 28 out of existence. If they could prevent the Justice Committee from completing its work, it would not be able to send the bill back to the House for third reading before parliament dissolved. To stall the bill in committee, they would have to resort to openly practising the parliamentary art of the filibuster, the resort to any possible procedural delay – especially lengthy speechifying – so as to run out the clock before a bill could be passed. One month of legislative hell, and the Liberals would be on the sunny side of the schools issue with their unity and momentum intact. But if the bill passed, the Liberals' new-found unity would be in peril and the election would likely come down to one broken machine fighting another.

The marathon Justice Committee sessions began on Monday, April 6, and continued without interruption, except for dinner breaks, from 3 p.m. that Monday until midnight on Saturday. Committee members rested on the Lord's Day, then debate resumed on the morning of April 13 and continued until 2:30 a.m. on Thursday. The Liberals deployed all possible filibustering tactics: procedural challenges strung end to end, books read out loud, childhood memories recounted. One observer described the battle: "Less a tourney of eloquence than a struggle of athleticism where the victory would belong to the more enduring, the teams of orators relayed themselves … as though formed in two enemy entrenchments, two teams of sentinels and riflemen."

John Charlton, the Liberals' parliamentary field marshal for the effort, kept a diary:

April 7: I spoke twice, as long each time as I could stand upon my feet.
April 8: The members are standing it well: we have four shifts, and each one has to hold the ground eight hours.
April 9: Our men are holding their ground easily.
April 13: It cannot possibly get through now. Our organization is perfect.
April 15: The Government shows signs of caving in.
April 16: The Government withdrew the Remedial Bill this morning at 2:00.

Tupper's breaking point had been reached. He had tested the Liberals' resolve and it was clear they would fight to the end of this parliament's life. Around the time of withdrawal, a backbencher addressed this remark to posterity. "There is one statement," he said, "that ought to be put on the Hansard, and that is that the opponents of this bill while on the floor of the House were not drunk. That ought to be put in for the simple reason that when future generations come to read the debates on this question it will be very hard to convince them that these honourable gentlemen were sober."

On April 23 parliament was dissolved and an election set for June 23, 1896. The first major move of the campaign came on April 2, when Bowell resigned his prime ministership and the governor general at last called on Charles Tupper to take over. The new prime minister spent the first few days after the writ was dropped attending to unfinished business – constructing a cabinet that could bring the Conservative machine together. In the West he recruited Hugh John Macdonald, a Winnipeg MLA and son of the late prime minister, but only with the secret understanding that the

Hugh John Macdonald (son of Sir John A.) backed up the remedialist Tupper in Manitoba. Note the weasel-wording of the National Policy for local consumption in the free-trading Prairies on this campaign button.

RETAIL POLITICS

TUPPER AND LAURIER ON THE CAMPAIGN TRAIL

Modern politicos distinguish between "wholesale" campaigning through the mass media and face-to-face or "retail" politicking. The distinction didn't exist in the 1890s; even newspaper coverage was fuelled by direct, live contact with voters. Tupper (*right*) offered his audiences a lordly, commanding, traditional presence. Laurier (*below*, in Prince Albert) gave off a courtly air, but could lift audiences to rapture with his elegant, classically structured, and passionately delivered speeches. He remained indisputably Canada's greatest political showman until John Diefenbaker sixty years later.

WELCOME

remedialist Macdonald could resign once the election was over. In Quebec, when Tupper's efforts failed to bring back Adolphe Chapleau, a fellow Macdonald-era hitter, the province was left in the hands of a lightweight *castor* group. The only star added to this dim constellation was Quebec's unpopular premier, Louis Taillion, whose machine was disintegrating. In effect, Tupper was abandoning Quebec to the bishops and their cabinet proxies, hoping they could stem the Laurier tide in the province.

The Liberal leader opened his writ campaign with *éclat*. On May 5 the Liberal Quebec City paper, *L'Électeur*, and its Toronto counterpart, the *Globe*, simultaneously announced that Sir Oliver Mowat had finally agreed to serve in a Laurier cabinet. Even though the premier had refused to resign and run as a candidate, his consent to a Senate appointment and a cabinet post in a new Liberal government was all that Laurier needed. The Liberal press trumpeted the new partnership with matching portraits of the giants of the two founding races.

Each party's pre-writ positioning determined its post-writ strategy: one for English Canada and one for French Canada (Quebec, Acadie, and parts of eastern Ontario and Manitoba). These were the days before opinion polls, but anyone could sense that, broadly speaking, the Liberals were in a sound, unified condition and the Tories still badly divided. The Conservatives did what losing campaigns do to this day: they went negative, aiming their Double Tribal Whipsaw entirely at trashing Laurier. In English Canada they would portray him as a dangerous French Catholic, alien to the majority interests of the Maritimes, Ontario, and the West. In Quebec the Tories and their ecclesiastical allies would slam the Liberal leader as a bad Catholic who was selling out his people in Manitoba. But Laurier's entire career had trained him for these attacks. From the naïve liberalism of

his days in provincial politics to the pro-British positioning of his 1894 western tour and, finally, his cunning yet masterful leadership positioning in his Torres Vedras speech and in the House debate on remedial legislation, Laurier had emerged as a truly national politician. His pre-writ positioning would ensure that, by the time the Tory slime started flying, little would stick.

Two big questions remained that would decide the election. The first applied to English Canada: How much damage would be caused, and to whom, by third-party or independent Protestant militant candidates in Ontario and Manitoba? Assorted splitters, including former Tories running as D'Alton McCarthy supporters and anti-Catholic Grits running as Patrons of Industry, mounted thirty-five candidacies in Ontario and four in Manitoba, making both provinces quite unpredictable. A McCarthyite candidate might attract votes from the Liberals and elect a Tory. A lapsed Liberal running as a Patron of Industry could do the same thing, or could just as easily wind up drawing anti-remedialist support away from the local Conservative and elect a Grit. In Quebec the big question was: Which would prove stronger, the people's hope for a *Canadien* prime minister or their Catholic fear of hellfire if they voted Liberal?

Now the carefully oiled party machines moved into high gear. Years later, Israël Tarte offered a rare insight into campaign financing in the Great Party era. "Let us glance discreetly at [the riding of] Maisonneuve …" he wrote in *La Presse* in 1904. "If Monsieur P. meets with an opponent of weight, can he expect to get off at less than $25,000 to $30,000?" Tarte estimated that $160,000 in electoral expenses were incurred in the City of Montreal alone during the 1904 campaign. All this cash came from the country's great corporations. "In 1872, Sir Hugh Allan, promoter of the Canadian Pacific, gave more than $300,000 to the Conservative Party for their campaign," continued Tarte. As a rule of thumb, an 1896 dollar was worth roughly thirty times its nominal value today. The CPR thus gave the Conservatives approximately $9 million worth of money in one election, sixty times the largest donations given today and vastly more than is now allowed by law. "In 1887 a sum of more than $100,000 [$3 million today] came out of the funds of several great companies eager for concessions and subventions for distribution in twenty-two constituencies in the province of Quebec. In 1891 the promoters of a huge dock enterprise supplied nearly $120,000 [$3.6 million today]."

The money paid for organizers to canvass the ridings and to identify supporters among the favourable voting blocs to be dragged to the polls on election day. The taxpayers footed some of the bill as well. Government enumerators were drawn from Conservative ranks to prepare the official lists of eligible voters. These partisans tended to be somewhat negligent in counting voters on the wrong side of town and rather diligent in enrolling the deceased. The money also helped pay for the party press. A newspaper served each community, and almost every newspaper was either Conservative or Liberal. Government patronage was intimately involved in the business of running a paper. In addition to carrying lucrative government advertising, many papers' presses thrived on government printing contracts. In return, the papers functioned as party house organs at all times.

In English Canada the provincial Liberal organizations were solid. And in Quebec, Tarte had been busy, creating political clubs in every part of the province, establishing a central office for Quebec to coordinate the flow of resources, and swelling the Liberal press with new party organs. While the Liberals tightened their organization, the Tories had fallen into disrepair. As the Tory *La Presse* lamented, "the ministers … were never in touch with any of the riding bosses." The problem was disunity; the long struggles between *bleu* and *castor* factions – over patronage, leadership, and the finer points of the Schools Question – had all left their damaging marks. The same problem existed in Ontario, where splitter candidacies and anti-remedial sentiment cut more deeply into Tupper's organization than into the Mowat–Laurier alliance.

Then, as now, the travelling medicine show at the heart of each campaign was the leader's tour. Rallies were like harvest fairs; in many communities, they were bigger. Their purpose was timeless: motivate the converted, and create a bandwagon effect for the doubtful. At Laurier's nine-hour campaign kick-off, twelve thousand Montrealers roared their support for the leader and a lavish fireworks display. The guest of honour invoked the spirits of Papineau, Baldwin, and Lafontaine – the liberal heroes who had stretched their hands across Canada's racial divide to bring responsible government to Canada in the 1830s and 1840s. Even *La Presse* conceded that the crowd ate it up.

On May 8, standing in Winnipeg with Sir John A.'s son, Tupper began his campaign by seizing on Laurier's vague assurances to Quebeckers of remedial action stronger than the government's. What was the logic, Tupper asked, of anyone who "oppressed a feeble minority, and that for the purpose of bringing

to power a Roman Catholic French premier, who declares he will do more?" The message was clear: you can't trust a Frenchman, even if he changes his spots.

Laurier was ready. On May 11 in Ste-Cunegonde, Quebec, he returned fire, accusing the prime minister of appealing to "the fanaticism of electors." By the end of the campaign's third week he was turning Tupper's slur to good use in front of English crowds, using his now-perfected routine of out-Britishing the British.

In the Montreal Anglo enclave of Westmount, Laurier declared: "When Sir Charles Tupper dares to say that I should not be entrusted with power because I am French and a Catholic, I hurl back the words in his face, as his greatest condemnation. It is not to my countrymen of French origin that I appeal, but it is to my fellow countrymen of British origin, because you belong to the race that has always been the champion of liberty." Nice one. Laurier now added his 1896 Champion of English Liberty at Westmount to his 1895 Duke of Wellington at Morrisburg and his 1894 Gladstone in Winnipeg. Having played these British roles for three years, he had defanged all attacks on his patriotism. Besides, the intensity with which Laurier fought back must have made a powerful impression. He was proclaiming his deepest convictions with all the eloquence and passion that Canada's greatest political orator could muster. He fought like a man who was through with losing, who could no longer be denied his dreams, whose hour had struck at last.

Each leader had time for one swing in

the Maritimes, Quebec, and Ontario. Laurier had got the West out of the way in 1894 and had covered Ontario so thoroughly in the fall of 1895 that he could concentrate on Quebec, while Mowat led the Liberal charge in his home province. Tupper was forced to make the haul to Manitoba and back at the campaign's front end. He would spend the rest of the time in the East, addressing thirty-one meetings in Ontario in the campaign's final two weeks. Laurier spent only ten of the campaign's sixty days in Ontario.

Laurier needed every minute he could spend in Quebec. On May 17 the bishops struck with a *mandement* read from every pulpit in every diocese of the province: "All Catholics shall vote only for candidates who formally and solemnly undertake to vote in Parliament,

This single-page flyer speaks volumes about Tupper's campaign. The recitation of Macdonald's 1891 slogan was a feeble attempt to make trade the big issue after the Schools Question had wrecked the Tory coalition.

in favour of legislation providing the Catholic minority in Manitoba the educational rights which have been recognized by the Privy Council in England. This grave duty imposes itself on all good Catholics, and you will be justified neither before your spiritual guides nor before God in foregoing this obligation." In a private circular, bishops were empowered to insist on written declarations of compliance from all candidates as a prerequisite for lifting the ban of the *mandement*. All but eight of the Liberal candidates in Quebec signed, one of the holdouts being the candidate in Québec-Est, Wilfrid Laurier. One day later Archbishop Laflèche of Trois-Rivières went a step further. At high mass in the cathedral the old prelate blasted Laurier's hoist speech and ordained that "a Catholic cannot under pain of sinning in a grave matter vote for the chief of a party who has formulated so publicly such an error."

Laurier and the Liberals fought back furiously, and the *rouge* press pilloried Laflèche for his dramatically partisan remarks. In the end the intervention of the church did not seem to sway Quebec voters one way or the other. But the Liberals worked hard to make sure that Ontarians heard about the company Tupper was keeping in Quebec. At a minimum the association of the Quebec church and the Tories made it difficult for an Ontario anti-Catholic bigot to know who his friends were. The overall result was the growing strength of splitter Tory candidates running as McCarthyites in the province.

The most important election dynamic in Quebec, however, was not the scrap between Laurier and Laflèche but the raw fact of Laurier's candidacy. No longer a rookie leader, no longer standing in Sir John A.'s shadow, and now looking like a real *chef* after weathering the Schools Question without any challenges to his leadership, Laurier had

emerged as Quebec's major political figure. He had come to personify the aspirations of his people.

The two leaders began election day, June 23, in suspense. Both knew that Ontario would be close, and neither was sure about Quebec. Tupper believed Angers's assurance that the province would deliver forty-five of sixty-five seats to the saviours of Catholicism. For his part Tarte had said: "Leave Quebec to Laurier and to me." The day broke fair in the Maritimes and across much of the country. At 9 a.m. local time the polls opened in each riding and remained so until 5 p.m. Polling hours coincided with work hours, making it difficult for many to get out to vote, especially in the urban centres.

"Near the poll at the house of a friendly neighbour was stationed the 'telephone man,'" wrote H.P. Ames, a Tory MP in an account of a municipal election day that captures the flavour of the era's politics well. "It is remarkable how many city electors can be reached during business hours by telephone. The necessary phone numbers of all presumably favourable electors had been ascertained prior to the day of election, and entered alphabetically upon a convenient card for the use of the 'telephone man.'

From 9 a.m. till 4 p.m. his telephone was never idle. 'Have you voted, sir?' 'When will you come up to vote, sir?' 'Shall we send someone to fetch you?' Such were the inevitable questions. And these constant reminders had their effect. Businessmen, realizing that work would be rendered impossible until they had performed their duty as citizens, came early to vote." In rural areas and small towns the same process was repeated face to face, with squads of paid workers combing the byways for friendly voters.

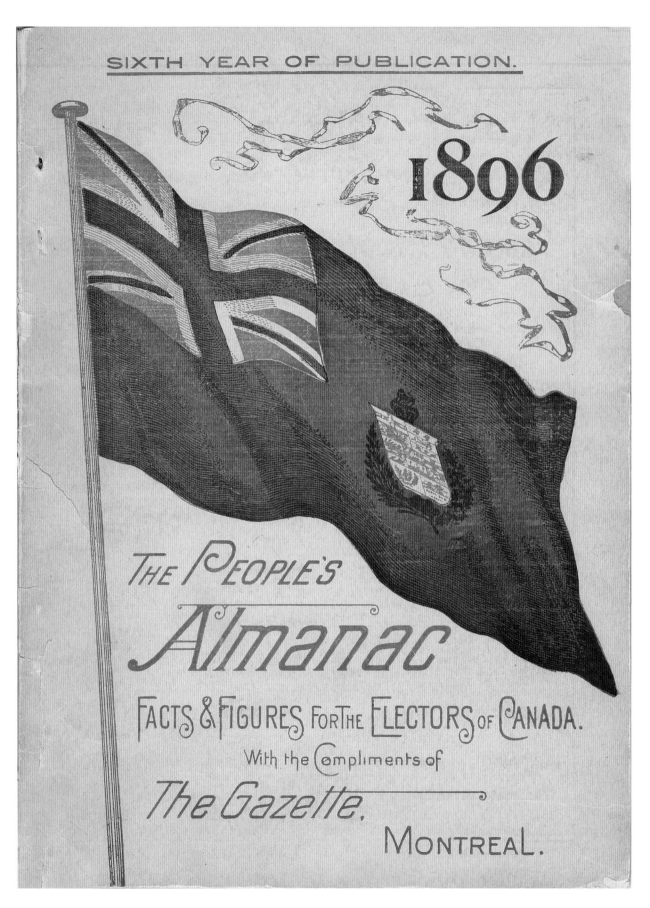

Voting took place in every imaginable location. Winnipeg electors could cast their ballots in Evan's Music Store, Conway's auction rooms, the Crystal Ice Company offices, and John Hanby's House on Donald Street. The *Globe* warned Toronto's Liberal scrutineers to guard against fraud in such loose circumstances, warning of plans "to give voters who have been tampered with a marked ballot before they enter the polling booth and they will be requested to take out with them the ballot they receive from the deputy returning officer."

In Ottawa Tupper awaited the results, while Laurier voted and waited in Quebec City. The *Globe*, optimistic as never before, ran quarter-page ads inviting folks to watch the returns on "an electric-lighted Stereopticon, from the *Globe* building, on a 30-foot square curtain" stretched on the opposite side of King Street.

That night the returns chattered over the telegraph wires. It took some time for the numbers to come in; some western and northern ridings would not be settled for days. When the dust cleared, however, the results were decisive: Liberals 118 seats; Conservatives 88; Independents 7. Near midnight in Quebec City a torchlight procession gathered for Laurier. The next morning his victory was celebrated in a thousand-carriage parade.

The national results showed a divided country. The electorate had grown by 15 per cent since 1891 – much more than had the

population – indicating strong organizational efforts on both sides. The raw Liberal vote went up by 10.5 per cent, while the Conservatives' rose a marginal 4 per cent. However, the big story was the decline in both parties' share of the total in English Canada, where the independents and splitters polled almost 9 per cent of the total vote, mainly in the sensitive spots of Ontario and Manitoba.

The lapsed Liberals running under the banner of the Patrons of Industry, the lapsed Tory McCarthyites, and the independents divided about 15 per cent of the Ontario vote and 18 per cent of Manitoba's. Both parties' share of the vote dropped, but the Tories' dropped more and "the splits" in the ridings usually broke against them. Seven splitter MPs were elected in Ontario and Manitoba. The Conservatives fell by five seats from their previous count in these critical provinces, while the Liberals lost one. In the West and the Maritimes the pattern was the same: modest Liberal gains and mild Tory losses. It fell to Quebec to give Laurier the election. *Canadiens* voted en masse for their native son, giving him 53.5 per cent of the popular vote and forty-nine of sixty-five seats. In almost every region of Quebec the Liberals advanced, gaining sixteen seats.

In English Canada, Laurier's adroit handling of the Schools Question had paid off. As in the pre-writ period, the Liberal

A hundred or so years ago election campaigns were treated as great civic celebrations. An election year was marked in red on the national calendar. This *People's Almanac (opposite)*, issued by the Tories at the *Montreal Gazette*, sold itself as a helpful tool for voters going about their sacred duty. This simple button *(right)* reminded Liberals of their real duty – to win after twenty years.

leader had let the Tories do the bleeding, counting on being left standing behind the lines of Torres Vedras once the Conservatives' strength had ebbed away. And in Quebec, Tarte's strategy of betting everything on the magic of a French Canadian leader with a real shot at power had worked magnificently. This promise represented a new dawn in Quebec politics, as well as the first appearance of the "Quebec advantage," which conferred then, as now, an immense head start to the party with the francophone leader.

It is tempting to argue that Canadians in 1896 cast their ballots for tolerance and unity. But the story of this first great Canadian election doesn't fit that bill. In 1896, as they had since 1867, Canadian voters generally supported their party, their tribe, and their church. A solid chunk of Ontario voters cast their ballots for their local anti-remedialist bigot, many of them stepping away from their traditional party loyalties to go with militant splitters. An even bigger segment of Quebec voted tribally, electing one of their own.

Yet these paradoxical results – moderation arising from extremism – grew out of a system of parliamentary politics that rewarded moderation both in the making of cabinets in Ottawa and, usually, out on the hustings at election time. This system of rewards, indeed the system itself, had been gravely threatened by the Manitoba Schools Question. The Tories' disunity, born of extreme positions taken by their French and English wings, made stable government impossible in Ottawa and doomed the party to disunity. Immoderate *castors* in Quebec sapped the party of energy and cohesion. Immoderate Tories in Ontario and Manitoba broke the government's effectiveness, then broke away from the party, then broke its hold on key ridings by running as McCarthyites and independents.

But the Liberals held the line. They mostly hung together in English Canada and were able to field a united, vigorous machine in Quebec, even under the extreme stress of attacks from that province's most powerful body. By winning the election this way, Laurier could count on implementing his moderate approach once in government, without losing members left and right; after all, he could argue, the people had spoken.

Of course the people hadn't so much spoken as they had worked through a complex representative system that was not really designed to reflect the popular will on issues. Our world, in which voters carefully track leaders' personalities, and large numbers of them connect issues to voting, was still a long way off. By and large, the voters of 1896 had chosen a government of elites that could, under less-talented leadership, have blown apart at almost any point in the lead-up to the campaign. The system worked, but Laurier and the Liberals had to work themselves pretty hard – and sacrifice Manitoba's Catholic minority – to save the system. They had rendered unto Caesar what was Caesar's, leaving God and the church to clean up the moral debris left in their wake.

The prize was worth the cost. The long, well-matched, closely fought battle that ended on June 23, 1896, directly addressed a fundamental nation-building question: the ability of Canada's two major racial/linguistic/religious groups to work together in a federal political structure. The intense fight leading up to 1896 came close to splitting the parties, deadlocking national politics, and, quite likely, taking down the structure of Confederation.

Instead, the system met the supreme challenge, defusing a threat to its democratic, parliamentary, and federal structure without recourse to undemocratic or extraparliamentary means. While 1896 clearly preserved the

PLAYBOOK II

The winning play in 1896 was the Quebec Bridge, the second entry in my imaginary political playbook. In 1896 Laurier countered the Tory whipsaw with a set of moves devised by Sir John A. Macdonald in the years leading up to Confederation. Macdonald realized that the surest route to electoral victory began by looking after the interests of Quebec, a region that tends to vote *en bloc*. He used the Quebec Bridge successfully in five of his six national election victories. The basic play, along with later variants still in use, has proven the most reliable way to win a Canadian election.

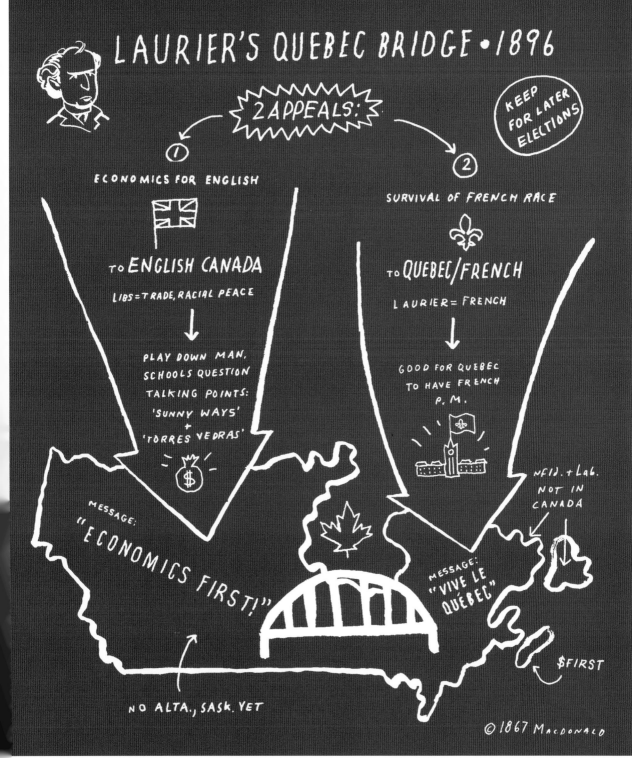

LAURIER'S QUEBEC BRIDGE • 1896

2 APPEALS:

KEEP FOR LATER ELECTIONS

① ECONOMICS FOR ENGLISH

② SURVIVAL OF FRENCH RACE

TO ENGLISH CANADA

LIBS = TRADE, RACIAL PEACE

PLAY DOWN MAN. SCHOOLS QUESTION
TALKING POINTS:
'SUNNY WAYS'
+
'TORRES VEDRAS'

MESSAGE: "ECONOMICS FIRST!"

TO QUEBEC/FRENCH

LAURIER = FRENCH

GOOD FOR QUEBEC TO HAVE FRENCH P.M.

NFLD. + LAB. NOT IN CANADA

MESSAGE: "VIVE LE QUÉBEC"

$ FIRST

NO ALTA., SASK. YET

© 1867 MACDONALD

outward forms of the two-party system, a critical evolution in Canadian politics took place beneath the surface: national electoral politics ceased to be a life-and-death proposition for the country itself. The centre held, and in the process the notion of "Canada" became stronger. Never again would Confederation itself be at stake in a federal election campaign.

The greatness of this achievement, and the fight from which it arose, is all the more impressive when compared with what other countries were going through at the time. The United States was still wrestling with the legacy of a massive Civil War in which 550,000 of its citizens were killed through combat and the rule of law was substantially suspended. In the 1890s Jim Crow laws were being drafted in the southern states, implementing a form of apartheid that barred black citizens from political participation for three-quarters of a century. In Britain the government of Laurier's avatar William Gladstone had just shivered to bits over the question of home rule for the Irish. Within a few years England and France would come to the brink of war in the struggle for colonies. And that was just in the earth's supposedly civilized parts.

The fight of 1896 was more than a battle for power or for our peculiar experiment in nation-building federalism. It was a struggle with a larger meaning. It is a cliché to speak now of Canada's unique tradition of tolerance and civilized reconciliation of our differences. But that's because a lot of the world has caught up with us. Something quietly magnificent happened here that June evening a century ago.

Arrival. House of Commons, May 1897, Ontario's Cartwright speaks as Laurier and Tarte (to his right), and New Brunswick's Blair and Manitoba's Sifton (to the left) look on. Almost four years after Macdonald's death, the country's sole national coalition is now Liberal.

ON BORROWED TIME

THE ELECTIONS OF
1900 / 1904 / 1908 / 1911 / 1917 / 1921

LAURIER GAVE THE GREAT party system a new lease on life in 1896, and, in the process, probably saved the country. For almost two decades more the delicate yet durable two-party system lumbered along, until the First World War finally threw the structure into a terminal crisis. Reconstructing a lasting order from postwar political chaos took almost a full decade thereafter.

Two of the six elections fought in the tumultuous period between 1896 and 1925 mark important moments in Canadian history, but neither truly passes the test of greatness. The free trade election of 1911 marked the end of the Laurier era and a climactic encounter over free trade, but in the final analysis it merely shifted the balance of power among the existing players. The political order stayed intact; it was never even challenged as it had been in 1896. The next campaign, the conscription election of 1917, smashed one of the great parties and plunged the Canadian political system into its time of troubles. But in no way was it an exciting match-up. It resembled a raw trial of strength between the French minority and the English majority and was thus over before it began. While the 1911 election saw the last of the old order and the 1917 contest set up a period of extreme voter and party volatility, both essentially looked backward to the race-based coalition politics of the nineteenth century, as the shadows lengthened and a political nightmare began.

October 1899
TROOPS OFF TO BOER WAR
The 2nd battalion of the Royal Canadian Regiment is dispatched to fight in the Boer War. The conflict, with its startling casualty rates and concentration camps, was really the first twentieth-century war. (*Above*) A "war cycle" designed to transport troops.

November 1896
GREAT IMMIGRATION DRIVE BEGINS
Interior Minister Clifford Sifton announces Canada's largest immigration drive. By the end of Laurier's tenure, Canada's population at Confederation will have doubled to seven million. (*Above*) Welsh immigrants on their way to Canada.

June 1898
KLONDIKE GOLD RUSH IN FULL SWING
On June 13 the booming Yukon becomes a separate territory. (*Above*) Dawson City's Palace Grand Theatre in November 1899.

November 7, 1900
LAURIER WINS SECOND TERM
Sir Wilfrid Laurier (*above*) and the Liberals take 132 seats to 81 for Sir Charles Tupper's Tories.

Canada's sun shone warmly during the long afternoon of the Laurier era. The "sunny ways" formula of 1896 set a pattern of easy compromises over painful issues and served the prime minister brilliantly during his first term in office. The Schools Question itself was resolved by Ottawa's abandonment of the Manitoba Catholics, with minor concession from the province to save Laurier's face. His cries in opposition for "commercial union" became a mere 2.4 per cent reduction in tariffs in his first budget. When the Boer War was declared in 1899, Laurier bowed to English Canada's urge to join in Britain's imperial adventure, but insisted that Canada's entry be a matter of independent choice. These straddles kept Laurier's French, English, agrarian, and industrial coalition partners in harness as he called an election in 1900. His Tory opponent was once again Sir Charles Tupper, whose scattergun attacks bounced harmlessly off the government during the run-up to the election and in the campaign itself. The Liberals were returned with increased seat-counts in every province except Ontario (where the vote-splitters of 1896 returned to the Tory fold) and British Columbia.

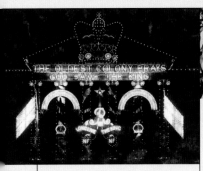

January 1901
QUEEN VICTORIA DIES
The queen's passing on January 22 marks the symbolic conclusion of the nineteenth century. (*Above*) The Crown colony of Newfoundland pays its respects to the new monarch.

March 1901
DOUKHOBORS LOSE THE VOTE
A legislative loophole allows Manitoba to disqualify Doukhobors and other unpopular immigrant groups from voting, creating Canada's version of the infamous Jim Crow laws in the US. (*Above*) Naked Doukhobors march during a 1903 protest.

September 1903
LAURIER GOES ON RAILROAD BINGE
Laurier's Railway Bill is passed, giving the green light to two new transcontinental lines, the Grand Trunk Pacific and the Canadian Northern (*above*), both of which proved financial disasters.

August 1904
FORD CANADA OPENS
More automobiles begin to appear on Canadian roads after the Ford Motor Company opens in Walkerville, Ontario. The plant would produce 117 cars in the first year.

Laurier continued to have an easy ride during his second term. But in one important area he seized the initiative: the settlement of the west. His aggressive encouragement of immigration helped fuel Canada's continuing economic prosperity and engendered in Canadians an unbridled optimism about the new century, which, the prime minister famously promised in January 1904, "shall be the century of Canada." He backed his expansionary rhetoric with two massive railway projects aimed at encouraging settlement and breaking the monopoly of the Canadian Pacific Railway, so hated by his western supporters.

In the 1904 election the new Conservative leader, fifty-year-old Robert Borden of Nova Scotia, faced a popular prime minister riding a continuing wave of prosperity. On election day, November 3, the Liberals won again, adding a solid western phalanx to their existing support. Laurier's third term capped his achievements with the creation of two new provinces, Alberta and Saskatchewan, in 1905. With continued prosperity – and, more important, having avoided any coalition-splitting issues in his third mandate – Laurier was able to repeat his 1904 triumph (in central Canada, anyway) in the next election, held on October 26, 1908.

But as the century's second decade opened, Sir Wilfrid was starting to look like yesterday's man, despite carrying his seventy years with characteristic elegance. His young protégé, William Lyon Mackenzie King, wrote in his diary: "He disliked the motor, telegraph, telephone, the real charm of the world had gone. He would rather have the eighteenth century." Laurier was running yesterday's government too; by their fourth mandate the Liberals had manifestly run out of ideas.

Then, in January 1911, Canada's tiny civil service delivered the Liberal prime minister an astounding coup, a draft free trade agreement – "reciprocity" in the parlance of the day – with the United States. Laurier had not forgotten the hard lessons of 1891, but he also knew that the deal would galvanize his farm support in Ontario and the West and put a little zip back into his drifting caucus. What's more, the highly favourable agreement provided for the free flow of raw materials, a sector where Canada had the advantage, but left in place the tariffs that protected Canada's manufacturers. Surely, thought Laurier, after almost fifty years of existence, the country had grown secure enough to enter a favourable commodities trade deal with the world's fastest-growing economy. Besides, putting the politics of principle at the centre of a campaign, rather than those of race and religion, had been his life-long goal. He decided he would make the trade deal the central plank of an early election campaign.

The deal posed a daunting challenge to the Conservative leader. Robert Borden had worked hard to outflank the Liberals' economic populism with progressive proposals such as government regulation of the electricity industry and the creation of a national telephone system, but his careful repositioning seemed set to tumble in the face of Laurier's attractive reciprocity deal. The Tories themselves were at odds over the issue. As one opposition MP was heard to mutter, "I just don't dare to vote against it." An alarmed Borden later wrote that "the difference of opinion which had developed seemed in itself to be a forerunner of disaster."

But Robert Borden was a fighter. On February 9, 1911, the Tory leader rose in the House of Commons to attack the deal's broad intent, charging that reciprocity meant turning away from the British Empire and towards the United States. "We should continue with firm heart and unabated hope upon the path which we entered nearly fifty years ago." Five days later, Borden's case was bolstered when Champ Clark, the Speaker of the US House of Representatives, declared of

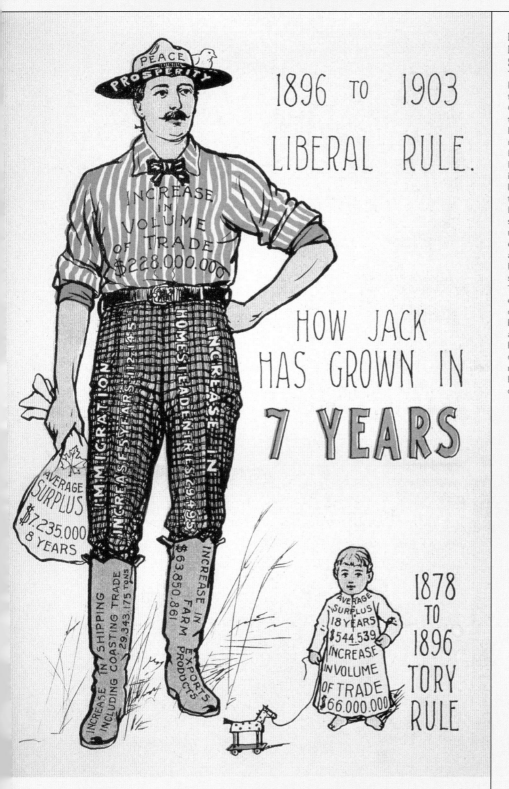

1896 TO 1903
LIBERAL RULE.

HOW JACK
HAS GROWN IN
7 YEARS

1878
TO
1896
TORY
RULE

PEACE
PROSPERITY

INCREASE IN VOLUME OF TRADE $228,000,000

INCREASE IN IMMIGRATION 121,145
INCREASE IN HOMESTEAD ENTRIES 29,495
AVERAGE SURPLUS $7,235,000 8 YEARS
INCREASE IN SHIPPING INCLUDING COASTING TRADE 29,343,175 TONS
INCREASE IN FARM EXPORTS PRODUCTS $63,850,861

AVERAGE SURPLUS 18 YEARS $544,539 INCREASE IN VOLUME OF TRADE $66,000,000

November 3, 1904
LAURIER WINS THIRD STRAIGHT MANDATE
The Liberals win their largest majority to date, taking 139 seats to the Conservatives' 75. During the campaign new Tory leader Robert Borden made little headway in English Canada against Laurier's record of prosperity, expansion, and railroad building, as depicted in this Liberal poster. In French Canada, Laurier's status as a native son was more than enough to overcome voter uneasiness about his support for British Empire projects such as the Boer War. The first *Canadien* PM expended a great deal of his political capital balancing Quebec's anti-imperialism with the hyper-imperialism of much of English Canada, adroitly managing to keep the English and French wings of his coalition happy.

September 1905
ALBERTA AND
SASKATCHEWAN JOIN
CONFEDERATION
Canada gets its eighth
and ninth provinces on
September 1 in recogni-
tion of the rush of settlers
to the "Last Best West."
(Above) A man who has
waited all night outside
the Dominion Lands
Office, Regina, for the
chance to register his
quarter-section of land.

MAY 1906
PUBLIC POWER IN ONTARIO
The government of
Ontario bows to public
and business pressure for
a publicly owned electrical
utility. Wiring the province
accelerates.

October 26, 1908
LAURIER ON TRACK
Laurier takes 133 seats to
85 for the Conservatives
under Borden. Despite
mounting French–English
discord over empire issues,
Laurier holds it all together
once again. *(Above)* The PM
drives the last spike of
Alberta's Central Northern
Railway on August 10, 1908.

January 1910
BOURASSA FOUNDS LE DEVOIR
On January 10 the first edition
of *Le Devoir*, former Liberal
MP Henri Bourassa's new
nationalist newspaper, appears
on the stands. *(Above)* Henri
Bourassa and his family.

reciprocity, "I am for it, because I hope to see the day when the American flag will float over every square foot of the British North American possessions clear to the north pole."

Laurier dithered over calling the election, giving his opponents time to rush into place the elements of a winning machine. Money came from the gentlemen's clubs and boardrooms of Montreal and Toronto. On February 20 a group of wealthy party stalwarts who became known as the "Toronto Eighteen" publicly broke with Laurier over the deal. A week later, on February 28, Clifford Sifton, Laurier's former western lieutenant, turned on his old boss.

In Quebec as well, prodigal sons bedevilled the prime minister. Another of his brilliant former protégés, the fiery Henri Bourassa, who had quit the Liberal caucus in 1899 over the Boer War, had by 1911 emerged as a challenger to Laurier for the leadership of French Canada. Bourassa, who had sat in the Quebec legisla-ture and had founded first the nationalist paper *Le Devoir* and then the

January 1911
CANADA–US TRADE AGREEMENT PROPOSED
Civil servants sign off on a reciprocity agreement. *(Above)* Program for a state dinner celebrating the agreement.

March 1910
CANADA CREATES NAVY
The Royal Canadian Navy is established, angering many Quebeckers. Henri Bourassa calls it "a national capitulation" to the pressure to fight British wars. *(Above)* Canadian Navy recruitment poster.

July 1911
LAURIER CALLS ELECTION
In English Canada the issue will be the Reciprocity Treaty with the United States; in French Canada, the navy and the empire. *(Above)* Tory campaign postcard showing the leader (Borden) and the local candidate.

Nationalistes, a federal party devoted solely to Quebec's interests, believed that Laurier was selling out the *Canadien* race to curry favour with Britain, and that nothing less than conscription of Quebec boys into British wars would be the end result. Laurier's big 1910 naval spending bill, which moved towards the development of a Canadian navy integrated in the defence of the British Empire, created a serious backlash that greatly enhanced Bourassa's standing.

In the late spring of 1911 Robert Borden authorized an informal alliance with Laurier's nationalist archrival. Borden and Bourassa never shook hands on a deal – it was concluded by lower-level players – but Bourassa would run twenty-eight Nationaliste candidates as Conservatives in winnable ridings, while the Tories provided money.

By mid-summer, having made this strategic alliance in Quebec, the Tory leader was well on his way to executing one of the classic Canadian political plays, the Double Tribal Whipsaw – invented and perfected by Sir John A. Macdonald in the early 1890s. In English Canada he would assault the free-trading Liberals as disloyal to the British; in Quebec Bourassa would rail against Laurier as a British toady disloyal to his fellow *Canadiens*. Laurier assumed he could defeat the Double Tribal Whipsaw as he had in 1896, 1900, and 1904, with the Quebec Bridge based on a secure base in his home province.

On July 10 the prime minister returned from a trip to London to confront a rapidly deteriorating political situation. Nonetheless he decided to plunge forward with an election campaign fought on free trade, hoping to carry the country by the force of his personality. At a welcome-home rally in Montreal on July 11, Laurier exhorted his troops into battle, invoking the ghost of France's warrior-conciliator king Henri IV: "Like Henry of Navarre, I say ... 'Follow my white plume.'"

On July 29, at Laurier's request, the new governor general, the Duke of Connaught, dissolved parliament and called a general election for September 21. The prime minister seems to have had no notion that it was an election he couldn't win. The man's political smarts were now rusted out, corroded by age and by fifteen years of unchallenged electoral supremacy.

The 1911 campaign unfolded predictably. Borden focused on Ontario, kicking off his tour in London, Ontario, on August 16, one day after he had published a powerful "Appeal to the People" in Toronto's Tory *Daily Mail and Empire*: "I appeal to the people ... that their verdict will be ... for the strengthening and not the loosening of the ties that bind this Dominion to the British Empire."

On August 17 Laurier commenced his effort in Trois-Rivières with the epigram that could stand as both his political catechism and his epitaph: "I am branded in Quebec as a traitor to the French and in Ontario as a traitor to the English ... I am neither. I am a Canadian." In Quebec he even tried out the nose-stretching argument that Quebec's interests and Britain's were identical: "The day when England's supremacy on the sea is destroyed your national and religious privileges will be endangered." Bourassa in reply scorned the prime minister as "the captain of the god-damned navy." On election eve, September 20, Rudyard Kipling, the Bard of Empire himself, publicly cabled his support for the Tory leader: "It is her own soul that Canada risks today."

On election night, September 21, Borden captured 133 of 221 seats. English Canada on its own almost gave the Tories a majority – their first since 1891 – but Quebec delivered the *coup de grâce*, electing 27 Conservatives/Nationalistes and

The "White Plume" of Canada's Grand Old Man

September 21, 1911
LAURIER DEFEATED
Laurier's July 1911 exhortation to "follow my white plume" was another of his little historical gags. The PM was not only making light of his advancing age but trying to quell Quebec's nationalist backlash against his naval bill as a "sellout" to the English. The quote, which appears on the cover of this booklet of speeches, came from King Henri IV, who healed France in the early 1600s after a century of religious war. In effect Laurier is saying to his fellow *Canadiens*, "I am a great leader and healer; if you betray me and vote *nationaliste*, you're risking religious/racial warfare with *les anglais*." Nice idea, but it didn't work.

The promise of free trade with the US, the English Canadian half of Laurier's strategy, didn't work either. Too many industrial interests were opposed, too many prominent Liberals were off-side, and too many voters were swayed by Borden's eloquent denunciations of Laurier's disloyalty to Mother Britain. Caught in a Tory trap straight out of Sir John A. Macdonald's playbook, Laurier went down to defeat on election night, 133 seats to 86, the steepest fall of a government since Confederation. The Laurier era was over.

Henry of Navarre, at the battle of Ivry, said, "Follow my white plume and you will find it always in the forefront of honor." Like Henry IV, I say to you young men: "Follow my white plume, the white hairs of sixty-nine years, and you will, I believe I can say without boasting, find it always in the forefront of honor."—Sir Wilfrid Laurier, to the great gathering in the Champ de Mars, Montreal, July 12, 1911.

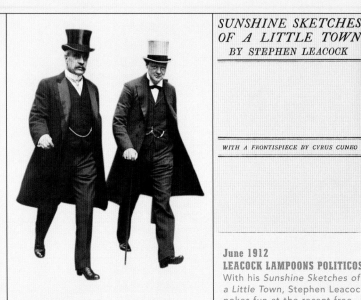

SUNSHINE SKETCHES OF A LITTLE TOWN
BY STEPHEN LEACOCK

WITH A FRONTISPIECE BY CYRUS CUNEO

October 1911
BORDEN BECOMES PRIME MINISTER
On October 10 Robert Borden is sworn in as prime minister. He will edge the country closer to Britain as the mother country seeks support in its maritime competition with Germany. *(Above)* Borden with UK naval minister Winston Churchill on a visit to London in 1912.

June 1912
LEACOCK LAMPOONS POLITICOS
With his *Sunshine Sketches of a Little Town*, Stephen Leacock pokes fun at the recent free trade election: "We can see – it's plain enough now – that in the great election Canada saved the British Empire."

August 1914
CANADA JOINS THE GREAT WAR
On August 4 Canada enters what will come to be known as the First World War. The first troops embark in October and become among the most respected fighters in the killing fields of France and Belgium. The war marked a coming-of-age for Canada – at least its English part – and a watershed in the country's politics. *(Above)* The legendary battlefield of Passchendaele.

reducing the Grits' national total to a paltry 88 seats. Laurier's prime ministership ended in a solitary train voyage from his Quebec City riding home to Ottawa, to his wife and a long twilight in opposition.

The free trade election of 1911 is memorable less for how it changed the country than how it didn't. Not only did a key national policy remain in place, but the form of national politics remained intact. Indeed, 1911 may be best understood as the last Great Party–era tussle fought in the familiar nineteenth-century way – with massive paid party machines dragging blocs of semi-inert voters to the polls. (Four per cent of the electorate switched sides – a big swing but a far cry from the volatility just ahead.) Thus, the 1911 election, while a great match-up over a nation-building issue, did nothing for the evolution of national politics and fell just short of greatness.

The 1917 election, as bitter and divisive a campaign as any Canada has ever witnessed, really began on August 4, 1914, just as Robert Borden's first government was getting ready to celebrate three years in power. On that

October 1917
CONSCRIPTION CRISIS ERUPTS
The conscription election begins, easily the most violent campaign in Canadian history. Ottawa's imposition of conscription brings mobs into the streets and divides the country more deeply than ever between its French and English citizens. (Above) Soldiers sit in front of pro-conscription graffiti.

December 1917
HALIFAX EXPLOSION
A munitions ship explodes in Halifax harbour, killing 2,000 and injuring thousands, including this boy.

December 1917
BLUEBIRDS VOTE AT THE FRONT
The Bluebirds – Canada's military nurses – become the first women to vote in a Canadian federal election when they cast their ballots at the front. At home, only women with relatives in the military will cast ballots in this election. (Above) Bluebirds line up to vote.

December 1915
WOMEN DEMAND THE VOTE
As women take a more active role on the home front, suffragist organizations clamour more loudly for the female franchise. (Above) Members of the Political Equality League.

date, the British Empire joined with her allies, France and Russia, in declaring war against the German Empire and Austria-Hungary. Canada was automatically at war.

The Great War instantly tore open the French–English fissure. French Canada did not support the war effort as intensely as did the country's English majority. It was clear to all from the outset that, should the effort come to require conscription of *Canadien* boys, Quebec would go one way and the rest of the country another. By April 1917 Borden's system of voluntary enlistment had failed to deliver the requisite soldiers, especially in Quebec, where enthusiasm for the war was lowest. Riots had repeatedly broken out in Quebec towns when recruiters arrived to sign up volunteers. At an April Imperial War Cabinet meeting in London, Borden committed to reinforcing the Canadian Corps, fully aware that his pledge meant conscription. On May 18, 1917, he announced that his government would shortly introduce legislation to conscript able-bodied males for service.

Borden's announcement put the pre-writ campaign into high gear. His first move, an effort to avoid a racially charged election, was to ask Laurier to join a coalition government. Laurier ultimately refused: the old *Canadien* would go down fighting for his people. The prime minister also began negotiating to bring a number of English Canadian Liberals across the floor to serve in a "Unionist" government of wartime solidarity. In June and July, as one Grit after another signalled he would support Borden, the opposition began to collapse. (In the end some thirty-eight out of forty-nine non-Quebec Liberals would desert Laurier and their Quebec brethren.) Only a few anglophone Grit MPs, notably the ambitious William Lyon Mackenzie King, would stand by their leader and with Quebec through the crisis. On July 24 Borden's Military Service Act was passed into law.

The parliament of 1911, now six years old thanks to extraordinary wartime extension measures, needed renewal to legitimize the government's conscription decision. This extension in turn required a Wartime Elections Act, which was passed in late September. The act, along with the concurrent Military Voters Act, broadened the franchise to include any British subject, male or female, who was an active or retired member of the Canadian armed forces – all servicemen and women – and the female relatives of anyone, living or dead, who had served in the armed forces. (As a result, the Bluebirds, Canada's military nurses, who cast their ballots at advance overseas polls, became the first women ever to vote in a Canadian election.) The Wartime Elections Act simultaneously stripped the franchise from recent immigrants from hostile countries. On October 6 an election was called for December 17 – an unusually long ten-week writ period to allow the overseas soldiers' vote to be solicited and counted. Six days after dissolution a new caretaker Unionist government was officially sworn in with a majority of 153 to 82, including ten Liberals in its eighteen-man cabinet. This forbidding line-up of both parties' English Canadian big guns glared imposingly at Laurier's small phalanx of mostly francophone MPs preparing to campaign as Liberals.

Laurier did what he could to raise the issues of government incompetence and corruption in the war effort, but the English Canadian population treated the conscription issue as Borden intended: loyalty versus treason. Conservative politicians throughout English Canada resorted to raw racial demonization, depicting Quebec as "the plague spot of the whole Dominion." The December 14 *Toronto Daily News* printed a map of the country with Quebec shaded in black under the heading "The Foul Blot on Canada." Toronto's Citizen's Union Committee took out ads that warned "Quebec must not rule Canada."

November 24, 1917

CANADA

DOMINION OF CANADA.

SOLDIERS' ELECTION.

A Selective Draft.

Not ALL liable to draft will be selected.

RELATIVES OF SOLDIERS will be sympathetically considered.

FOR

THE LEADER OF THE GOVERNMENT has given this PLEDGE:—

In enforcing this Act the Government will proceed upon the principle that the SERVICE and SACRIFICE of any FAMILY which has already SENT men to the Front MUST be taken into account in considering the exemption of other MEMBERS OF THE SAME FAMILY.

AS THERE ARE IN THE CLASS LIABLE TO SELECTION

MORE THAN FIVE TIMES THE NUMBER OF MEN REQUIRED

THIS MEANS THAT

SOLDIERS' RELATIVES WILL BE EXEMPTED FROM SERVICE.

WOMEN VOTERS IN CANADA.

Under the new Act the wife, widow, mother, sister or daughter of any person, male or female, living or dead, who is serving or has served Overseas in the Military Forces, HAS A VOTE IN CANADA.

WRITE AT ONCE to all your RELATIVES AND FRIENDS in Canada, telling them that

THE BOYS AT THE FRONT EXPECT ALL OF THEM TO VOTE FOR THE UNION GOVERNMENT.

SHOULDER TO SHOULDER SHOULD BE THEIR WATCHWORD AS WELL AS YOURS!

231

December 17, 1917
UNION GOVERNMENT
WINS LANDSLIDE
Borden triumphs at the polls 153 to 82, but he knows his victory has come at a fearful cost. Conscription posed the gravest political crisis since the Manitoba Schools Question, carrying a popular impact as great as the hanging of Louis Riel. The 1917 campaign (from which this appeal to voting soldiers is drawn) immediately deteriorated into a raw trial of strength between overwhelmingly pro-conscription English Canada, united behind Borden's coalition government, and overwhelmingly anti-conscription French Canada, united in bitter opposition to forcible involvement in a war it didn't fully support. The crisis destroyed the old party system based on accommodation between the races within each of the two parties. Now, an English party called "Unionist" glared at a French party called "Liberal." The old order was gone; a decade would pass before the emergence of a new one.

March 1918
MPS SIT IN TEMPORARY HOUSE
Borden's first session of parliament
takes place in temporary quarters.
The original Parliament Buildings,
nearly destroyed by a fire in early
1916, were still being rebuilt.
Members of parliament convene
in the auditorium of the Victoria
Museum *(above)* while the Senate
sits in the museum's Hall of
Invertebrate Fossils.

July 1918
BORDEN KEEPS FAITH
Prime Minister Robert Borden
addresses the Third Canadian
Infantry Brigade in France.
Many of the men in his audience
had been drafted into the armed
forces under the Military Service
Act of 1917, which had precipi-
tated the conscription crisis.

May 1919
WINNIPEG WORKERS
START GENERAL STRIKE
Winnipeg comes to a
standstill as most of the
city's workers join a general
strike called to protest poor
wages, long hours, and abom-
inable working conditions.
Their numbers are swelled by
the legions of unemployed
soldiers returned from the
war. *(Above left)* A Winnipeg
streetcar overturned in the
Bloody Saturday riots of June
21 in which Mounties shot
and killed two strikers.
(Above right) Unemployed
men looking for work
in Toronto.

In parts of French Canada, voters reacted with physical as well as
verbal violence. In Montreal, so many Unionist rallies were broken up by rioting
mobs that the government gave up organizing them. Tory editorialists were
threatened with lynching. Violent demonstrations broke out in Quebec City
and Sherbrooke.

When the ballots had all been counted, the Unionist government was
returned with 153 of 235 seats, 150 of them in English Canada, to the Liberals' 82.
The Liberals' share came overwhelmingly from Quebec. (Interestingly, the initial
election returns showed a much closer result than the lopsided final tally: 141 seats
to 96. But the day after the election the Union government took advantage of a
controversial clause in the Military Voters Act that allowed the overwhelmingly
English Canadian servicemen and servicewomen overseas to vote simply for a party.
These party votes could be distributed to whatever riding the party wished, thus
tipping the balance to the Union side in a number of close races.)

The wartime election of December 17, 1917, smashed the political system
that had lasted since Confederation. In it, two massive, diametrically opposed waves

May 1921
QUEBEC DROPS PROHIBITION
After a brief flirtation with the national wartime trend of prohibiting alcohol, the government of Quebec nationalizes the sale of beer and wine. The tide turns, and prohibition all but disappears in Canada by 1927.

December 1921
MRS. MACPHAIL GOES TO OTTAWA
Agnes Campbell Macphail, an Ontario Progressive, becomes the first woman elected to the House of Commons.

August 1919
KING WINS LIBERAL LEADERSHIP
William Lyon Mackenzie King succeeds Sir Wilfrid Laurier (who had died in February) as leader of the Liberal Party. *(Above)* King hobnobs with delegates at Canada's first-ever federal party leadership convention.

of popular opinion on the issue of conscription swamped the powerful but delicate party machines, with their elite-level interconnections across the lines of race and religion. High-level players deserted their coalition partners in the rush to the racial ramparts. For the first time in Canadian history the public got into the game as well. In 1917 voter opinion played a huge role in forcing the politicians' moves.

Yet the explosion of 1917 falls short of electoral greatness; as a fight, it was no contest between the English majority and the French minority. The election blew up the Victorian party system and unleashed powerful political energies kept confined under the old order; it was surely the big bang that ended the old political order, but it did not mark the transition to the new. The shape of that future would begin to emerge only in the great double-header election of 1925–26.

Sir Wilfrid Laurier barely outlived the war that broke his party, his dreams, and his heart; he died, still leader of the opposition, in February 1919. After his Ottawa funeral, some 50,000 Canadians lined the streets of Ottawa, as if to say goodbye not only to a great leader but to the half-century-long Great Party era that he had represented so well.

A new generation took centre stage. In Canada's first leadership convention that August, the Liberal Party chose the forty-four-year-old William Lyon Mackenzie King. Prime Minister Borden, whose Union government tottered through a sharp post-war economic downturn, retired on July 1, 1920. The Unionist caucus gave the crown to the brilliant, controversial minister of the interior, Manitoba's Arthur Meighen – the man who had quarterbacked conscription through the Commons.

But if the parliamentary cast had changed, the surrounding political scene was shifting even more rapidly. Industrial workers who had been radicalized by the war and by worker-led revolutions in Europe formed a Labour Party in Ontario. This new group acquired a taste of power as junior member of a coalition with the United Farmers of Ontario, which took provincial power in 1919. The English Canadian agrarian voters and politicians who had quit the Liberals over conscription rose up, electing not only Ontario's farmer government and one in Alberta in 1921, but forcing the Liberal governments of Manitoba and Saskatchewan to adopt their policies holus bolus. At the dominion level, a former Laurier supporter and key Manitoba agrarian leader, T.A. Crerar, who had been brought into the Unionist cabinet in 1917, led eight other farmer MPs out of the government to sit "cross benches" as neither Tory nor Grit. By 1920 Crerar's group had grown to eleven and constituted itself as the caucus of the National Progressive Party, with Crerar as leader. Canada's first authentic federal third party had been born.

The Meighen government staggered through a year and a half of political defections and an economic downturn before calling an election for December 6, 1921. King campaigned against its economic record and, borrowing from the radicalism sweeping English Canada, railed against the "continued autocracy" of the wealthy under the Tories. The political whirlwind that had nearly blown away the Liberals in 1917 now tore into the other great party. The rouges swept Quebec, while English Canada split three ways between the two old-line parties and the Progressives. Voters elected 116 Liberals, 69 Progressives, and a miserable 50 Tories alongside 5 Independents, to reveal unprecedented voter volatility. The Tory vote was slashed to 30 per cent, and the other parties' share exploded tenfold to 29 per cent. Mackenzie King was one shy of a majority. Sworn in as the new prime minister on December 29, 1921, he set out across the no-man's land of minority government – the first in the history of the world's British-style parliaments – taking the initial halting steps to the new political order that would become visible only a half-decade later.

HON. W. L. MACKENZIE KING
Leader of the Liberal Party

Speakers' Handbook

ECONOMY
RETRENCHMENT
REFORM

December 6, 1921
LIBERALS FORM FIRST
MINORITY GOVERNMENT
Under new leader William Lyon Mackenzie King, the Liberals take 116 seats, the Progressives 69, and the Tories a mere 50. King forms the first minority government in Canadian history. Conservative prime minister Arthur Meighen's heavy hand in implementing conscription had made him a pariah in Quebec, while the growing farmers' movement shifted Tory support in Ontario and the prairies to T.A. Crerar's Progressives.

King had run a classic opposition campaign aimed at harnessing discontent while keeping his own plans vague. This 1921 handbook for Liberal candidates trumpets three limp themes: "economy" (obvious enough with a near-depression under way); "retrenchment" (a hazy promise to get things more or less back to normal); and King's perennial favourite, "reform" (a broad commitment to bring about social "progress" for "the working man"). Armed with such fuzzy ideas and the kind of weak mandate they generated, the rookie prime minister set out to forge a new political order.

KINGDOM COME

OCT. 29 | SEPT. 14
1925 | 1926

WILLIAM LYON MACKENZIE KING VS. *ARTHUR MEIGHEN*

ELECTIONS ARE SUPPOSED to settle things, but when the votes cast on October 29, 1925, were counted, they had settled nothing at all. The Canadian electorate had given itself the second minority parliament since 1867, the second in a row in only four years, electing 116 Conservatives, 101 Liberals, and 28 others (including the Independent Henri Bourassa). The English Canadian splinter parties – Progressives, Liberal Progressives, Labour, and Independents – once again held the balance of power. Halloween 1925 dawned with no one knowing who would form the government. Most expected it would be the upright Conservative Arthur Meighen. But in our parliamentary system, the prime minister remains in office until he either resigns or is defeated on a vote of confidence in the House of Commons. And anyone who had observed the wily Liberal leader, Prime Minister William Lyon Mackenzie King, knew that if he was good at anything, it was at hanging onto power.

From the day after the 1925 election until the votes of the subsequent election were tallied on September 14, 1926, the game would be played for the highest stakes. Two of the most compelling figures ever to mount our political stage would fight the climactic round of their ten-year duel. This duel would decide whether the Tories or the Grits would rule and whether a stable party system would re-emerge from the chaos following the First World War, or whether Canada would suffer the anarchic, revolving-door governments that characterized postwar Europe. Finally, the double-header election of 1925–26 would decide whether Canadian parliamentary politics – indeed, Canada itself – would break away from the legacy of British colonial rule.

For the Liberal leader, the 1925 election was supposed to put a triumphant end to four frustrating years of minority government. Between 1921 and 1925, the King government had limped from vote to vote with the support of the Progressives. As the party's name implied, many Progressives were lapsed Liberals. They were content to maintain the government in power, yet many of the

Mackenzie King set out on campaign trails in the 1920s with a party system in disarray, a country in rapid transition, and an electorate transformed. In this 1922 photograph, he courts women, now part of the new electorate.

party's voters and a healthy minority of its MPs were more Conservative in inclination. King showed a remarkable ability to keep this shaky arrangement intact, doing whatever was necessary to hold onto power by reaching out to the friendly Progressives, especially the more than half of their MPs who came from the West. (Those from Ontario were much more likely to have been voted in by lapsed Tories who had parked their vote with the Progressives in 1921.) King had managed to avoid defeat in parliament, but at the cost of failing to give the country any clear path out of its postwar political confusion.

The political volatility that had followed the splitting up of the Union government and led to the birth of the Progressives was fuelled by massive social changes. By 1926 Canada's 1891 population of 4.8 million would have almost doubled. By 1921, 45 per cent of Canadians lived in communities of over one thousand people. Much of the press had thrown off its financial ties to governments; now newspapers carried more information than ever before about both sides of the issues. In May 1918, all female citizens twenty-one years of age or older gained the right to vote in federal elections, further weakening the hold of the old parties that had been loosened by the war and by conscription. The popular vote swing between elections, starting in 1917 and ending in 1940, averaged 11 per cent, with shifts

THE PROGRESSIVES' PROGRESS

The Progressives' run of success in the early 1920s was a long time coming. The movement had deep roots in both the agrarian and industrial protest movements of the late nineteenth century.

LABOUR TURMOIL IN CANADA
Angry over the postwar slump and continued poor pay and working conditions, Canada's labour movement came into its own immediately following the war. The Winnipeg General Strike of 1919 was harshly suppressed, but gave warning that urban labour was now a force to be reckoned with.

WINNIPEG RIOT

REVOLUTION IN EUROPE
Communist takeovers (Russia, 1917, *above*) and coup attempts (Germany and Hungary, 1918) spell a world spiralling into turmoil following the Great War. Canada's urban, industrial radicals were inspired by the overthrow of many such *anciens régimes*.

FARM PROTESTS IN THE STATES
Agrarian populism had been a driving force in American politics since the 1870s. *(Above)* The Grange and the Illinois State Farmer's Association organized farmers throughout the country to meet on July 4, 1873, for a Fourth of July celebration.

occurring of up to 20 per cent. This figure was almost four times the average swing in the country's first twenty years, and twice the average over the fifty-year span of the Great Party era. Some traditional patterns remained, however. Voters tended to migrate between one of the two old parties and the third; direct switching between the Conservative and the Liberal poles was less frequent. Still, the electorate had abandoned its old reliability.

In policy terms the Progressives offered a mix of practical fixes and wild-eyed populist millenarianism, but the essence of their program was to get national politics off the old race/religion axis that left farmers' concerns ignored and to organize the national debate

around the largely economic questions that mattered to English Canadians, especially in the West. At a partisan level, the basic question in the early 1920s for the Progressives and their leader, T.A. Crerar, was whether the Laurier coalition could be re-established by uniting Progressives and Liberals, and, if so, on which party's terms. Would the western splitters be reabsorbed into the established, central Canadian mother party? Or would the remnants of the mother party become junior partners to the triumphant western splitters? (A variation on this same question was posed by the Reform Party/Canadian Alliance and the Tories in the federal elections of 1997 and 2000.) By 1925 the four western provinces had grown to represent

ECONOMIC SLUMP ON THE PRAIRIES
After the First World War, wheat prices collapsed – and with them the wheat boom that had followed the massive immigration to the Canadian West in the Laurier years. The golden age of agrarian progress – and prosperity – was over.

UNREST EVERYWHERE As the 1920s dawned, the revolutionary impulse, the rise of urban labour, and the rural collapse all came together. One of the results was a powerful new political force on the Canadian scene: the Progressive Party.

CITY LIGHTS

Rural protest was accompanied by urban innovation as an increasing number of Canadian city dwellers embraced modern postwar ways. Technological, social, moral, and political change in the 1920s included (*clockwise top left to bottom left*) the ballroom craze; the Canadian National Exhibition midway; women at the races in flapper attire; and the bustling corner of Toronto's Bay and Adelaide Streets. Urban life helped dissolve the traditional political structures rooted in family, religion, and local community. The twentieth century would be the age of "mass man" – and the mass politics of reaching out to large groups of voters, male and female, now free to make their own choices for the first time.

28 per cent of the House of Commons, slightly more than Quebec. In theory it was now possible for the West as a region to exert the kind of dominance over national politics that Quebec always had.

The prospect of political realignment left two questions hanging in the 1920s: Whither Quebec? Whither the federal Liberal Party? They were in many ways the same question. When Prime Minister King called the election in September 1925 his Liberals were a Quebec-dominated rump, holding all but four of the

NAME: W.L.M. King

PARTY: Liberal

ROLE: Prime minister since 1921. Leader of second-place party after 1925 election. Seatless. Determined to hang on.

province's seats but very little else except in Saskatchewan. Following war's end, King had faced a brutal choice: try to reconstruct the Liberal Party as one of economic principles or salvage its role as the race-based party of French Canada. For as long as Quebec society remained in the grip of the conservative Catholic Church, the progressive half of Laurier's national dream would never win there. (Only Quebec had failed to grant women provincial voting rights after the First World War.)

As a good disciple of Laurier, King would have preferred to orient his party around the axis of ideas. Throughout the industrialized world, businessmen, labour leaders, intellectuals, and governments were struggling with the massive social changes wrought by one hundred years of economic transformation. As a young man, King had devoted immense energy to wrestling with this elemental complex of issues. He had written extensively on the subject and worked as a senior mediator in

industrial disputes after 1911 on behalf of the Rockefellers. He had left the United States and many tempting offers there to serve as a deputy minister, then a minister, in the Laurier government, where he had created legislative frameworks for collective bargaining. Moreover, he had social reform in his blood; his grandfather was William Lyon Mackenzie, leader of the Upper Canada Rebellion in 1837 against the power of the Family Compact, the wealthy elite that controlled the province on behalf of the British Crown and thwarted all attempts to establish democracy and responsible government. It is not surprising, then, that King saw politics as a battle between forward-looking folks like himself and the reactionaries – men like Tory leader Arthur Meighen.

There was just one hitch: King owed his political skin to Quebec. He had paid a high price in 1917 for standing by Laurier and against conscription, losing his seat and enduring accusations of treason. But two years later, at the first national leadership convention in Canadian history, he reaped a

NAME: T.A. Crerar

PARTY: Progressive

ROLE: Progressive leader, 1920–22. Unionist minister, 1917–20. MP for Marquette, Manitoba. Farmer.

rich reward. Quebec's federal Liberals stood staunchly behind the unilingual King and elected him as leader. As his campaign manager, Sir Allen Aylesworth, breathlessly wrote to a friend: "The Frenchmen did the grand thing … they voted – practically solid – to stand by Fisher and me [King's agents] because we were English and had stood by Laurier and the French Canadian ... Dozens of them hugged me. They'd have kissed me if I would have

KING'S
PATH TO POWER

STEP 1 Birth into a political family. Mackenzie King, the grandson of the reformer William Lyon Mackenzie, was born in 1874 in this house *(left)* in Berlin, Ontario (later renamed Kitchener in 1916 in patriotic recognition of the British general). King's parents, Isobel Mackenzie and John King *(above, with King, circa 1910)*, were Presbyterians and Liberals. King senior ran for political office five times and lost. His mother doted on her precocious favourite son.

STEP 2 King studied at the universities of Toronto, Harvard, Oxford, and Cambridge. He became an industrial mediator, then Canada's first deputy minister of labour, before successfully running for parliament in 1908 and quickly rising to become minister of labour. After his defeat in the free trade election of 1911, King moved to New York City, where he became top mediator for the Rockefeller interests *(above right, with John D. Rockefeller Jr. in 1915)*.

let them – and they voted – every man Jack among them – just to stand by the men who had stood by Laurier."

So, while King dreamed of making the Liberals the party of reconciliation between capital and labour, East and West, factory and farm, he owed everything to the Grits' status as the party of French, Catholic Canada. Besides, as the heir of Laurier, he had a sacred duty to reconcile the races. What to do? Adopt the politics of ideas or of race? Do the right thing or the expedient thing? Build the country or build the Liberal Party? King's answer was yes – to everything. He would stand four-square for Quebec and he would extend one olive branch after another to those "Liberals in a hurry," the Progressives.

The olive branches took many forms. In the 1921 election King had pulled Liberal

candidates from races where he thought it necessary to unite the anti-Tory vote. He had also cultivated relationships with Progressive MPS and their key supporters back home on the farm. He had co-opted Progressive MPS into the Liberal caucus, and he helped induce their leader, Crerar, to leave politics in 1922 (he would return in the late 20s, as a Liberal, while Robert Forke of Manitoba took Crerar's place at the head of the parliamentary Progressive caucus). On the policy side, King carefully crafted each move to meet Progressive needs.

But parliamentary survival came at an electoral price. Not only had all these political manoeuvres aimed at placating the western core of the Progressive Party robbed King's government of any direction or message of its own, but they caused it to come across as a tool of the western interests,

STEP 3 Stay loyal to the leader in and out of parliament. He fancied himself the political heir of his idol, Sir Wilfrid Laurier (below, centre) and stood by the old man during the conscription crisis in 1917, finally earning Laurier's full respect.

STEP 4 Run for the top job. When Laurier's death in 1919 threw open the Liberal leadership, King was ready to make his move. Here he is seen buttonholing delegates to Canada's first-ever national party leadership convention in Ottawa. He won on the third ballot.

always electorally dangerous in Ontario. The government gave off a stale odour, unmoved by principle or purpose, that was captured by Tory leader Arthur Meighen when he groaned about yet another of King's legislative compromises: "Oh, I would like to have been present when this amendment was being fixed up. I would like to have been around when the pruning, and the sandpapering, and the varnishing, were being applied to the verbiage in order to get the amendment in such shape that they could all get in on the vote."

When the 1925 election campaign finally came, it proved to be a boring affair. King ran on an ill-defined record of good government. Meighen made an issue of King's legitimacy in office, attacking the Liberal government furiously, calling King's efforts at a "common sense tariff" – the PM's effort at achieving a

balance between the Liberals' industrial and agrarian support – "the twisting and shifting practices of Mr. King." The election results were uneven, but clearly showed a nationwide collapse in Progressive support. In the West, those voters moved smartly towards the Liberals, but in Ontario, defecting Progressive voters took the Tories to a shattering 57 per cent of the vote and pushed the party to a dominant position across the Maritimes. In Quebec, in contrast, the Liberals held firm against the hated Meighen, whom they had pilloried as the archfiend of conscription. Overall, the 1925 results looked more like 1917's than anything else, except for the West's three-way split. Mackenzie King's experiment with co-opting the Progressives had clearly failed its first real test. At the time it also looked to be its last.

KING: MAN OF THE PEOPLE

Despite hob-nobbing with Rockefellers and Lauriers, King's path to power involved sending out the message that he was a man of the masses – such as these mummers and friends at a 1908 campaign picnic in Berlin, Ontario. As leader he would struggle with both twentieth-century class politics and the old French-English battles that had consumed Laurier. His prowess at the new multi-dimensional Canadian political game came slowly, but he was an eager learner.

Now that the strategy lay in ruins, what of the strategist? The day after the 1925 election, Mackenzie King was still prime minister of Canada, even though he now led the second-place party. He would remain in office until he handed Governor General Viscount Byng his resignation or the new House convened and defeated his government in a vote of confidence. When the prime minister contemplated the lopsided and grim election results – his party had fallen from 116 seats to 101, he had lost his own seat of North York, and eight of his ministers had gone down to defeat – he considered two options: resign immediately or try to hang on with third party support. (I will treat the twenty-eight third-party MPs the way King did: as a loosely organized single party.)

Resignation looked unattractive to King. The surprisingly poor results had left many Liberal power brokers inside and outside parliament eager to dump the leader. If he resigned the government, he would lose the initiative and likely be toppled. But if he could stay in office, he would retain the power to shape events and might even achieve a lasting and stable Liberal government. Moreover, if an early election happened – always a possibility in a minority parliament – King would still hold the levers of election administration, the

immense advantage given by the government's control over enumeration and election day personnel. In sum, by remaining, King made success in the next round a little more possible. Even if staying on couldn't guarantee victory, resigning would definitely mean his personal defeat. Staying was his only viable course.

But just how practical was hanging tough when the Tories held fifteen more seats? King figured he had a good shot at gaining the parliamentary support of the Progressives, whose Conservative-leaning voters (mostly in Ontario) had already defected to the Tories. The MPs who remained were mostly lapsed agrarian Liberals and deeply opposed to the pro-business, high-tariff polices of Arthur Meighen. And so Mackenzie King pondered his future into the wee hours past election night, as usual committing his thoughts to his diary. "It looks like a heavy road ahead," wrote this self-disciplined loner, "but the Progressives may come with us … then if he [Meighen] wins in the H. of C. it looks like another election or great uncertainty for a while."

King's sense that a heavy road lay ahead was an understatement; he was, in fact, very near the end of the road. His hold on the hearts and minds of Liberals was weak. His style – to command from behind the lines, devoting his abundant energy and talent to intelligence gathering, strategic positioning, and developing consensus among his followers – had cost him in government and at the polls. Now he was a seatless prime minister. Leadership rivals had already begun manoeuvring to succeed him.

Even if he kept the party under his control, he faced the serious problem of reconciling his short-term parliamentary needs with his long-term electoral objectives. The sheer and unprecedented cheekiness of holding onto power despite a second-place finish was bound to provoke public concern, which Meighen would certainly seek to fan into outrage.

At Vimy Ridge, Canadian troops, under one command for the first time, take on the Germans and win a rare Allied victory on the Western front. English Canadian nationalism is born.

King could not afford to face the next election with the main issue in the public's mind being his clinging to power. Somehow, he would have to find another issue to place front and centre.

But that reckoning seemed far off as King set about cobbling together the Progressive support he urgently needed to survive parliament's opening days. His first move was to put pressure on the Liberal-cum-Progressive premier of Saskatchewan, Charles Dunning, to reverse an earlier decision and come to Ottawa to serve in a Liberal cabinet following parliament's return. Renewing his outreach to the western Progressives may have seemed counter-intuitive, given how poorly the strategy had paid off at the ballot box, but inside the House there was no option: King would cast his line where the loose fish swam and hope to keep himself alive to fight another day.

On October 30, the day after the election, King went to Rideau Hall to visit the governor general. After tea and a discussion of the weather, the two men retired into the library. Julian, Viscount Byng of Vimy, was a pleasant and easy-going sixty-three-year-old British nobleman. Born an earl, his particular title had been awarded as a result of his command of the Canadian Corps during the April 1917 storming of Vimy Ridge. Vimy was a defining moment in the development of Canadian national feeling, and it was fitting that one of its central figures, Byng, became governor general after the war. Like most British gentlemen of his era, Byng had a profound belief in fair play (his wife donated the NHL trophy awarded to this day to the year's most sportsmanlike player). According to King's diary, when he began to explain his intention to stay on, Byng interrupted to clarify the possibilities as he saw them: "The first is dissolution [and another election] ... the next is that Mr. Meighen having the largest

THE REF: VISCOUNT BYNG OF VIMY

The governor general's great-great-great-uncle, Admiral John Byng, was unjustly executed in 1757 for botching the battle of Minorca. Great Uncle John took it like a man. Family moral: play by the rules. But what happens when the ref gets drawn into the game?

GENTLEMAN Born in England, 1862, seventh son of the second Earl of Stafford. Educated at Eton. Nickname: "Bungo."

OFFICER Byng's c.v. read like a roll-call of imperial engagements. Captain, India; Lt.-Col., South African War, 1899–01; Maj.-Gen., Belgium, 1914, First Ypres, 1915; temp. Lt.-Gen., Gallipoli, 1915; Lt.-Gen. Canadian Corps, Vimy, 1916–17, Cambrai, 1917.

JOURNEYMAN Appointed twelfth governor general of Canada – no one's first choice, but not a bad catch nonetheless – in 1921. After Ottawa will become commissioner of the London Metropolitan Police.

MEIGHEN ACCORDING TO MEIGHEN

The Tory *Montreal Star* of 1920 portrays Meighen as a commanding prime minister, but the newspaper is guilty of wishful thinking. As the nation's navigator, he rode only the economic and social tides, the politics of ideas based on the interplay of class and trade interests. When it came to navigating Canada's racial currents, he was totally at sea.

CHAOTIC TRADING CONDITIONS

WILD IDE

TARIFF THEORISTS

CLA
CONSCIOU

SOCIA

FINANCIAL UNEASINESS

WORLD UNREST

SHIP OF STATE

solid group should be called on, and the third that you should continue."

The ability to change governments without an election was a legacy of the system Canada inherited from Great Britain. Throughout the eighteenth and nineteenth centuries, British ministries – composed of hereditary lords and elected members of the House of Commons – frequently rose and fell without any re-election of the lower house's members. In the United Kingdom, as in Canada, the authority to name the government still rests with the Crown, and our governor general still occasionally exercises this power.

The atmosphere in the library grew cooler as Byng said he hoped King would choose the "dignified" course of resigning and allowing Meighen a chance to govern. King replied that he would first see whether parliament would back his government. And if it did not? At this point King's account and Byng's diverge. According to Byng, the prime minister accepted that he "must not at any time ask for a dissolution unless Mr. Meighen is first given a chance." Put another way, "We were both agreed that all alternative forms of Government should be tried before resorting to another election." That night, however, King wrote in his diary that the two men had merely canvassed some scenarios based on a defeat in parliament, including both dissolution and resignation in Meighen's favour, but that no promises had been made.

Neither account is truly reliable: Byng's was written a year later; and King's notorious talent for rationalization was never better

deployed than in his private diaries. It's entirely possible that both men drew totally different conclusions from the same words. One thing King got right, however, was his sense of what would happen if Meighen ever accepted office from the governor general: "I did not say anything but I thought at once that if he did – that would be his doom forever."

King went home to Laurier House, his predecessor's residence, which had served as an official home for the Liberal leader since 1922 (24 Sussex would not become the official residence of the prime minister until 1951), to ponder his decision. By Monday, November 2, whatever doubts remained about the wisdom of muscling the Crown's representative and striking out into unknown constitutional ground had been pushed aside: he would stay on and face parliament. That evening, when he informed Byng of his decision, the disappointed governor general asked the prime minister to sleep on it first. For the next two days King worked on Byng. Finally, on November 4, the viceroy gave in. In a press release, King stated that he had asked for parliament's return to determine "the very important question raised by the numerical position of the respective political parties," and that Byng "has been pleased to accept this advice."

Arthur Meighen lashed out in response on November 5, calling King's statement a crass attempt to remain in office "in defiance of a heavily adverse verdict from the people of Canada." The Tory leader sincerely believed that King was contemptibly clinging to power in spite of the public will: Meighen had more

Meighen and King (*right*, in college days) both attended the University of Toronto in the mid-1890s and clashed in debates and mock parliaments. Their mutual loathing was as much a clash of personalities as of ideas. A friend wrote to Meighen, "King was always a noisy fellow, although brainy, and had ideas. Just the opposite to you, that is, as to the noise."

Le trafiquant de chair humaine

MEIGHEN ACCORDING TO KING

The 1925 cartoonist of Quebec City's Liberal *Le Soleil* sees the Tory leader as an unrepentant enemy of the French Canadian. Meighen never lost the baggage he acquired from his major role in the 1917 conscription crisis. He thought *les Canadiens* should just get over it.

seats; his MPs had more than doubled in number; and his popular vote had leapt from 30.3 per cent to 46.5 per cent, giving his Tories substantially more than the Grits' 40 per cent – a seemingly clear mandate to govern.

Meighen thought, as he usually did, that King was being a grasping little bounder. After Meighen was elected MP for Portage la Prairie, Manitoba, in 1908, he had risen swiftly, emerging as the unquestioned workhorse of the Borden cabinet and its chief parliamentary star. Borden had handpicked him to implement the conscription program, and, when Borden retired in ill health in 1920, the caucus elected Meighen to succeed Borden. It did so grudgingly; one shrewd minister warned, prophetically, that he was "absolutely out of the question in so far as Quebec was concerned."

Meighen didn't last long as prime minister. He led the Tories to the brink of extinction in the December 1921 election. There were mitigating circumstances to explain this catastrophe: the party had governed for ten years; it was hated in francophone Quebec; the party had no senior figures in many of the dominion's nine provinces; and the economy was in a postwar slump. But the prime minister's style had contributed to his electoral misfortune. Arthur Meighen had a talent for annoying people. He possessed the deadly clarity and logic of a high school mathematics teacher turned lawyer – and the charm of both. He wielded a cruel and piercing wit, and he conveyed none of the warmth that was the glue of the close-knit worlds of caucus, cabinet, and party.

Meighen was also something of a reactionary, intellectually capable of understanding that the world had changed irrevocably in the Great War but unable emotionally to accept the fact. In August 1920 he said to a crowd in Truro, NS: "The great task before the people of Canada is to get back not to old conditions but to old time sanity of thought and action …

A great many people seem to have lost all sense of values, of proportion and of numbers. Dangerous doctrines taught by dangerous men, enemies of the State, poison and pollute the air." Fortunately for Meighen, the Tories' core constituencies had nowhere else to go. As a result, the small caucus remained solid throughout King's first government, rebounding brilliantly in the fall 1925 election when the country had soured on King's thin, tentative record as prime minister and when former Tories who had voted Progressive in 1921 came home.

The Tory leader spent the rest of the fall of 1925 seeking to undermine King's legitimacy in anticipation of parliament's return. Although Meighen was in a much stronger position than King, he, too, faced grumblings from his caucus and party establishment. The election results had bolstered the doubters, fulfilling yet again the prophecy that Meighen couldn't win in Quebec and, without that province, couldn't win a majority. He was now forced to share decision-making power with a caucus "Board of Strategy" – always a sign of a leader on probation.

An early opportunity to spike his critics' guns was handed to him on November 5, when the Liberal MP for Bagot died and a by-election was called for December 7, 1925, barely a month after the general election. Meighen wanted badly to win this francophone seat to the east of Montreal. He was convinced he'd taken a bum rap for conscription in Quebec, and he believed that if he could just get *Canadiens* to stop thinking of him as some imperialist, *habitant*-gobbling war god, he had an excellent opportunity to bring Quebec into a long-term Tory coalition.

Meighen's aim was nothing less than to re-create the coalition of Macdonald and Borden, with the Tories as the party of the Ontario-Quebec manufacturing economy ranged in opposition to the agrarian Liberals and Progressives. Hadn't the Tories' 1911 defence of the protective tariff swept Ontario, given them their best Maritime showing this century, split the Liberal West, and even made inroads in Quebec? And could not the issue be used to squeeze the Liberals into abandoning their "tariff for revenue only" straddle and make them choose between alienating anti-protectionist western Progressives on the one hand and protectionist supporters in Montreal and southern Ontario on the other? Wasn't pushing the tariff the Right Thing, the only fit and proper issue that, logic demanded,

NAME: Arthur Meighen

PARTY: Conservative

ROLE: Prime minister, 1920–21, MP for Portage la Prairie. Leader of the opposition since 1921. Has more seats than King after 1925 election.

must be placed unambiguously front and centre? "If," said Meighen in a speech to his riding in 1921, "I can but get the people in this country to see that the issue is Protection or no Protection, the battle will be won."

Meighen's dream of a tariff-dominated national politics could be achieved, he thought, if only that annoying race question could be set aside. Fine, then, he would sweep it off the table once and for all by proving to Quebec that he was no bloodthirsty warmonger. This would be no easy task, however, because, along with conscription, Meighen's other memorable contribution to national politics had been in the same vein. In 1922, when Britain and Turkey confronted each other in the eastern Mediterranean, the mother country had put out a public feeler for military assistance from the dominions (Canada, Australia, New Zealand, and South Africa). Prime Minister King had

dodged, hoping the crisis would solve itself, which it eventually did, but Meighen had plunged blindly into the issue with a grand rhetorical flourish: "Ready, aye ready; we stand by you." This anachronistically jingo position had damaged Meighen severely among all but the core Tory vote of Ontario and the Maritimes.

Imagine the surprise when, on November 16, 1925, Meighen explained in a speech in Hamilton, Ontario, that in any future conflict he would impose conscription if required, but would ensure that an election took place before he sent the army to the front. This "heresy at Hamilton" was not only a startling turnabout but absurd policy. As the editor of the Tory *Orange Sentinel* pointed out, no one had a problem with an election before imposing conscription, but holding one after the fact and before deployment made no sense at all. What would the government do if it lost? Send the conscripts home? Meighen's foolish tilt at the Quebec windmill yielded him nothing. The Tories decisively lost a by-election in Bagot, Quebec, thus suffering their second emphatic defeat in the francophone riding in the space of five weeks.

The Conservative leader was out of his depth. It wasn't so much that Meighen's vision of political realignment around the tariff question was a mirage, but that, aside from a few opportunists and business leaders, he had no authentic power base in francophone Quebec. His hopes for national political realignment along the lines of ideological principle were based on the idea that French Quebec was ready and willing to give up bloc voting for *la survivance* and to set farmers in the Beauce to fight rail workers in East Montreal over tariff policy. This scenario was about as likely as a Catholic Power party taking over Alberta. Worse, by raising the tariff issue, Meighen drove Liberals and Progressives together in parliament. "Why not join right up?" he had asked them witheringly during the 1920 budget debate. "Am I to be told that I am anxious to keep these people divided?" Principled? Perhaps. Politically stupid? Definitely.

NAME: Ernest Lapointe

PARTY: Liberal

ROLE: King's Quebec lieutenant, the greatest since Cartier. MP for Québec-Est. King's sole strategic adviser and ultimate loyalist.

The autumn political season ended with the Liberal win in Bagot on December 7. Prime Minister King announced that the new parliament – with its old government – would sit starting Thursday, January 7, 1926, "under conditions unprecedented in British or Canadian history," in the words of the Toronto *Globe*. The freakish political atmosphere was reflected by unusually warm winds and springtime skies that turned Ottawa's snowdrifts into curbside creeks. At 3 p.m. all parliamentarians were summoned to the red chamber of the Senate, splendidly rebuilt after the 1916 fire, whereupon the Commons dispersed and reassembled in the green chamber to elect a Speaker. The next day all reconvened in the Senate Chamber to hear Governor General Byng deliver the Speech from the Throne. The government's legislative program had been developed through extensive informal consultations with key Progressives – notably Robert Forke, their leader in the House of Commons. The King government promised to establish an independent commission to review tariffs, to instruct the Board of Railway Commissioners to gear decisions towards western producer interests, and to implement a previous agreement to hand Ottawa's control of natural resources over to Alberta.

When the speech concluded, the *Globe* reported: "Society leaders hasten[ed] from placid Senate to pack crowded galleries of Commons," where the fireworks were about to begin. Still unable to sit in the House, Mackenzie King kept himself busy dictating letters in his second-floor office. "Being in office and out of parliament is not a pleasant business," he wrote, but until parliament met and voted the government up or down, there was no point calling a by-election to get himself a seat.

Out on the floor of the green chamber his tall, lumbering point man, Ernest Lapointe, who was also justice minister and government leader in the House, rose to be recognized. As King's Quebec lieutenant, the articulate, bilingual Lapointe kept the Quebec Liberal machine purring, represented the province's concerns in the government, and, as Laurier's successor in the riding of Québec-Est, carried the flame of King's mentor. His faithful, self-effacing execution of these sacred trusts made Lapointe King's only truly close collaborator. At his leader's instructions, Lapointe immediately moved a motion of confidence on the question of the government's right to retain office.

In a minority parliament, if the government loses a vote on a major bill, a key motion, or a budget, it is deemed to have "lost the confidence of the House." The task of managing a minority situation is infinitely more complicated than with a majority, for the government must craft its policies and parliamentary manoeuvres to keep the opposition parties from combining to force a new election. The government must also consider how each manoeuvre will look to voters on the day of its possible defeat, attempting to prevent the opposition parties from forcing an election over an issue that makes the government look bad. This balancing act entails knowing when to force a vote and when to arrange for a few members' absence. Sometimes a minority government deliberately tries to engineer its own defeat on an issue that will launch a winning campaign.

In a minority parliament, every action has a double meaning – how it will play in the Commons and how it may play on the campaign trail. The entire life of a minority government is one long pre-writ campaign fought on the floor of the House. King understood this truth implicitly, factoring into all his planning how the parliamentary action might play publicly in an early election. "Of course

NAME: James Woodsworth

PARTY: Progressive

ROLE: Canada's first socialist MP for Winnipeg North Centre since 1921. Former Methodist minister, Winnipeg General Strike leader. Key Progressive.

what he [Meighen] will seek will be to [take power and] get control of the election machinery – let him have that if I have the people." King had glimpsed at a great opportunity: if he could make Meighen's grab at power into an issue, his own similar manoeuvres might not seem so bad in voters' eyes.

Meighen, a consummate "House of Commons man," didn't keep the voters much in mind. He acted as though the political game began and ended in the green chamber, seeming to think that if he could push King out and take power, all would be well. Some of Meighen's doggedness may have been motivated by his own vulnerability to a leadership challenge – he needed to keep the party moving towards power lest the doubters catch up with him. The Tory leader's other problem, though, resembled that of a dog chasing a car: What if he caught it? Had anyone told him about the bad optics of a British aristocrat appointing a reactionary Tory,

beloved of big business, to the office of prime minister without an election? Did he see the danger of putting his own power-grab in the spotlight and overshadowing King's? Did it occur to him that this move might drive Liberal and Progressive MPs and voters together? If so, Meighen didn't seem to care. It was all legal, he said, the Progressives would understand, and the people had spoken.

And Meighen would speak for them. The Conservative leader was the finest debater in the House, perhaps the finest in Canada's history, though he spoke without any particular flourish and certainly with no charm. Rather, he wielded a precise, deadly logic that often sliced through Mackenzie King's logorrhea, straight to the heart of the matter. Sometimes Meighen's attacks literally made King squirm. Watching a debate during King's first minority government, *Manitoba Free Press* reporter Grant Dexter wrote, "Meighen would carry his controversial speech to the point where he really infuriated the Liberals. Mackenzie King … would bow over his desk and you could see the blood coming up his neck … The members would be the same and they would begin to mutter and growl. Nobody would say anything. Meighen – I have seen him many times … would stop in the course of a speech and say 'You're growling over there. Now anybody there speak up. If you have anything you want to say, say it; don't behave as your ancestors did ten thousand years ago.'"

On January 8, eager to seize the parliamentary initiative, Meighen leapt to his feet, interrupting Lapointe's confidence motion with a point of order and inserting his own want-of-confidence motion in the form of a Throne Speech amendment. The Speaker, Gaspé Liberal Rodolphe Lemieux, set aside Lapointe's motion for consideration over the weekend and began debate on Meighen's. This debate lasted a week, with the performance on the Commons floor a sideshow compared with the offstage drama, as both major parties frantically sought to line up Progressive support. Two key Labour/Progressives from Winnipeg, Abe Heaps and James Woodsworth (Canada's first socialist MP, who would found the Co-operative Commonwealth Federation in 1932), presented both King and Meighen with an inquiry as to their policies on old age pensions. Nothing came of the approach to Meighen, but King personally promised immediate implementation (and would have Lapointe pledge it in the House on Tuesday, January 28). Such prompt action sealed Progressive support for both the Throne Speech and the government.

On Friday, January 15, the House divided on Meighen's amendment: Ayes 120, Nays 123 – propped up by twenty-three Progressives. Though a bare majority had sustained the Liberal government, King heaved a sigh of relief and, that day, called a by-election for February 15 in the riding of Prince Albert, Saskatchewan. It was a safe seat, where the Liberals and Progressives had creamed a young Tory named John Diefenbaker in the fall campaign.

King's successful tiptoe through the parliamentary minefield didn't last long. On February 2, 1926, Vancouver Tory H.H. Stevens informed the House of very damaging allegations about the Montreal federal Customs Office. It seemed that, with an appropriate payment in the right hands, liquor smugglers evading prohibition laws could move as much

While prohibition wound down in Canada through the 1920s, it remained in force in the United States. Legal Canadian liquor (like the shipment below) could be smuggled to the States for millions in profit.

business as they pleased straight through the federal warehouses in the country's largest city. And the hand being greased in each transaction belonged to the chief preventative officer of the Montreal office, J.-E. Bisaillon. In early 1924 Bisaillon had been tried for bribery and other offences but was acquitted. He held onto his job for another six months before he was sacked by the Liberal customs minister, Jacques Bureau. In September 1925, just before the election, King quietly elevated Bureau to the Senate. Now, with Bureau safely out of the way, the new minister, George Boivin of the Eastern Townships riding of Shefford, could truthfully claim to have stepped into a difficult challenge, with a mandate from the PM to clean house.

But here was Stevens, three weeks into a precarious minority situation, demanding a full parliamentary inquiry into corruption in the customs service. King searched for a way out. He knew that the Progressives held the corrupt habits of the "old-line parties" in particular horror, and that by raising the spectre of scandal the Conservatives hoped to drive a wedge between his shaky government and the idealistic Progressive MPs who kept it alive. The prime minister would have loved to stonewall the Tories on this one, but in a minority situation he couldn't afford to alienate the Progressives. At the same time, sacrificing Boivin was unacceptable to his Quebec wing.

As in so many of the tricky situations he faced that year, King decided to play for time, keeping open the maximum number of options while allowing only the absolutely inevitable things to take place. He agreed to strike a special parliamentary committee under Stevens to investigate – four Liberals, four Tories, and one Progressive – and hoped that the issue would burn itself out before it blew up.

On every other front, as winter turned into spring, events unfolded according to King's plan. On February 15 he was elected MP for

Prince Albert (Diefenbaker wisely didn't run). In early March, Dunning won his by-election by acclamation in Regina, having already been appointed minister of railways and canals in anticipation on February 20. That month an old age pension bill, Canada's first, was introduced. (To King's delight it would be voted down by the Tory-dominated Senate in June.) On April 15 Finance Minister James Robb of Quebec brought down a soundly Liberal-Progressive budget that bashed the Ontario automobile business by lowering the tariff on cars, reduced personal income taxes (always a popular measure), and slightly raised corporate taxes. Each legislative step was taken in consultation with a group of key Progressives, who registered their satisfaction in the only way King cared about.

NAME: Henry H. Stevens

PARTY: Conservative

ROLE: MP for Vancouver Centre since 1911. Blows whistle in 1926 on Liberal customs scandal.

Throughout the spring the government survived one no-confidence motion of Meighen's after another by ever widening margins, as the tone in the House grew nastier and the Progressives became more impatient to get on with the government's pro-farm agenda. Meighen repeatedly excoriated King for his "bribery" of the third party, portraying it as political prostitution of the worst kind. But King was far too canny to see issues such as railways and the tariff in terms of right and wrong. The various players on these matters were simply arguing their interests, just as righteous unions and crafty employers might do, and King could never get passionate about a predictable interplay of interests. No wonder moralizers like Meighen repeatedly portrayed

KING'S GAME

OCTOBER 29, 1925, TO JANUARY 27, 1926

start here

TALK TO BYNG

PERMISSION REFUSED

LIBERALS FALL. MEIGHEN IN POWER?

PERMISSION TO FORM GOVERNMENT

RECRUIT DUNNING AND SUCK UP TO PROGRESSIVES LIKE WOODSWORTH

HOLD VOTE

OFFER OLD AGE PENSIONS

YOU WIN, STAY IN POWER

CALL A BY-ELECTION FOR DUNNING

Mackenzie King faced a tortuous series of moves as he struggled to retain power following his second-place election finish in the 1925 election. As if these stakes weren't high enough, King knew that if he failed to hang on to the prime ministership, his party would probably dump him, putting him out of the game for good at the young age of fifty-one. Through the game's opening moves, King stayed on course. He persuaded Governor General Byng to let him test the confidence of the House (it passed the test), recruited the Saskatchewan premier Charles Dunning to shore up his Progressive flank, brought in old age pensions to please the Progressives, and got himself back into parliament by way of a by-election. But with the eruption of a seamy scandal in January, all bets were off.

KING RUNS IN A BY-ELECTION

WHOOPS

SCANDAL!

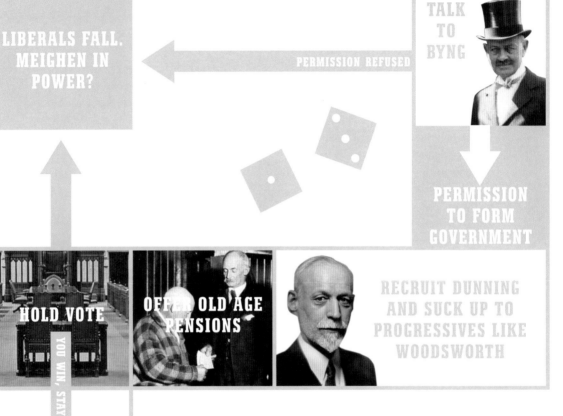

the prime minister as unprincipled. The accusation stung, but King could console himself with success. It seemed that the session might limp peacefully into a summer recess and that a stable, working minority government might carry on for at least another year.

But as June approached, the Stevens Committee's report still loomed. It had heard from over two hundred witnesses, who collectively painted a lurid picture of official corruption, and incompetent senior management under former minister Jacques Bureau. Moreover, the testimony had exposed a more recent incident in which the new minister, George Boivin, had interfered in the case of a convicted New Brunswick bootlegger with close Liberal ties. Pressing their advantage, the Conservative members moved that the committee's report censure Boivin. They knew that if a report censuring a sitting minister came up for adoption before the whole House, the Progressives would almost certainly vote against corruption and with the Tories – and that the vote would surely be a matter of confidence.

Into mid-June the battle inside the committee raged over the Conservatives' proposed censure of Boivin. With Tory and Liberal MPs split evenly, the question would be decided by northern Alberta farmer D.M. Kennedy, the committee's lone Progressive swing vote. King wasted no time: "At once," his diary entry of June 16 reads, "we all got busy with Prog. Friends … I got Forke, Gardiner, Evans, Spencer to my room at midnight, to have them work on Kennedy." King was very good at organizing this kind of lobbying, crafting just the right arguments and issuing precise, yet diplomatic instructions to supporters and temporary allies alike. The next day Kennedy sided with the Liberals, and Stevens's motion failed five to four. The deeply religious and somewhat mystical King, ever alive to the presence of "the Unseen Hand" in his affairs,

wrote that night: "The Govt was again saved as if by a miracle."

On Tuesday, June 22, Stevens presented the committee's report to the House, at the same time moving to amend it to include a denunciation of Boivin's conduct as "utterly unjustifiable." If carried, the amendment spelled doom for the government. A lengthy debate got under way. On Wednesday J.S. Woodsworth, who had been so helpful in sustaining the government back in January, gave an agonized speech reflecting the acute dilemma before the Progressives. He decried the obvious Liberal corruption but could not bring himself to hand power to the Tories, whose policies were anathema to the socialist MP. Instead, he moved his own amendment to Stevens's amendment: the reference to Boivin would be struck and a royal commission called to investigate further. Meighen challenged the motion, and the House went into severe disorder and was adjourned. It was one o'clock on Thursday morning, June 24.

When the House reconvened that afternoon, Speaker Lemieux ruled that Woodsworth's amendment was in order, meaning it would be debated and then voted on. To the Speaker's right, King rose to rally his stricken government. He was not a great orator or even a particularly good one. His speeches rambled; his logic was often obscure; his phrasing habitually sacrificed clarity to nuance; and his clichés, pieties, and sanctimonious insistence on his own virtue were annoying at all times. When he deployed his little homilies in defence of a nakedly partisan position, the spectacle was thoroughly irksome. Good Canadians that they were, his peers tended to conduct the grabbing of power quietly, almost apologetically. King placed his hand on his heart, rolled out the scriptural quotations, and lunged at power for all he was worth. If anyone noted the low aims to which his high ideals were being directed, King would react with wounded shock and surprise that anyone could suspect him of such base motives.

That afternoon the prime minister went on for two hours, pleading for sympathy for Boivin, weakly poking at possible collusion between the scandal's original whistle-blowers and the Conservatives, and lamely defending Bureau's qualifications for his senatorship. At one point a Tory heckler accused King of making a cheap point. "Yes," he replied candidly, "if my hon. Friend wishes to follow these methods I will admit that they are cheap. The whole business is pretty cheap when you get to the bottom of it." Getting back on his message, King ended with a scriptural quotation: "For with what judgment ye judge, ye shall be judged." Heckled again, King assumed his favourite Christian-before-the-lions pose, saying: "My hon. Friends may laugh. They laugh at Scripture. They laugh at anything and everything but they will find the truth of the words I have just uttered, because those words have stood through many centuries and will stand for many centuries to come." Quoting the Bible to defend a scandal was typical King; trying to distinguish this prime minister's idea of his own interests, the Liberal Party's, Canada's, and God's was like trying to slice fog. An observer could never tell where the high-minded aims ended and the crass politics began. Neither could King, which made his whole routine both more convincing and more exasperating – especially to Meighen, a numbers man and fond of nice, clean slices.

The pale figure of Arthur Meighen now rose and set about destroying King's argument that the corruption didn't matter and that the real issue was the Tories playing politics to take power. For almost three hours the Conservative leader dismantled King's position piece by piece, remorselessly pushing the Progressives into a logical corner where they would have to side with him whether they liked it or not: "If we are going to yield to this insidious appeal that every time an hon. Member seeks to hold those in the seats of the mighty responsible, then he is playing politics, he is seeking to 'get' his enemy … then parliament is paralyzed and is no longer the guardian of the honour of the state. Between these two positions I place every hon. Member of the House to-night, and I put my fellow members there with confidence that parliament at this momentous time will fulfill its high purpose in our land and vindicate its name to the people of Canada."

The Tories cheered. Progressives stirred. The hour of Meighen's triumph seemed at hand. He stood poised to return to office from the wilderness of opposition – the first man to do so since Sir John A. Macdonald almost fifty years before. The extraordinary afternoon of Thursday, June 24, ended with Meighen standing like an avenging angel over the King government's twitching corpse, which was still clutching at power with what appeared to be its dying breath.

All day on Friday the atmosphere in Ottawa was electric. "Great Crowds Surge to Parliament Hill for Fateful Division," reported the Toronto *Globe*. "Scores upon scores of people from … [late afternoon] up until midnight vainly clamoured for admittance to the galleries." Hallway line-ups formed as the public crowded into Centre Block and packed the public galleries to witness the crucial vote. Inside the House, the *Globe* reported, "the two party lobbies present scenes just as animated … The same whispered conferences, the same significant gatherings in corridors." One Liberal member, whose wife had died the previous day, was forced to cut short his mourning period; the opposition had refused to pull a member to "pair off" the Liberal's absence.

Shortly after 8 p.m. the House came to order. First came the division

OTTAWA

PHOTO. JAMES.

HOUSE OF COMMONS DURING A SESSION.

Night sittings of the House of Commons (seen here in 1915) helped create the atmosphere of a closed gents' club. Not until the 1980s was the House schedule of sittings lightened to allow MPs more time with their constituents (!) and their families (!!).

on Woodsworth's pro-government amendment: defeated by two votes. The Tories whooped. Next came Stevens's amendment, censuring Customs Minister Boivin. Suddenly an intricate procedural donnybrook broke out, with motions and amendments ricocheting around the green chamber and the gallery crowds "remaining in their seats, eagerly at attention, for … hours without interruption." Finally, at 4:50 on Saturday morning, with the government having lost two more procedural

motions, the House was adjourned. Stevens's amendment would be voted on when the Commons reconvened on Monday, June 28.

On Saturday morning, June 26, King considered his predicament, working through the problem in his diary. Having now lost three votes in a row, he had clearly lost control of the Commons. The likelihood of the House censuring Boivin increased by the hour and the price of hanging tough was rising, as the wheeling and dealing for Progressive support became more and more risky from a broader electoral standpoint. Today, blatant clinging to power is considered crass, but hardly surprising. The less cynical voters of the 1920s felt differently. They expected their parliamentarians to display an upright British sense of fair play. "The bargaining, bartering, bribing that is going on is something that cannot be cont'd," King wrote that morning. If he held on for too much longer, he'd appear before the public exactly as Meighen had portrayed him in the fall: a power-hungry usurper.

William Lyon Mackenzie King was in the blind heart of his darkest labyrinth. If he let the House proceed on its present course, the Tory motion of censure would pass and his government would fall in disgrace. If Meighen got his censure motion through, took office but then could not hold the support of the House, an election would follow in which the scandal and

King's attempts to hang onto power would be the main issue. Key Liberals were already moving openly to prepare Dunning to take the leadership on King's seemingly inevitable exit. King had foreseen this pass in his diary entry on election night 1925: to keep the people onside, he would have to surrender the government. The simplest course was to hand it over to Meighen by resigning and recommending the opposition leader's appointment to the governor general. But the Tories would undoubtedly pass the censure amendment, putting the stain of official parliamentary condemnation on the Liberals in any forthcoming campaign.

The prime minister had one more card to play. If the most important goal was to avoid censure, he would have to ask the governor general to dissolve parliament and call an election – now. No one could accuse him of clinging to power if he asked that the people

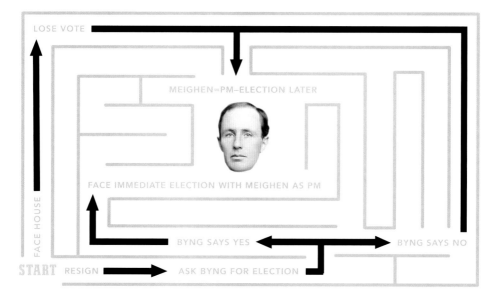

LOSE VOTE

MEIGHEN=PM–ELECTION LATER

FACE HOUSE

FACE IMMEDIATE ELECTION WITH MEIGHEN AS PM

BYNG SAYS YES   BYNG SAYS NO

START   RESIGN   ASK BYNG FOR ELECTION

LABYRINTH: KING'S OPTIONS ON JUNE 28

With King's grip on power loosening by the hour, all roads seemed to lead to Meighen as PM – the outcome King had laboured so mightily for eight months to avoid.

decide. That afternoon, King met with his cabinet members to announce his decision. They agreed that dissolution was the only course.

As the prime minister set out for Rideau Hall, he was entering unknown constitutional territory. The law was obscure on the fine points of governors general and minority parliaments. Canada had no written constitution beyond 1867's British North America Act, which was silent on the matter. There were no precedents. King had already achieved a parliamentary first by forming a government after finishing second in an election. A recommendation for dissolution might be legal or it might not. Byng might say yes or he might not. Yet King does not seem to have considered the possibility that Byng might refuse. The prime minister did what he usually did when he was on shaky ground: he worked himself into a froth of conviction, to the point where, if he didn't actually believe he was legally justified in demanding dissolution, he might as well have.

When King recommended an election that afternoon, Lord Byng was taken aback. He quickly informed the prime minister that he would not grant dissolution, but would instead invite the leader of the opposition to attempt to form a Conservative minority government. King was shocked at Byng's adamant refusal to accept the recommendation of his prime minister. Byng was not only amazed that King appeared to be reneging on their January deal but disgusted that he was doing so to dodge a sleazy scandal. Moreover, the governor general felt that the law was clearly against King. Suppose a dying government was granted dissolution only nine months after an election and after barely two months' worth of parliamentary sitting. Why, then, would not some future prime minister, defeated at the polls, stroll in on election night and ask for another election? The two went at each other for hours. King, believing himself in the right, pleaded with the viceroy to consult constitutional experts before setting his decision in stone. Finally, he left.

On Sunday, after another gruelling, high-stakes argument, King left Government House convinced that he could not change Byng's mind. That night in his diary he wrote of "a great peace in my heart … If [Meighen] seeks to carry on I believe he will not go far. Our chances of winning out in a general election are good. I feel I am right, and so am happy. May God guide me in every step."

King paid one final visit to Lord Byng, who received him at 1 p.m. on Monday, June 28. Once more King requested dissolution. Once more Byng refused. Then the prime minister drew out his letter of resignation.

The governor general accepted the prime minister's resignation and would sum up the argument in a note sent the next day: "As, in your opinion, Mr. Meighen is unable to govern the country, there should be another election with the present machinery to enable the people to decide. My contention is that Mr. Meighen has not been given a chance of trying to govern, or saying that he cannot do so, and that all reasonable expedients should be tried before resorting to another election." Byng later cabled a copy of his letter to London, adding the following postscript. "Mr. King, whose bitterness was very marked Monday, will probably take a very vitriolic line against myself – that seems only natural. But I have to wait the verdict of history to prove my having

Byng's post-mortem on the constitutional tussle with Mackenzie King, which was sent the day after the governor general refused the prime minister's request for an election. By the time King received it, he had already made the next move and resigned.

GOVERNMENT HOUSE,
OTTAWA.

June 29th 1926

My dear Mr. King,

I must acknowledge on paper, with many thanks,
the receipt of your letter handed to me at our meeting
yesterday.

In trying to condense all that has passed between
us during the last week, it seems to my mind that there is
really only one point at issue.

You advise me "that as, in your opinion,
Mr.Meighen is unable to govern the country, there should be
another Election with the present machinery to enable the
people to decide". My contention is that Mr. Meighen has not
been given a chance of trying to govern, or saying that he
cannot do so, and that all reasonable expedients should be
tried before resorting to another Election.

Permit me to say once more that, before deciding
on my constitutional course on this matter, I gave the subject
the most fairminded and painstaking consideration which it
was in my power to apply.

I can only add how sincerely I regret the
severence of our official companionship, and how gratefully
I acknowledge the help of your counsel and co-operation.

With warmest wishes.

Byng of Vimy.

The Right Hon.W.L.Mackenzie King, C.M.G.,
                Etc., Etc.,
        OTTAWA.

adopted a wrong course and this I do with an easy conscience."

Throughout the preceding weekend, Meighen had weighed advice regarding his constitutional rights from various Tory legal experts and from Sir Robert Borden. All agreed that Meighen should by law be invited to form a government, but Borden expressed deep political misgivings over accepting. No one was aware that King had already hatched a plan for his deathbed recovery.

NAME: Sir Robert Borden

PARTY: Conservative

ROLE: Prime minister, 1911–20. Informal adviser to Meighen in constitutional crisis.

At two o'clock that Monday afternoon King rose before the Speaker and the reconvened House. In an uncharacteristically pithy 105 words he asserted that dissolution was necessary, explained that Byng had refused his recommendation, and, fighting back tears, announced his resignation as prime minister. The shocked House was silent. As a private member, King then moved that the House adjourn. Again, silence as every member struggled furiously to understand King's latest surprise move. All eyes fell on Meighen.

The Conservative leader rose to intervene, but King cut him off, stating correctly that his adjournment motion was not debatable. He added that it was impossible for the House to carry on because, at the present time, no government existed. In effect, King was implying that no legal government *could* exist. He was daring the Tories to grab at the power he had just ostentatiously given up. His adjournment motion had brought parliament

to a standstill. The House rose after only fifteen minutes.

The Tories began celebrating that afternoon. On the fifth floor of Centre Block, backbench MPs formed up into a kind of conga line and paraded downstairs past the offices of the party's Board of Strategy, singing songs of triumph.

Arthur Meighen, with power now at last within reach, repaired to Rideau Hall, where he was formally invited by Viscount Byng to form a government. The Tory leader had taken Borden's warnings seriously but decided to go ahead anyway: a refusal would have made a laughingstock of the governor general, who had overruled a sitting prime minister. If Meighen forced Byng to call an election, he would have forced the viceroy to bow to King's point. Any emasculation of the Crown in Canada was anathema to Meighen, who was pro-British to his fingertips. He accepted Byng's commission to form a government.

Canada's prime minister-designate now set about organizing a cabinet – a procedure that, in 1926, presented an arcane technical hurdle. Under the laws of the time, an MP being appointed to the status of a salaried minister was considered to be switching jobs: changing from a people's representative to a king's minister. To legitimize this change in status, the minister-designate was required to resign and run in a by-election so that constituents could sanction the switch. Ordinarily, these by-elections took place between the election of a new government and the convening of parliament some months later. But with Meighen's new government coming to power mid-session, not to mention the precariousness of his working majority, even the temporary resignation of a cabinet's worth of his MPs would expose his government to certain defeat in the House.

Anticipating this problem, Meighen consulted with Department of Justice lawyers and arrived at a solution. Instead of fifteen ministers, he would divide all the departments among just six, who would function in cabinet as ministers without portfolio. They would

NAME: Robert Forke

PARTY: Progressive

ROLE: Party parliamentary leader since 1922. MP for Brandon, Manitoba, since 1921.

take no oaths, run their departments merely as acting ministers, and draw no salaries. Once the deposed King regime had been censured and parliament went into summer recess, the six acting ministers would resign, the new prime minister would name a full cabinet, and by-elections would be held before parliament returned. Meighen himself did not have this option: he had to resign his seat immediately so he could be sworn in as prime minister, and he did so that very afternoon.

It was now Meighen's turn to watch from the sidelines as his new government sought to consolidate its support in the House. On June 29, the day after King's surprise resignation and Meighen's accession, an amendment moved by the pro-Tory Progressive W.R. Fansher was attached to Stevens's still-outstanding amendment of censure, and the whole package was put to a vote. It passed with a majority of ten. On June 30 the new leader of the opposition, Mackenzie King, moved non-confidence in the government's tariff policy. This predictable Liberal move to peel the Progressives from the Conservatives was defeated by seven votes. Dismayed at his party's drift towards the Tories, Forke resigned as Progressive leader.

Thus, when the House recessed for dinner on June 30, the new government seemed to be taking hold. Meighen's Tories had won power

the way the Canadian Corps had taken Vimy Ridge in April 1917: hard-slogging through the barbed wire, with no finesse and at a methodical pace, directly towards the enemy trenches. Deserted by their Progressive allies, the Liberals were now condemned by the House, out of power, and on the run. All that remained was for the new government to pass a money bill to fund its operations, adjourn, prorogue the House, and then enjoy a long, sweet summer of triumph – punctuated with a string of by-election victories by its new ministers, who would return in the fall to restore honour and prudence to the administration of the dominion's affairs.

After dinner the House reconvened for the evening sitting. Meighen watched from the curtained door of the government members' lobby behind the Tory benches. The long-overdue supply bill was up for debate, and King was droning on about its provisions. Then Sir Henry Drayton of Toronto, the Conservative House leader, sat

NAME: Sir Henry Drayton

PARTY: Conservative

ROLE: MP for York West (Toronto) since 1921; in 1926, new minister without portfolio (Finance, Railways, Immigration).

up in puzzlement. The opposition leader had wandered farther than usual from his topic and was now posing a question directly to him.

KING: Before we proceed any further … I would like to ask my hon. Friend who is leading the House whether he has taken any oath of office of any kind since he undertook to lead the House …
DRAYTON: No.
KING: Will my hon. Friend tell me what

departments he is administering? …
DRAYTON: … I have been regularly
appointed by order in council as a member
of the king's Privy Council to act in the present occasion in the Department of Finance
and the Department of Railways and Canals.
KING: … My hon. Friend has told me that he
has taken no oath this year. May I ask the hon.
Member for Argenteuil (Sir George Perley)
what departments he is administering?
PERLEY: I am Acting Secretary of State
and Acting Minister of Public Works.
KING: May I ask my hon. Friend if he
has taken any oath of office this year?
PERLEY: No …
KING: Perhaps I could shorten the questions
by asking my hon. Friend whether all of the
acting ministers have been appointed acting
ministers by order in council [the only means
of appointing an acting minister] …
DRAYTON: Yes …

Although the House was not in Question
Period, government members strove one after
another to explain away the complexities of
their ingenious arrangement for forming a
cabinet without resorting to by-elections.
Behind the curtain, an alarmed Prime Minister
Meighen paced back and forth. He knew exactly
where King was headed: an assertion that
Meighen's government did not legally exist;
that absent the oaths and assigned portfolios,
no cabinet existed; and, therefore, that the
non-existent cabinet could not have legally
appointed the acting ministers now asking
parliament for funds.

KING: … It is not a secret in any way of the
Privy Council that an order in council to be
regular, to have any force, must be carried by
a quorum of the cabinet. I can understand how
the right hon. The Prime Minister may have
taken his oaths and been sworn in as a minister,
but he was then, as I would understand it, the
sole member of council entitled to act in an
executive capacity … Privy Councillors are not
permitted to walk into the council chamber, sit
around the table, and pass whatever orders they

SHALL WE DANCE?

The wild, yet intricate parliamentary dance of King and Meighen in June/July 1926 involved an immense amount of fancy procedural footwork. But stepping back, its broad shape becomes clear: an effort by each to portray the other as a power-hungry usurper.

may like to give each other official positions … But what I want to make clear to the House and to the country this evening is that of this entire cabinet there is not a single member who has taken an oath to administer a single department of the government; and yet these gentlemen come before us with estimates and ask us to vote hundreds of millions of dollars … I say there is not a single member of this administration sitting in his seat tonight who is entitled to ask the House to vote him a single dollar … to expend … on the public service of the country.

King was wrong, legally; ample precedent existed for both oathless ministers and acting ministers to ask parliament for supply. From his lookout, Meighen ran into a friendly Progressive and muttered, "Lord. How I wish I was in there!" Had Meighen been on the floor, he could have laid out these facts and slapped down King's latest attempt as the whining of a sore loser. The Tories would have cheered, the Progressives would have nodded, and all would have been well. But Meighen was

trapped in the wings while, out on the stage, King was making his case brilliantly. He was doing so before an unstable House of Commons, already exhausted from two weeks of high drama, one that held more than a few leaderless, uncertain Progressives liable to be swayed by King's argument when it came to a vote. And the flustered Tories, leaderless in the House, were leaving his charges essentially unanswered.

That June evening William Lyon Mackenzie King became a leader. Up until then, no one could ever have imagined him exhorting his troops, as had Wilfrid Laurier, to "follow my white plume." The day before, everyone had written him off as a has-been. But on June 30, 1926, King single-handedly led the countercharge, sweeping along behind him Liberals and Progressives alike. For the first time he found his true political voice, attacking with the bravura of a supple-minded man who, for once, believes himself to be on the right side of a clear-cut moral situation. In contrast to his usually cool, analytical approach to most issues, the Liberal leader saw Meighen's ascension as a matter of liberty versus tyranny: the royal colonial power was imposing a big-business, imperialist puppet on the people of Canada without an election.

Faced with such an issue, King did not bargain or bribe but became the soldier of Christ he was born and raised to be. This fight brought out King's wounded pride in his oft-besmirched principles: he'd show Meighen and all the others who was noble, by God! Another, deeper chord was struck too: his beloved mother had raised him on stories of his rebel grandfather's courage and sacrifice in the cause of Canadian freedom. Byng and Meighen were obviously nothing more or less than the old Family Compact. Now a Mackenzie would once again lead the forces of freedom and reform against the British overlords, their Tory toadies, and the privileged classes they represented.

One hour into his magnificent rant, King was in full campaign mode. "Yes I am thinking of '37," he roared, "and I tell my hon. Friend that I was never prouder in my life than to have the privilege of standing in this parliament to-night and on behalf of British parliamentary institutions denouncing the irresponsible government of his party … 1837 was bad enough, but it was not a circumstance on the present condition of affairs. If at the instance of one individual a prime minister can be put into office and with a ministry which is not yet formed be permitted to vote all the supplies necessary to carry on the government of Canada for a year, we have reached a condition in this country that threatens constitutional liberty, freedom and right in all parts of the world." He was going after not only Meighen and his government but also Byng himself, whose action, he charged, "reduces this Dominion of Canada from the status of a self-governing Dominion to the status of a Crown Colony."

The parliamentary storm King had unleashed raged for two days. The House sat in extraordinary session on July 1, Dominion Day, and through the evening into the wee hours of Friday, July 2, debating a Liberal motion that, in effect, asserted that either of two propositions was true: that Meighen's cabinet ministers had been legally appointed and had effectively resigned their Commons seats, or that they had been appointed illegally and did not hold office. King needed twenty-three out of twenty-seven Progressive votes to topple Meighen. The motion was ingeniously designed to gain the support of both those who thought that the new ministers should resign their seats and those who thought the new ministers weren't ministers at all. Heads: King wins; tails: Meighen loses. These fine points aside, the real lever forcing the Progressives' support was fear of the election that now seemed imminent, and the consequences back home if they voted for an appointed right-wing government whose legality was in question.

As the vote drew near, the wheeling and dealing reached frenzied proportions. Taking absences into account, the Liberals and their allies could muster ninety-five votes. The Tories could pull together eighty-seven members, and nine Progressives were prepared to support them. The rest would vote with the Liberals or abstain, making for a dead heat. One pro-government Progressive, however, the same Kennedy who had wavered in the Stevens committee, was unavailable at voting time. To cover his absence, he arranged a "pair" with T.W. Bird of British Columbia, who would abstain from voting, leaving the two sides tied at ninety-five apiece. The Speaker (a Liberal) would be forced to cast the deciding vote, thereby absolving the Progressives of responsibility for the outcome but perhaps causing a government to fall

WILFRID LAURIER

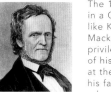

WILLIAM LYON MACKENZIE

KING BECOMES A LEADER

The 1837 Upper Canada rebellion, here recalled in a C.W. Jefferys drawing, pitted reformers like King's maternal grandfather, William Lyon Mackenzie, against the British Crown and its privileged agents in Ontario. King's worship of his grandfather, nurtured by his mother, lay at the heart of his social reformist politics. But his father figure, Laurier, offered a different role model: accommodation with the Crown and emphasis on racial harmony. When the governor general appointed Meighen as prime minister over King's objections, King saw them as attacking both his grandfather Mackenzie's belief in liberty and his "father" Laurier's vision of Canadian nationhood. Byng and Meighen brought the two sides of King's political personality together, transforming the consummate ditherer into a passionate crusader.

through a dubious use of the Speaker's power.

At 1:55 a.m. the division bells rang. Speaker Lemieux called on the ayes to stand. Liberals and Progressives rose, sitting down one by one as the Speaker called their names. As the counting reached the third party's benches, Bird suddenly leapt to his feet and was recorded as an aye. Some said he had been sleeping and jumped up, confused, when the count drew near him. Others suspected something darker. We'll never know, but when the votes were all counted, Bird's timely leap gave the Liberals their margin: the motion passed ninety-six to ninety-five.

Conservatives cried out "shame" and "tie vote" as Bird stated he had cast his vote inadvertently. Lemieux ruled that Bird's vote must stand, and wild celebration broke out on the Liberal benches. Lapointe and Drayton bellowed at each other across the floor. The Speaker adjourned the House amid thunderous Liberal cheers.

For the first time in Canadian history a government had been defeated on a motion of confidence. It broke the Tories' will to carry on. While the government could carry the House on motions of policy, it had just lost a vote on its legal right to exist. No party could now retain control of the Commons.

The next morning, July 3, after a rumoured three-hour interview with Meighen, Governor General Byng bowed to the inevitable, accepted his prime minister's advice, and dissolved the fifteenth parliament. Meighen would lead a caretaker government. As acting prime minister, he could call an election any time within the next eleven months, but he was eager to get going as soon as his party could prepare for battle. In anticipation of the writ's issuance, parliamentarians scattered to their ridings to begin campaign preparations. Newspapers speculated on a September 21 election, noting it was for Tories

the anniversary of their 1911 free trade election victory, but soon it became widely known that the vote would take place on September 14.

The Meighen government, still in power despite its brief run in the Commons, could console itself with the control it had gained of election machinery. Enumeration would be handled by Tory appointees, who could be relied upon to put good Tories on the voters' lists and as few Liberals as humanly possible. This taxpayer-funded work was only the tip of the organizational iceberg. Canvassing needed to be done, voters' lists had to be marked, and the voters themselves had to be herded to the polls. However, volunteers now did much of the work. The partisan complexion of the civil service had largely been eradicated in the previous decades, eliminating much of the enormous reservoir of paid political operatives for governments to draw on at election time. Corporations still made impressive (and unrecorded) contributions, but the heyday of the paid riding organizer was over. Much of the money now went to advertising in newspapers and magazines and to the printing and distribution of campaign literature in the ridings (Canada's first radio networks were still a few years away). As in previous campaigns, organization would be a major factor, but victory would likely go to whichever leader could persuade undecided and third-party voters to come his way.

Each leader planned to explain to bewildered voters what the hell had just happened up there in Ottawa, to guide voters' intentions by shaping their understanding of the issues at stake. "I see it all so clearly," wrote King in his diary the morning of Sunday, July 4. "From now on, I go forward in the strength of God & His Might and Right to battle as my forefathers battled for the rights of the people." Meighen looked forward to clarifying matters as well. In modern parlance, both were playing a "frame game," a political battle in which both sides seek to frame events into a story that has only one possible moral: vote for me. Meighen's story about sleazy Liberals clinging to power so as to pillage the public estate was squaring off against King's tale of usurpation by the forces of privilege and colonialism.

In 1926 this frame game was played for the benefit of a vital audience of undecided voters. While the old verities of race and religion still drove a great deal of electoral behaviour (especially in rural areas and in Quebec), the ever-fluctuating third-party scene made for a relatively large pool of highly persuadable electors. In 1925 some 282,000 Canadians had voted Progressive, and another 148,000 had voted for fourth- or fifth-party candidates, for a total of 14 per cent of the votes cast. These swing voters were concentrated in Ontario and on the prairies. King may have failed in luring Progressives to his cause in 1925, but the Tory gains in the last election at the expense of the Progressives told him that the bulk of Progressive voters that remained had a Liberal leaning. In other words, every vote squeezed from the Progressives in this campaign would be likely to go to him. While King hoped to milk Progressive votes and pick up a number of seats, Meighen had little reason to expect much in Ontario, where he had scant room to grow. Despite the Tories' hostility to prairie interests, he still hoped to improve his count in the West. That left Quebec; if the Tory leader could add to his 1925 total just seven Quebec seats, a secure majority would be his.

Meighen spent most of the two weeks between his government's fall and the campaign's official start trying to sort out factional struggles in Quebec. When his caretaker cabinet was announced on July 14, its Quebec slots had not been filled, and the task was only partially completed a week later. That night, at a "special convention" of Conservatives in the heat of the old Ottawa Auditorium, four thousand support-

ers heard Meighen announce an eight-week campaign with an election date of September 14. He kicked off with a stirring attack on the King government's "utter absence of elementary essentials of honest fiscal administration." He planned to run hard on the corruption question, insisting, "there is no constitutional issue."

King picked up the frame game on July 23, kicking off his campaign at the same Ottawa venue as Meighen. He put the constitutional issue front and centre, arguing as he would for the rest of the campaign that Meighen had "usurped power." He promised that Meighen "will find before the present campaign is over that there is a constitutional issue greater than any that has been raised in Canada since the founding of this Dominion … and Mr. Meighen has only himself to thank that it overshadows everything else."

King prepared to sound the grace note of Canadian nationalism in his clarion call against Meighen's usurpation. On July 25, departing his Gatineau retreat of "Kingsmere" for the campaign trail, King wrote: "Spent the last hour tonight singing hymns … I go into the battle of another election – believing we have a great issue – that the people will respond to – that is the making of our nation." Out on the hustings in Ontario through to the end of July, he drove home again and again the link between Meighen's usurpation and British colonialism. Not many voters were able to follow the twists and turns of his detailed legal disquisitions on what everyone now called "the King–Byng affair," but they could easily grasp his message of Tory usurpation versus independence and freedom. "It is the one thing," said King, "the people rise to above all else when it is explained." He was tapping into the same kind of plucky, underdog, Canuck nationalism that the Tories usually used to slam the Grits as pro-American – only now he was using it against the British.

This new English Canadian nationalism had been a long time coming. One by one the political milestones had been passed: in 1922, Canada had said no to a British request for military aid; in 1923 came the first Canadian signature on a treaty; 1926 saw the Balfour Declaration establish the dominions as equal and independent partners of Britain in the empire. Laurier's long quest to build a distinct Canadian identity had laid the foundations of a nationalist sentiment in English Canada. Now King was both drawing from and adding to that tendency at each campaign stop. Of course, the deposed prime minister took pains to counter the inevitable charges of disloyalty by couching his crusade against Meighen's usurpation as a loyal preservation of the rights and liberties of British subjects.

Campaigning in week two in Ontario, King supplemented his constitutional message with reminders of his springtime budget, with its lower tariff on cars and reduced personal income taxes. These bon-bons were particularly aimed at Progressive voters and were featured prominently in Liberal communications in rural Ontario. Through these messages, King saw in the 1926 election fight the chance to bring a five-year strategy to fruition. Since 1921, the year the Progressives took second place, King had staked his future on leaving a candle in the window for wandering liberals. Now he sensed that many of them were ready to come home. For many reform-minded electors, the three-day Meighen government of 1926 had shown that the hated Tories had a chance at power as long as Liberals and Progressives remained divided; voting Progressive seemed a luxury to be indulged when the Tories were safely off in third place, as in 1921, but not now. In Ontario, where King would spend more than three weeks on tour by election day, and to a lesser extent in Manitoba, Progressive-cum-Liberal voters would at last have to choose between voting

Progressive, and thereby helping to elect a Tory government, or voting Liberal. Many Ontario Grits favoured a direct attack on the weakened third party, but King exercised restraint. Only four of the province's eighty-two seats saw a three-way race. The Liberals stood aside in eight ridings, while in five they fielded a Liberal-Progressive candidate. Everything depended on ending the Liberal diaspora.

King stuck to his formula as he rolled west in week three. In Manitoba he and his lieutenants arranged matters so well that Liberal and Progressive candidates did not face each other in even one riding, leaving the Tories to face a united front in every district. In several ridings Progressives even made the link official, running under the banner of Liberal-Progressive. In Saskatchewan, however, where King stood in Prince Albert against the thirty-year-old Diefenbaker, the Liberal Party was judged strong enough to take on both the Tories and the Progressives directly.

By week four, Meighen's attacks on Liberal corruption, delivered first in the Maritimes, then throughout a high-speed continental rail odyssey to his other bastion in British Columbia, had fizzled. On August 11 in Kamloops the prime minister not only cut the scandal message right out of his speeches but dropped his original position that there was no constitutional issue. Instead, he resurrected the Tory cry of loyalty to Britain, accusing Mackenzie King of trying "to raise the spirit which actuated in his old grandfather, William Lyon Mackenzie – that of rebellion. His motive is to stir up feelings against the British and Lord Byng and we are determined to let the people know where he will lead them ... into the hands of the United States." The Liberals blasted back, with speeches and newspaper ads that cited Meighen's heresy in Hamilton to mock his pro-British credentials.

King reluctantly spent week four campaigning in British Columbia and Alberta,

DEATH-STARE: MEIGHEN ON THE CAMPAIGN TRAIL

Meighen in his riding of Portage la Prairie in 1920. This photo captures the man's Darth Vader-esque campaign technique. He seems to regard everything he sees with contempt: the local men around him, the whole messy democratic process. Meighen's elitist, intimidating style of campaigning did not serve him well and has long been out of fashion.

TO BE A KING

MACKENZIE KING ON THE CAMPAIGN TRAIL

Mackenzie King was generally a weak campaigner, with a "portly, prosaic look on the platform," in the words of journalist Bruce Hutchison, who covered him in the 1920s. His tedious, platitudinous speechifying had been disappointing crowds, such as the one that turned out to hear him in Kitchener (below, right), since he first entered electoral politics. And just look at the staid image he presents in the 1925 motorcade picture (below) or his awkward attempt to look like a leader during a rally in Brampton (right). In the 1926 Campaign, people saw a new King. The strain of ten months on the political knife-edge had taken pounds off his overstuffed frame. His exhausting tour schedule – adopted against the advice and the wishes of a battered campaign staff – kept him lean. As Hutchison wrote of Campaign '26, "King, the sedentary student, tired out all the ex-farmers and athletes in his entourage." What kept him going? Above all, the belief that he was leading a righteous crusade. Nothing else can explain his alpha-male swagger as he chugs a glass of water before roaring into a late-campaign rally in Cobourg, Ontario (top left) or the vigour of his outflung arm as he speaks to the big crowd (below left). In 1926 King was a changed man. He knew it and the voters could feel it.

THE U.F.A.

OFFICIAL ORGAN

THE UNITED FARMERS OF ALBERTA
ALBERTA CO-OPERATIVE MARKETING POOLS

Vol. V.   CALGARY, ALBERTA, SEPTEMBER 7, 1926   No. 24

THE DAWN OF SEPTEMBER 14th

having been persuaded that a once and future prime minister must, on principle, campaign nationwide. In Alberta the Liberals were getting behind the Progressives, who now constituted themselves as the United Farmers of Alberta. Let the Tories fight the UFA if they wished. In the coastal province he lamented the Tory strength, which he attributed to warfare between Liberals and Progressives and "a waste of a fine province." He left British Columbia on August 14 and returned to Ontario and Quebec, before proceeding to the Maritimes.

In Quebec the Liberal hold remained secure. The nationalists' quiescence left Liberals in francophone ridings a clear field in which to run against the bogeyman Meighen – whose sins now included the recent death in Pittsburgh of the hapless former customs minister, George Boivin. (Boivin had died of natural causes, but Meighen was found guilty by association. As the leader of the party that had attacked him and as a still-hated figure for pushing through conscription, Meighen might as well have put poison in Boivin's soup.) Quebeckers had no difficulty buying King's version of the Tories' "usurpation" of power. Even old Henri Bourassa in *Le Devoir* endorsed the Liberals. King's brief appearance in the province was highlighted by a silent vigil over Boivin's grave on August 23, the consecration of yet another *Canadien* martyred by that terrible Meighen.

For his part, the Tory leader continued lavishing time on the West, visiting his Manitoba riding and speaking in Winnipeg before heading east for the final two weeks. He visited Montreal on September 4, then hurried back to Ontario, where King was pouring it on for the campaign's final ten days. By now the Liberal leader had honed to perfection his recitation of the election's meaning: freedom versus tyranny, the common folk versus the privileged few, colonial status versus nationhood. King's passion was making a difference on the campaign trail. Voters could see that the Liberal leader meant what he said – a far cry from the tortured defender of a middling minority record the previous year and light years from the fussy, tentative figure of the early 1920s. Whatever he may have thought of his legal arguments, he knew he was on the right side of history, and he played like a champion at the top of his game. King had become a leader – and it showed.

At the campaign's finish, counters in the Tories' Ottawa headquarters told reporters to expect 132 Conservatives, with 70 from Ontario, 26 from the Maritimes, 7 from Quebec, and 29 from the West. They were effectively admitting that their Quebec strategy had failed – a concession that left only wildly optimistic predictions on the Prairies to make the case for victory. On more solid ground, the Liberals predicted they would win 133 seats, with 21 in Ontario, 12 in the Maritimes, 63 in Quebec, and 37 from the West.

Voting began in Cape Breton at 8 a.m. on September 14, 1926, and rolled west from there. There were as yet no standard voting rules, as the provinces administered elections, but, in the main, every British subject twenty-one years or older who had resided in Canada for a year before the issuance of the writ was entitled to vote. Arthur Meighen voted in Portage la Prairie, where rain fell for most of the day.

By midnight in Manitoba, the results from Ontario were in and Meighen knew his party

Last stand. In 1926 the Progressives and their allies were weakened by the 1925 defections to the Tories in Ontario and besieged by King's assaults in the West. This campaign poster's paranoid imagery suggests a movement facing defeat.

had been defeated at the polls. An hour later he knew he was also on his way to personal defeat, trailing by four hundred votes in his own riding. In Ottawa, King and a few political friends, including industrialist Vincent Massey and his party treasurer and top English Canadian fixer Andrew Haydon, were holed up in his Parliament Hill office, where he had installed a dedicated telegraph service. Using the maps and charts spread out on his desk, he began piecing together the results until the national picture was reasonably clear to him. Only at 4 a.m. did a victorious King return to Laurier House and sleep.

In the end the Liberals fell slightly short of their pre-election prediction, winning 128 seats, 11 of them under the indistinguishable Liberal-Progressive banner, for a viable majority in the 245-seat House of Commons. Quebec had come through with 60 seats, and, while King fell slightly short of expectations in the Maritimes and on the Prairies, he had exceeded his hopes in Ontario, winning 26 of the province's 82 seats. Ontario failed Meighen, with a reduced Tory turnout that delivered him only 53 MPS in the face of King's Liberal-cum-Progressive vote. In the West the Tories dropped by ten seats, leaving them shut out of Manitoba and Saskatchewan and with one seat in Alberta – future prime minister Richard Bennett's Calgary stronghold. Nationwide, the Tories elected only 91 MPS.

The Tory percentage of the popular vote had fallen very slightly, but the Liberals had leapt from 40 per cent to 46 per cent as a result of three factors. Voter turnout had increased to 3.25 million from 1925's total of 3.15 million, with the Liberals receiving the larger share of the increase. The third-party vote had col-

lapsed by more than half, with the bulk of it going Liberal. Finally, the Tories' total had dropped by 5 per cent in Ontario, while their share of that province's vote fell 3 per cent to 54 per cent. Votes for the splinter parties in Ontario fell from 12 per cent to 7 per cent. Ontario Progressives had come home to the Liberals, making the crucial difference in many of the Grits' eleven new seats there.

The collapse of the Progressive vote was repeated in the West, where effective riding-level deals and improved Liberal performance robbed the Tories of seat after seat and often added directly to the Liberal column. In the three Prairie provinces the Liberals enjoyed an extremely efficient translation of popular votes into seats. In Manitoba the Liberals' support increased by less than five thousand votes, but their seat count went from one to four, while the Conservatives, despite a leap in the popular vote, fell from seven seats to zero. In Saskatchewan the Tories improved their popular vote performance by 20 per cent, but didn't win a seat, whereas the Liberals, who merely held steady, retained fifteen of the twenty-one seats. In Alberta the Tories fell from three seats to one, as the United Farmers of Alberta carried eleven of the province's sixteen seats. Only on the west coast did the splits play right for the Tories: in British Columbia the shifts from Progressive to Liberal were negated by a surge in the Tory turnout, increasing Meighen's coastal strength from ten to twelve out of a possible fourteen. In Atlantic Canada a smallish Liberal increase sparked a gain of three seats, while in Quebec the Tories' modest popular vote gains were buried under the usual Liberal landslide. King's strategy of co-opting the Progressives – a loser at the polls in 1925 and

On election night, 1926, a crowd of Winnipeggers watches the national results as they are posted on the *Free Press*'s billboard, a newspaper-era equivalent of today's election-night telecasts.

frustrated by scandal in June 1926 – had held up for him both in the House on July 2 and in the ballot box on September 14. He had held his course through fierce political storms and sailed triumphantly into safe harbour.

You can still get a good argument going among historians and politicians about the 1926 election. For one thing, it produced the kind of results that get proportional representation enthusiasts all hot and bothered. The spread between popular vote and seat count was unusually large: Liberals got 46 per cent of the votes and 52 per cent of the seats; the Tories' 45 per cent of the votes yielded just 37 per cent of the seats. And the argument gets louder when you start in on the campaign's key issue, the King–Byng crisis. To this day Tories believe that King was dead wrong in asking for dissolution, that Byng did the right thing, and that King proved himself the original slippery Liberal: a Canadian political stereotype as recognizable as the red-faced Orangeman Tory, the elbow-padded New Democrat professor, and the beret-wearing, Gitanes-smoking militant of the Parti Québécois. Liberals counter by painting Meighen as a brick-headed clod who bet the farm on a narrow legal interpretation in a fast-moving, primarily political situation. The King–Byng battle is also a bone of contention between monarchists and Canadian nationalists, the former believing that we abandoned a glorious tradition in 1926, and the latter arguing that Canada grew up when it chose King over Meighen, Byng, and obedience to the Crown of England in the 1926 election campaign.

Neither side has it totally right, mainly because too many factors contributed to the outcome for any one cause to predominate. Consider all-important Ontario, where the Tory drop and Liberal surge can be attributed to any or all of the following: riding-level vote splits, King's spring budget, general economic prosperity, and disaffection over Meighen's heresy at Hamilton. Voters responded to the King–Byng affair not so much on its merits as on the way King used it to position himself as the only means by which progressive voters could avert the evils of an illegitimate Tory government. He ran on nationalism, economic populism, and democracy, and a mass migration of Progressive votes followed to the Grit column in Ontario and on the prairies.

But there was another crucial factor: King's crusade also transformed him into a compelling leader. In both the 1921 and 1925 campaigns he had been the old, windy, foggy King. In 1926 he was passionate and forceful, rendering a complex issue into a simple, clear, and compelling message and generally acting the way a leader is expected to act. People responded.

Not that leader-driven politics was new, of course. Meighen had used his public performance to good effect in 1925. As early as 1921 the Tory slogan was "Canada needs Meighen." And as far back as 1891 the image of Macdonald, with the slogan "The Old Flag, The Old Policy, The Old Leader," had been plastered on telegraph poles from coast to coast. What was new in 1926 was the size of the swing vote, which was strongly influenced by leadership. As society changed and horizons expanded, more and more voters were looking beyond the little worlds around them to their province, to their country, and even, since the war, to lands overseas. So, when it came time to choose a govern-

This postcard cartoon from 1925 mocks Mackenzie King's flexible approach to policy issues. Before King, Liberals stood or fell on causes such as free trade, provincial rights, and anti-conscription. From King's day onward, they would be labelled as slippery, unprincipled, and – more often than not – victorious.

ment, they tended increasingly to look beyond their community, with its local political figures, and to the national leaders. The world of the all-powerful party machine was gone and something like modern politics was starting to happen. The Siamese twin of this more direct relationship between voters and leaders was more direct democratic involvement in the big questions. In the 1890s people voted the local man, who then went to Ottawa where the caucus and the cabinet brokered the national issues. In the 1920s many people still voted that way, but ever larger numbers were now voting directly for the national leader and, by extension, the leader's position on national questions.

Within this overall trend, some parts of the country were more volatile, leader-oriented, and geared to the politics of ideas than others. Small-town Ontario and rural Quebec would remain locked in their tribal and religious loyalties well into the 1960s. King's genius was to realize that, for all he might wish to align national politics around the battle between Liberal progress and Tory reaction, he needed always to account for the stubborn fact of Quebec's unique political needs. (It was also Mackenzie King's luck to be up against a Tory leader so hated and feared in Quebec that the Liberals needed little to maintain their grip on the province.) In the electoral struggles of the 1920s the broad pattern of subsequent national politics was established – a battle along ideological lines across English Canada; a related struggle to reconcile western regional priorities with central Canada's; then in Quebec something completely different: a contest to choose who could best answer French Canada's unique requirement of *la survivance*.

King understood this complex game in a way Meighen never could. The Tory leader's dream of realigning national politics along ideological lines foundered on the hard facts of race. But Meighen failed as well at even

the relatively straightforward game of English Canadian issue politics. His arrogant logician's brain simply could not master the obvious political maxim that "the enemy of my enemy is my friend" – and that maybe, by fighting tariff battles, he was driving both his enemies, Progressives and Liberals, into each other's arms. Finally, Meighen misunderstood the limited role of parliament in a modern democracy. On June 24, 1926, he thought he had won his duel with King on the floor of the House of Commons, but in reality the duel was only beginning to attract the audience that would ultimately decide its outcome. Meighen showed a woeful disregard for public reaction to his parliamentary swordplay, overestimated the declining importance of parliament, and underestimated the rising power of the volatile electorate.

There was one other fight that Meighen really could not win. Canada's ongoing evolution as an independent country was bound to sunder his nostalgic, umbilical bond to the mother country. In the end King gave as good as he got in the indoor fencing match, and he rolled right over Meighen in the broader struggle over the shape of national politics and the future of the country.

The ever fascinating Mackenzie King was at his best and his worst in the fight of 1925–26. He showed considerable courage and tenacity in a seemingly hopeless situation. At the same time his use of legally unsound arguments to demand dissolution and to challenge the constitutionality of Meighen's government presents him as an amoral twentieth-century politician, devoid of the decency and honour that had heretofore characterized public life. No wonder that Lady Byng, the epitome of honourable grace, expected of King "a goodish deal of filth, once his power was in danger." That his filth was clad in the pieties of Victorian, small-town Ontario adds a further unpleasant air to King's behav-

PLAYBOOK III

The Canadian political playbook may be timeless, but it isn't static. Each new generation of leaders adapts the basic strategies to changing social and political realities. In 1926 Mackenzie King recycled his mentor Laurier's favourite play – the Quebec Bridge – but gave it a new wrinkle. The core strategy of representing Quebec's interests stayed the same, but King also had to navigate the new politics of class in English Canada. To do so, he reached out to urban workers and progressive farmers, adding them to his Quebec core to rack up a record of five electoral wins and two losses.

iour in the crisis. But while King the man presents a low moral spectacle in 1925–26, his achievements as a nation builder more than redeem him in my mind.

Between assuming the leadership in 1919 and winning his first majority in 1926, King saved the Liberal Party and, in so doing, salvaged the common ground where both racial and regional politics and the new politics of class could be amicably sorted out. Had King's Liberal Party died, three mutually hostile power blocs would have remained in national politics: English Canada's Tories, English Canada's Progressives, and Quebec. How could any of them have worked together? The Tories' British imperialism ruled out their long-term accommodation of Quebec; that province's conservative, Catholic culture made cooperation with socialists equally improbable; and, of course, the Tories and the socialists couldn't get together at all. Canadian politics would have been deadlocked, leaving the country perilously disunited for the challenges of the 1930s and 1940s, and likely freezing social progress in the face of Tory and Quebec opposition. King restored the Liberal Party as the common ground on which Quebec's traditionalist power structure and English Canada's reformers could do business together. King brought the Quebec Bridge play to perfection. Yet there was more to its use than electoral advantage. In our invented country, whose very existence is a political arrangement, the configurations of Mackenzie King proved durable and beneficial in ways that far outshine the shadowy means by which they were sometimes achieved.

On all counts, the twin elections of 1925 and 1926 pass the test of greatness. They were a glorious see-saw fight, with the probability of victory changing hands at least four times over the twelve months from the first election's call to the counting of the second's results. They marked the end of the political system's time of troubles (which began in 1917) and the commencement of a new period in national politics – one based on Ottawa's brokering not of the races so much as the regions – that would last three decades and come to be known as the King Era.

Finally, King's 1926 campaign breathed a little life into the arrangement called Canada. In English Canada anyway, King's nation-building message caught the spirit of the age. His New World nationalism, economic populism, and democracy look quite modern alongside Meighen's colonial chest-thumps about Great Britain and the Crown. The young dominion had nobly fought a war; it was becoming a real country, one that could make its own decisions without some foreign aristocrat deciding who ruled the roost. King felt this emerging nationhood in his bones. He was a Laurier Canadian, not an English Protestant or a French Catholic. He had served as a deputy minister in the infant civil service; he lived in Ottawa, the physical monument to the new country's emerging identity; and he had chosen his home country over a life of influential ease in London or New York. If anyone believed in an independent, distinct Canada, it was William Lyon Mackenzie King. And, in 1926, he got a whole lot of people to believe in it with him. A nation was coming into being.

On a trip to England, Mackenzie King poses for a photo in front of a casting destined for the National War Memorial in Ottawa. With monuments like these, King sought to forge a national consciousness distinct from old colonial ties. The 1926 campaign marked a milestone in this lifelong effort.

THE KINGDOM AT HAND

THE ELECTIONS OF
1930 / 1935 / 1940 / 1945 / 1949 / 1953

MACKENZIE KING'S 1926 ELECTION TRIUMPH forced Arthur Meighen's exit from the national stage and rang down the curtain on the Progressives as a serious federal force. At first it looked like a restoration of the two-party order to the federal scene – with the post-colonial, moderately progressive, pro-Quebec Liberals on top in a system based on regional brokerage. Only three years into King's new administration, however, the great Wall Street crash of October 28 and 29, 1929, sent stock prices plummeting 25 per cent, triggering economic panic. Policy makers worldwide, including Canada's prime minister, assumed they were witnessing a normal cyclical downturn. Within months they turned it into an economic collapse through a series of blunders that throttled trade, collapsed prices, and sent unemployment soaring to unprecedented heights. Canada, as a trading nation, was hit hard and fast. Within a year, employment had fallen 5 per cent and was dropping at an accelerating rate. On the prairies and particularly in Saskatchewan, a drought that had begun in 1928 combined disastrously with the wider collapse of trade. (These events would ultimately slash that province's per capita income by 72 per cent.) By July 1930 almost 20 per cent of Canada's workforce was out of a job.

Hon. R.B. Bennett receiving nomination at Convention of Conservatives Winnipeg. 1927.

**July 1927
CANADA
CELEBRATES
DIAMOND JUBILEE**
Festivities from coast to coast mark the sixtieth anniversary of Confederation. *(Above)* Lapel pin commemorating the jubilee and depicting the PM in 1867 (Macdonald) and the PM in 1927 (King).

**October 1927
BENNETT WINS TORY LEADERSHIP**
Wealthy Calgary bachelor Richard Bedford Bennett succeeds Arthur Meighen as leader of the Conservative Party at the Tories' first leadership convention in Winnipeg.

**October 1929
CRASH HERALDS
DEPRESSION**
Wall Street meltdown and botched government responses trigger a global "Great Depression." Farm prices collapse and prairie drought and dust-bowls *(above)* deepen the misery in rural Canada.

**June 1930
BENNETT
CAMPAIGNS ON
RADIO**
R.B. Bennett kicks off his campaign with a nationally broadcast election speech. Radio had come to Canada in 1919, but Bennett's was the first campaign speech to be broadcast nationally. *(Above)* Children listening to radio.

King and his government responded weakly. He tinkered with trade policy, mainly in a bid to outflank the Tories on the perennial tariff issue while doing little to address the economic slump. In the House at the end of March 1930, with relief rolls soaring, he primly reminded the opposition that welfare was a provincial responsibility, then added brutally that he would not give a five-cent piece to any provincial Tory government. Such outrageous partisanship showed how detached King was from both the human and the political realities of the Great Depression.

The prime minister called an election for July 28, 1930. In this context he would for the first time face R.B. Bennett, the Calgary millionaire MP who had succeeded Arthur Meighen at the Tory leadership convention in 1927. During the writ campaign, Bennett lit up the country with his commanding rhetoric – for example, promising to "use tariffs to blast a way into the markets" of the world. The Tory leader's policy may have been nonsensical – tariffs are designed to keep goods out of one country, not force goods into another – but in contrast to King's limp slogan, "a record of faithful stewardship," the Bennett formula sounded like salvation. Bennett showed he was a man of the future by taking to the airwaves, becoming the first federal leader to campaign over national radio. Swing voters tilted towards the Tories on election day, and

THE WELDER

July 28, 1930
KING GETS HAMMERED
Bennett takes 137 seats and wins 49 per cent of the popular vote, the Liberals take 91 seats, and the dwindling Progressives 17. *(Above)* Liberal campaign poster deifying the soon-to-be-defeated leader.

August 1932
CCF COMES TOGETHER
Labour MPs and farmers' representatives gather in Calgary to form the democratic socialist Co-operative Commonwealth Federation (CCF). The CCF later reconstituted itself as the New Democratic Party. *(Above)* Newly elected leader J.S. Woodsworth addresses a meeting.

December 1934
COMMUNIST NIGHT IN CANADA
Canadian Communist Party leader Tim Buck, recently released from prison, speaks to a packed Toronto Maple Leaf Gardens under comrade Stalin's watchful gaze.

August 1935
SOCIAL CREDIT ROLLS IN
The Social Credit Party under William "Bible Bill" Aberhart wins the Alberta provincial election. Soon the party will sweep the province's federal seats. *(Above)* Socred poster on the back of a railroad flatcar.

the first-past-the-post system magnified the party's 49 per cent of the vote to 56 per cent of the seats: 137 for the Tories to 91 for the Liberals and 17 for the Progressives and others. Even Quebec elected 24 Tory MPs. King's new political order of 1926 – Liberal dominance in Quebec and among progressive voters – seemed to have been shattered by the crisis.

In power, however, Bennett could not turn his political opportunity into achievement. He proved no better than King at solving the Depression (nor, to be fair, did any other leader in the world). As unemployment climbed towards the one-third of the workforce it would reach in early 1933, Bennett frantically worked the traditional fiscal toggles of tariffs and budget balancing. From the opposition benches, King offered no real alternatives. When a truly rancid scandal erupted in 1931 over the previous Liberal government's award of hydroelectric power contracts in Quebec, the opposition leader just lay low.

King's uneven performance – from the peak of the 1926 election to what he called the "valley of humiliation" in the early 1930s – made him seem like one of those politicians who was good at getting elected but bad at governing. He had figured out the tactical side of politics – no one could question that after the crisis and triumph of

1926 – but his failure to score any significant policy achievements in nine years of office showed that the purpose of power had eluded him. Now, as the Depression deepened, he sought intellectual renewal. Sitting at "Kingsmere," his estate outside Ottawa, the manipulator of the 1920s reacquainted himself with the idealist of the 1900s, rekindling his passion for social justice and the healing power of government.

He was not alone. Across the industrialized world, intellectual and political leaders were embracing the idea of a massive state response to the economic crisis. The economist Maynard Keynes's prescriptions for Britain, Roosevelt's New Deal, Hitler's massive program of public works, and even Stalin's forced industrialization all seemed exciting responses to the popular demand for radical action. In Canada, intellectuals, farmers, and trade unionists formed the country's first socialist party, the Co-operative Commonwealth Federation (CCF) in Calgary in 1932, placing J.S. Woodsworth at its head. The same year, Alberta preacher William "Bible Bill" Aberhart began the radio addresses that would sweep him into the premiership three years later. He pledged a radical populism based on eccentric "social credit" ideas out of Britain, most notably that a "social dividend" built up by society as a whole should be converted into cash and paid to individuals. Bennett's Tories could smile at a revival of left-wing populism in Liberal Saskatchewan, but the populist splitters in Alberta posed a direct threat. Action was required.

Prime Minister Bennett's deathbed conversion to a new way of thinking came five months later in January 1935, but only after four-and-a-half years in power and far too late for his prospects of re-election. The Depression at last was easing, but Bennett's name had by now become synonymous with misery. In the 1935 election King re-emerged with a new commitment to dynamic government and a memorable slogan, "It's King or Chaos," that positioned him as the alternative to both the doomed Bennett and the gaggle of instant parties that had sprung up across the country. On election day, October 14, 1935, the Conservatives crashed to 39 seats and fell ten points to 30 per cent of the popular vote. Only the Liberals' vote held steady, which was sufficient to yield them a whopping 171 seats. The CCF polled 9 per cent of the vote and elected seven MPs in Saskatchewan, Manitoba, and British Columbia while the Alberta-concentrated Social Credit converted only 4 per cent of the vote into 17 seats. As in the past, King had built his majority on the rock of Quebec, but now Manitoba and Saskatchewan came firmly into the Liberal fold and would remain pillars of King's coalition for a decade and more.

VOTE LIBERAL

BECAUSE—

1. You do <u>not</u> want a one-man government at Ottawa.

2. You want your representatives to make a contribution to the Government in your interest.

3. You want a People's Government.

4. You do <u>not</u> want to elect mere rubber stamps.

5. You do <u>not</u> want the **"iron heel of ruthlessness"** in Canada.

VOTE LIBERAL!

Issued by the

National Liberal Federation

114 Wellington St. - - Ottawa

PRINTED BY THE DADSON-MERRILL PRESS LIMITED, OTTAWA, CANADA.

October 14, 1935
KING RESTORED
Mackenzie King's Liberals win 171 seats, the largest majority thus far in Canadian history, reducing R.B. Bennett's Conservatives to a paltry 39 seats. King's campaign was actually much simpler than this Liberal pamphlet's obscurely worded copy would suggest. The Grits built their comeback around the slogan "It's King or Chaos," a compelling pitch amid political and economic disarray. But King's victory was deceptive. The Liberal percentage of the popular vote actually stayed at about 44 per cent. But the new splinter parties tore into the Tories, especially in the West, leaving King's Liberals solid in Quebec and the only party left standing nationwide. In classic fashion, King never for a moment questioned the legitimacy of his vast majority, and he only strengthened his grip on power over the next thirteen years.

June 1937
KING CALLS ON THE FÜHRER
The Canadian prime minister makes an official visit to Nazi
Germany and comes away impressed with Herr Hitler and
with a message of "understanding, friendship and goodwill."
(Above) King at a Nazi labour rally with Ernest Lapointe, his
Quebec lieutenant and right-hand man.

May 1939
ROYALS VISIT CANADA
King George VI and
Queen Elizabeth make
a month-long tour of
Canada, during which
they unveil Ottawa's
National War Memorial
and stop to open the
Canada Pavilion at the
New York World's Fair.
(Above) The king and
queen arrive at an
event in Regina.

September 1939
CANADA AT WAR
On September 10
Canada declares
war on Germany,
one week after
Britain and France.
(Above) A Canadian
munitions worker
inspects just-
manufactured
artillery shells.

The 1935 election brought two lasting forces onto the federal scene: the western Social Crediters, who would remain a force until the mid-1960s, and the CCF that survives as the NDP to this day. The Liberal campaign's focus on King-the-strongman also took to a new level the role of the leader in winning an election. Yet the 1935 election wasn't a very good fight. The only real policy clash on the question of economic recovery took place out on the campaign's margins as the new parties floated their radical solutions. The main players had little of importance to say on the greatest issue of the day.

Still, Mackenzie King seized the opportunity seemingly granted, yet again, by his "Unseen Hand" of providence. He laid the human and intellectual foundations of the Liberal dynasty that would outlive him. His 1935 cabinet included new men – Saskatchewan's Jimmy Gardiner, Ontario's C.D. Howe, Nova Scotia's James Isley, and Quebec's Charles "Chubby" Power – who would serve in senior portfolios and as regional barons for the Liberal Party for up to twenty years and more. King also started out – ever so slowly lest he offend conservative, Catholic Quebec – on the path of social reform, paving the way for a federal role in social policy. And at long last he began engaging in international affairs, as the world again headed towards war.

UNITY
Not an Accident...
but an Achievement

[The REALITY of Canada's unity in this day of great national effort is a source of dismay to our enemies and a factor of strength to ourselves and to our Allies ... What Canadians should realise more fully is that their national unity does not exist through accident ... It is the direct emergence of resourceful, determined and painstaking administration during recent years by an experienced and nationally-minded federal government ... During the past few years the proactive policies of the Mackenzie King Government with respect to both foreign affairs and domestic affairs — reflect the interests of the whole people and give proof to the world at large — that our unity does not exist through accident.]

A Program of Trade Treaties — ...

Development of the Trans-Canada Airways — ...

Support for the Canadian National Railways System — ...

A National Agricultural Policy — ...

Publicly-Owned Central Bank — ...

Co-operative Action on Unemployment Problem — ...

Parliament's Right to Decide on War — ...

No Prior Commitments — ...

The Quebec Election — ...

ACTION
Since the outbreak of war

First Division ....
Second Division ....
Coastal Waters ....
War Supply Board ....
$100,000,000 War Expenditure ....
Voluntary War Services ......
Agricultural Supplies Committee ....
Foreign Exchange Control ....
Commonwealth Air Training Plan ......
Food Shortages Prevented ......
Wheat ....
Ships ....
Public Information Bureau ......
Internal benefits ......
V.C.A. Atlantic State Available ......
Canadian Farms Under Arms ......

FORWARD WITH
MACKENZIE KING

March 26, 1940
KING'S MAJORITY GROWS
King's commitment to wartime unity without conscription boosts the Liberals to 178 seats. The Tories under Manion take 39, Social Credit 10, and the CCF 8. *(Above)* A Liberal campaign poster rallies voters to King's wartime cause.

The Bearer, whose photograph and specimen of signature appear hereon, has been duly registered in compliance with the provisions of Order-in-Council P. C. 117.

Vancouver
(Date) March 12 1941.

JAPANESE NATIONAL

Issuing Officer
INSPECTOR J.C.M.P.

December 1941
WAR WITH JAPAN
In response to the Pearl Harbor sneak attack, Canada joins Britain and the US in declaring war on Japan. As war approached, identity cards *(above)* were issued to Japanese Canadians. After December 8 they were herded into prison camps.

"SUPPORT OUR SONS"
Vote
MEIGHEN
MONDAY FEB. 9TH
9.00 a.m. to 7.00 p.m.
(DAYLIGHT TIME)

February 1942
MEIGHEN'S COMEBACK CRASHES
Arthur Meighen, recently restored to the Tory leadership, loses a Toronto by-election to the CCF – with a little help from King. The Tories go shopping for a leader once again. *(Above)* A Meighen campaign flyer.

The years leading up to the Second World War showed Mackenzie King at his worst. He failed to understand the forces at play and, in a time of cowardly western appeasement, King was at least as cynical as his fellow statesmen and perhaps even more naïve. He completely neglected to prepare Canadians for the coming struggle and, adding turpitude to folly, played the most crass sort of politics over acceptance of Jewish refugees from Nazism. When war did come, in 1939, King yet again demonstrated a shocking blindness to the great events unfolding. His 1926-style concern for the forms of national independence caused him to delay Canada's declaration of war a full week after Great Britain's.

King's first major move of the war was to fight an election in 1940, in part on his 1939 pledge that he would not introduce conscription. This campaign was classic King – the execution of a Quebec Bridge strategy that rallied wartime English Canada to its government while reassuring a less enthusiastic Quebec that its vital interests would be protected. The Conservatives had a new leader in Robert Manion, and they pounced on King as insufficiently committed to the war effort. However, the public sided with its wartime PM, and in the election of March 26, 1940, the Liberal coalition delivered an even stronger majority than five years before.

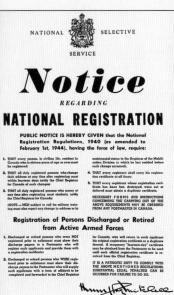

December 1942
BRACKEN TURNS
CONSERVATIVES PROGRESSIVE
Former Progressive premier of Manitoba John Bracken becomes Conservative leader at the party convention in Winnipeg – on the condition that the party will be known henceforth as the Progressive Conservatives. *(Above)* Bracken with third-place finisher John Diefenbaker *(on right)*.

February 1943
WOMEN GO TO WAR
Members of the Canadian Women's Army Corps take a break after a firefighting demonstration in London, England. Canadian women took to factory and field as the war's demand for labour ballooned.

September 1943
CCF REACHES THE TOP
A poll puts the CCF in first place, sparking a wave of anti-socialist propaganda and causing King to move faster in the direction of the welfare state. *(Above)* A pamphlet satirizing socialism.

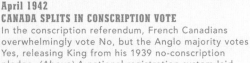

April 1942
CANADA SPLITS IN CONSCRIPTION VOTE
In the conscription referendum, French Canadians overwhelmingly vote No, but the Anglo majority votes Yes, releasing King from his 1939 no-conscription pledge. *(Above)* A national registration system laid the groundwork for possible conscription.

For the rest of the Second World War, the Liberal prime minister successfully waged a two-front struggle that would ensure his victory in the 1945 election and in the broader arena of nation building. Against the Tories he fought on the familiar, scarred battlefield of conscription. With the socialist CCF party he struggled across the new terrain of class politics and the role of government in society.

The conscription issue dominated the first phase of this five-year campaign. As the war intensified, the Liberal cabinet and caucus began dividing along racial lines into pro- and anti-conscription wings. In Quebec an anti-conscription political movement, the Bloc Populaire, sprang up. In English Canada the Tories flayed the government for not being conscriptionist enough. By 1942 King needed room to manoeuvre and he hit upon the novel scheme of holding a referendum on conscription on April 27, 1942, to ease the pressure inside his party. The referendum passed, releasing King from his "no conscription" pledge. Quoting the *Toronto Star*, he said the vote meant "conscription if necessary but not necessarily conscription."

John Bracken, who became Tory leader in 1942, did his best to drive a wedge into the Liberal Party by continuing to push for immediate overseas con-

August 1944
KING DELIVERS BABY BONUS
The King government passes the
Family Allowances Act, providing
the "Baby Bonus" to parents of
children under eighteen years.
(Above) War brides and their
children in Calgary in 1946.

June 1944
ALLIES INVADE NORMANDY
On June 6, 1944, the
Allied invasion of Europe
– D-Day – commences
with a massive landing
along the Normandy
coast. *(Above)* The Second
Canadian Flotilla trans-
ports troops.

May 1945
GERMANY SURRENDERS
The unconditional surrender of Nazi Germany marks
Victory in Europe, or "VE Day." Japan would surrender
on September 2. *(Above)* Torontonians celebrate.

scription. Bracken, the Progressive premier of Manitoba for the previous twenty years, made the leap to Ottawa reluctantly and only after the sixty-eight-year-old Arthur Meighen had attempted an ill-considered comeback. (Meighen had been named to replace Manion but was immediately defeated in a 1942 by-election attempt to enter parliament.) Bracken accepted the Tory helm only on the condition that the party add the word "Progressive" to its name. (The Tories have been known as the Progressive Conservatives ever since.)

With such a half-hearted opponent, King's main challenge was to keep his party and his cabinet together. Mostly, the prime minister played for time, banking on a German defeat before his bluff was called. In his other key political battle, King faced off against fast-rising forces on the left. M.J. Coldwell's calls for government creation of five million new jobs, universal health care, a million government-built homes, and a massive program of hospital and university construction were cutting into the progressive segment of Liberal support. But the kicker came in the September 1943 Gallup poll that put the CCF in first place among the three national parties, with 29 per cent support to 28 for each of the Liberals and Tories.

The prime minister responded with a sharp leftward turn. He established an expert Committee on Reconstruction whose proposals for a postwar welfare state were embodied in the government's 1944 Throne Speech. King pledged his government to a "high, stable level of employment," budgetary flexibility including deficit financing, full collective bargaining for labour, and a set of income supports, the most important of which was the family allowance, or "baby bonus." The CCF poll numbers started to fall, dropping in April 1945 below 20 per cent.

Ever cautious, King continued to manoeuvre on the conscription issue right through the spring of 1945, when he took parliament to the end of its legal life before calling the election on April 16 for June 11. The Tories entered the 1945 campaign already behind the eight ball. The war in Europe – the part of the conflict Canadians really cared about – ended on May 7. For the rest of the campaign the Tory leader Bracken tried to make an issue out of who would go to fight alongside the Americans in the anticipated invasion of Japan. But this gambit went nowhere.

With the conscription issue defused in Quebec and victory in Europe conveniently arriving halfway through the campaign, King could spend the home stretch straight-arming the threat to his left. His campaign slogan, "Vote Liberal and keep building a New Social Order in Canada," could almost have been Coldwell's, but for the word denoting continuity. Cockfield Brown, the country's largest advertising agency and biggest producer of federal advertising, marketed the whole package. Aided by this propaganda, King made sure to stake out for the Liberals the symbolic middle ground while squatting on the CCF's platform turf.

When the results were in, King had narrowly retained his majority, with 125 seats out of 245. The Tories had climbed significantly in Ontario but were flattened in the Prairies and British Columbia by the CCF and Social Credit. Coldwell's party leapt to 28 out of the region's 72 seats and Social Credit took 13 out of 17 in Alberta. King's was a Quebec-based government with a good-sized following in Ontario, Manitoba, and the Maritimes. However, the seeds of the Liberal decline in the West were planted: support in Saskatchewan fell and King himself lost his seat in Prince Albert.

The political questions that had hung in the balance as the war had progressed were grave and far-reaching: the country's wartime unity; the country's postwar social and economic system. Nor were the outcomes inevitable on either front. If King had failed to manage the conscription issue so adroitly, Canada might well

June 11, 1945
KING WINS THIRD
STRAIGHT MAJORITY
Mackenzie King's Liberals
eke out a narrow majority,
winning 125 of 245
Commons seats. The
Conservatives take 67,
CCF 28, and Social Credit
13. With the war over, the
country's leftward turn
transformed the political
landscape, as indicated in
this photograph of rookie
Liberal candidate Ernest
Bogart's campaign head-
quarters in west Toronto's
working-class riding of
Trinity. His campaign signage promises to "complete
the job" of reform. In the
election, Bogart split
the left-wing vote with
Communist Tim Buck and
a CCF candidate, allowing
the Tory Larry Skey, veteran
of the war just ended, to
squeak through by just
eighty-nine votes. Four
years later, in a calmer
political landscape under
a new Liberal leader, the
star candidate and sports
hero Lionel "The Big Train"
Conacher would return the
riding to the Liberal fold.

September 1945
CHALK RIVER LAB OPENS
The ZEEP (Zero Energy Experimental Pile) reactor *(above)* begins operation at the Chalk River, Ontario, nuclear research facility, ushering in the nuclear age in Canada.

February 1949
THE ASBESTOS STRIKE BEGINS
An illegal strike by five thousand members of the Canadian Catholic Confederation of Labour begins at Asbestos, Quebec. The strike marks the debut of the new generation, including the editor of this book *(above)*, that would overturn Quebec's power structure.

June 27, 1949
LOUIS ST. LAURENT CARRIES THE TORCH
Under new leader Louis St. Laurent, the Liberals take 50.1 per cent of the vote and a massive majority of 190 seats. The PCs win a mere 41 seats, the CCF drops to 13, and the Socreds win 10. *(Above)* St. Laurent on the hustings in 1949.

have been plunged into a national nightmare as bad as those of 1911 and 1917. If the CCF had won, or even held the balance of power in Canada's first postwar government, our country might have imitated Great Britain's long, unhappy experiment with socialism. King instead played for time and defused the conflicts he faced, allowing military victory to look after the conscription file and co-opting the socialist program on his own terms and timetable. By avoiding a big battle, he ensured victory in the broader struggle.

For King, the war's end brought him near the end of his political journey. In 1948, after twenty-two years as prime minister and almost thirty as Liberal leader, the cagey veteran retired at the top of his game – the only prime minister ever to do so. The rock-solid political foundations he had laid were more than enough for his successor, Louis St. Laurent, to continue building on. In 1949 the new prime minister outdid his mentor, taking a record-setting 190 of 264 seats. The Liberal machine presided over by St. Laurent began to look like a permanent government, annoyed but never really challenged by the Tories with their usual forty to fifty seats and 30 per cent of the vote, and the ragtag band of western protest parties that

December 1950
CANADIAN TROOPS
IN KOREA
The 2nd battalion
of Princess
Patricia's Canadian
Light Infantry land
in Pusan, the first
Canadian troops
to fight in the
Korean War.

September 1952
CANADA ENTERS
TV ERA
The first local CBC
television stations,
CBFT Montreal and
CBLT Toronto, begin
transmitting.

August 10, 1953
LIBERALS RETAIN
STRANGLEHOLD
St. Laurent's Liberals
win big again by putting
their leader front and
centre, taking 50.0 per
cent of the popular
vote and 171 seats to
51 for Drew's Tories, 23
for Coldwell's CCF, and
15 for Solon Low's
Socreds. *(Above)* St.
Laurent speaks in 1953.

December 1956
JOHN DIEFENBAKER
FINALLY WINS
At the Progressive
Conservative Party con-
vention, John George
Diefenbaker wins the lead-
ership on his third try.
Everyone knows he'll be
creamed by St. Laurent.
(Above) The victorious
Dief flanked by defeated
rivals Donald Fleming
(left) and E. Davie Fulton.

September 1957
CANADA SWOONS
AS ANKA CROONS
Ottawa's first con-
tribution to rock-
'n'roll, Paul Anka,
zooms to number
one across North
America with his
hit song "Diana,"
the beginning of a
stupendous music
career. *(Above)*
Anka in front of
Ottawa's Château
Laurier Hotel.

each commanded less than 10 per cent support and generally held about thirty seats between them. The election of August 10, 1953, reaffirmed this structure, albeit with some strengthening of the PCs and the third parties. King could have asked for no more fitting memorial than the continuance of his political system long after his death.

In an era when leaders lasted, King outlasted them all. His political steward-ship formed the long bridge between the horse-and-buggy Canada that staggered from the wreckage of the First World War and the industrial society that motored into the century's second half. Across that span of decades, this bridge was buffeted by the winds of war, sagged under the weight of depression and scandal, and twisted and turned endlessly on its route to the far shore of a better, modern world. Built on the solid footings of conservative, Catholic Quebec, yet soaring to visions of universal social progress, King's exquisitely balanced edifice looked as though it would last forever.

FOLLOW JOHN

JUNE 10 1957 | MAR. 31 1958

LOUIS ST. LAURENT

VS.

JOHN DIEFENBAKER

LESTER PEARSON

VS.

"I'LL TELL YOU EXACTLY when the turning point was," Tory MP George Hees would recall many years later. "It was three weeks before election day and, up to this point, we were just going along, ho hum … people thought that this was okay, and we were going to get some more seats, and so on. That's it, we had not taken off until this point, and we went to Vancouver …"

The date is May 24, 1957, two-and-a-half weeks before election day. Outside the Georgia Street Auditorium, people have been gathering for hours to hear the leader of the opposition, John Diefenbaker. "Dief," as he has come to be known since his election as Tory leader six months ago, is the clear underdog in this election, given little to no chance of turfing the "natural governing party" out of office. With the sole aberration of 1930–35, the Liberals have held power since 1926. Although the political master Mackenzie King is dead, his chosen successor, the avuncular two-term prime minister Louis St. Laurent, looks like a shoo-in. Through the lengthening afternoon into the cool of a Lower Mainland springtime night, two thousand late-arriving Vancouverites stand craning their necks, sit on curbs, or even perch in trees, but they can still listen to the speech on hastily installed outdoor loudspeakers. Inside, the hall is jammed with another three thousand men and women.

Those lucky enough to have found a spot inside the sweltering auditorium don't know it yet, but the future of Canadian politics stands before them. Maybe they figure it out during the warm-up speeches, and maybe they get the sense when he strides onto the stage and they all roar their greeting. They give Diefenbaker the greatest acclamation he has ever received, and he does not disappoint. "I think tonight across Canada something is happening," he begins, his deep, rich voice quivering with anticipation. "I think the Liberal Party is now realizing Canada is aroused as it has not been aroused in many years." The voice rolls across the hushed crowd, out through the loudspeakers onto the

John Diefenbaker in full rhetorical flight at the historic Vancouver rally, May 24, 1957. With the 1957 campaign, Dief single-handedly rewrote the rules of national politics. Before this election the leader and his image mattered; after 1957 they became paramount.

street, and over the airwaves into radios nation-wide. It calls on its listeners to sweep away the dangerously arrogant Liberal regime, to get Canada moving again, to bring the country together to achieve its magnificent destiny.

The people listening to Diefenbaker's speech in Vancouver that night belonged to a city and a country on the move. Vancouver was burgeoning, midway through a decade in which its population would increase by an astounding 75 per cent. Much of this surge had come from Canada's other provinces, and almost 100,000 foreign immigrants had arrived in the city since 1945. All these urban British Columbians were living the changes of the mid-twentieth century. New machines were transforming their factories; women were pouring into offices, revolutionizing the rules between the sexes; the city's five radio stations and now a local CBC television channel fed the sounds and sights of the electronic age into the living rooms of their new suburban homes.

They had left behind their old countries, their native provinces, the faiths of their fathers, and the certainties that had shaped

politics for generations. These were "go-ahead" folks, eager for the future to come. It was people like these who made the difference in what was, arguably, the most exciting election in Canadian history. And, a year later in 1958, they would follow Diefenbaker to his massive nationwide majority victory.

These two elections make up a single fight that marked both the eclipse of the political system that had prevailed for thirty years and the birth of the modern in Canadian politics. Moreover, something critical was at stake. The Liberals offered Canadians continued techno-cratic management by an entrenched political and bureaucratic elite that skillfully balanced regional and class interests, but was prepared in the name of governmental efficiency to cut corners when it came to democracy and the rule of law. John Diefenbaker responded to this dangerous approach with something new to federal politics – a visionary populism that val-ued dynamism over management, nation over region, and, above all, the people over the elite.

Everyone knew there would be a federal election in 1957, just as there had been every four years since 1945. The only question was who the two major leaders would be. Until the summer of 1955 it looked as though the Tory warhorse, George Drew, would be matched up against a new Liberal leader – perhaps the press gallery's darling, Lester "Mike" Pearson. But on July 4, 1955, leading the government in a heated Commons debate, St. Laurent slipped in the statement that "all of us on this side expect to be here three years from now to carry out any undertaking that we give to the House."

St. Laurent had decided to run again, and why not? Through the final years of King's tenure, then from 1948 under St. Laurent, the

Beneath Laurier's approving gaze, Louis St. Laurent accepts the prime ministership from Mackenzie King, who blatantly stage-managed the succession at the 1948 convention.

Liberals had continued to successfully apply King's formula for holding power. The party retained its mastery of the race-based politics of French Canada while occupying a vast swath of English Canada's left-centre-right political spectrum. Concocted in the chaos of the 1920s, this formula for power had evolved over time into a comprehensive system of politics and government as highly structured and distinct as the Great Party system of Confederation's first fifty years. Balancing all these interests – English and French, eastern and western, capital and labour – required a strong group of like-minded leaders sitting around the cabinet table under the master balancer. In St. Laurent's small cabinets of twenty or so members, men like Quebec's Jean Lesage and Nova Scotia's Robert Winters could speak for Catholics and Presbyterians, Industry Minister C.D. Howe and Agriculture Minister Jimmy Gardiner could sort out matters between their respective constituents, and Finance Minister Walter Harris could square off on behalf of big business against Paul Martin and his Windsor trade union supporters. Each of the country's major interests could count on at least one middle-aged white male to represent it at the cabinet table.

Down the hall a generation of brilliant, liberal-minded, Oxbridge-educated civil service "mandarins" churned out policy for one Grit minister after another. This class of deputy ministers headed what was reputed to be the world's most efficient civil service. It functioned with particular effectiveness under the highly centralized Canadian parliamentary system. With only a weak, divided opposition to criticize their ministers in parliament, and with the provinces in thrall after the wartime expansion of Ottawa's powers, the mandarins held unprecedented power to reshape Canadian life according to their ideas. They did so in a way that was "far more liberal than democratic,

MANDARIN RULE

The technocratic elite that ran Liberal Ottawa were proud – of their ironic sense of history, their top-flight education, and their track record of practical success.

Real mandarins. Ottawa's elite deputy ministers were called mandarins after imperial China's omnipotent civil servants.

Mandarin in training. Future mandarins like Lester Pearson studied at Oxford or Cambridge, hotbeds of ideas about state planning.

do not hoard

RATIONED
SUGAR ½ lb. a week PER PERSON
TEA ½ of the usual PURCHASE
COFFEE ¾ of the USUAL PURCHASE

Liberal mandarinism in action. Allied governments managed wartime economies by putting their Oxbridge economic theories to work.

THE KING AND HIS BARONS

Cabinet power peaked under St. Laurent. The twenty political heavyweights who sat around the cabinet table balanced the nation's regional and economic interests (at least among white males) and sometimes even its religions. And the St. Laurent cabinet gave as much weight to the dynasty's past as to its future, with 1930s veterans such as Howe and Gardiner rubbing elbows with 1960s players like Pearson, Martin, and Winters.

STUART GARSON
Justice. Ex-Manitoba premier. Former Liberal-Progressive.

LESTER PEARSON
External Affairs. MP from Northern Ontario, but really represents the mandarins. Golden boy.

ROBERT WINTERS
Public Works. Nova Scotia up-and-comer. Represents Maritime business.

Uncle Louis and the kids. Paternalistic photos like this one were part of 50s politics. The image wouldn't have been out of place in Russia, China, or even the good ole USA.

and not at all populist," in the words of Lester Pearson's biographer John English.

In many respects the Liberal technocratic machine was an authentic reflection of the values of its era, which was dominated by the generations of voters who had lived through the boom and bust of the 1920s and 1930s and the sacrifices of the Second World War. For these people, stability and progress were the watchwords. In the United States and Britain, as well as in Canada, the same kind of mildly progressive, brokerage-oriented, don't-rock-

the-boat governments served year in and year out. The Canadian electorate appeared to have attained a level of inert satisfaction, satiated by consumer goods to the point where politics no longer mattered. Political scientists spoke of "the end of ideology." The future belonged to the social engineer, the scientist, and the organization man. The whole political style of the era was summed up by a professor, Paul Fox, who wrote: "The Liberal government aims at operating noiselessly, like a respectable mammoth business corporation which fears

NAME: Louis St. Laurent

PARTY: Liberal

ROLE: Prime minister since 1948. Ex-corporate lawyer. Dignified, managerial, apolitical. At seventy-four, will lead Liberals into third election.

nothing more than making people aware that it is there."

If the government could be called Liberal Inc., its continuing board chairman in 1955 was Louis St. Laurent. Born in 1882, St. Laurent was the most successful corporate lawyer in French Canadian history when Mackenzie King persuaded him to enter politics in a 1942 by-election triggered by the death of Ernest Lapointe. King groomed him for succession and shamelessly orchestrated his victory at the 1948 Liberal leadership convention – the first in thirty years. St. Laurent was a class act, a very able prime minister conducting the nation's affairs with intelligence, integrity, and almost regal dignity. At the same time his natural graciousness and warmth put a human face on the imposing Liberal power structure. In the 1949 election campaign a Toronto *Telegram* reporter, watching St. Laurent play with children at a campaign stop, immediately coined the moniker "Uncle Louis." So perfectly did it sum up the paternal, reassuring persona the Liberals sought to project that they incorporated the phrase into their 1953 campaign advertising, a campaign Uncle Louis handily won.

The new politics of image was a response to the increased fickleness of voters, whose support could be won only by persuasion. The relentless urbanization of the country – 70 per cent of Canadians would be living in cities and towns by 1961 – the wave of postwar immigration, greater physical and income mobility, decreased churchgoing, and the ever more

rapid diffusion of new ideas and influences through the growth of print and electronic media had all helped erode the bedrock of racial and religious loyalties that had underpinned national politics since before Confederation. In this more fluid society, voter opinion could and did shift massively during the life of a government, and even during a campaign. No such shift had occurred at the federal level, but, over St. Laurent's two terms in government, the Liberals had lost provincial power in British Columbia, Nova Scotia, and New Brunswick.

The new system had changed the role of MPs as well. They no longer delivered at their discretion hundreds of government jobs to individual voters whose loyalties they commanded.

HMCS One Party State. The Liberals' century-long cruise was never more smooth than under Louis St. Laurent. In 1966 his grateful political heirs honoured his success by naming this imposing Coast Guard ice breaker after him. The Liberal ship sails on.

THE LONG, GOOD DAY

Canada experienced astonishing economic development during the 1950s, completing its transformation from an agrarian society to an urban-industrial one. C.D. Howe's government-driven mega-projects, such as the St. Lawrence hydroelectric complex (being opened *above*), helped power the growth of resource towns like Chicoutimi *(bottom)*. Growth was also fuelled by immigrants from war-torn Europe, such as these two kids on Halifax's Pier 21 *(bottom left)*. The result: better living! – celebrated by this 1954 Eaton's salute *(left)* to "Canadian achievement." Chairman Louis has won The People a happy life!

Instead, they came across with universal entitlements such as unemployment insurance and baby bonuses. Accordingly, St. Laurent's backbenchers had less power than those under Macdonald or Laurier; their role had shifted from serving as the party's area general managers to being the government's salesmen, market researchers, and spokespersons in the ridings. Not that this work wasn't critical. Polling was still in its infancy, so MPs were the principal means by which the government kept tabs on evolving public opinion around the country. Similarly, they were valuable messengers. The media through which Ottawa could speak to the people were limited and expensive: only one nightly television newscast on the CBC's seven local stations, two or three major newsmagazines, and a string of newspapers and radio stations. There was only so much the government could pump out through the funnel of Ottawa's small press gallery. To hammer the message home, the local MP needed to get back into the riding and work those local channels of communication: the afternoon newspaper, community radio, and the timeless "retail politicking" of ribbon-cuttings, town-hall meetings, and coffee parties.

On a good day – and the period from 1945 to 1957 was mostly a very long, good day – the entire King–St. Laurent system of politics and government worked beautifully, with wise mandarin-authored policies delivering the goods at an impressive pace: postwar economic recovery, the beginnings of the welfare state, impressive GNP growth, strong employment, and a sound currency. Voters saw tangible results in new houses, better appliances, bigger cars, must-have television sets, and efficient telephones – the panoply of mid-century abundance. They returned their Liberal governments at election time, keeping the whole smooth machine humming along. Such was the situation in the debate on

July 4, 1955, when St. Laurent quietly announced he would stay on.

The debate that day centred on the Defence Production Act, a law passed during the Korean War that gave the minister of defence production such extraordinary emergency powers as the expropriation of private property. Now, two years after the war had wound down, the hard-charging minister, Clarence Decatur Howe, was asking parliament to extend his wartime powers for another five years. In parliament the opposition parties

NAME: Clarence Decatur Howe

PARTY: Liberal

ROLE: Cabinet minister since 1935. Runs Canada's industrial economy from Ottawa. You-can't-make-an-omelette-without-breaking-parliament kind of guy.

filibustered, then offered Howe a compromise: extension for three years. Howe blew them off: "That would mean coming back to Parliament in three years, and I've more to do than spend my time amusing Parliament."

Howe's contempt for parliament was part of the darker side of Uncle Louis's technocratic rule, which placed government efficiency ahead of every concern. St. Laurent disdained party politicking; his own minister Jimmy Gardiner said that the prime minister was "a lawyer's lawyer, he wasn't a politician at all." In cabinet battles the prime minister tended to choose policies that enjoyed bureaucratic support, dismissing political concerns raised by the ministers. In the House, St. Laurent despised the partisan jockeying as cheap politics rather than an essential part of a democratic system based on the rule of law through parliament. If St. Laurent occasionally lost sight of parliament's crucial role, Howe was blind to it. In 1951 he had gleefully asked the opposition:

Rideau - Ottawa - Wed. morning (cold drizzle)

"If we wanted to get away with it, who would stop us?" In 1953 he had defended an abuse of an order-in-council authority by saying, "If we have overstepped our powers, I make no apology for doing so." The occasional degeneration of the government's respect for democracy and the rule of law was straight out of a 1950s sci-fi B-movie. A cheerful, big, slightly clunky domestic robot, beloved for its efficient performing of mundane household tasks, drops a plate in the kitchen. "Gosh honey, I'm a little worried about Robot-O. He just doesn't seem to be … himself."

The Defence Production Act was rammed through, bringing down on the government heavy press criticism before the summer recess began on July 28. The fall 1955 sitting of parliament was fairly quiet, but in the spring of 1956 the Liberal machine once again went berserk and started trashing the House. The result was the 1956 Pipeline Debate, one of the most dramatic confrontations in Canadian parliamentary history. From May 3 to June 5 the Liberals tried to drive through legislation to finance construction by American interests of a cross-country gas pipeline. For Howe it was a chance to cap his career with a final, glorious megaproject. For George Drew's Tories, and the CCFers under M.J. Coldwell, it was a bitter struggle to uphold the right of parliament to scrutinize government legislation or lay bare in the attempt the Liberals' contempt for the democratic process. The mostly Albertan Social Credit MPs stayed uncomfortably on the fence, torn between their

opposition to the government and the benefits the project would bring to their province.

Day after day the Liberal majority passed closure motions to cut off debate; day after day the Tories and the CCF filibustered. "In one sense, the period resembled a Wagnerian opera …" wrote Michael Barkway in the *Waterloo Review*, "with the mediocrity of the performance covered by an armoury of theatrical mechanics. Dark clouds scudded across the cyclorama; orange spotlights flashed hither and thither as though a platoon of demented lighthouse-keepers was making up for a lifetime of sober regularity; smoke bombs exploded alongside the pounding tympanies as the orchestra crashed its way to the climax of the pipeline debate."

"Through all this hubbub," wrote Dexter Grant in the *Winnipeg Free Press*, "the most arresting figure on the Government side is Prime Minister Louis St. Laurent. He sits,

Off With Their Heads! The Liberals' trampling of parliament peaked with the 1956 Pipeline Debate. This Globe and Mail *cartoon (opposite) uses the image of the Peace Tower turned into a guillotine – parliamentary jargon for a government closing off debate by invoking closure – to pillory the Liberal government's tyrannical behaviour. (Right) The 1954 cover of one of the popular Tom Swift series of books for boys could have been a poster for Liberal technocrats running amok.*

impassive, expressionless, chin on hand, an open book on his desk. His aloofness is almost unbelievable. Especially at a time of high controversy, prime ministers always dominate proceedings and lead their party. Mr. St. Laurent does neither." Howe was equally diffident, muttering one wild afternoon, "I've never been so bored in all my life."

The opposition felt rather differently about the government's untrammelled exercise of its majority power. "At last I understand the meaning of revolution," Diefenbaker told a friend on June 1, the most disorderly and intense day of the crisis. "I am wondering," mused the famously steady Coldwell, "whether we are in the old German Reichstag or the Canadian Parliament." "This is Black Friday, boy," said a Tory MP, Thomas Bell. The press

NAME: M.J. Coldwell

PARTY: CCF

ROLE: Socialist party leader since 1939. Saskatchewan moderate. Leading party through slow decline from mid-1940s heights.

agreed with the opposition. On Saturday, June 2, even the reliably Liberal *Ottawa Citizen* carried the headline, "An Axe Falling on the Rights of Parliament." The *Globe and Mail*'s cartoonist, Jim Reidford, depicted the Peace Tower as a giant guillotine.

The public agreed with the opposition. When Tory MP Donald Fleming flew home to Toronto after being expelled temporarily by the Speaker, five hundred supporters came out to greet him at Malton Airport. "They didn't seem to know when to stop," a Toronto lawyer told a pollster, "the arrogance, and that closure business." A Vancouver homemaker said, "I really thought Parliament was in danger with

the Pipeline." Although the legislation was passed on schedule and pipeline construction began that summer as planned, the Liberals had paid a heavy price, dropping 10 per cent in one opinion poll.

After the rampage of the Pipeline Debate, the Liberal machine quietened down for a while. During the summer the gentlemanly St. Laurent gave word that the next election would be held in June 1957, surrendering the crucial prime ministerial control of election timing for no other reason than that the opposition parties "may not be taken by surprise." (Six feet underground in Toronto's Mount Pleasant Cemetery the body of Mackenzie King did a quiet quarter-turn.) With the election date known, and the issue on which the election would undoubtedly be fought set up in the Pipeline Debate, the pre-writ campaign was on.

But the cast changed suddenly in September, when George Drew's doctor told him either to quit politics immediately or to face death within six months. He announced his resignation late that month, and a leadership convention was set for December 10–14, 1956. Three major candidates quickly came forward. The front-runner was Saskatchewan's sixty-one-year-old John Diefenbaker, MP from Prince Albert since 1940 and the second-place finisher at the 1948 convention that had elected Drew. The outgoing leader's two key parliamentary lieutenants, Torontonian Donald Fleming and British Columbia's Davie Fulton, filled out the field, although neither seemed particularly hopeful of winning. "It had become a philosophy for the reconciled – Diefenbaker could not be stopped," wrote a youthful Dalton Camp, then the Progressive Conservative Party's publicity director. "After the election he would retire and the party could then find a younger, abler man. Diefenbaker had been around a long time, so let him have it. The Grits would win the next election anyway."

A young Brian Mulroney rubs shoulders with the about-to-be Chief at the 1956 Conservative convention that elected John Diefenbaker leader. By abandoning his party's starchy, anglomaniac identity, Dief repositioned the Tories to attract all sorts of newcomers. Many, Mulroney among them, would later turn against him.

The real battle in the Tory leadership campaign was not among the candidates but between the front-runner and the party "establishment," the men around Drew who had treated Diefenbaker with, at best, modest respect while they continued losing election after election. The Tory Old Guard may have been something of an invention. "Ah yes, the Old Guard," laughed one of its supposed members to a reporter at the convention. "We had a full-dress regimental parade in front of the Toronto armoury, but only two of us

turned out. The rest of us are all dead or spavined." But the establishment lived a vivid existence in Dief's mind, even though it was less a group of men than a set of intellectual tendencies that had kept his party in the wilderness for a generation. Among these tendencies were a Bay Street obsession with low taxes that alienated the subsidy-seeking farmers out West, including many of the voters in Diefenbaker's riding of Prince Albert; a United Empire Loyalist tone that set English and French against each other and left no room for Canadians with foreign-sounding names like Diefenbaker; and a hostility to the welfare state that offered no comfort to the dirt farmers and hard-luck railway workers Dief had represented as a prairie defence lawyer going back to 1919. These Old Guard postures and approaches, Diefenbaker believed, had consigned the Tory Party to permanent minority status in national politics. Let the Old Guard with its wicked ways organize liquor-filled hospitality suites for Fleming and Fulton. Diefenbaker the prairie teetotaller would keep his reception rooms at the Château Laurier Hotel bone-dry.

NAME: John Diefenbaker

PARTY: PC

ROLE: Opposition leader since December 1956. Prairie populist – more progressive than conservative. Looks like a sure loser.

On the day before the climactic leadership vote, December 13, inside the creaky old agricultural Coliseum at the Central Canadian Exhibition grounds, the convention's pro-Diefenbaker majority set about correcting the party's position in the political firmament. Delegates passed resolutions dropping their party's opposition to Mackenzie King's 1944 baby bonus and called for low-interest government loans to homebuyers. They expressed unqualified support for the state-operated Wheat Board, and even cleansed their policy book of traditional calls for "free enterprise" and the banning of "communist activity." At a time when most Canadians automatically

equated social welfare measures with "progress," the new Tory moderation sent an important message: the old party was finally getting with the modern swing of things.

On the snowy afternoon of Saturday, December 14, Diefenbaker flattened Fleming and Fulton on the first ballot, 774 votes to 393 and 117. In his acceptance speech, broadcast nationwide as part of Canada's first televised political convention, the new leader clearly sounded the note of populist humility. "I will make mistakes, but I hope it will be said of me … he wasn't always right, sometimes he was on the wrong side, but never on the side of wrong." Up in the press booth, Dalton Camp, a Diefenbaker sceptic, heard "the first, quavering notes of evangelism, the muffled sounds of angels' wings, hints of martyrdom and invocations of righteousness." "This will be my attitude," the new leader went on. "This will be the stand that I shall take, 'Whosoever of you will be the chiefest shall be the servant of all." Diefenbaker's acceptance speech that December evening sounded the notes that would resonate throughout the next six months, during which voters would compare the new Tory leader with the continuing Liberal one. Diefenbaker understood the power of ideas to persuade voters and he was determined to get his message right: his populist forelock tugging made a lovely contrast with the Liberals' smug purring.

Day after day that spring St. Laurent sat impassively on the Liberal front bench across the aisle from the new PC leader, who glared and scowled back at him. Around St. Laurent were clustered the mighty cabinet barons: Pickersgill of Newfoundland; MacLean of Nova Scotia; the Ontario triumvirate of Owen

Crying in the wilderness. Diefenbaker addresses the 1948 Tory leadership convention. His speech was the usual barn-burner and, as usual, he lost, this time to George Drew. Dief's many defeats turned him into a long-running joke among the political elites. Turned out the joke was on them.

Selling Liberalism. In the 1950s, no self-respecting ruling party went without a guiding ideology. (Today our parties sell "values.") In Quebec (where this 1956 fundraising dinner was held), the party's economic and social welfare achievements were trumpeted alongside the national unity message, here encoded by the "fleur d'érable" – a hybrid of fleur de lys and maple leaf – behind the head table. In another kind of one-party state, the banner might have read: "All Glory to Laurier–King–St. Laurent Thought."

Sound's Harris, Windsor's Martin, and Port Arthur's Howe; Manitoba's Stuart Garson; Saskatchewan's redoubtable Gardiner; and British Columbia's boss, Big Jim Sinclair (whose daughter, Margaret, would marry Pierre Trudeau in 1970). St. Laurent let his team do the heavy lifting while his schedule was kept easy, his diet carefully regulated so as not to upset his digestion, and his smoking cut back to a few cigarettes a day. The highlight of his winter was a 1,400-person tribute dinner to celebrate his seventy-fifth birthday on February 2 in Quebec City. There he was presented with a giant birthday cake, although he was unable to blow out all the candles and he smeared his suit with icing in the attempt.

Meanwhile, Diefenbaker was reorganizing party headquarters, retaining Camp but letting most of the Drew team go, and attacking the government in the House. In a January debate over an impending railway strike, Dief, as he was now coming to be known, pushed his message that the government was adrift and arrogant. Journalist Patrick Nicholson described Diefenbaker's attack: "With right hand on hip, in his familiar stance holding back the imagined counsel's gown, he asked innocently: 'What does the government do?' Then the accusing forefinger shot out towards the Prime Minister and he charged: 'It continues its policy of being resolute in irresolution.' When the Prime Minister smiled at his words, he snarled back: 'The Prime Minister smiles regarding a problem that affects the hearts and purses of Canadians everywhere.'"

Day after day the drama played itself out: some blithe act of Liberal complacency, followed by a Tory pounce. A political neophyte could have seen that the 1957 budget would have to be an election budget, a budget crafted to include a number of vote-getting items such as tax cuts or popular spending programs, as well as one to meet the economic challenge of a mild but perceptible slowdown. But instead of forging it into an electoral weapon, St. Laurent allowed the economic plan to become a political football between Trade and Commerce Minister C.D. Howe (who held that portfolio as well as Defence Production) and Finance Minister Walter Harris. The mandarins were divided, with bright-eyed Trade and Commerce bureaucrats calling for new spending to stimulate growth, and grim-faced Finance officials pushing against any stimulus out of fear that it would spur inflation. Harris and Howe finally settled on a compromise budget, which the youthful and ambitious finance minister delivered on March 15, 1957. The plan increased spending, but not by as much as Howe wanted, and not nearly enough for Diefenbaker's born-again pro-welfare Tories. The opposition had been pushing hard for a $10 increase in the $40 per month old age pension, yet in the budget Harris announced a disappointing $6 hike, which led to his immediate branding as "six-buck Harris." Once again the government had

put its public policy concerns first and virtually ignored the political consequences.

Perhaps the Liberals could have gotten away with this lackadaisical, smug performance if Drew had still been on the scene or, better yet, if they had symbolized renewal and change by replacing St. Laurent. But first they had thrown away the renewal card when St. Laurent decided to run again in mid-1955 and, a year later, the Tories picked it up when Drew exited and Dief took the helm. Diefenbaker himself wasn't really new; he'd been in parliament for seventeen years and was a familiar public figure. But as people began to see more of him in his new role in early 1957, the vigour, indignation, and confidence of this man definitely amounted to something new under Ottawa's pale, late-winter sun. If Canadians wanted more of the same, the Liberals couldn't lose. But if the mood was different, if change was in the wind, if the public had had enough of the overbearing Liberal government, the underdog might just have a chance.

NAME: Dalton Camp

PARTY: PC

ROLE: Tory publicity director. Ad man by trade. Maritimer. Young Turk.

Once the budget splash was over, both the government and the opposition tensed for the election call, which was sure to come soon in accordance with St. Laurent's already announced timetable. A public poll showed the Liberals miles ahead, with 47 per cent, and the PCs at 32 per cent. Both campaign teams were already in place, both party headquarters in election mode, and each side committed to its plan for fighting the writ campaign.

The right man in the right job

LOUIS ST. LAURENT sees for Canada's future an exciting adventure of national development . . . to provide here in this rich land a more abundant life for all our people.

Under his leadership, Canada has moved ahead further and faster than ever before . . . our population has increased over 25 per cent . . . a million new homes have been built . . . our standard of living is higher . . . and we have undertaken national developments that will bring great benefits to every part of our land.

Above all, Louis St. Laurent has the human sympathy and understanding to know the needs of our people. The Government he leads has provided greater social protection to the Canadian people . . . social security benefits have been increased . . . federal legislation for a nation-wide system of hospital insurance has been proclaimed.

Canada's progress shows that Louis St. Laurent is the right man in the right job. Vote for your Liberal candidate and keep Louis St. Laurent at work helping to create a better life for *all* Canadians.

For a greater Canada...for tomorrow's opportunities...

VOTE LIBERAL

The secretary of the National Liberal Federation, H.E. Kidd, would officially direct the Liberal effort out of party headquarters on Cooper Street. He sat at the centre of an elaborate network of committees and information exchange systems that reflected the very loose structure of the Liberal campaign. This system gave the maximum latitude for St. Laurent and his chief strategic adviser, Jack Pickersgill, to make the real decisions. In 1957 "Jack the Nimble," the fifty-two-year-old minister of citizenship and immigration, was at the summit of a brilliant career in Liberalism, running for re-election in the Newfoundland riding into

NAME: Jack Pickersgill

PARTY: Liberal

ROLE: Campaign manager, 1957. Bureaucrat, King's principal secretary, backroom operator, Newfoundland cabinet minister. St. Laurent's chief strategic adviser.

which St. Laurent had parachuted him in 1953. Before that he had served for more than a decade in the corridors of Liberal power, first as Mackenzie King's speechwriter and private political assistant, then as St. Laurent's clerk of the Privy Council. Long before he ran for office, Pickersgill was more influential than many cabinet ministers – the first of the Liberals' long line of senior, unelected backroom players. But like every such player before him, Pickersgill felt that cabinet was the right place from which to call the strategic shots.

Over at Tory headquarters on Laurier Avenue West, Allister Grosart and Dalton Camp didn't feel the same way; neither of them

had any intention of running. They were prototypes of the new backroomers, unelected professionals bringing private-sector marketing experience into the political game. (While advertising professionals from the Cockfield Brown and McKim agencies had been playing key roles in national campaigns since the early 1940s, the top management had remained in the hands of elected MPs and ministers. The Tories in 1957 were the first to give "non-electeds" a share of the top slots.) Along with Winnipeg MP Gordon Churchill, the two Toronto advertising men made up the strategic troika running the Tory campaign. Churchill was there to keep the caucus in line and had already proven his strategic skills with a 1955 memorandum, which then–party maverick Dief had thought excellent, advising the party to stop wasting resources in the hopeless cause of winning Quebec seats and to concentrate instead on Ontario and the West. Grosart and Camp provided the marketing brains and the campaign's heart. Grosart, at fifty a successful Toronto advertising executive who handled government and party advertising for Tory administrations in Ontario, intended to replicate the leader-driven strategies he had run for Premiers George Drew and Leslie Frost. Camp, thirty-six, a New Brunswick whiz kid who had built a successful career in Toronto advertising while shuttling back to the Maritimes for the campaigns that had toppled long-serving Liberal governments, coordinated the paid advertising and party print materials. Although the ebullient Camp was approached to run in 1957, he had decided to stick to the backrooms.

The two strategic teams – Pickersgill, the former bureaucrat and regional minister,

Leader as institution. Big man. Big ideas. Big government. The classic mid-century institutional appeal. St. Laurent is front and centre in this 1957 magazine ad, but the Liberals are really selling the party and the government itself: a pair of mega-institutions towering above the lowly voter.

versus Grosart and Camp, the private-sector ad men – reflected the campaigns each party would run. The Liberal show was suffused with the production values of the House of Commons: ministerial speaking tours; the stately, even remote figure of a prime minister; and the low-key deflation of opponents' charges through irony and a gentlemanly smile. It was all very Question Period. The Tory effort and its architects anticipated the future generation of private-sector political hit men, TV-pundit strategists, and million-dollar pollsters. Its style was Madison Avenue North: single-minded pro-motion of the pitchman, relegation of secondary players to the shadows, and abandonment of the brand itself in favour of the spokesperson.

The Liberal strategy came down to one simple concept: stand pat. Pickersgill and Cockfield Brown would once again rock voters to sleep on the kindly knee of Uncle Louis. "Even if we have to run him stuffed," C.D. Howe had allegedly said that spring, the Liberals would win with St. Laurent. A spring 1957 poll had seemed to bear him out, report-ing that Prime Minister St. Laurent enjoyed a 74 per cent approval rating. "To the extent that any over-all plan of the campaign was formu-lated at all," wrote political scientist John Meisel, "it seemed to consist of the notion that nothing dramatic was to be attempted, that a quiet campaign was desirable." As the campaign was about to get under way, the Liberal bet looked like a sure thing.

The Tories' long-shot wager was equally simple: put all your money on the leader, as in a Marlboro print ad with 250 square inches of cowboy and 3 square inches of logo. It was Diefenbaker's only hope. His party was locked

at 30 per cent of voter support, barely alive in Quebec and caught out West in endless three-way struggles with the CCF and the Social Credit Party for the anti-Liberal vote. If the party couldn't carry the leader, the leader would have to carry the party.

The Chief (as they had already begun to call him) had a mix of shrewd political instinct and messianic self-aggrandizement that drew him naturally to the idea of a new kind of campaign. Let the Liberals waste their time and money on big ministerial speaking tours. The PCs would put everything into selling Diefenbaker. Given St. Laurent's approval numbers, staking the campaign on winning a match-up with Uncle Louis seemed like attacking the enemy at his strongest point. But Diefenbaker and his handlers understood something that few Liberals had grasped: lead-ership wasn't *a* card any more; it was *the* card.

Modern voters had long ago stopped following their local chieftains or even their parties. Voters increasingly expressed their desires through the medium of the leader. During election campaigns the Liberals seemed to understand this point. In 1953 their Uncle Louis strategy was a state-of-the-art exercise in driving voter approval through marketing the image of the leader. St. Laurent under-stood it too; in 1957 he told a young speechwriter that "the important thing was not to make statements of policy ... but to give people a chance to see him and judge for themselves if he was likely to be able to lead them for another four years." Once the election lights were killed and the stage struck, however, the Grits would revert to the type of remote, colourless cabinet government that King had

Leader as individual. The Tory 1957 campaign pitch couldn't have been more different. As in this 1957 ad, every piece of party propaganda presented Diefenbaker's human qualities: intelli-gence, intensity, passion. These qualities are sung in the third-party endorsements, a proxy for voters' voices. Power to the People!

"A Canadian with a spirit of true Canadianism . . . a reformer with a keen sensing of changing needs for his country . . . a man of breadth who has been tested in the trials of pioneering and progress."

"He is an indefatigable worker. He is independent enough not to be swayed by sectional appeals. And he is buttressed in his task by the declared loyalty of exceedingly able lieutenants."

"An incorrigible defender of human rights. His record pleads eloquently for him. Since the day when he first hung out his shingle as a young lawyer in Saskatchewan, in 1919, he has been fighting with clear-sighted vision for those elements in Canadian life which he believes are vital for the well-being of the individual."

"He has first-hand knowledge of the trials and problems, the hopes and dreams of ordinary people. He is profoundly dedicated to belief in individual rights and human dignity."

"John Diefenbaker would fill the post of Prime Minister with dignity, with courage, with fairness and with honor, those same inflexible qualities which already won for him the instinctive trust of ordinary people everywhere."

excerpts from the editorial pages of Canadian newspapers

... IT'S TIME FOR

a Diefenbaker government !

invented thirty years before when nobody even owned a radio. As Diefenbaker had shown from the moment he became leader, he instinctively understood that he had to project a strong, human image and a complementary message to the people throughout the crucial winter and spring of the pre-writ campaign. In 1957 Dief's opportunity lay in the fact that while St. Laurent would be marketed well in the writ campaign, he and the Tory team had already undermined the prime minister's image by highlighting his faults in the pre-writ period.

In strategic terms, the Tories had set the Liberal leader up for the kill. Diefenbaker's job in the writ-period campaign would be to finish him off gracefully. As a naturally gifted political animal, Dief knew that going negative on kindly Uncle Louis would come across like elder abuse. The trick was to deliberately arrange for favourable contrasts to be drawn during the campaign, but not to take any direct shots. A contemporary strategist would say that during the pre-writ campaign Diefenbaker had positioned himself as the anti-St. Laurent in several key dimensions of leadership that resonated with the public. Of course, executing this strategy meant throwing some traditional Tory messages out the window. When Finance Minister Harris penny-pinched on the budget, Diefenbaker played the big-hearted spender to make St. Laurent look like an old miser, a neat reversal of the usual party roles. When diplomat Herbert Norman mysteriously committed suicide on April 4, Dief made government secretiveness the issue, rather than go after Norman's previous communist associations.

Above all, Dief sought to capitalize on the public outrage that had been briefly stirred by the Pipeline Debate the previous year. A few weeks before the election was called, a Tory campaign committee took issue with the leader's plan to play up the episode in the forthcoming writ campaign. "One fellow got

up and said, 'Well, John, that's a year ago, that pipeline thing. People have forgotten about it.' A lot of them said, 'People don't care that much about what goes in Parliament.' He said, 'That's the issue and I'm making it.'" Diefenbaker knew that the Pipeline Debate best demonstrated the contrast he was trying to draw: technocratic elite versus democratic populace; arrogant Liberals versus earnest Tories; and, above all, spaced-out old Uncle Louis versus that young John Diefenbaker, the man with the vision.

Here was the final piece of brilliance in the Tories' 1957 strategy: when Diefenbaker hit the campaign trail, he wouldn't simply be asking Canadians to vote for him because he was a new man, but because he had a vision of the future. This vision was the brainchild of Dr. Merrill Menzies, a young economist who had worked for the Liberals' Manitoba baron, Justice Minister Stuart Garson, but quit in frustration when the Liberals rejected his bold plans. Menzies took his ideas to Diefenbaker through his father-in-law, a Prince Albert pal of the new leader, in a series of memos written that winter and spring. They pulsed with a sweep and turn of phrase that appealed powerfully to Dief's personality and values. "From Confederation until the early 1930's, there was a powerful unifying force in the nation … This unifying force was the challenge and the development of the West. It engendered a powerful but not xenophobic nationalism and was made possible and given shape and direction by Macdonald's National Policy." Thereafter, Menzies went on, "we have had no national policy – and we have had no transcending sense of national purpose, no national myth, no unifying force." The Liberals "have never understood the significance of national policy and the imperative need for a transcending sense of national purpose … That is why I have proposed a new national policy – the NEW FRONTIER POLICY; a new national strategy … a new national myth – the 'North' in the place of the 'West.'"

Menzies hung a number of specific schemes onto his visionary structure: a new province to include the southern Yukon, the southern Mackenzie Valley, and Great Slave Lake; hydro projects and mining developments, financed by both the public and the private sector, to kick-start new communities; and the promotion of agriculture, forestry, and local markets, to give the communities life. To realize this dream, the vision required railways, highways, dams – the panoply of development tools favoured by government planners from Appalachia to Zambia.

Diefenbaker immediately embraced Menzies's vision as his own. Here was the Tory answer to the Liberals' frequent crowing about solving Canada's problems of race and religion, region and class. Now the Tories could argue that, in so doing, the Grits had made of Canada just another country, cynically managing the nation to some technocratic template and robbing her of her distinctness, her unique mission, her chance at greatness. The vision would restore the singularity of the Canadian experience as well as the Conservatives' claim to a share in the country's grand nation-building tradition. Diefenbaker would offer something different, something more than the comforts delivered by the Liberal system. Drawing on the 1953 coronation of Queen Elizabeth II and harkening back to the glorious era of her sixteenth-century namesake, he wrote later: "We wanted to make ours an Elizabethan Age worthy of its predecessor, an age of adventure and high endeavour." Only twelve years earlier the young nation had triumphed in a world war. With his vision, Diefenbaker could promise new worlds to conquer.

Menzies's vision – modified by the leader to accommodate the odd inescapable practical reality – became the election program of the Progressive Conservatives without significant discussion in caucus or in the shadow cabinet. (Imagine St. Laurent trying that!) No one will ever know whether, left to his own devices, Dief would not have ended up where Menzies pointed him: going on about wonder and challenge and espousing imaginative national policy. But Menzies's ideas brought a narrative line and specific content to Diefenbaker's impulses towards greatness and destiny. They made of Diefenbaker something more than a vehicle of anti-Liberal protest; they made him into a great man, a man you could imagine as prime minister. That was the key – the vision became policy because it fit not only with Dief's own views but also with the Tories' leader-centred campaign strategy. It contrasted with the Liberals' "steady-as-she-goes" message but offered more, not fewer, of the benefits Liberalism had brought. It fit the national mood: a frustrated longing for change. Above all, it fit with the image of Diefenbaker that Grosart and Camp had been crafting: youthful, dynamic, bold, and new, full of prairie pioneering populism, grounded in tradition but with an eye to the future. Put the vision in the man's mouth, and the whole Tory selling proposition fell into place.

When John Diefenbaker embraced his vision, he made a brilliant intuitive political move. From a purely electoral standpoint, the fact that the ideas were unworkable and poorly thought-out is irrelevant. The vision was something more than policy or even strategy. It was a window into Dief's soul, allowing a vital bond to form between politician and voter. As Dief, Grosart, and Camp understood, that bond had become more important than ever in a world where diminished party loyalties left voters free to choose but uncertain where to go. That bond, they began daring to dream, might perhaps be strong enough actually to win them the election.

MYTH BUILDING, DIEFENBAKER STYLE

Diefenbaker's 1957–58 vision called for massive development of Canada's North through intensive exploitation of natural resources.

The vision was a conscious attempt to renew the frontier spirit that had built the Canadian Pacific Railway, settled the West, and filled Canada's early years with high purpose.

The Tory leader's "vision" of heroic development – "the North" in place of "the West" – was rooted in both the Canadian nationalist and British imperial traditions.

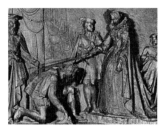

Diefenbaker saw himself as a latter-day Sir Francis Drake (here being knighted by Queen Elizabeth I), winning new worlds for his Queen Elizabeth.

Diefenbaker's Queen Elizabeth (here opening parliament in 1957, with the prime minister looking on) no longer knighted Canadian PMs, but would surely be pleased at the new worlds her northern knight hoped to win for her.

On April 8 the twenty-second parliament was dissolved. That Friday, April 12, the election was called for Monday, June 10. In the country's 265 ridings, the campaign effort began immediately. As always, the job of identifying supporters through door-to-door and telephone canvassing was the focus of party workers at the riding level. To these local organizations fell the task of tying the local candidate to the national party leader. The incumbent-rich Liberals held a clear advantage at the constituency level, as MPs remained quite important in their communities and a significant number of electors still voted the local man, not the party or the national leader. Moreover, the Liberals' long tenure had built many of these figures into formidable local forces. Thus, in a riding such as Ontario's rural Lincoln, the backbench Liberal incum-

bent, Harry Cavers, took out newspaper ads featuring long-winded missives that now would seem ridiculously self-important: "Eight years ago Harry Cavers made up his mind to serve all the people of Lincoln equally well regardless of who they were and what they were … he has drawn no barrier between the factory worker and the tiller of the soil … the shop keeper or the manufacturer … neither race, colour or creed has swayed him from this determination. There is only one way to judge a man … and that is by the sum total of his works on your behalf … with this you must agree … and in doing so decide to once again vote for Harry P. Cavers. There can be no other choice." The Tory ads in Lincoln had a tighter focus, bluntly linking their man to the national leader: "ON MONDAY JUNE 10, MAKE A DATE WITH DIEFENBAKER AND ELECT JOHN SMITH." Riding

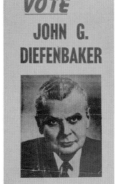

The Diefenbaker campaign reached out in many directions at once. Campus women could be drawn to this tasteful, yet hep sweater (left). Those tired of Liberal atrophy would respond to an energetic promise of "good government." Tories in Ontario were reminded that Premier Leslie Frost was supporting the federal party as never before.

Massey Hall, Toronto, April 25, 1957. The Chief rocks a secular temple full of Toronto Tories, who have, by now, swallowed the "Diefenbaker government" angle hook, line, and sinker.

campaigns generated lots of this kind of print, radio, and even TV advertising. Most of it simply served to remind voters of how to translate their national preference onto the riding's ballot, but, sometimes, when a candidate like John Smith stuck to the national message, it could actually help change minds.

The national headquarters hives buzzed with organizational effort, fundraising, and preparation of publicity materials. Above all, they hammered together the details of their leaders' tours, the essence of the campaign. For most of the writ period's first two weeks, both major leaders were absent from the national stage while the details of their lives for the next six weeks were settled. St. Laurent used the time to rest and to clean up government business in Ottawa. Diefenbaker spent most of the writ period's second week campaigning in his home riding of Prince Albert, where the Liberals were mounting a strong challenge to take advantage of his anticipated absence on the national campaign.

In late April the caravans finally got under way, marking the true launch of the national campaign. Here, the contrast between the Liberals' traditionalism and the Tories' modernity was inescapable. Diefenbaker was first off the mark, speaking at a boisterous rally at Toronto's Massey Hall on Thursday, April 25. Premier Leslie Frost warmed up the partisan crowd in the Tory stronghold, praising his federal leader to the skies. (Dief had taken care to mend his provincial fences, promising to side with the provinces on federal-provincial tax negotiations.) Then came the new man himself, tall, striding to the podium, which bristled with radio microphones. Behind him hung a giant blow-up of the official campaign poster featuring a massive photo of the Chief and emblazoned with the bold, black slogan, "It's time for a Diefenbaker Government." Barely visible and printed down in the poster's corner were the words "Progressive Conservative Party." They had come for a Tory event, but wound up rallying for a retooled, rebranded entity that could only be called the Diefenbaker party.

The leader rolled confidently into his speech, promising that the Progressive Conservative Party would recover "all the wisdom, all the faith and all the vision" of Sir John A. Macdonald. There was no mention of the ten intervening Tory leaders, not Borden, Meighen, or the whole blue-blooded Tory brand. Nor was there any of the usual Quebec bashing. Instead, Diefenbaker made a ringing call for "one Canada – with equality of opportunity for every citizen and equality for every province from the Atlantic to the Pacific." Next, he ripped into the Liberals for their arrogance during the Pipeline Debate, for tyrannizing parliament, for their cheapskate budget. The crowd roared at each turn.

Then came the vision. "We intend to launch a new National Policy of development in the northern areas which may be called the New Frontier Policy. Macdonald was concerned with the opening of the west. We are concerned with developments in the provinces and with provincial cooperation, and in our Northern Frontier in particular. The North – with its vast resources and hidden wealth – the wonder and challenge of the North must become our national consciousness. All that is needed, as I see it today, is an imaginative policy that will open its doors to Canadian initiative and enterprise. We believe in a positive National Policy of development, in contrast with the negative and haphazard one of today." The crowd responded enthusiastically and, as the people filed out into the night, they could pick up copies of the party's major campaign brochure, *A New National Policy*, which spelled out the Diefenbaker program amid a heavy emphasis on the man himself.

Louis St. Laurent kicked off his campaign four days later, on April 29, in Winnipeg.

Someone in the Liberal team had actually suggested a launch out on the northern frontier in the Arctic, but the idea was rejected as too strenuous for the aging PM. (And too expensive – an odd concern, given that the Liberals would spend a whopping $6–10 million on the campaign, or between $40 million and $70 million in today's dollars. The Tories' $3–3.5 million [$21–25 million today] effort was comparatively modest.) After a restful, two-day train journey from Ottawa to Manitoba, St. Laurent spoke to a half-filled auditorium. The prime minister droned through an auditor's report disguised as a campaign speech, reeling off reams of statistics and reading from a *Winnipeg Free Press* editorial that warned of "grave dangers" to Liberalism attendant upon another four years of power, but nonetheless supported the Grits on the grounds of the "superiority of the present government, compared with any possible group or grouping that might take its place."

To call this performance uninspiring is an understatement. But then, wasn't that the secret plan of those tricky Liberals? Pickersgill wasn't worried; he was selling to the voters the pure product of the King–St. Laurent Liberal system: the silent, efficient management they knew and supposedly still loved. When he called the election, St. Laurent promised a campaign of "no nonsense; no promises," a look-ma-no-hands prelude to an encounter with an electoral lamp post. Cockfield Brown recycled an earlier, suitably bland slogan – "Unity, Security, Freedom" – and generally presented it with a photo of a young family walking towards the words. The main campaign brochure, headlined *Liberalism … A Fighting Faith*, was largely a reprint of policy materials prepared for the party's 1948 convention. As the campaign progressed, another eight pamphlets would spew forth from Cooper Street, each highlighting a different policy area, including such classics as "Atlantic fishermen are making STEADY GAINS UNDER LIBERAL POLICY"

and "CANADIAN WOMEN have confidence in
St. Laurent." The whole approach was an
almost deliberately boring, *de minimus* soft sell.

The campaign's first free-time television
broadcasts aired the same week that the leaders
launched their national tours. St. Laurent's first
such broadcast was a tape of his Winnipeg
speech, aired that night, April 29. In it, he
echoed his flat live oratory with such zingers
as "Good times and good government have a
habit of going together" and a promise to "keep
up the kind of work that has helped make the
past four years such really outstanding ones."
Diefenbaker, in his April 30 broadcast, managed to put across a more compelling message,
balancing his concern over "the very real threat
that Canada would become a one-party state"
with his positive pledge to "do something for
the average man and woman across the country,
and to carry out the development policy for the
benefit of Canadians as a whole."

Radio and TV advertising (later dubbed
"bought media") were significant, although not

dominant parts of both campaigns. The PCs
purchased five fifty-second spots featuring
Diefenbaker reading a text in a studio and
produced four fifteen-minute presentations
by Diefenbaker, which were played a total of
seven times, for the CBC's free-time political
broadcasts. The Liberals, despite investing in
a mini-studio in a garage next to their national
headquarters in Ottawa, rotated three free-time
presentations by an uncomfortable, leaden St.
Laurent and produced few bought spots. Dief
was excellent on both radio and on television,
cooling his oratorical fireworks for the intimacy
of family living rooms. While St. Laurent found
radio addresses a useful means of communication with the public, he was distinctly averse
to television, considering its use of make-up
and teleprompters to be fundamentally dishonest. On one occasion he sarcastically agreed to
wear the make-up and use the teleprompter, but
swore he would begin his televised statement
by explaining that he was using these tools. His
aides backed down, allowing him to tape with-

Early in the campaign, with the pundits predicting an
easy Liberal win, the Tories had to attract attention –
by any means necessary. In this case the means is a
hired clown at a campaign office opening.

"EVEN IF WE HAVE TO RUN HIM STUFFED"

LOUIS ST. LAURENT ON THE CAMPAIGN TRAIL

C.D. Howe's tasteless promise to run on the St. Laurent image no matter what his condition seemed to become reality as Campaign '57 unfolded. The machine could still dredge up the crowds, like this one in Quebec (*top centre*), but they were thin and disengaged (like these bored motorcade watchers in New Westminster, BC, *top right*). Sloppy advance work led to un-prime-ministerial chintz like the cheap, taped-on signage on the car (*right*). Once he got out of the car, St. Laurent frequently lost track of where he was (in this case, *lower right*, he's in Drummondville, Quebec). Normally, a candidate who's bad in crowds can be cleaned up in the television studio, but not St. Laurent. He detested television as artificial and dishonest, which made for some interesting challenges as puzzled aides, like the one in the studio with St. Laurent (*below*), struggled to get the old man to use a tele-prompter instead of looking down at his notes.

out make-up and reading from a sheaf of notes in his hands, eyes down.

By May 5, the end of week three, the election campaign was moving into gear. While the local party volunteers and candidates went about their business, each leader had gotten out of the way the task of touring a low-priority region – for St. Laurent the unpromising West and appearances before flat crowds in Edmonton and Vancouver; for Dief the hopeful but vote-poor Maritimes, where his oratorical fireworks enthralled and delighted crowds. The Chief was getting into the swing of his simple task on the tour – to create an impression among voters that the race that had begun with him so far behind was not already over, that a choice was possible, that a Tory vote could make a difference. Crucial to this task was the travelling press corps that had begun to accompany each leader in campaigns since the war. Dief needed the touring reporters and pundits to tell the voters that the election was up for grabs. To convince these professional sceptics, he needed surprisingly big crowds and surprisingly good reactions. It was all aimed at convincing the media that the polls were wrong, or at least stale-dated, that something was happening out there.

While Dief charged from one event to the next whipping up momentum, St. Laurent was just trying to kill time. He wasted much of weeks four and five in rock-solid Quebec. Dief spent the same two weeks out West wrestling with the debilitating vote-splitting between Tories, CCFers, and Social Crediters, so as to consolidate anti-Liberal support behind him. In Winnipeg he laid out his message of momentum to a cheering crowd, saying that his campaign was assuming "something of the nature of a crusade." "All across the country," he continued, "men and women who previously supported other parties are coming forward to say to me and many of our candidates, 'This time I am voting Conservative.'"

By the time Diefenbaker reached Vancouver at the end of week six, the momentum prophecy had become a statement of fact. The precise means by which hundreds of thousands of people strung along thousands of miles of country begin coming to the same conclusion have never been detailed and proven, despite all the time and effort that brilliant minds have devoted to this question over the years. Media and advertising play a role, but so do word-of-mouth endorsement and even the solitary process of logical reflection. By whatever means, Diefenbaker's crowds by late May had been growing and their enthusiasm waxing – though not enough to convince the all-important media that Diefenbaker might actually have a chance.

Vancouver changed all that. Lately a bad city for the Tories, it had elected just one PC among its nine MPs in 1953. Yet here, on May 24, were five thousand people jammed into the hall and crowded outside to hear a Tory leader speak. And if the size of the crowd didn't tell the story, the response to Diefenbaker's inspiring performance certainly did. As MP George Hees put it: "It was the crowd that did it. The word came back across the country that Diefenbaker had had a tremendous meeting in Vancouver, and the crowd went wild, and people were excited and so on. Everybody said suddenly, 'Maybe this guy could do it.'"

The opposite dynamic was at work on St. Laurent's effort, as people stayed away in droves or came and went home bored. The same night as Dief's triumph in Vancouver, St. Laurent drew a meagre four hundred people to a rally in his home province, the Liberal citadel of Quebec. His speeches had by now degenerated into a series of disjointed anecdotes and musings. As his personal secretary later wrote, "He ended invariably with a lecture on the benefits of the Canadian democratic system, and a reminder that if the audience did not feel that the Liberals could do the best job for them over the next four years, it was their duty to vote for some other party. But, he would add with a shrug of his shoulders … 'I don't know where you will find anyone who can do any better.'" St. Laurent's attention seemed to be straying badly, both on and off the podium. At one point he confided to an aide that he feared that the Social Credit would form the official opposition. At a stopover in Jarvis, Ontario, he shook hands enthusiastically with reporters he'd been travelling with, clearly mistaking them for local electors. Uncle Louis was losing his marbles.

So were some of the Liberal bullhorns. C.D. Howe made a spectacularly inept foray into Manitoba in week six, poking an angry farmer's belly in the town of Carman and saying, "Looks to me like you've been eating pretty well under a Liberal government." Later that day, in Morris, Manitoba, Howe tried to silence a persistent questioner by exclaiming, "When your party organizes a meeting, you'll have the platform, and we'll ask the questions." The heckler mounted the stage, revealed that he was the head of the local Liberal association, and set about denouncing Howe as full of "baloney." Howe tried to elbow his way from the hall but was blocked at the door. "Look here, my good man," hissed the minister, "when the election comes, why don't you just go away and vote for the party you support? In fact, why don't you just go away?" Maybe something *was* happening out there.

Even the Liberal high command finally figured that one out. Although Pickersgill was safely insulated in Liberal Newfoundland, Ministers Walter Harris, Robert Winters, Milton Gregg, and Stuart Garson were all reporting voter hostility in their regions of Ontario, Nova Scotia, New Brunswick, and Manitoba. Finance Minister Harris was the first to panic, suggesting that his infamous six-buck pension increase be hiked by another $4 to the level Diefenbaker had demanded

back in March. St. Laurent contemptuously dismissed the idea, but at least, with two crucial weeks to go until voting day, he broke out of a small-halls tour of eastern Quebec and the Maritimes to deliver a major live address in Ottawa on May 27. In this speech St. Laurent did what most stumbling front-runners do: he went negative, ridiculing the "Tory election promise to spend more and tax less," defending the government's handling of the Pipeline Debate, and mocking the opposition's role as "certainly a black Friday in the history of the Tory and socialist parties." The prime minister made fun of the Conservatives' campaign materials for their downplaying of the Progressive Conservative brand, joking that their slogan should have been "Now is the time for all good Diefenbakers to come to the aid of their party."

St. Laurent's May 27 address is a good example of how not to go negative. By showing the usually cheerful and boring St. Laurent deviating from his strategy, the speech confirmed what the Tory tour had been trying to demonstrate – that something big was happening. The prime minister resembled some besieged generalissimo trying to rally his troops while his wife, just off camera, is packing her shoes. Moreover, by discussing the pipeline, he was reminding voters of what they liked least about his government. And by agreeing with the Tories that they were burying their party and playing up their leader, he gave the prime ministerial endorsement to the idea that a vote for Diefenbaker wasn't really a vote for those awful old Tories. Reading the newspaper reports the next day, Grosart thought, "If these fellows want to start this, it is exactly what I am trying to get across: 'It's Diefenbaker. It's Diefenbaker.'" Grosart sent the newspaper report of St. Laurent's speech to Tory candidates all across the country, instructing them to use it in persuading voters that the Tory Party had indeed become the Diefenbaker party.

ROCK
AROUND
THE CLOCK

JOHN DIEFENBAKER ON
THE CAMPAIGN TRAIL

John Diefenbaker was the best campaigner in Canadian history, a relentless, upbeat dynamo who could will political momentum into being by his simple physical presence. His enthusiasm was boundless, his schedule punishing, his energy infectious – and exhausting. Diefenbaker was one of the few larger-than-life politicians Canada has produced, and he carried Canadians along with him – sometimes literally, as in the plane-boarding picture (top, left). Showboating for reporters (top, centre), his charm fills the room. Sitting in a hotel room (centre row, lower), he looks ready to leap out and force the television to say what he wants it to. Hustling down a rainy Main Street, Anytown, Canada (top, right), his staff can barely keep up. A stagey photo with a typewriter (bottom, right) shows Dief's energy threatening to pound the little machine to bits. And the poor devil at the other end of the telephone (bottom, left) is doubtless reeling under the assault of the Chief's bullhorn voice, his love of the game, his will to win.

Keeper of the flame. No medium was too small for the Liberals to use to portray their leader as a god, not even this campaign matchbook.

The lowest point of the Liberal campaign came on Friday, June 6, at a mammoth rally organized in Toronto's Maple Leaf Gardens. John Meisel re-created the scene: "Each [local] candidate had groups placed in the audience at Maple Leaf Gardens carrying banners. Some of the groups were costumed. One, dressed like Indians, performed a war-dance in the aisles when its candidate was introduced. But this feathered claque apparently proved less popular with the electorate than a group of short-skirted blondes. There were massed bands, bagpipes, dancing girls, the Leslie Bell Singers, drum majorettes, cheer leaders, cow bells, noise makers, Lorne Green as master of ceremonies, and a tandem bicycle." So far, so good. Then, halfway through St. Laurent's address, a fifteen-year-old heckler mounted the stage and began tearing up a poster of the prime minister. The crowd stared speechlessly. So did the prime minister. The event chairman moved on the youth and accidentally knocked him backwards, sending the young man tumbling down the stairs, smashing his head on the concrete floor, and knocking him unconscious. The crowd waited in horror for a few minutes until attendants revived the young martyr and escorted him gently from the hall. It was Black Friday all over again.

Diefenbaker leapt on the episode: "The next day I devoted part of my speech to new methods for quieting perverse people who did not agree with government policy: 'Shove them off the platform. If they break their necks, that's just too bad.'"

In the campaign's two final weeks, Diefenbaker rolled to a frenzied close, sleeping in airplanes on overnight flights so as to squeeze in more events with an electorate he felt was coming his way. With a little over a week to go, the Chief celebrated the anniversary of Black Friday with a barn-burner of a speech in Ontario's Bruce County in which he told 2,100 rural voters: "If you send this government back to office, don't ask Her Majesty's loyal Opposition to stand up for your rights. For you no longer will have any rights." The pace was exhausting. "Near the end," recalled a *Globe* reporter, "he was in Edmonton and he made a speech that was absolutely incomprehensible. It was gibberish." The crowd cheered wildly just the same.

The party leaders both knew the race was tightening; each pleaded for a majority result in his week seven TV address. The pre-election Canadian Institute of Public Opinion poll, published on June 7, showed a tightening as well, with the Liberals at 43.5 per cent, down from 46 at the campaign's start, and the PCs up from 33 per cent to 37.5. But while no one could deny that Dief had run a good campaign and would pick up seats, it looked as though the Grits would certainly survive. *Maclean's* magazine went to press on June 8 with an editorial saying, "We Canadians have once more elected one of the most powerful governments ever created by the free will of a free electorate." Off the record, Diefenbaker predicted to the Toronto *Telegram* that the PCs would win ninety-seven seats. The reporter thought he was joking.

Election night showed just how wrong everyone was. The PCs triumphed in 112 seats, the Liberals in 105, the CCF in 25, and Social Credit in 19. (Four independents were also elected, for a total of 265.) The Liberal share of the popular vote fell 7.8 per cent to 40 per cent, while the Tories' increased by the same amount. The real story, however, lay beneath those numbers. Turnout had shot up by 6 per cent from the previous election, and while the Liberal vote had declined only slightly – indeed the Grits had won the most votes – Tory support leapt by 820,000. The electorate had expanded, turnout had increased, and the total Progressive Conservative vote had sky-rocketed by more than 40 per cent over its 1953 result. In other words, the Liberals mainly held onto their vote from 1953, while new voters and voters who had sat out the last election mostly flocked to the Diefenbaker party.

As the night wore on and the results moved west, one Liberal baron after another was unhorsed – nine ministers in all, almost half the cabinet, a whole generation of Liberal power brokers. On the Lakehead, Howe went down to spectacular defeat at the hands of a CCF schoolteacher, ending a twenty-two-year cabinet career. Walter Harris was bested in Ontario's Bruce riding, Stuart Garson in Winnipeg, and Robert Winters in Queens-Lunenburg. In northern Ontario, Lester Pearson survived as MP for Algoma East, to the dismay of his politics-hating wife, Maryon.

At home in Quebec City, with Pickersgill at his side, St. Laurent was befuddled, even uncomprehending at the news. Driven to a temporary television studio in the Château Frontenac, St. Laurent delivered the first televised concession speech by a prime minister in Canadian history. Across the

Up in smoke. A panicky-looking Louis St. Laurent at the disastrous Maple Leaf Gardens rally in early June. In the campaign's final stretch, the PM went negative on Diefenbaker – and looked like a fool doing it.

On election night, Diefenbaker's win surprised everybody – including himself.

country the flickering screens showed a ghostly old man with only a tentative grip on what had befallen him. In Port Arthur, Howe is reported to have "characteristically delivered himself of the opinion that the nation was being swept by some strange disease and he was going to bed."

In Regina, Dief awaited the outcome at the CBC studio, where he would deliver an address of either victory or concession. By 8:15 central time (10:15 eastern) he knew he had fulfilled his life's dream. At 9:00 he spoke to the nation from an empty television studio. "Our task is not finished," said the new prime minister– elect. "In many respects it has only just begun." Then he raced to the airport, got back on the plane, and returned to a hero's welcome from three thousand Prince Albertans. Dief was so engulfed in the throng of joyous supporters that he didn't even get a chance to make a speech.

The 1957 election was the first in Canadian history in which the campaign itself undeniably made the difference. When the writs were dropped, Diefenbaker's own top managers believed victory was out of reach, yet a mere eight weeks later it lay in their hands. What happened? The Conservatives caught the national mood and the Liberals did not. Too long in power, the Grits had complacently assumed that none of the three sub-national parties – the Tories, the CCF, and Social Credit – presented a plausible alternative, and they acted accordingly. In the pre-writ campaign they put good policy over good politics, as if offending big chunks of the Canadian population wouldn't affect the outcome of the looming election. In the campaign proper they ran under a set of platitudes that didn't amount to a positive message, with a shop-worn leader

St. Laurent was stunned and bewildered by the loss, unable at first to grasp what had happened.

incapable of articulating a compelling reason to support him.

Diefenbaker – almost alone among the Tories – had sensed the opportunity to cast himself as the hero opposite the Liberal villains in the coming public drama. During the pre-writ campaign Diefenbaker framed each major issue on the public's mind – the memory of the Pipeline Debate, the budget, even the Herbert Norman affair – in terms of actions, not ideas. The Grits, he charged, were acting badly, like a complacent, arrogant government that had forgotten about democracy after too long a time in power. The frame fit: the Liberals occupied the position the Tories assigned them in what they did and what they failed to do. And when the voters looked at the Tory leader, they saw not only the energy and humility St. Laurent lacked but also something more: a positive, even inspiring look into the future. The combi-

nation of a new leader and new ideas proved irresistible to a large swath of voters – particularly the volatile young moderns of English Canada's big cities.

Had Dief come up short in 1957, or had St. Laurent done a King and tried to govern with fewer seats than the Tories, the election still would have marked a watershed: the close of the decades-old King–St. Laurent system, the end of region-based rule by a technocratic elite, and the beginning of something completely different. Dief had also devised the first new entry in decades into the Canadian political playbook, the Populist Rush, which has proven the only really successful counter to the Quebec Bridge. Yet Diefenbaker's "One Canada" still took a wide detour around Quebec. The next campaign would change all that.

The 1958 campaign should never have happened. It was triggered by remarkably

WILLIAM HAMILTON
Montreal. Postmaster general. Dief supporter since 1942. Trusted.

DAVIE FULTON
Kamloops, BC. Justice. Smart guy. Rhodes Scholar and all that. Ran against Dief in '56. Deeply mistrusted.

GEORGE HEES
Toronto. Transportation. Nicknamed "Gorgeous George." Considered a lightweight. Not trusted.

GORDON CHURCHILL
Winnipeg. Trade and Commerce. Campaign manager. Strategist. Trusted somewhat.

MIKE STARR
Oshawa, Ontario. Labour. First Ukrainian-Canadian minister. Trusted.

DONALD FLEMING
Toronto. Finance. Lawyer. Windbag. Ran against Dief in '56. Deeply mistrusted.

THE CHIEF
Prince Albert, Saskatchewan. Prime minister. Barnstormer. Saviour. Trusts no one. Okay, maybe his wife.

TEAM DIEFENBAKER...SORT OF

Dief had won on the strength of his personal campaign, but many of the most talented members of his thin and inexperienced caucus – remember, his was a bare minority – had until recently been his sworn enemies. He had no choice but to appoint some of them to cabinet. But he didn't trust them. And they didn't like him.

GEORGE PEARKES
Esquimalt, BC. Defence.
Dief supporter from
'48. Trusted.

ELLEN FAIRCLOUGH
Hamilton, Ontario. Secretary
of state. First female
minister. Mistrusted.

LÉON BALCER
Trois-Rivières, Quebec.
Solicitor general. Led anti-
Diefenbaker walkout at '56
convention. Deeply mistrusted.

stupid Liberal blunders that were seized upon brilliantly by the Tory prime minister. Liberal ineptitude allowed Diefenbaker to take his innovative politics into uncharted territory.

From the morning of June 11, when he invited reporters and photographers to come with him on a brief fishing trip, Diefenbaker fully understood, as had Mackenzie King in 1925, that in a minority parliament the pre-writ campaign begins immediately. So intense was his continuing touring schedule that he hardly had time to form a cabinet and present his new program in a Throne Speech delivered by Canada's new queen, Elizabeth II. Indeed, throughout the fall he acted as though election day had never happened, maintaining an almost campaign-like regimen of appearances, cere-monies, and speeches, criss-crossing the country by air as none of his predecessors had done.

In parliament the opposition parties mostly just got out of the way as the Diefenbaker government expanded coverage under the Unemployment Insurance Act; hiked pensions; cut taxes on incomes, automobile sales, and small businesses; established a royal commission on price spreads; pushed through new housing loans; extended benefits for shipyards – the list of dervish-like activities whirled on and on. As never before, Diefenbaker put into action the power of the prime minister to project the government's desired image. It was the same as in the 1957 campaign: change-oriented, youth-ful, full of populist energy and the vigour of democratic renewal. The polls reflected a surge of approval for the new government: by the end of the summer of 1957 the PCs commanded the support of half the electorate, and retained this level throughout the fall.

Most political observers expected an election sometime in late 1959 or early 1960. Surely no politician with any brains would want to take on Diefenbaker in the midst of his honeymoon with the electorate. Besides, the Liberals were in no shape for a rematch. They had lost office, much of their front bench, and a generation's worth of the people who sustained a party's power – grateful patronage appointees, friendly businessmen, and civil servants who brought them fine new policies to implement. Most of all, the Liberals needed a new leader. On September 15 Louis St. Laurent finally resigned the leadership, paving the way for a convention that was called for January 14–16, 1958.

Mike Pearson became the immediate front-runner. Urged on by such powerful friends as former US secretary of state Dean Acheson, backed by much of the remaining Liberal caucus, and with an influential clique of journalists acting as a kind of fan club, Pearson seemed headed for a coronation. On October 14 his lustre increased further when he was awarded the Nobel Peace Prize – surely the nicest mid-campaign profile-booster a leader-ship candidate could wish for. The sole caucus member who stood against Pearson's jugger-naut was Paul Martin, the southwest Ontario regional heavyweight and crusading former welfare minister who had run unsuccessfully against St. Laurent ten years earlier. But Martin's chances of succeeding St. Laurent were poor, given that he was another francophone in a party that had alternated between English Protestant and French Catholic leaders since the 1880s. To no one's surprise, on Thursday, January 16, in Ottawa, Pearson won on the first ballot, 1,074 to 305.

NAME: Lester Bowles Pearson

PARTY: Liberal

ROLE: Opposition leader since January 1958. Ex-mandarin. Nobel Peace Prize winner. Political greenhorn.

The new leader left the convention in a bellicose mood, having found the delegates surprisingly eager for a fresh election fight. By January 1958 the economy had softened somewhat, with growth slowing and unemployment rising to a postwar high of almost 8 per cent. Walter "Six Buck" Harris, now a mere delegate, charged that "the Tories didn't inherit unemployment from us; they created it." Perhaps Pearson let the mood of the crowd go to his head. In an off-the-record chat with some friendly reporters he announced, "We're going to force an election. That's final." The newly crowned leader in his acceptance speech whipped up the party's fighting mood, calling the convention "the full, complete and final answer to the idle and partisan chatter that this party is downhearted and defeatist. Who dares say so now?" Delegates left Ottawa anticipating an early drive to force an election.

Four days later, on Monday, January 20, facing the Commons as leader for the first time, Pearson changed his tune. As he recalled in his memoirs, his debut "should have been a day memorable for the pleasant tributes paid me by the Prime Minister, by other party leaders, and by St. Laurent as I assumed my position as Leader of the Opposition. Memorable it was; pleasant it was not." The new leader rose to offer a Liberal amendment to a government supply motion, but, instead of putting forward a simple question of confidence, he moved a bizarre amendment that began by blaming Diefenbaker's seven-month-old government for a litany of economic woes. It continued:

"In view of the desirability, at this time, of having a government pledged to implement Liberal policies, His Excellency's advisers should, in the opinion of this House, submit their resignation forthwith." Huh? The amendment called for the Tories to vacate office and allow the Liberals to form a government without an election. Pearson was doing an Arthur Meighen!

What had brought Pearson to this absurd position? By the Monday after the convention his belligerent rhetoric had run into the hard fact of a caucus dead set against an election for which the party was totally unprepared, to be waged against an opponent sitting at 50 per cent in the polls. In his memoirs Pearson blamed the entire mess on an over-reliance on the advice of "the experts, our professional politicians," who urged him to follow "the practice … of defeating one minority to replace it with another." This interpretation doesn't accord with the recollection of Pickersgill, the Liberal "professional politician" par excellence. "Having gotten ourselves into this mess by breathing fire and slaughter and saying we were going to try to bring the government down, we had to find some weaselling motion that we would be sure the small parties would not vote for so that Diefenbaker would not be defeated." We'll never know which version is closer to the truth, but I suspect that Pearson was exercising a former–prime minister's prerogative to rewrite history. Both are silent, though, on a vastly more important question: How they expected their weaselling motion would play with the public.

Herein lay the Liberal Party's real problem: its members had not collectively figured out why they'd lost power the previous June. Pickersgill's rationalization was typical: "The electorate got bored. St. Laurent made it seem so easy to govern Canada that the electorate decided that anybody could do it." This explanation was not only wrong but it perpetuated

Remembering everything, and learning nothing,
the Liberal convention showed that the party's
monolithic instincts were unshaken by defeat.
Same bad slogan – Unity, Security, Freedom.
Same herd mentality. Changed country.

the very undemocratic arrogance that was the real cause of the Liberal defeat. Even in opposition, the Grits with their outrageous demand to be reinstated were once again taking the voters for granted, as though Liberal government was a permanent condition that needed no popular sanction. In modern parlance, they just didn't get it. And even worse for them, they didn't understand that they were handing Diefenbaker the political opportunity of a lifetime. "When I took my seat," recalled Pearson, "I knew immediately that my first attack on the government had been a failure, a fiasco."

Across the aisle, Diefenbaker's eyes burned with hungry anticipation. "I turned to Howard Green," he wrote in his memoirs, "and said, 'This is it.'" With superb, animal-like political instinct, Diefenbaker had sensed the bare throat Pearson was offering him. If he could make enough of this blunder and frame it as the ultimate example of Liberal arrogance, he would have both an election pretext and an election-winning message before day's end.

The House hushed as the prime minister rose to reply. He began, predictably enough, by eloquently mocking Pearson's flip-flop: "On Thursday there was shrieking defiance; on the following Monday there is shrinking indecision … The only reason that this motion is worded as it is is that my honourable friends opposite quake when they think of what will happen if an election comes."

On his feet, improvising with the assurance of a parliamentary master, Diefenbaker now tore into the Liberals' request to return to power, calling Pearson's amendment "the resignation from responsibility of a great party … the resignation amendment of a party saturated with fear of what the electorate will do to it." Finally, he drew forth from his ever-present heap of papers a document called "Canadian Economic Outlook." It was dated March 1957, produced for the then-Liberal cab-

inet's use by the Department of Trade and Commerce, and stamped "Confidential." It contained the department's warnings of a slump which had helped shape Walter Harris's pre-election budget, sharply at odds with the sunny economic picture painted by the Liberals for their 1957 campaign. Dief stood, his arm on his hip in finest courtroom style, and brandished the incriminating document at Pearson, twenty feet away. "You secured the advice of the economists in your own departments and were advised what the situation was in March 1957. This record was given to every one of you … They had a warning … Did they tell us that? No, Mr. Speaker, why did they not reveal this? Why did they not act when the House was sitting in January, February, March and April? They had the information … You concealed the facts, that is what you did. What plans did you make? Where was that shelf of works that was going to be made available whenever conditions should deteriorate? … When we came to power and looked for the so-called shelf there was not one solitary suggestion of a program available to meet the situation." It was a savage, yet magnificent performance. At the small price of flouting the sacred protocol that a previous government's cabinet documents remain confidential, Diefenbaker had turned the opposition Liberals' only issue, the economic slowdown, against them. The economy, the Liberal amendment, the new leader – everything Diefenbaker could think of – was fashioned into another claw with which to slash at the undemocratic arrogance of the Grits. When he sat down after two hours, nothing remained of the Liberals' credibility.

Ten days later the rookie prime minister visited the governor general, Vincent Massey, at the vice-regal residence in the Citadel at Quebec City to ask for an election. Although Diefenbaker had no real constitutional grounds to recommend the vote, to have refused him

DEE-FENCE! DEE-FENCE!

In parliament, Diefenbaker's courtroom style, honed as a prairie defender of the underdog, presented an image eerily like that of television's most famous defence attorney, Perry Mason. In a day when defence lawyers were heroes – Mason stood up for the little guy – Dief's style touched a chord. When he tore into the Liberals in '57 and '58, he did it with the gusto of a crusading public defender taking on the anti-democratic Liberal powers that were about to be cast down.

would have triggered a second King–Byng crisis. Massey, who had spent election night 1926 beside King, watching him triumph over Governor General Byng, must have had no appetite to re-fight the old battle. He obligingly dissolved parliament and called an election for March 31, 1958.

From the start, Diefenbaker's 1958 campaign was a triumphant reprise of 1957, with the volume pumped way up. From the previous year's "It's Time for a Diefenbaker Government," the slogan became, simply, "Follow John," superimposed on a poster showing a set of black footprints. (Grosart lifted the slogan from a Vancouver Tory candidate, John Taylor, who had used it successfully in 1957.) It was a simpler appeal, almost biblical in tone, an invitation to walk on water together. Similarly, in party documents and transcripts of Dief's speeches, the vision of 1957 became the "Vision" of 1958, upgraded to upper case to reflect the leader's apotheosis.

Donations poured in, allowing the PCs to double their spending and lavish money on both national publicity and grants to local riding campaigns. Gordon Churchill's English Canada–only strategy of 1957 was replaced with an all-out drive to add Quebec to the Tory win column. In time-honoured Conservative fashion, this goal was met by making an arrangement with the nationalists in Quebec, in this case the Union Nationale government of Premier Maurice Duplessis, a formidable *bleu* who swung his weight decisively behind the PCs. Bags of UN money were distributed, seasoned UN organizers muscled aside the cheerful losers of the Quebec PC Party, and candidates were recruited and introduced on platforms by UN *députés* from the National Assembly.

"It's generally true," recalled Quebec Tory stalwart Jacques Flynn, "that the Duplessis machine was behind Diefenbaker in '58." Allister Grosart, who presumably knew

exactly what arrangements were made, contradicted Flynn, saying, "There was no deal with Duplessis in 1958." One wonders by what narrow definition of "deal" the Tory campaign manager might have been truthful. Regardless, the 1958 deal was a good one for the Tories,

NAME: Maurice Duplessis

PARTY: Union Nationale

ROLE: Premier, 1936–39, and since 1944. Authoritarian. Conservative Catholic.

since it came with no price tag. Dief needed, Duplessis had, Duplessis gave – the Quebec premier would decide how to collect later. "I am completely convinced," Diefenbaker minister William Hamilton said later, "and I think all the evidence indicates that Mr. Duplessis, at that particular point in time, saw a way by which he could dominate and control the federal Parliament. No one in his right mind could have conceived of the Conservatives obtaining a majority without Quebec … twenty or thirty seats in Quebec would make the difference. Now it's pretty clear that if you, as a provincial leader, can put twenty or thirty people who really believe that they owe their presence there and their allegiance to you, rather than to their federal leader and federal party, your power on the federal level will be tremendous."

This Tory–UN alliance was something new in Canadian politics. The players may have been the same as in the Tory–Nationalist deal of 1911, but the substance was different. This was not a reprise of the Double Tribal Whipsaw or even a deal to pander to Quebec: Diefenbaker made the same pre-election offer to Duplessis on revenue sharing that he made to Ontario's Leslie Frost and everyone else. He didn't need to offer special treatment. "It was so obvious," recalled Flynn, "that the Conservatives would win, that Mr. Diefenbaker would win a majority, that I used to tell the [Quebec] candidates, 'Talk about anything, but conclude, when you speak on a given matter, "Whether you like it or not, the Conservatives are going to win, so why not be with him?"'" For the more recalcitrant, Flynn had another pitch: "'I know that people describe Mr. Diefenbaker in different ways. Even if he was a devil, don't you think you would do a good thing to elect people to keep him – to circle him in other words?' People agreed. They said, 'That's true, and the Liberals have been there for such a long time.'" Through intermediaries and with the considerable expectation of mutual benefit to be sure – but still in return for nothing other than the same wave of change he had generated in English Canada in the summer of 1957 – Diefenbaker enrolled Quebec in his crusade.

In Quebec, as he did throughout the country during the 1958 campaign, Diefenbaker amplified his preferred themes, albeit in fragments of execrable French. During the 1957 campaign in Montreal, the Tory leader had pledged that his party's first aim was "ONE CANADA," in which there would be an equalization of opportunity for all parts of the country. At the time, One Canada was presented to Quebeckers as a promise to share in the postwar prosperity the province was missing out on, with its per capita income of only 80 per cent of the national average. Swiftly following came the pledge that its minority prerogatives would be respected. "My reading of the discussions prior to Confederation," wrote Diefenbaker later, "revealed convincing evidence that the Fathers of Confederation intended to build 'One Canada.'" It wasn't totally clear what Diefenbaker meant in 1957, but, when the Chief was campaigning, substance didn't much matter.

In 1958 Dief pumped the One Canada theme up to gigantic proportions. "One day we

had a big meeting," recalled Pierre Sévigny, Diefenbaker's chief Quebec organizer and himself a candidate in 1958, " … and we were sitting around discussing what the slogan should be … Anyway, at one point, Diefenbaker was talking in his inimitable way about Canada, the dream of a greater and bigger Canada. I told him: 'Well, let's leave it at this. One Canada where everybody will live in harmony.'" Sévigny had recommended simply retaining the language and meaning of Diefenbaker's Montreal speech from 1957. But the penny dropped for Diefenbaker. "My God, it was as if I had put a bomb under his seat," said Sévigny. "He got up and said, 'That's it! Yes. One Canada.' Then, he started right there in front of us all and he said, 'One Canada! What we can build around that slogan!'" Diefenbaker had flashed onto a broader meaning implicit in his earlier words. "One Canada" now became more than a pledge of economic equality; it became the starting point and the destination of the Vision itself. The pursuit and fulfilment of the Vision would unite the country into One Canada, just as One Canada would implement the Vision. The two ideas were his Alpha and Omega, in the great Canadian tradition that had linked

"Let's Not Isolate Quebec." In 1958 the Tory appeal to Quebec voters was simple – and effective: We're going to win, so you might as well join us.

PAT BOONE VS. ELVIS

PEARSON AND DIEFENBAKER ON THE CAMPAIGN TRAIL

Running Lester Pearson against John Diefenbaker in 1958 was like booking Pat Boone versus Elvis – a dull crooner opposite a rock star. Pearson's image was remote and impersonal to begin with *(top left)*, and the reality disappointingly prosaic. By contrast, Dief had emerged as the free world's first political superstar. Sociologists are still trying to figure out what was in the water in the late 50s and 60s that caused this kind of mass hysteria. Elvis and the Beatles drew on it and so would politicians like Jack Kennedy, but Diefenbaker was the first one in.

He tore about the country at an even wilder pace than in 1957. Tory events always started out as orderly, typically Canadian exercises in decorum, until Diefenbaker hit the stage and started rolling. By the time he was done, crowds were mobbing him, literally kissing the hem of his coat. People screamed and wept.

Pearson didn't stand a chance against this mass phenomenon. Neither charismatic nor visionary (his vision would come later), Pearson in 1958 seemed nothing more than a disused, tarnished bit of silver out of the King era's Liberal war chest.

Confederation and the railway for Macdonald, unity and progress for King, and, later, would link unity and human rights for Trudeau.

Diefenbaker's yoking of One Canada to the Vision was a feat of political imagination that completed his transformation of national politics. For the first time there would be but one campaign message – One Canada tied to the Vision – in every part of the country, English or French, Protestant or Catholic. According to Grosart, "I think that everybody would agree that at this time Mr. Diefenbaker had raised the level of policy-making, policy-thinking, policy decision-making to a highly creative and imaginative level that caught the imagination of the public." That's one way of putting things. Dief had big, important ideas, all right, but they were impossible dreams. When, for example, he told Newfoundlanders, "We'll build a nation of fifty million people within the lifetime of many of you here," he was making it up. In the long history of Canadian political hyperbole, no one before or since has made wilder or more irresponsible promises.

At a purely electoral level, the One Canada rap was great campaign stuff. And it sounded best when it came from Diefenbaker himself because the Chief believed it heart and soul. He came from the Prairies, where French versus English wasn't so much at issue as who was English and who was not. Although his mother was related to a British prime minister, he had suffered for his German surname, particularly during the two world wars. Dief believed passionately in equality: of citizenship, of provinces, and of individual economic opportunity. Good Prairie populist that he was, he implicitly saw the world in terms of the broad mass of ordinary folks, undifferentiated by race, religion, or language, struggling for their dignity and opportunity against entrenched elites. He believed that this universal struggle, common to every part of the

country, would be won at last through the achievement of One Canada. Dief's intense belief in the idea of One Canada energized his already commanding leadership profile.

Once again, Diefenbaker the leader would be at the heart of the Tory campaign. There had been a strong element of anti-government protest vote in the 1957 election. Seven months later the leader and his troops would accentuate the positive aspects of voting Tory, talking less about punishing the self-satisfied Grits and more about following the leader to Canada's national destiny. Even the sceptical Pickersgill later conceded the point. In 1957, he said, "I think people just voted against us. In '58 there is no doubt that they voted for Diefenbaker."

As political fights go, the 1958 campaign was no contest. A January 1958 Gallup poll put the government at 50 per cent to the Grits' 35 per cent, which was pretty much how the campaign ended. The Tory re-election crusade kicked off on February 11, when the Chief departed Ottawa for Winnipeg. He was supposed to begin his campaign in the Manitoba capital, but when his train rolled through the northern Ontario village of Capreol, he braved frigid weather to go and shake hands with the small crowd that had gathered to watch his train go by. In several towns along the route, the same routine was repeated.

On the night of February 12 in Winnipeg he addressed an auditorium jammed with 5,000 people, who interrupted his fifty-four-minute speech with laughter and applause forty-six times. "I will never forget that meeting," said Pierre Sévigny. "It was one of the most incredible meetings I ever saw. He got there and the arena where the meeting was held was packed to the roof. I mean there were kids sitting on the rafters. Diefenbaker was in his finest form and let go with a speech where he saw that bigger, that greater Canada, where he saw high-rise buildings in the north. Then, he started with this One Canada that he repeated – One Canada where people will live in harmony, One Canada where everything will be great. The people were stirred up by this magnificent flurry of eloquence of his … When he had finished that speech, as he was walking to the door, I saw people kneel and kiss his coat. Not one, but many. People were in tears. People were delirious. And this happened many a time after."

Over the campaign's forty-five-day course, the PM would journey seventeen thousand miles by train and airplane, giving eighty-five speeches. In Edmonton and Fredericton, people tried to touch his coat. In Penticton folks closed their umbrellas when he rose, bareheaded, to speak in the rain. Even in Quebec the people rallied to him. "There is no doubt," said an admiring William Hamilton, "that the rally in the huge Craig Street armoury in Montreal was one of the great political meetings. I remember Pierre Sévigny, who introduced Diefenbaker, just churning that crowd over and finally challenging them: 'Levez-vous, levez-vous, saluez votre chef! Rise, rise and salute your chief!' And that whole place, thousands upon thousands of people, jammed into that auditorium, just tore the roof off in a frenzy."

For Pearson, the 1958 campaign was one of the cruellest courses of on-the-job training imaginable. "Initially, I thought we might win," he wrote in his memoirs. "It is very easy to be deceived in these things, especially when there are many kind people who do not want to tell you what is in fact going on." Voters were less kind. "We had a good rally in Kingston," he went on. "What I now remember in particular about that meeting, however, was our cavalcade through the streets of the city. As we slowed down for a light, a gentleman offered a very friendly but rather discouraging observation: 'Mr. Pearson, you are a very nice man, but go home, you're wasting your time.'" Pearson was a lacklustre campaigner at the

best of times; he looked like a one-watt bulb in comparison with the incandescent Diefenbaker.

Trying to make a virtue of necessity, the Liberals wrapped their effort around Pearson's self-effacement and forthrightness. At one rally at the University of Toronto, Pearson admitted that he couldn't compete with the "agitated eloquence" of his opponent and preferred a "quiet, reasoned approach." His new-found humility came far too late, however, and was broken up by Dief's savage ripostes from the road. When Pearson accused the Tories of imposing a winter election upon the country, the PC leader responded by blaming the Liberal no-confidence amendment for bringing the election about in the first place. When Pearson ridiculed Diefenbaker's Vision with its "roads to resources" as building "from igloo to igloo," he came across as flippant. Pearson's flat leadership profile was not helped by the dreary Liberal platform: a laundry list of piecemeal promises for tax cuts and more social programs. His slogan was just as lame as St. Laurent's had been the previous year: "Vote the Pearson Plan … For Jobs … For Peace."

On election night, the Diefenbaker party took an astounding 208 seats to the Liberals' 49 and the CCF's 8. Social Credit was wiped off the federal political map. Canadians had given the man with the Vision the largest majority in Canadian history. With turnout up again, the Tory vote had soared even higher, to 53.6 per cent of the popular vote versus the Grits' 33.6 per cent. In Algoma East the rookie Liberal leader survived another close race, causing Maryon Pearson to sob: "We've lost everything. We've even won our own constituency."

Canada's one-ness was confirmed that night in the sweeping, nationwide majority, and Diefenbaker reprised the theme in his televised victory address. "The Conservative Party has become a truly national party composed of all the people of Canada of all races united in the concept of one Canada." For the first time in the history of Canadian elections a leader had won by running a unified national campaign with a single message – and, in every region, the people responded.

The 1957–58 fight had several effects that long outlasted Diefenbaker's disastrous full turn at government. His landslide buried the remains of the political system of the

A worker for the chief electoral officer takes a tally of the metal ballot boxes about to be shipped out to the ridings. Not until the 1988 election were cardboard boxes introduced (that year only in central Canada). In 1992 they replaced the cumbersome metal boxes completely.

King–St. Laurent era, replacing that system's incremental co-optation of regions, classes, and language groups with a new politics of national purpose. In 1957 English Canadians voted for change and vision. In 1958 Quebec voters signed onto the same deal, something totally unprecedented. In every campaign since Confederation, Quebec's separateness had been an unavoidable fact, expressed through appointing a single national party to represent

the French Canadian race or, less frequently, through fielding an explicitly Québécois nationalist party of its own at the federal level. In 1958 Quebec did neither. Intentionally or not, it joined fully in the national trend.

Diefenbaker was the first leader (and remains one of the only ones) to successfully court Quebec on the same principles and ideas familiar to voters throughout English Canada and the free world: economic development, populism versus elitism, and human rights. In so doing he fulfilled the King–St. Laurent system's noblest dream: that Quebec would someday join in the politics of the rest of Canada. St. Laurent, at his seventy-fifth birthday banquet, had suggested to his fellow French Canadians that it was "perhaps time that we … stopped wondering with too much anxiety about our future; it will be what we ourselves make of it by our work, our perse-verance, our confidence that there is a place for us in the Canadian nation, that we are capable of filling that place, and that it is a place which is growing larger and is becoming more and more assured as the nation expands." He hoped the time had come for Quebeckers to join with other Canadians in building a future together.

Yet the King–St. Laurent Liberals' hold on Quebec could never transcend its tribal character – not when the hold stretched unbroken from the hanging of Louis Riel and not when the leader was himself a French Canadian. If, however, an Anglo – a unilingual Anglo from the Prairies no less – could fight and win in Quebec by selling the same issues and messages as in the rest of the country, maybe the ancient political axis of race and religion was at last fading away, blurred into meaninglessness by the endless smooth ministrations of King and St. Laurent.

Diefenbaker's novel Populist Rush was driven by the presentation of a vision that symbolized change. Over the next two

PLAYBOOK IV

If Diefenbaker had seen a copy of my imaginary playbook, he would have been horrified; the Chief didn't like to play by the book. He threw out the two standard political plays used over and over since Confederation. By doing so and winning, he added a new play to the book – the Populist Rush. Diefenbaker invented it in 1957 and perfected it a year later, using the populist traditions of a burgeoning western Canada as the motor of his drives against Liberal Ottawa. As the diagram shows, the Populist Rush mobilizes voters who don't generally like Ottawa and so are opposed to whatever government happens to be in office. It was the emergence of highly alienated western Canada as an electoral force that made this new play possible.

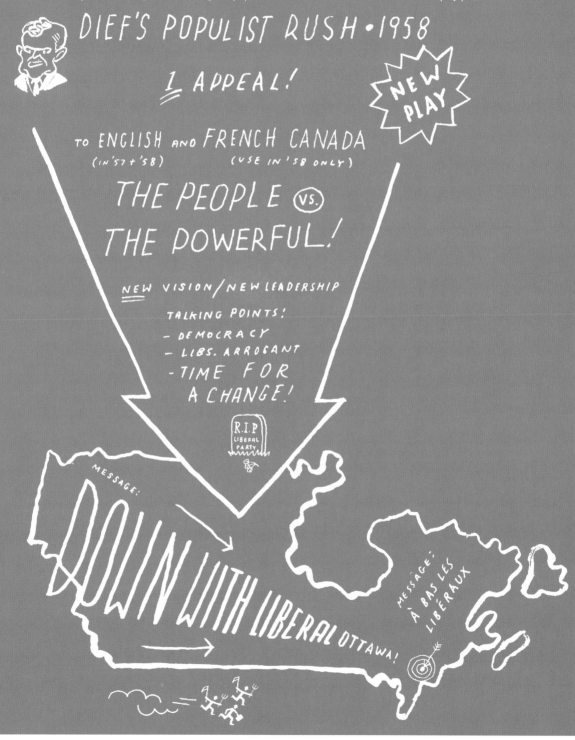

DIEF'S POPULIST RUSH • 1958

<u>1</u> APPEAL!

NEW PLAY

TO ENGLISH AND FRENCH CANADA
(IN '57 + '58)   (USE IN '58 ONLY)

THE PEOPLE (VS.)
THE POWERFUL!

<u>NEW</u> VISION / NEW LEADERSHIP

TALKING POINTS:
- DEMOCRACY
- LIBS. ARROGANT
- TIME FOR
  A CHANGE!

R.I.P
LIBERAL
PARTY

MESSAGE:
DOWN WITH LIBERAL OTTAWA!

MESSAGE:
À BAS LES
LIBÉRAUX

decades, federal politics would be dominated by such overarching national visions: Diefenbaker's Northern Destiny; Pearson's compassionate internationalism; Trudeau's Just Society; and, finally, the idea of Canada as a nation of rights-bearing individuals to which Trudeau's broader vision was eventually boiled down. The racial coalitions of the post-Confederation era and the minutely balanced combinations of the King system had required political operators like Macdonald, Laurier, Borden, and King. The new national politics of purpose would be delivered by visionary leaders like Diefenbaker, Pearson, and Trudeau (up until 1980, when he became distinctly an operator). Seen in this light, St. Laurent was a transitional figure, thinking about a national politics based on standard issues while sitting atop a King-era structure based partly on his status as Quebec's native son and partly on the Tories' failure to reach out meaningfully to Quebec. Once Diefenbaker became leader and remade the Tory Party in his image, the obstacle of traditional Tory hostility to Quebec was gone. St. Laurent's retirement effectively removed the "native son" factor. Thus, in 1958, Canada suddenly found itself in a new political era with a viable two-party system. By erasing the Liberals' "Quebec advantage," Dief completed the destruction of the King era political order he had commenced in 1957. The first election showed that a powerful leader image could roll over all the intricate brokerage arrangements of the King–St. Laurent government by cabinet. The second election finished off the regional basis

of the King era's politics by vaulting the Tories into first place not only in their traditional heartland of Ontario and the swing zones on both coasts, but also in the Liberal strongholds of Quebec and the Prairies.

The politics of "One Canada" under a towering leader figure had supplanted the regional political structure that had prevailed for three decades of depression, war, and reconstruction. This evolution had taken place around the fundamental nation-building issue of maintaining democratic freedom in the face of an increasingly undemocratic Liberal technocracy. Finally, the whole business had been accomplished in the course of a rousing struggle that included the most dramatic upset in Canadian political history. A greater fight could hardly be imagined.

In this new era the great divide would henceforth fall between urban and rural, not English and French or East and West. And this modern, urban impulse towards diversity and equality would attach itself at times to either of the two national parties. So it was that twenty-four years after his 1958 triumph, the Diefenbaker vision of Canada came to pass at a Liberal's hand. Not his dreams of tundra metropolises, but the enshrinement of the rights of the individual Canadian, so dear to Diefenbaker, became a concrete reality on April 17, 1982, when Queen Elizabeth and Pierre Trudeau enacted the Charter of Rights and Freedoms. It was the Promised Land – the One Canada of which Diefenbaker had been the Moses, had been permitted a glimpse, yet was fated never to enter. We followed him, after all.

Diefenbaker's wins in 1957 and 1958 ushered in the modern era of national politics, where leaders relate directly to individual voters. This style fit with Dief's commitment to individual rights for Canadians. This commitment would become a bedrock value for people like this child in Moose Jaw when he grew old enough to vote.

BEYOND REGION

THE ELECTIONS OF
1962 / 1963 / 1965 / 1968 / 1972 / 1974

FROM THE DIZZYING HEIGHTS OF 1958, Diefenbaker's descent was long and hard, taking almost a decade and littering the political landscape with rubble that took a long time to clear. Indeed, the memory of Diefenbaker's epic fall looms so large that it often obscures the underlying reality of Canada's political landscape in the 1960s: a new and enduring political order, based on leadership and vision, established in 1957 and 1958.

Diefenbaker wielded his own leadership and vision to gather for the Tories the political energies of Social Credit and the CCF in the West and the Duplessis tendency in Quebec. In so doing, however, he fathered a wild electoral beast that he was unable to tame into a sustainable coalition. Once he was in office, Diefenbaker's unifying yet totally unrealizable Vision faded away, revealing the stubborn contradictions it had glossed over: a fierce loyalty to Britain and the Crown at odds with the nationalism of his Quebec MPs; the crude anti-Americanism amid the realities of the Cold War; the nostalgic, anti-modern streak during a period of sweeping social and technological change. By 1962, with an election in the offing, John Diefenbaker was already the doomed Tory hero, wrapped in a Union Jack and battling alone against the dragons of Americanization, big business, and technology itself, the tragic figure who would be celebrated by historian Donald Creighton and philosopher George Grant.

June 1960
LÉVESQUE STEPS OUT
The election of Jean Lesage's Liberals marks the end of traditional Quebec. New leaders, like broadcaster René Lévesque, begin to make their mark. *(Above)* Lévesque being made up before going on air.

June 1959
ST. LAWRENCE SEAWAY OPENS
Queen Elizabeth II officially opens the St. Lawrence Seaway – one of North America's most important shipping routes – at a ceremony in St-Lambert, Quebec.

August 1960
BILL OF RIGHTS PASSED
The Canadian Bill of Rights, which set out rights and freedoms in areas of federal control, becomes law. *(Above)* A copy of the bill being presented to students by Quebec Tory MP William Hamilton *(centre).*

May 1961
KENNEDY VISITS OTTAWA
President Jack Kennedy and wife Jacqueline are greeted by Prime Minister and Mrs. Diefenbaker.

T.C. DOUGLA
FEDERAL LEAI

NEW DEMOCRATIC PAR

August 1961
DOUGLAS LEADS NDP
Saskatchewan premier Tommy Douglas is elected leader of the New Democratic Party at an Ottawa convention.

Meanwhile, Lester Pearson's Liberals had taken unusual advantage of their period in opposition to hammer together a strong national vision, based on progressive social welfare and internationalist outreach, that might compensate for Pearson's weak hold on the public imagination. Fearful of the New Democratic Party, into which the CCF had morphed with the formal support of organized labour in 1961, and its new leader, former Saskatchewan premier Tommy Douglas, the party's English wing was ready to embrace creative policies aimed at "progressive" voters. As a bonus, the Diefenbaker sweep had released the Liberals from their forty-year clinch with the conservative, Catholic power structure of Quebec. When that power structure was overthrown in the provincial election of 1960, the federal Liberals were free to embrace the province's new order. Quebec's societal sea-change – an astonishingly rapid rush to modernity known as the Quiet Revolution – transformed the province from a static, reactionary anchor in national politics to a sail billowing with the winds of change. Pearson caught these gusts with progressive new policies and with a new generation of candidates and organizers.

September 1962
OPENING OF TRANS-CANADA HIGHWAY
At the Rogers Pass, Prime Minister Diefenbaker (with shovel) opens the Trans-Canada Highway, in the works since 1949.

June 18, 1962
PEARSON COMES CLOSE
John Diefenbaker's PCs drop from 208 to 116 seats and form a minority government. Lester Pearson's Liberals win 99 seats, Social Credit 30, and the fledgling NDP elects 19 MPs. *(Above)* Pearson.

Mike for me in '63

September 1962
CANADA LAUNCHES ALOUETTE
Canada enters the space race with the launching of its first orbiting communications satellite, *Alouette 1. (Above)* Dr. John Chapman stands with his baby.

February 1963
SNAP ELECTION AS PCS FALL
In disarray over nuclear defence, the fractious Diefenbaker government is defeated by the opposition in the House. Lester Pearson *(above)* gets his third shot at beating Dief.

The 1962 election registered both an impressive Liberal rebound and the stubborn strength of Diefenbaker's bedrock support. His government was reduced to a minority with 116 of 265 seats, while the Liberals doubled their seat count to 99, electing a majority of Ontario's MPs, regaining a foothold in British Columbia, and winning almost half of Quebec's ridings. Dief's transformation between 1957–58 and 1962 – from a national bolt of modernity to an English-only anachronism – peeled away two of his key constituencies. To the NDP and the Liberals he lost his support among the forward-looking urban sets of both English and French Canada. The Liberals gained in urban Quebec as well, while the province's rural zones went to the conservative-populist Ralliement des Créditistes under Réal Caouette, who won 26 per cent of Quebec voters and 26 Quebec ridings. The Chief's only reasonably solid regional bloc lay in the still largely rural Prairies, where he held on despite a marginal Liberal comeback and an impressive 12 seats for the NDP. This important but muddled election left a bad taste in much of the nation's mouth, setting the stage for an even less edifying spectacle ten months later.

Diefenbaker's minority government staggered along through almost constant chaos, as a rolling cabinet mutiny over Canada–US nuclear defence rocked his administration week by week. On February 5, 1963, the opposition won a vote of no-confidence, triggering the second such fall of a government in Canadian history. An election was called for April 8. Convinced that "everybody's against me but the people," Diefenbaker took his cause to the electorate again, but the rising tides of 1962 now carried his Liberal opponents to a minority victory with 129 seats, the Tories at 95, the NDP at 17, and Social Credit's Quebec contingent at 20 and its western cousins at 4.

The 1962–63 fight was as close and as intense as any in Canadian history. However, there was no fundamental issue of nation building at stake. The integration of Canadian and US defence systems echoed the old free trade debates of Canada's first fifty years and their anxiety over US domination. But while this touched a chord, it did not dominate the campaign. Moreover, this double-header stayed strictly within the confines of the new political system – based on leadership and vision – that had taken hold in 1957–58. The issue of 1962–63 was Diefenbaker and the disappointment he had come to represent. That disappointment left a bad taste in Canadians' mouths. In the post-election soul-searching, pundits fretted further over the country's unwillingness to grant Lester Pearson a clear majority. Some focused on the leadership question: political scientist Samuel Lubell reported that, everywhere, people were saying, "Diefenbaker has shown he isn't fit to be prime minister but Pearson is no leader either."

The inconclusive, divided results of 1962–63 were reflected throughout Pearson's prime ministership. On the policy side, Pearson's years in office marked an outstandingly creative period. The Liberal government's moves were self-consciously progressive and popular in urban Canada: national medicare, the Canada Pension Plan, the first powerful female cabinet minister in Judy LaMarsh, a new flag for Canadians (conveniently, in a Liberal red), and a major outreach to meet the aspirations of Quiet Revolution Quebec. Much of the country bitterly resisted these changes, but any hope of a clear, resonant clash of the old and the new Canada was buried by a mudslide of scandals that undermined the government's credibility and often made it out to be the repository of the worst old-style politics.

April 8, 1963
RENEGADE OUT OF POWER
In the second election in less than a year, Lester Bowles Pearson and his Liberals win 129 seats to form a minority government. The Tories take 95 seats, the Socreds 24, and the NDP 17. This montage of Diefenbaker and Pearson nicely captures the intensity of their unprecedented, four-election rivalry, which would continue throughout most of Pearson's bumpy tenure in office. The new prime minister promised voters "Sixty Days of Decision," a foolish pledge that became a joke when his friend and finance minister Walter Gordon withdrew his budget and offered his resignation on the government's sixtieth indecisive day in office. These opening stumbles set up Pearson's weak leadership profile, which he proceeded to cement with an often shaky control of an inexperienced cabinet and a diffident public demeanour. Yet his tenure was extraordinarily creative, giving Canada national medicare, a new flag, and a strong effort to reconcile the new Quebec with English Canada. Diefenbaker, increasingly an anachronism, raged on in opposition.

September 1963
CRÉDITISTES
BREAK FROM
SOCREDS
Réal Caouette, the rising leader of Quebec's Ralliement des Créditistes, breaks away from his western Social Credit cousins, leaving the party with a tiny contingent of four MPs. *(Above)* Caouette campaigns at Montreal's Atwater Market.

December 1963
NUCLEAR WARHEADS
ARRIVE
The first nuclear warheads for US Bomarc missiles arrive in Canada. Among the many voices raised in protest, a Montreal academic named Trudeau calls Pearson "the de-frocked Prince of Peace." *(Above)* Anti-nuke poster implies that Pearson is doing the US president's bidding.

February 1965
NEW FLAG FLIES
On February 15, at a moving ceremony in front of the Peace Tower, Canada's new maple leaf flag is officially raised for the first time. The flag debate had raged for six months and split the nation, but the new banner gained almost instant acceptance. *(Above)* Parliament Hill demonstrators show their support for a maple leaf flag.

November 8, 1965
PEARSON FALLS SHORT – AGAIN
In a snap election designed to convert his bare minority into a working majority, Pearson gains only two seats over 1963. The result: Liberals 131, Tories 97, NDP 21, Créditistes 9, Social Credit 5. *(Above)* Protesters greet Pearson on a western campaign swing.

Now, ideas mattered in 60s politics, and when it came to ideas, Dief was now pointed the wrong way, while Pearson – however dynamic his policies and however snazzy a campaign the men around him could cook up – didn't appear to be moving in the right direction fast enough. Pearson acted as a powerful agent of substantive public policy change – which enabled him to govern with de facto NDP support – but he could neither fire the English Canadian imagination nor connect with French Canada sufficiently to take the commanding role in the whole country's evolution.

These shortcomings became clearer than ever when Pearson called a snap election for November 8, 1965, and voters returned an almost identical parliament, as if to confirm the idea that Canadian politics was deadlocked in some strange and unprecedented way. Perhaps the dazzling parabola of Dief's rise and fall blinded observers to the underlying pattern that now reasserted itself: as in the 1930s, 40s, and 50s, in the mid-60s the Liberals governed as the only national party, while the opposition was split into warring camps. The only big difference was Quebec. Had Pearson matched the Quebec performance of St. Laurent or even King, he would have tied or beaten Dief in 1962 and won back-to-back majorities in 1963 and 1965.

April 1967
PEARSON BRINGS IN NEW BLOOD
The prime minister shuffles his cabinet to include three young men who will each become prime minister. *(Above)* A happy Pearson *(far right)* welcomes the new members of his team: Pierre Trudeau *(left)*, John Turner, and Jean Chrétien.

April 1967
EXPO 67 OPENS
Montreal's World's Fair, the highlight of Canada's Centennial celebrations, opens. *(Above)* A mini-skirted visitor approaches Buckminster Fuller's geodesic dome that houses the United States Pavilion.

July 1967
DIEF DUMPED
The leader of the opposition packs up his office *(above)* as he is ousted from the Tory leadership by a party coup. He is succeeded by Nova Scotia premier Robert Stanfield.

Small wonder that, after the 1965 election, as Pearson began to prepare for his expected retirement, he resolved to be succeeded by a francophone Quebecker and said publicly that he believed he would be the last unilingual prime minister.

By the time Dief was finally driven to resign the Tory leadership in 1967, only the prairie West remained with him. Their populist prophet's downward ride left a residue of profound bitterness among rural westerners towards the Babylons of the East, where their hero had been dishonoured. In time, this resentment would fertilize the seeds of other historic grievances that would ultimately bring about the flowering of the distinctive, oppositional western political culture that shapes our national politics today.

The breakdown of monolithic Quebec and the marginalization of Diefenbaker's die-hard support into a relatively small voting bloc temporarily submerged the regional/racial axis that was and remains the basis of our national politics. Canada's urban–rural divide was more important in 1960s politics, as were demographic categories, especially age groups. The Liberals' next opportunity could come along either axis, through a renewed outreach to Quebec or with a concerted drive to consolidate the party's progressive credentials. The stage was set for something or someone to cement the coalition Pearson had laid out, but not quite glued together.

That something turned out to be the Centennial year and its defining episode, Expo 67, when our adolescent country discovered itself. And that someone emerged in 1968, when forty-eight-year-old Pierre Elliott Trudeau glided to the centre of the national stage. In journalist Richard Gwyn's memorable phrase, "Trudeau won because, if Expo had been a person, that person would have been Trudeau."

On December 14, 1967, Lester Pearson announced he would resign office. A leadership convention was swiftly set for April 4–6, 1968. The outgoing prime minister's desire for a Quebec-based leader was initially stymied when the most likely candidate, Minister of Manpower Jean Marchand, refused to run. Marchand recommended his friend, Justice Minister Pierre Trudeau, who had risen swiftly but quietly in the caucus since first being elected in 1965. Pearson was unsure, but soon gave up on finding a francophone alternative and began showcasing Trudeau, who announced his candidacy in mid-February. His fans among the media and the intellectual elites of Montreal, Ottawa, and Toronto weren't exactly Liberal organizers, but when Pearson "let a few friends know I was well disposed towards him," Trudeau soon found himself with the organization he needed.

No fewer than eight English-Canadian ministers came forward to run against him, but none had the stature to unite the others. When the voting ended on the fourth ballot on April 6, the convention had chosen Trudeau over St. Laurent alumnus Robert Winters 1,203 to 954. The well-established Liberals swiftly set about re-branding themselves in their leader's image. The Tories, who had briefly shot ahead in the polls after Nova Scotia premier Robert Stanfield succeeded Diefenbaker, had no chance to adjust. Trudeau called the election on April 23, the day after his swearing-in, for June 25.

The 1968 election was the first truly made-for-TV campaign, complete with the first televised leaders' debate (a boring, inconclusive affair). Everywhere his jet touched down, Trudeau was greeted like a rock star, complete with screaming girls and people straining to touch his sports coat. It was 1958 all over again, but delivered in mod style: Diefenbaker in Ray-Bans. Trudeau even had a Diefenbaker-style Vision, albeit more cerebral and less sweeping than the prairie messiah's. He spoke often about the "Just Society" he wanted to build north of the 49th parallel, promising full social, economic, and legal equality to all Canadians.

COME WORK WITH ME

April 1968
TRUDEAU SQUEAKS
PAST THE PARTY

On April 6, at the end of an emotional and bitterly contested four-ballot Liberal leadership race, the delegates gathered in the Ottawa Civic Centre narrowly choose Pierre Elliott Trudeau – an MP for only three years – over Bay Street darling and former Louis St. Laurent cabinet minister Robert Winters. In selecting Trudeau, the Liberals make a brilliant choice, at a stroke correcting their party's two biggest weaknesses under Pearson: a flat image and an inability to connect to Quebec. The dashing, effortlessly bilingual forty-eight-year-old Montrealer promises to cement the new Liberal coalition of urbanites and the young and to attach to it the energy and full support of post–Quiet Revolution Quebec.

From the start, Stanfield played the tortoise to Trudeau's hare. He crossed the country in a 1959-vintage DC-7 turboprop instead of a jet. His handlers sent him primarily to traditional events, dominated by motorcades on main streets and bean suppers in local arenas. In a campaign where Trudeau embodied the go-go spirit of Expo, Stanfield felt like a visit to the Royal Agricultural Winter Fair.

It didn't help Stanfield's cause that the most daring plank of his campaign platform was made of very soft intellectual wood: "the concept of *deux nations* not in the sense of two political states, but as a recognition of the country's two founding peoples: an English and French community with distinct cultural and linguistic backgrounds." "These ideas are difficult to express, but easy to distort," Tory backroom strategist Eddie Goodman later admitted. That's because *deux nations* was a slogan, not a policy.

Trudeau, in contrast, had thought through his approach to Quebec much more thoroughly. As the 60s progressed, the victorious quiet revolutionaries had split into two wings: radicals who favoured social democracy and, increasingly, an independent Quebec; and moderates, many of whom had gravitated to Ottawa. Stanfield's approach was to offer concessions to provincial moderates; Trudeau's was to tell Quebec's citizens to choose between separatism and Canada, *point final*. And when he spoke to his Anglo audiences of his attitude towards Quebec, he convinced English Canadians that this guy knew how to "*deal* with" the "Quebec problem."

When the votes were counted, Trudeau had won the majority that eluded Pearson and had gone some distance towards re-establishing Liberal dominance in almost every region. The Liberals' basically urban coalition expanded for Trudeau in English Canada, sweeping British Columbia and making strong showings in the urban centres of Manitoba, Saskatchewan, and Ontario. He took the Liberals over the top with 155 seats, compared with 72 for the Tories, 22 New Democrats, and 14 Social Credit.

Trudeau's majority triumph in 1968 completed the transfer – begun after 1958 – of the mantle of modernity and "progress" from the Diefenbaker party to the Liberals. The outcome of the campaign was never really in doubt, not with almost 80 per cent of the country's 21 million people living in the urban settings that were so fertile for the Liberals. The one-sidedness of Campaign '68 alone robs it of any true claim to greatness.

June 25, 1968
TRUDEAU SWEEPS
THE NATION

Trudeau's rock-star image and go-go campaign swamps the plodding efforts of Progressive Conservative leader Robert Stanfield. The Grits win 155 seats, the Tories 72, the New Democrats, still led by Tommy Douglas, 22, and the Créditistes 14. Canadians (young, urban, liberal-minded ones who wrote newspaper articles, anyway) were enchanted by Trudeau's style more than his substance, "the Mercedes sports car, the ascot ties and sandals. The racy reputation as wealthy bachelor surrounded by beautiful women. The academic achievements at some of the world's best universities. The judo brown belt, and acquaintance with yoga," to quote the usually buttoned-down (and Tory) *Globe and Mail*. Equally important, many believed that this ardent federalist from Quebec could satisfy his province's increasing demands for autonomy through a combination of French affirmation in English Canada and a tough attitude towards separatists in Quebec. It was the stuff political dreams are made of, brought together in a single compelling figure.

October 1970
OCTOBER CRISIS BEGINS
On October 5, members of an FLQ cell kidnap British trade commissioner James Cross. The subsequent kidnapping of Quebec's minister of labour Pierre Laporte soon leads Prime Minister Trudeau to invoke the War Measures Act. (Above) Canadian Army troops patrol Ottawa.

April 1971
LEWIS INHERITS NDP
Long-time party organizational mainspring David Lewis is elected leader of the NDP, becoming Canada's first, and so far the only, Jewish leader of a major national party. (Above) Lewis gets a victory kiss from his wife.

June 1970
VOTING AGE LOWERED
Amendments to the Canada Elections Act lower the voting age to eighteen. (Above) Student protestors.

As a somewhat sexier version of Diefenbaker's 1958 triumph, the 1968 election didn't change politics (another reason it cannot be rated a great one) from its post-Dief orientation towards leadership and vision. The election did, however, crown a singular collective episode in the country's existence. Much as every European of a certain age could remember years later the long, beautiful summer of 1914, so too can every Canadian now over fifty recall the quickening of our shared national life in those twelve months from the opening of Expo 67 to election night. Like all perfect things, it couldn't last. But for the generation of voters who lived through that heady, hopeful time, the 1968 campaign retains the luminous quality of a treasured memory.

Trudeau in power fell cruelly short of his advance billing. Despite a surge of popularity when the country rallied to him in the October Crisis of 1970, his remote, analytical style and aggressive implementation of official bilingualism created a severe backlash in English Canada. In the election of 1972, Trudeau and a coterie of professorial advisers ran a diffident, unfocused campaign whose wretched slogan, "The Land is Strong," unwittingly captured how out-of-touch the Trudeau Liberals had grown in office. On election night, October 30, the Liberals came in for a shock: initial results gave Stanfield's PCs 109 seats to the Liberals' 107, while the NDP vaulted to 31, and the

The
land is
strong

Vote Liberal

September 1972
CANADA SCORES!
On September 25, in Moscow, with 34 seconds to go, Paul Henderson puts the puck in the net and Canada over the top in the final and deciding game of the first Canada-Russia hockey series. *(Above)* Trudeau encourages Team Canada before the first game, played at the Montreal Forum on September 2.

October 30, 1972
STANFIELD COMES CLOSE
The final 1972 election results gave a narrow victory to the Liberals, 109 to the Tories' 107. But Trudeau hangs onto power with support from the NDP's 31 members. (The Créditistes hold 15 seats.) *(Above left)* Conservative Leader Robert Stanfield campaigning in Vancouver's Chinatown. *(Above right)* The Liberals' lousy slogan, "The Land is Strong," unintentionally captures the aimlessness of their campaign.

Créditistes retained 15. Many of Ontario's ridings and all of British Columbia's went against the Liberals, with a surprising number going to the NDP and its rookie leader, long-time party organizer David Lewis. (Had there been a fundamental issue at stake in the campaign, it could easily have been a great one.)

The next day, the count evened to 108 apiece, then 109 Liberal to 107 PC. Suddenly interested in such trivialities as smart politics, Trudeau arranged for the overt support of the NDP in exchange for a set of left-wing policy initiatives to be implemented over the two years of his minority government. Then in 1974, with this progressive legislative record in place, the Liberals engineered their own defeat over the annual budget and went to the people. This time, Trudeau turned on the charisma that had served him so well in 1968, campaigning alongside his beautiful young wife, Margaret, at every venue, rally, and contrived event the campaign pros he had banished in '72 could cook up for him. The dynamic Liberal campaign, coupled with Stanfield's ill-advised pledge to implement wage-and-price controls (which Trudeau trashed on the hustings but would cynically implement a year later), worked brilliantly. On July 8 Trudeau won back a solid majority of 141 to Stanfield's 95, just 16 for Lewis, and a dangerously low 11 for Caouette.

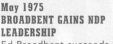

May 1975
BROADBENT GAINS NDP
LEADERSHIP
Ed Broadbent succeeds David
Lewis as federal leader at an
NDP convention in Ottawa.
(Above) Broadbent and fellow-
candidate Rosemary Brown, who
would place a strong second.

July 8, 1974
TRUDEAU REGAINS MAJORITY
With the help of his wife,
Margaret *(above left)*, Trudeau
leads the Liberals to a 141-seat
"solid majority." The Tories take
95 seats, the Créditistes 11, and
the NDP 16.

August 1975
TURNER QUITS
Finance Minister John
Turner *(left)* resigns
over long-running
policy differences and
power struggles with
Trudeau. With this last
of the Pearson era
players gone, it's
Trudeau's party now.

Beneath the ups and downs of Trudeau's first three elections, the tectonic plates of the Liberal coalition were shifting. The party of Laurier was slowly fading in western Canada while steadily regaining its hegemony in Quebec. By the mid-70s, the prime minister stood poised between an approach that seemed to emphasize the politics of ideas, especially in battling the NDP in Ontario and British Columbia, and a return to the traditional political playbook, in particular the Quebec Bridge. Canadians heard less and less about the Just Society and more and more about national unity – especially after the November 1976 election of a separatist Parti Québécois provincial government under René Lévesque. The nature of the times and of the men at the top of the Liberal Party were forcing it back to its roots as a regional coalition.

The Tories, under Joe Clark, their new leader since 1976, also stood poised between traditional regional politics and the politics of ideas and leadership. They consolidated their western regional base while staking a strong claim on economic issues and aggressively challenging the increasing power of the Liberal state in Canadian society, in a manner distinctly reminiscent of Dief's attacks on the Liberal power structure of the 1950s. By 1974 they had rebuilt their popular vote from

July 1976
MONTREAL HOSTS OLYMPICS
The first Olympic Games to be held in Canada kick off in Montreal.

November 1976
SEPARATISTS ELECTED
The separatist Parti Québécois under René Lévesque is elected in Quebec.

August 1979
FAREWELL TO THE CHIEF
Canadians line the route of the funeral train carrying John Diefenbaker from Ottawa home to Saskatchewan, following his death at age eighty-three.

its 1968 low of 31 per cent to a healthy 35 per cent and could reasonably hope for more – especially in Ontario – in elections to come.

As for the New Democrats, they weren't really in the regional game – their base of support was too small and concentrated. However, they were eager to grow and saw opportunity in the Liberals' post-1945 drift away from dynamic, progressive policies. In 1975 they selected as successor to the retiring David Lewis a leader almost twenty years younger than Trudeau, a bright, yet avuncular and homey MP named Ed Broadbent.

By the mid-point of Trudeau's third mandate, the Liberals were clearly vulnerable. The big forces in Canada were converging. Economic woes, western power, and Quebec separatism had all featured in elections since the early 60s, but each jockeyed now for centre stage as the final months of Trudeau's mandate ticked away. Which to run on? Economic ideas or the old politics of region? The next campaign would force the Liberals and the Conservatives to choose what kind of politics would shape the fights of the future.

HE STOOPS TO CONQUER

MAY 22
1979

FEB. 18
1980

PIERRE TRUDEAU

VS.

JOE CLARK

ED BROADBENT

ON THE SURFACE, the double-header, revolving-door elections of 1979 and 1980 appear to be little more than a personality contest between leaders: Joe Clark, the wimpy conciliator who won a minority in 1979, versus Pierre Trudeau, the arrogant gunslinger who came back in 1980. Seen this way, both fights appear as minor variations on the modern, leader-dominated, nationwide campaign pioneered by John Diefenbaker in 1957 and 1958 and reprised by Trudeau himself from 1968 on. Looking more closely, we see something deeper: a contest between two fundamentally different visions of the country. Trudeau stood for Big Ottawa: a central government with constitutional clout over the provinces and economic clout over Canadian and foreign big business. Joe Clark stood for Little Ottawa: a less centralized federation that he called "a community of communities" and a greater role for private enterprise in the economy. When Trudeau prevailed, so did his vision of Canada, elements of which continue as the law of the land to this day.

The leaders' duel and the tale of Ottawa's strong central government versus the community of communities are both well known. But there's another story these elections tell, a chapter in Canada's distinct saga of racial and regional conflict. The twin elections of 1979 and 1980 played out a brutal power struggle between Quebec and the West, with Ontario – the province with more seats than any other – holding the balance. This was a winner-take-all battle, with no means of reconciling the interests of the two combatant regions.

It wasn't supposed to be that way. After Diefenbaker swept to power it had seemed that Canadian politics would henceforth be organized around the questions common to all advanced democracies: the play of interests between capitalists and socialists, populists and elitists, urbanites and rural folk. Put another way, in the late 50s and early 60s it looked as though Canada's distinguishing political feature – the gnarly French Canadian fact – had finally been worked smoothly into the grain of a single national politics based on the clash of visions. But by the 1970s the wrenching politics of French versus English had returned in full force, with an out-and-out

Facing single-parenthood, Trudeau watches the Montreal Olympics with his son. Mayor Jean Drapeau pledged the '76 games "could no more have a deficit than a man could have a baby." They ran a deficit, along with the once-prosperous Canada.

separatist government installed in Quebec City and anger over official bilingualism raging throughout English Canada. In addition, the West had roared to life as a newly powerful centre of profound discontent within Canada. The racial axis – now called "the language question" – was back and, bound tightly to the axis of regional discontent in the West, it was bigger than it had been for thirty years. The complementary forces of Quebec separatism and western alienation threatened the broad consensus about Ottawa's dominant role that had underpinned the politics of national purpose for two decades. The twin elections that rang out the 1970s marked the end of that consensus and the beginning of a new period of tough regional struggle, more complex than before, that continues into the twenty-first century.

The return of the old politics of regional manipulation and linguistic rivalry, and the fading of the politics of national purpose, ushered off the stage the visionary leaders of the 1950s, 1960s, and 1970s. In their place came new men, armed with a formidable technological arsenal with which to fight the old regional battles. Joe Clark emerged triumphantly in 1979 as one of these new/old political operators.

Yet inside this Pandora's box of regional warfare lies a final, hopeful tale. A working plurality of voters effectively opted for a Constitution that completed Canada's passage from colony to nation, and with it a Charter of Rights and Freedoms that has transformed Canadian society. In 1979 Trudeau-the-Visionary tried to sell the Constitution and the Charter directly. He lost the election. In 1980, facing the extinction of his political dreams, Trudeau reluctantly took up the

weaponry of this new/old politics. To achieve his cherished vision, he became the kind of politician he had previously scorned. He stooped to conquer, running an overt, regional operator's campaign straight out of the old playbook, but winning the power he needed to make his national vision of the Constitution and the Charter a reality. It was quite a stoop, but quite a conquest as well. True, his achievements deepened the country's overt regional divisions. Yet, paradoxically, the vast majority of citizens are now united in their acceptance of his dream of human rights and individual liberty. Somehow, a divided electorate made the right choice.

The pre-writ campaign began on September 1, 1978, when Prime Minister Pierre Elliott Trudeau called a set of seven by-elections for October 16. They would coincide with eight others already called for the same date, making the October canvass the largest cluster of by-elections in Canadian history. The contests, from Halifax to Vancouver, were instantly dubbed a single "mini-election" by the media. Trudeau kept postponing the general election out of fear that he could not win it. Trudeau's mandate, his third, had gone badly, with mounting economic problems and the election in November 1976 of Quebec's first separatist government under René Lévesque. Trudeau almost called an election in July 1978, but the positive Liberal support was soft, so he delayed facing the people in the hope that the economy would improve and, with it, the party's standing. That had left a number of vacant seats which had to be filled. At the end of August, faced with the decision of calling a general election or playing for time, Trudeau had chosen the

"The Just Society is above all the right to work," protested Canadians in the late 1970s. Trudeau's soaring national dream for 1968 is dashed against hard economic reality.

NAME: Pierre Trudeau

PARTY: Liberal

ROLE: Prime minister since 1968. Brilliant, charismatic, aloof, facing divorce, lost soul.

latter, leaving him no option but to face the mini-election.

Trudeau had no choice but to campaign personally. The entire government – the cabinet, the caucus, and the party, even the civil service – was viewed by the public as a simple extension of the prime minister. In his early days in power, Trudeau had struggled against this centralizing tendency. He ran his cabinet meetings "like a graduate seminar"; as one of his ministers later recalled, "on most questions he would not force his views on the meeting." Another wrote, "he wanted the team to govern." But the years had taken their toll, and Trudeau had come increasingly to rely on unilateral action. The most famous example of this increasingly autocratic behaviour involved Jean Chrétien, Trudeau's new finance minister, in the summer of 1978. Chrétien had delivered a free-spending budget in April at the PM's direction, only to flip on the television one day in August to find his boss announcing $2 billion in spending cuts because "Canadians are fed up." There was no way for the Liberals to downplay Trudeau in 1978; the Liberals were Trudeau – at least as far as the public was concerned.

Unfortunately, this meant that if October 16 went badly, the public would link Trudeau with the defeat, damaging the aura of invincibility that had been his strongest weapon since he had shot to power in the spring of 1968. Trudeau was entering very choppy political waters. Hanging around into the fifth year of a

mandate offended the public's taste for an election every four years. Such delays tended to presage defeat, and the air of impending doom was heavy in Liberal Ottawa in the summer and fall of 1978. The public polls generally showed the Liberals behind – sometimes by as much as 10 per cent. Governments everywhere were in trouble. Prime Minister James Callaghan's Britain staggered towards its strike-bound "winter of discontent." To the south, a beleaguered President Jimmy Carter gave televised addresses about the "malaise" gripping America. And in the bungalows and ranch-style houses of middle-class Canada, a decade's worth of economic "stagflation" – stagnant growth plus high inflation – had created a powerful current for political change.

Once begun, the Liberal mini-campaign went badly – and the problem was Trudeau. Loyal Liberals refused to come out and work while he was leader. Rallies went awry. At an event in the critical swing riding of York-Scarborough, an Italian Canadian – from one of the Grits' most stalwart voting bases – took the mike and said, "I respect you and I know you are my prime minister … but I think it is time you stepped down." The loss of confidence in Trudeau was underpinned by the sputtering economy and the prime minister's seeming lack of concern. His mind was on other things than Canadian families' struggle to make ends meet. Trudeau's best approximate understanding of that struggle would have been from the analytical briefings of his close friend Michael Pitfield, the clerk of the Privy Council and the country's top civil servant. In Pitfield's view, "the mid-1970s saw a classic explosion of inflation, a blowout of expectations followed by a fierce battle for shares. It had been building for decades. It had to come." The fatalist in Trudeau – the man who saw the forces of capitalism flagging around the world, narrow regionalism and xenophobic nationalism rising at home, and reason itself collapsing in the break-up of his own marriage to Margaret – may well have thought there was little he could do in the face of Pitfield's bleak prognosis. Besides, it wasn't his top priority; what he really cared about was winning the upcoming Quebec referendum on separation.

On October 16 the government lost every one of the thirteen English Canadian seats up for grabs, winning, predictably, only the two Quebec constituencies. A riding-by-riding analysis made it all the worse. Losing an ethnic bastion like York-Scarborough or, worse, the Franco-Manitoban enclave of St. Boniface, which had been Liberal with one exception since 1925, spelled real trouble. Over at his office on Parliament Hill the leader of the opposition, with eleven wins under his belt, was jubilant. As reporters eagerly sought his reaction, the thirty-nine-year-old Joe Clark, a physically awkward Albertan with the pallor of a career backroom politico, glowed preternaturally in the spotlight.

It was hard to believe that this uninspiring rookie had just whupped the heavyweight champ – albeit in an exhibition match. Just two years earlier, in 1976, Clark had run to succeed Robert Stanfield as Tory leader and won with a model "everybody's second choice" candidacy. He'd been the MP for the Alberta riding of Rocky Mountain since 1972 and a paid party staffer before that. Clark's political operator's background made him the polar opposite of the academic visionary Trudeau. He was a product of the murderous backroom politics of the Tory Party in the 1960s: the internal wars that ended with Diefenbaker's ouster in 1967 and the recriminations that followed. These experiences had

(Right) Everybody's second choice, Joe Clark wins the 1976 PC convention with tactical skill, not charismatic appeal.

taught Clark to place an extremely high value on party unity. He drew on his struggles and his own characteristics – a fine mind but zero personal magnetism – to develop a political approach that emphasized the workmanlike, incremental knitting of consensus among more forceful personalities and factions.

Clark's approach was to out-listen, out-smart, and out-work his flashier rivals. He was naturally drawn to a deep study of the new political technologies, particularly polling, which had become infinitely more precise and complex than the crude yardsticks of the 1950s and 1960s. "I arrived in the House of Commons at the same time as [modern] polling," said Clark, "which caused us to understand the electorate in its component parts. Polling made us realize that there were deliberate as well as charismatic ways of appealing to the larger electorate and knitting the country together." A Joe Clark armed with modern polling was like some high school science geek who'd just discovered a secret chemical formula for dating girls. "I'll show those charismatic guys on the football team!" But, of course, he wouldn't just use this power for his own

NAME: Joe Clark

PARTY: PC

ROLE: Leader since 1976. Heads fractious caucus. Gets a shot at the title. If he loses, he's gone.

gratification. Oh no, he'd use the formula so everyone could score, "knitting the country together" into one happy heap of deliberately arranged component parts.

Clark is too Tory to admit it, but he'd probably found the formula in the back of a dusty old volume entitled "How to Succeed at Politics Without Charisma" written by a batty old alchemist named William Lyon Mackenzie King. Clark could relate not only to King's style of leadership but also to King's obsession with reconciling conflicting regional groups. Clark came from an alienated region that wanted its particular needs addressed before signing onto encompassing national visions from Ottawa. During the Pearson/Trudeau years the four western provinces had grown more populous, and more wealthy, as Vancouver boomed and as Alberta's

Joe'll show those eastern bastards!

CORRALLING THE EAST

As an Albertan, Clark presented himself as the heir to Diefenbaker's western populist crusades. In truth, he was always seen more as Ottawa's man.

Funny, I thought he was one of those eastern bastards ...

and Saskatchewan's oil and gas discoveries of the 1950s and 1960s came on-stream in concert with soaring world prices. A great chunk of the country, with its own aspirations and a distinct political culture, was suddenly rich and powerful beyond its wildest dreams.

Yet the power of the new West was barely felt in Ottawa, where the region's presence was concentrated on the back-benches of the official opposition and the NDP. The true power of the new West was instead displayed in the region's gleaming, steel-and-glass provincial capitals. Western assertiveness showed up in fierce struggles with the federal government over taxes, revenue sharing, and program financing. The power and anger of the West was felt most surely whenever Ottawa tried to introduce some big new Liberal program that would centralize power, give all the boodle to Ontario and Quebec, replicate the hated National Policy of Sir John A. Macdonald, and screw the West once again. Scratch a national vision, most westerners believed, and you would find some dirty deal to feather the central Canadian nest.

Indeed, as the long years and tough times of the 1970s chipped away at Trudeau's 1968 egalitarian vision of the Just Society, it became increasingly clear what a Quebec-centred proposition the whole idea really was. Trudeau's embrace of Canada from his Quebec milieu involved the conscious assertion of "French power" on the national stage. From the imperative of defeating separatism came an important by-product: the need for a powerful, federalist Ottawa to serve as a counterweight to the gravitational pull of Quebec City and separation. French power was also good politics for the Liberals. Their Quebec Bridge was sturdy; Trudeau never won less than three-quarters of its seats. And he relied upon it; from 1972 on, between

40 and 50 per cent of his caucus had been made up of Quebec MPs.

With the passage of time, Trudeau's visionary approach to governing looked to many like, at best, a scam to bribe Quebec into staying in Canada and, at worst, just old-fashioned abuse of power. Regional economic development became Liberal pork barrelling. Social welfare came suspiciously to resemble vote buying. Official bilingualism looked like a plot (particularly in the English-speaking West) to put Quebeckers in charge of everything, from air traffic control to the detested post office. Conservative sage Dalton Camp encapsulated this view in 1979: "One could quantify the dimensions of the day's crises by counting the 'dese' and 'dose,' the casual damns, hells, my gods and goddams emerging in curls of smoke from the mouths of Frenchmen often in their shirtsleeves … For a decade, all the troubles in Canada had appeared in a French accent." Even Trudeau's concern over national unity began to look like just another sleazy Quebec-oriented way to keep power. "Who will speak for Canada?" was the national visionary's rhetorical question at the heart of Trudeau's speeches in the late 1970s. His withering depiction of Clark as "head-waiter to the premiers" stemmed from the same commitment to a national purpose led by Ottawa. When, however, he proposed the patriation of the Constitution – removing the last vestige of colonialism by ending Britain's sole legal authority to amend the Canadian Constitution and placing it in Canada's hands –

NAME: René Lévesque

PARTY: Parti Québécois

ROLE: Since 1976, Quebec's first separatist premier. Preparing for referendum on separation. Trudeau's nemesis.

THE NDP: CANADA'S VELVET UNDERGROUND

Rocker Lou Reed's epitaph for the Velvet Underground's first album – "Not many people bought it, but everybody who did started a band" – is the story of the federal NDP. The party was far more influential than electable, thanks to the elites it attracted – academics, writers, media people, union leaders – allowing it to shape the national agenda over four decades. Ed Broadbent (seen here campaigning in a Toronto by-election) was determined to translate influence into power.

it seemed to many just another pre-referendum sop to *la belle province*.

The fight between Clark and Trudeau went beyond the clash of visions, regions, or languages. It was a struggle between two fundamentally different approaches to national politics. Clark represented the original Canadian tradition of regional brokerage, pioneered by Macdonald and expanded by Laurier and King. Trudeau represented the new politics of unified national purpose, haltingly pioneered by St. Laurent and perfected by Diefenbaker. Their disagreement was therefore total: Clark saw Trudeau's vision as a highfalutin cover for an interregional scam; Trudeau saw Clark's brokerage approach as a petty operator's chicanery fluffed up to resemble a political principle.

For the public, the choice between these two approaches was bound up in the figures of the men themselves. Trudeau put his finger right on the heart of the matter a few weeks after the mini-election debacle. In a December 1978 press conference, his first since the by-elections, he faced reporters' questions about his own political future. "Considering the alternatives," he reasoned, "I think I'm the best man." (To Liberals with memories, the remark must have ominously echoed St. Laurent's "I don't know where you will find anyone who can do any better.") By 1979, leadership had almost come to overwhelm all other aspects of the electoral game. Ever since Diefenbaker, the leader had been the prism through which voters considered things political, from visions and policies to regions and races. This tendency had accelerated wildly as television came to dominate all other media in the 1960s.

In 1957, 63 per cent of households had a television set. Twenty years later, that penetration was nearly total. Television wasn't much good at giving facts and figures; it wasn't even all that great at telling a story. But TV could really give the viewer a sense of character. One look at Trudeau on the nightly news and you could tell what he stood for: French power, elite rule, big ideas. One look at Clark would fix his coordinates as well: Anglo, an average Joe with workaday concerns. Other characteristics came through the little box as well, such as "arrogant bastard" or "bumbling turkey." These repeated up-close views of the leaders had become the means by which voters' political decisions were made. This emphasis on individuals over parties made for a high degree of volatility under the seemingly smooth surface of Liberal rule. Voters went to the polls nine times from 1958 to 1980, electing five minority governments out of eight and never once awarding two consecutive majorities. In this volatile environment, campaigns mattered. In the late 1970s the rule of thumb was that a really good writ-period campaign could shift 8 to 10 per cent of the vote, more than enough to turn an election one way or the other. More than ever before, it was leadership that counted on election day.

In developing their strategies as the election approached, the Liberals, the Conservatives, and the New Democratic Party each believed they could work the politics of leadership to their advantage. The NDP's forty-two-year-old leader had gotten off to a fairly respectable start since winning the leadership in 1975. Broadbent was a political science professor who fit easily into the union-hall culture of his Oshawa, Ontario, riding and possessed a fresh, likeable personality that gave him a knack for relating to ordinary voters.

For the NDP, the 1979 election was a chance to restart the march towards power that had recently been going backwards. The party had been created in 1960 to put new life in the prairie-based CCF by formally linking it to the industrial trade union movements of Ontario, Quebec, and, to a lesser extent,

British Columbia. Since then, while Quebec had remained deaf to its message, the NDP had come tantalizingly close to breaking through in Ontario and had even succeeded in forming a government in British Columbia. But the heady days of 1972–74, when the party had held the balance of power in parliament and driven Trudeau's minority government's progressive agenda, now seemed all too far away. Broadbent's minimum goal for the 1979 campaign was to return the party to the position it had held under Lewis, from which it could resume its long march towards becoming the dominant party of the left. Like Britain's Labour Party, he wanted it to be part of a rational, ideologically organized two-party system, with capital represented by the Tories, labour by the NDP, and the squishy-centrist Liberals left out in the cold.

In 1979 the omens for an NDP comeback looked reasonably promising. The political situation in the country was similar to that of 1972: a pooped-out Trudeau regime faced a Tory Party headed by an uninspiring leader. The "universe" of potential NDP voters included few who would consider voting PC, so the party needed to waste little time attacking Joe Clark. During the campaign, Broadbent's job would be to accuse Trudeau of betraying the hopes of the working people who had voted for him in 1974 by abandoning good, progressive (read NDP-inspired) policies for bad, "old-line" pro-capitalist ones. There was no need for Broadbent to get too far into constitutional minutiae, or even into Clark's less-technical attacks on arrogant centralization. All he needed was a sharp, uni-dimensional attack at Trudeau's disappointing record on pocketbook issues. That would take voters straight to that nice, new-Chevy kind of guy from right next door, Oshawa Ed.

The Tories' opportunity was much greater, but their problems more complex,

NAME: Bill Neville

PARTY: PC

ROLE: Clark's main operations man. Puts Murray and Gregg's strategies into action. Disillusioned former Liberal.

especially when it came to the all-important question of leadership. On the face of it, Clark was not much of a leader, but that's exactly what Allan Gregg intended to make of him. The Tories' new pollster was an improbably longhaired rock'n'roller who would have been a nonentity in the Conservative Party of old – some college kid with a computer. But the advance of polling techniques had made those who understood the new tools extremely powerful. Gregg later told of one old pro's lament that, "in the old days, if you wanted to know what your prospects were in, say, Alberta, you called Old Bob and he'd tell you. Now some pollster will tell you 'Bob's full of shit,' and that's that." Old Bobs had dominated the Tory Party. Gregg told them all they were full of shit, and he was usually right.

Gregg's polling numbers showed two basic facts: the public was very disappointed with Trudeau's failings, and yet people retained an underlying optimism despite the difficult times. "People were wondering what had gone wrong," Gregg recalled. "But they still believed that increasing prosperity was the norm." And if these conditions didn't obtain, voters believed that the national government could change its policies to make prosperity and progress return. So why wasn't this economic fix happening? Why hadn't the Liberals set things right? The answer that folks gave to Gregg was "because Trudeau doesn't care." On one of the central questions by which modern voters measure a politician – "Does he care about my prob-

lems?" – Trudeau placed third behind NDP leader Ed Broadbent and Clark. He didn't care about the economy, didn't care about the little guy, didn't care about ordinary people. Gregg's data suggested that voters would accept a weaker leader than Trudeau as long as they believed he did care, devoting his attention to the economy and bringing back the good times they expected.

Gregg reported with his polling data to Lowell Murray, Clark's closest personal friend and topmost adviser, a fastidious intellectual and career Nova Scotia Tory apparatchik who had been Clark's boss in various party roles before the young Albertan ran for parliament. While Gregg knew the public opinion numbers, Murray knew how well the data might fit in with party policy, the egos of the caucus members, the forces and factions among the grassroots, and the million other

NAME: Lowell Murray

PARTY: PC

ROLE: Clark's chief strategist. Cerebral Halifax intellectual. Determined to outsmart the Liberals.

details that transmit political strategy into electoral results. The third member of Clark's team was Bill Neville, a former Liberal who excelled at both strategy and the nuts and bolts of running a party. Clark's backroom players got along well with the leader, who was hardworking and took advice – even tough stuff that wasn't pleasant to hear – with good cheer and a determination to do better the next time.

A simple equation drove the Tory message: Canada minus Trudeau equals a better future. The party ad men cleverly worked the message into a slogan: "Give the Future a Chance."

NAME: Allan Gregg

PARTY: PC

ROLE: Pollster. Strategic guru. Smart-aleck kid with a com-puter.

It put the focus on a decade of Trudeau's rule, and conveyed a kind of battered-but-cheerful optimism that synched with the mood of the voters the PCs wanted to reach.

The slogan and the strategy were great as far as they went, but that was no farther than the Quebec border. If Clark was lucky, he might win a handful of seats inside Trudeau's fortress. To win a majority of the House of Commons' 282 seats, therefore, he would have to thrash the Liberals in English Canada, taking nothing less than 68 per cent of non-Quebec ridings. A Conservative victory would have to be an Anglos-only affair, delivered by the West, by cleaning up in the swing ridings of Atlantic Canada, and, above all, by creating a tide of victory in Ontario.

The genius of the Tories' master plan was that it set a trap the Liberals could not avoid. Trudeau's economic record was mid-dling at best, and he had no plans to develop a credible economic platform to run on. The Grits would thus have no choice but to rely on the prime minister's leadership qualities to do the job for them. That would mean building the campaign around his personality alone, putting him in the spotlight, which was exactly what Clark, Murray, Gregg, and Neville wanted. If the issue was Trudeau, the Tories could use his very profile against him by pointing out his economic failings and seeming lack of concern. It was the political equivalent of a judo flip: turning the force

of an opponent against him to bring him down.

There was only one major weak spot in the Clark strategy: it depended entirely on his opponent being the unrepentantly arrogant Trudeau. And in December 1978, as the House went into its Christmas recess, the prime minis-ter had not made up his mind about his future. He told his top political advisers he would decide over the holiday: stay or go. Most expected him to quit, yet when he returned from vacation he announced to his staff that he would stay on. And to make sure he would face no backbiting, he extracted a promise from the Liberal Party's national executive council that it would back his leadership. He even added a crucial caveat – he intended to fight the election on national unity. Anyone got a problem with that? No one spoke up, and suddenly the leadership and the basic strategy were settled.

Why did Trudeau stay? In retrospect it seems an odd choice. Borden and Pearson had weighed similar odds, and chosen to go out on their own two feet, turning the party over to some younger legs. In fact, he didn't have much choice. Regardless of their leader, the next election did not look winnable for the Liberals. Whether Trudeau stayed or went, the loss would inevitably be blamed on him. At least by staying, he avoided being pinned with the tag of "quitter," a most unappetizing prospect for this prickly, proud personality. Exiting wasn't really an option, which meant that the only question was *how* to go down: scrabbling to win or seeking a kind of moral triumph in glorious defeat. Trudeau chose the noble gesture. He would rage against the fail-ing of the light – the dimming of his personal vision for a united Canada.

In choosing to stay on as leader, Trudeau had presented his party with an impossible paradox. Liberals genuinely believed that he was their strongest suit, and most were

JUDO FLIP

THE TORY PLAN TO TURN TRUDEAU'S STRENGTHS INTO WEAKNESSES

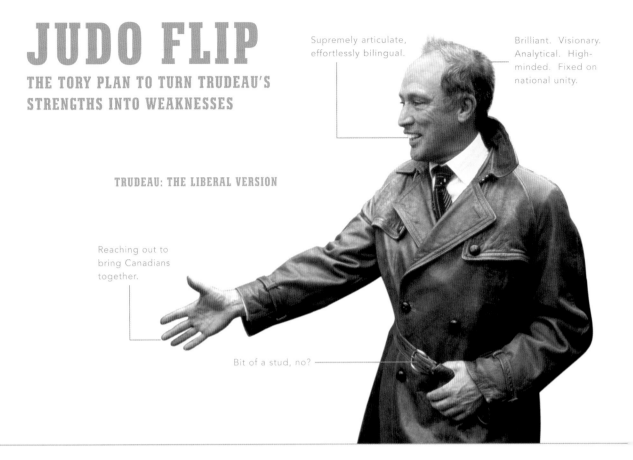

Supremely articulate, effortlessly bilingual.

Brilliant. Visionary. Analytical. High-minded. Fixed on national unity.

TRUDEAU: THE LIBERAL VERSION

Reaching out to bring Canadians together.

Bit of a stud, no?

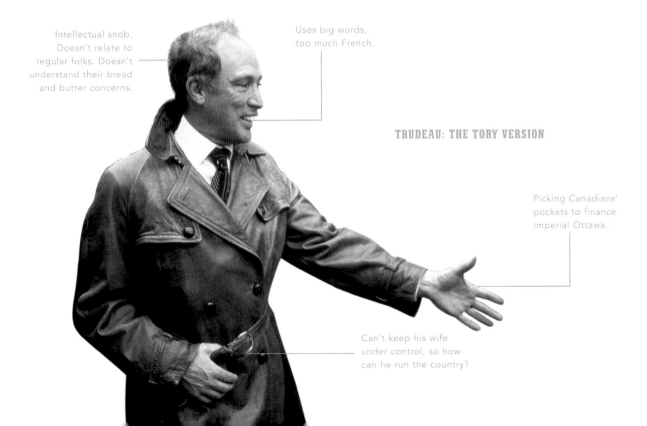

Intellectual snob. Doesn't relate to regular folks. Doesn't understand their bread and butter concerns.

Uses big words, too much French.

TRUDEAU: THE TORY VERSION

Picking Canadians' pockets to finance imperial Ottawa.

Can't keep his wife under control, so how can he run the country?

NAME: Keith Davey

PARTY: Liberal

ROLE: Campaign co-chair responsible for English Canada since 1973. Senator. Organizer. Ex-Toronto ad salesman.

terrified at the prospect of facing an election without him. (The few who wanted him gone were either too afraid or too respectful to give him a push.) Yet this towering figure, so obviously made of stronger leadership timber than Clark, was clearly losing to the lesser man. The paradox only deepened in February 1979, when Clark went on a much-publicized tour of the Middle East and Asia to meet foreign leaders and acquaint himself with foreign policy concerns. The trip quickly degenerated into a PR nightmare of lost luggage and timing screw-ups. Clark himself performed badly, making dopey remarks such as "Jerusalem is a very holy city" and asking an Indian peasant, "What is the totality of your land?"

The Liberal strategy team, led by Jim Coutts and Keith Davey, prayed that the public was simply peeved with Trudeau and had merely sent a traditional by-election message of protest the previous October. Both principal secretary Coutts and Senator Davey, chairman of the national campaign committee, were professional political operatives who had come a long way since their debut as players in the Pearson years. Davey was a former salesman of advertising space on radio who had got his political start during the 1950s in then-Tory Toronto, risen swiftly as Pearson rebuilt the party with new men, and been elevated to the Senate when Pearson finally squeaked into 24 Sussex. Coutts, slightly younger and more cerebral, was a former Pearson staffer who had become a Harvard-trained management consultant after his boss's retirement. Both sat out Trudeau's

shaky first mandate, but were soon approached by the prime minister, chastened by his near defeat in 1972, to take charge of his political fortunes in English Canada. (Trudeau minister Marc Lalonde would look after Quebec.)

Coutts and Davey were delighted to be invited back into the centre of the action, and, by delivering a resounding victory in the 1974 election, they cemented positions with Trudeau even more commanding than they had enjoyed under his predecessor. In the process, they became true believers: the ambitious Coutts was profoundly impressed by Trudeau's charisma, and Davey was in awe of his intellect. Martin Goldfarb, an exuberant exponent of the science of polling, backed up Coutts and Davey, as did broadcasting lawyer

NAME: Jim Coutts

PARTY: Liberal

ROLE: Principal secretary to Trudeau since 1975. Runs PMO. Link between government, party, campaign. Ex-management consultant.

Gerry Grafstein, who ran the advertising, visual image-making, and general communications sides of the Liberal campaign.

Much as Coutts and Davey were talented professionals, they could not manage their man as Murray and Neville directed Clark. Their preferred strategy would have been for Trudeau to soften his "negatives" by showing that he actually did care about the economy and the plight of middle-class Canadians, thereby cancelling out Clark's advantage as a caring politician. Then voters could decide how to vote on the basis of which leader was smarter, or tougher, or made them prouder on the world stage. But Trudeau simply refused. He insisted on talking unity and the Constitution, which ranked low on English Canadians' list of national priorities. His handlers knew that by putting his agenda ahead of everyone else's, he would highlight his own worst negatives, thereby walking into the Tories' trap. But they also knew that their man didn't care; he didn't want to talk about inflation and fish prices. "I understand what you are saying," he sighed to his aides when told no one wanted to hear about national unity, "but my God, what does it say about this country?" Able to stride the national stage only one last time, Trudeau decided he would stand, or more likely fall, on the constitutional issue he really cared about. Deep in the political gutter, he decided to reach for the stars.

When the thirtieth parliament resumed in January after the winter recess, everyone could see the Tory strategy starting to work. The atmosphere of those last weeks before the

election call was nicely encapsulated on February 7, 1979, one of those rare occasions when Clark, usually eager to showcase the talent around him to make up for his own thin leadership image, asked the lead-off question in Question Period. Even more rare was the presence of Prime Minister Trudeau to answer him.

Clark began. "Mr. Speaker, in the absence of the Minister of Finance, my question is to the Prime Minister." The Tory leader spoke with staccato precision, in tones that suggested a knock-off of John Diefenbaker. "The Prime Minister will know that on Monday the Minister of Finance revised upwards his estimate of inflation this year … I wonder if our Prime Minister can tell us whether the government is also now revising downward its forecasts of real growth?"

Trudeau rose to answer. Cheers and whoops broke out on the government benches

MESSAGE: "I CARE"

In contrast with the remote, unity-obsessed Trudeau, Joe Clark's campaign strategy stressed his shared concern for voters' pocketbook issues, especially inflation.

as their champion waded in. The opposition hollered back their scorn. One Liberal shouted, "This is what a leader looks like, Joe."

Trudeau addressed Clark's question directly. "I have some difficulty understanding it myself, Mr. Speaker. I was not in the House, I did not hear the speech of the Minister of Finance and I was not briefed on it."

A perfect little Clark–Trudeau moment. The opposition leader asks a dead-earnest question on the number one national issue, the flagging economy. With a shrug, the prime minister admits that he isn't on top of the file, and advises Clark to address his question to the appropriate underling at a more convenient time. Trudeau's implication is clear: this isn't prime minister stuff, Joe; it's only the economy. Clark would have known a straight answer was unlikely, but that didn't matter. In fact, Trudeau's failure to answer illustrated exactly the point Clark wanted to make: the PM doesn't care about the average guy's money woes.

With this exchange – the last time the two would cross parliamentary swords before the election – and in a thousand other little mini-dramas and statements acted out over the three-year pre-writ period, Clark gained exclusive ownership of the economic issue – beach-front real estate in the election to come. (This kind of preparatory activity had now come to be known as "positioning" – a product marketing term. The concept is ancient – think of Laurier laying out his pro-British credentials a year before the 1896 election. But the word was new, introduced into political parlance by the Madison Avenue guys who ran Richard Nixon's 1968 campaign, and written about in Joe McGinniss's bible, *The Selling of the President: 1968*, which was eagerly read by every Canadian backroomer thereafter.)

If Trudeau was going to play the election that way, the Tories could start measuring the drapes for their new offices. The Liberal team knew that, but, unlike Clark, Trudeau was very selective about advice. Sometimes he followed it; sometimes he just said no, full stop. What could you do? The guy was going through a divorce. He had won three elections. He was prime minister. End of discussion.

Still, if Trudeau insisted on talking unity, perhaps his handlers might just be able to build a decent campaign around the positive aspects of his leadership: courage, decisiveness, and that impressive intellect. Maybe he could turn the strength of the Tory attack back against

Joe McGinniss's best-selling 1970 manual on how to market a US politician – widely read and followed by Canadian political operators.

them. So they came up with the slogan, "A Leader Has to Be a Leader," and ordered large-sized posters depicting a lone Trudeau, thumbs hooked in his belt, smirking at the camera and daring the viewer to take him on. The poster image became known as the "gun-slinger" pose, destined to join the Trudeau iconography alongside Pierre the pirouetting imp, the "noble savage" canoeist, and half-a-dozen other visual personae that defined the passages of his career.

The evening of March 26, 1979, though cold and clear, carried the promise of spring as Prime Minister Trudeau was driven in his black Cadillac limousine from Rideau Hall to the National Press Theatre facing the Parliament Buildings. Before a room packed with reporters, he announced that he had asked Governor General Ed Schreyer to call an election for May 22. The call surprised

Wild thing. Her marriage to Pierre on the rocks, Maggie bares all – in books, movies, and photos.

many observers. No one was really sure why the prime minister decided to go when he did. The Gallup poll showed the Grits a point ahead of the PCs at 39 per cent to 38 per cent, but the Liberals' private polling showed they were around ten points behind the Tories in English Canada – putting a renewed majority well out of reach. Many had come to expect that Trudeau would wait until the fall, testing the constitutional limits of his mandate. Some speculated that the impending April publication

of Margaret's tell-all memoir, *Beyond Reason*, might have induced him to bundle all his troubles into one two-month period, get them over with, and go on with his life. There really was no answer, but it can be stated with assurance that political calculation had little to do with this election call. Trudeau apparently approached the decision in the same way he had decided to run again on the unity issue: he put the personal above the political, believing that as long as he fought for what he believed in, he could retain his dignity even if he went down to defeat. If anyone ever doubted that Pierre Trudeau was an unusual politician, the wholly unstrategic timing of the 1979 election call made it clear how very odd a leader he was.

The prime minister's televised statement that evening was low-key, befitting the sombre mood in Ottawa. He spelled out five challenges facing the country: national unity, a "decade of economic development," social policy, fiscal discipline to fight inflation, and a secure energy supply. His remarks left no doubt which he considered most important: "First, there is the challenge of ensuring the unity of our country. The government you elect will have to cope – perhaps just a few months after the federal election – with the Quebec referendum." It's easy to picture the reaction in living rooms across English Canada. Husbands and wives, their kids asleep in bed, watching the news, listening to Trudeau's message, then turning to each other. National unity, eh? A pause. A sigh. "You won't believe what I paid at the gas station today."

By the late 1970s Canadian federal election campaigns had assumed the pattern that more or less prevails to this day. The traditional eight-week writ period (today it's as brief as thirty-five days) was broken down into three phases, demarcated by the types of marketing techniques the parties were permitted to use and the methods by which they would try to communicate a winning message to voters. This marketing-driven campaign highlights how much the art of electioneering had evolved since Laurier's day, when organization was paramount. Even organizational guys like Davey now worked hard to master the rudiments of polling and advertising. The elections of 1957, 1965, and 1972 had all been decided during the writ period. With a possible swing of 8 to 10 per cent of voters changing their minds during the campaign proper, voter persuasion had become all-important. A local riding organizer could still mount a convincing case that a close riding would be lost without doing some basic tasks such as voter identification. But new mavens like Allan Gregg and Liberal pollster Marty Goldfarb would tell those Old Bobs to get lost. One could win a persuasive campaign with a weak organization; but absent a persuasive campaign, no amount of organization could possibly deliver the goods.

Campaign directors had two basic ways of reaching voters: earned media and bought media. "Earned media" means the communication of the campaign's message through news coverage of the leader's tour. "Bought media" means paid advertising. During the campaign's first phase, lasting about four weeks and often called the "phoney war," the parties focused on earned media through coverage of the leader's tour. Once the four-week blackout imposed by law was lifted, the second phase began with the deployment of paid television and radio commercials. The third phase was the home stretch, in which the networks broadcast tour events every night, the parties put their commercials into heavy rotation, and major media outlets stepped up their schedule of published public opinion polls.

Tough guy. Trudeau's strengths are indelibly captured here in *Weekend* magazine's famous January 1978 "gunslinger" photo.

As the 1979 campaign got under way, there was also talk of a televised leaders' debate. Since the lacklustre debate of 1968, the idea had fallen into disrepute. But the most recent US presidential campaign in 1976 had seen the first TV debate in sixteen years: a critical encounter in which President Gerald Ford stumbled badly before challenger Jimmy Carter and may well have lost a close election in the process. Canada's broadcasters were ready to take another chance, so once the writ was dropped the parties dispatched high-level negotiating teams to hammer out debate rules, production requirements, and timing. They ultimately agreed on the date of Sunday, May 13, almost exactly the point at which the home stretch would begin – with the big, wind-up rallies scheduled by each of the two major parties to generate momentum for the final ten days.

There were two keys to victory in the writ-period campaign: hammering home a winning message and winning the leadership sweepstakes. The requirements of the first had been clear for years – set up your message through careful pre-writ positioning, then relentlessly broadcast the message from that position throughout the campaign. That's what Diefenbaker had done in 1957 with his pre-writ message of democratic, populist outrage. Now Joe Clark would remind voters over and over again that he shared their workaday economic concerns and Trudeau didn't. Trudeau, for his part, had never bothered with this kind of strategizing. His message of unity from before and after the campaign began was consistent, but it wasn't really part of a strategy. It was just Trudeau continuing to talk unity, with Coutts and Davey hoping he'd do it so well that voters would decide they just couldn't stomach replacing their man with a loser like Clark or giving their votes to the untried Broadbent.

Given this leadership imperative, winning the image wars was critical, on both fronts

of earned and bought media. Ever since Diefenbaker, campaigns had focused very tightly on the leaders, a focus that grew more and more intense as television newsgathering became cheaper and more comprehensive. In 1979 Canadian voters got to see the party leaders speechifying, working crowds, moving in and out of events, answering reporters' questions, and even "taking time off" with their families. (Trudeau refused to do family events, holding as sacred his private time with his sons.) This increasingly intense coverage of the leaders forced the campaign teams to devote increasing energy to feeding the cameras' voracious appetite for "good visuals." The Liberals and the Tories obliged by mounting complex, occasionally even amphibious events – Trudeau's Halifax boat ride in week six and Clark's waterborne entrance at an outdoor Montreal event in week seven – to create compelling television.

But while the TV cameras lapped up the pretty pictures, they loved most of all to feast on the candidates themselves. How a leader walked, the way his face moved, what his eyes did, how his voice sounded became vital measures of the man's ability. What came out of his mouth mattered as well, along with how restrained he stayed when faced with hecklers and aggressive reporters, and how well he used the two languages – all contributed to voters' understanding of the man and were taken as demonstrations of his capacity to lead. The quality of the tour itself had also become a measure of leadership ability, on the doubtful logic that good baggage handling indicates sound public policy skills. Lousy logistics could kill a tour, as they had in Clark's nightmare foreign junket of January and February 1979 by taking the earned media story away from Clark hobnobbing with world leaders. A well-operated tour, in contrast, contributed to a leader's aura, bringing all the pieces together, as in a successful speech or the graceful lifting of a smiling baby for a well-received kiss.

Both elements of the campaign – message and performance – were crucial. In 1979 the Tories were counting on a strong message to offset their weakness in the leadership sweeps. The Liberals were hoping for the reverse. The goal of both campaigns was to use message and performance to sell voters on a desired "ballot box question" (another imported Americanism). If the Tories could herd enough electors into the polling station asking themselves "Do I want four more years like the last eleven?" they would win. But if folks went behind the little cardboard screen asking "Which of these two guys has got the moxie to lead?" the Liberals were back in.

The Tory tour therefore had two imperatives: stay on message and avoid logistical and personal screw-ups that would make Clark's performance the issue. On his first day of campaigning, March 28, Joe Clark did a nice job of both delivering his strategic message and coming across like a leader. He began with a swell send-off at Ottawa airport from two hundred cheering supporters. That afternoon in Thunder Bay he was received enthusiastically by five hundred Progressive Conservatives – a good turnout in a union town represented by Bob Andras, a heavyweight Liberal cabinet minister. The event was well arranged and ran smoothly – no lost luggage or baffled peasants. Clark looked confident and delivered his lines impeccably, going right to the heart of Trudeau's weakness: the prime minister's economic record and its relationship to Canadians' sense of missed opportunity. Blasting the Liberals, he said: "Their record speaks for itself. What I intend to do is to remind Canadians of the great potential of this country, because Canada has more potential than any country in the world … We are going to build on the strength of Canada that they have been wasting." In a press confer-

ence, he added: "This is where the campaign begins – with the record of the Trudeau government. Mr. Trudeau obviously wants to avoid that subject … Canadians will know what a Trudeau decade has already done."

Clark was no spellbinder. He moved clumsily, with stiff chops of the hand to emphasize his points, and delivered his lines with a solemn, eyes-over-the-glasses intensity interrupted by his contrived, barking laugh. He was obviously trying to conform to some Coles Notes entitled "How Prime Ministers Act," and thus came across as a phoney. But phoniness alone isn't enough to sink a leader, and Clark wasn't making any major mistakes. His tour ran like clockwork. He delivered his lines. And his message was right, even if it came through the wrong medium.

Meanwhile, Pierre Trudeau, the right medium with the wrong message, went straight off course in week one. The Liberal strategy permitted him to talk unity, but the way he delivered it must have made his handlers wince. The same day that Joe Clark talked national potential in Thunder Bay, Trudeau went on an open-line radio show in Toronto and accused a caller of being "almost treasonable" for rating unity as a low priority. Clark jumped on the remark that afternoon in Kitchener. Speaking to reporters, he said: "At the risk of being called a traitor by the Prime Minister of this country, I think it [national unity] is an important issue, but there are other issues."

This kind of rapid response, made possible by improved technology, had accelerated the pace of the campaign well beyond that of 1957 or even 1968. Dief had not seized until his speech the next day upon St. Laurent's Maple Leaf Gardens catastrophe, when a young heckler was knocked off the stage. Clark's pile-on appeared side by side with Trudeau's gaffe on the evening news. The immediacy and drama at which television excels drew producers towards

GO, JOE, GO! GO, JOE, GO! GO, JOE, GO!
ON THE CAMPAIGN TRAIL

If the Tories could have avoided the campaigning part of Election '79, they would have. Clark on the campaign trail was physically awkward and looked uncomfortable – even in friendly settings like with his daughter, Catherine (at the Calgary Stampede, *above*), an interested oil worker *(right)*, or tartan-clad cheerleaders at a pre-election rally near Barrie, Ontario *(opposite top)*. Faced with so bad a show, the crowds, like the one that came to hear him in Hamilton, Ontario *(below)*, sat on their hands. Clark (as in this badly staged photo, *bottom right*) underwhelmed at performance art, but he understood the game's new rules. Had he remained in the backrooms, he would probably be remembered as another Dalton Camp or Allister Grosart. Instead, he reached for the top.

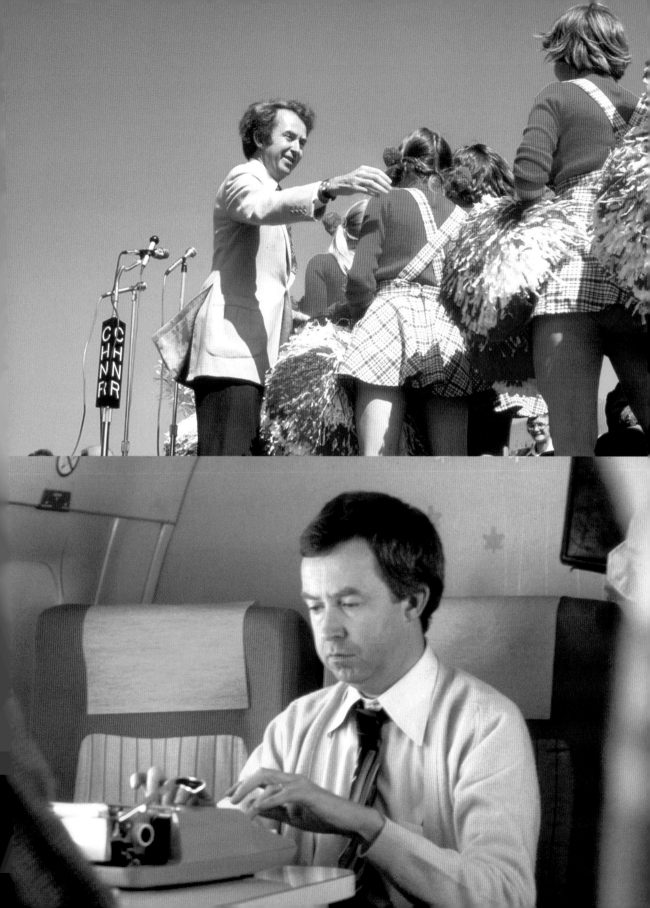

these call-and-answer stories and away from other aspects of the fight. The result was an even tighter TV focus on the leaders and their tours, one the newspapers also followed.

That Saturday a *Globe and Mail* columnist parodied Trudeau's concerns, breathlessly reporting an outbreak of "traitorous talk" and "the names of two of the ringleaders in the conspiracy to destroy Canada" by airing other issues: Joe Clark and Ed Broadbent. Trudeau could pose as a gunslinger and assert leadership all he wanted, but if he couldn't act decently to Canadians, he was playing right into the Tories' hands.

Both of the major campaigns used the tour to outline key policies that supported their broader positioning. These frequent announcements were known to backroomers as "Gainesburgers" – after the dog food – prefabricated bits of policy substance to be stuck in front of the hungry newshounds on the tour. Following this logic, Clark rolled out bread-and-butter economic policies through the campaign's first month: tokens of concern for middle-class families such as tax deductions for mortgage-interest payments and property taxes, exemptions from the capital gains tax for shares of Canadian-owned companies, tax incentives for employee share-ownership, and a $2 billion tax cut. The list of strategically targeted goodies went on and on, pictures in a storybook about Joe Clark's concern and underlying optimism.

The Tories had an economic policy all right. One could argue that they had three: one for their anti-spending fans of the hot new "monetarist" economics; another for their regional development fans from poorer ridings; a third for their small businessmen who abhorred deficits. The resulting contradictions and fuzziness didn't matter. What mattered was that Clark would talk economics, and he would do so in a way that showed he

cared, while Trudeau didn't. You judged the book by its cover – or its coverage.

These kinds of policies were hard to fathom if you believed that Tories were cruel fascists in blue suits who woke up wondering how they might feast on the bones of the poor that day. They also puzzled and frustrated the economically conservative members of the Tory Party. Too bad for those Old Bobs. The hard fact that policy wonks need to understand is that most real people don't think in terms of left and right. And there are a lot more of these real people than there are economic conservatives. So if Joe Clark wanted to win, he would have to do as Diefenbaker had done: leave aside the stereotypical Tory positions and use policy as a tool to illustrate his priorities to voters, rather than as an ideological program for governing to please his core supporters.

So went the campaign through the four weeks of phase one. Under the election rules of 1979, the second phase, with its "bought media," began with twenty-nine days to go before the election. Modern consumer advertising techniques had supplanted the static, talking-head broadcasts of the Diefenbaker era, yet the song remained the same as in the Chief's day: pound home the message from the pre-writ campaign. The best of the Tory ads showed the Canadian flag being lowered down a pole, while a voice-over reprised some of Trudeau's mid-mandate calls for Canadians to lower their expectations. The ad clinched its point when a meaty hand firmly halted the downward hauling of the flag, while the voice-over trumpeted the Tories' determination to fulfil Canada's potential. The Liberal ads soldiered along with their message of Trudeau's leadership ability, backed up by the gunslinger visual. Like the Liberal leader himself, the ads were more stylish than their PC counterparts but did nothing more than assert Trudeau's well-known strengths.

They simply rammed the Grits' pre-writ pseudo-strategy: the message that raw leadership ability was the election's only issue.

The Tory commercials were viewed as hard hitting by Canadian standards of the day. One spot scrolled a series of callous Trudeau quotations over slowed-down footage of the prime minister in the House – obviously on a very bad day – looking semi-coherent, perhaps drunk. These weren't, however, nearly as tough as contemporary American spots. In the New York Republican primary of early 1980, senatorial challenger Al D'Amato attacked the capacities of his venerable opponent, Jacob Javits, by showing a Javits look-alike keeling over on camera. D'Amato won. (It's easy to feel nostalgic for the gentler style of our old campaign ads. There's nothing quite so distasteful as today's thuggish, lowbrow attack ads that hammer away crudely on some obvious poll-driven theme. These kinds of spots drive voters away, which is much too high a price to pay in the long run.)

By the beginning of phase two in mid-April, the Tories' internal polling showed that the crucial battleground of Ontario was going Tory by 39 per cent to 31 for the Grits, with the NDP static at 17 per cent and 15 per cent still undecided. If Clark could protect this Ontario lead against a Liberal surge among the undecided, he would be prime minister within a month. Anticipating victory, he gave his most substantive policy address of the campaign – a full-dress speech before Toronto's blue-chip Empire Club on April 19 entitled "Building a Nation." The Tory leader broadsided Trudeau's idea of what a constitution and a charter could mean for Canadians' sense of identity: "We are a nation that is too big for simple symbols. Our preoccupation with the symbol of a single national identity has, in my judgment, obscured the great wealth we have in several local identities." He held up an

COMING DOWN

This Tory TV ad symbolized Trudeau's calls for Canadians to lower their expectations as a lowering of the flag. In the final frames, a strong hand halts the decline as the voice-over asks for a Tory vote.

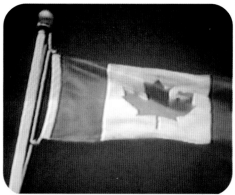

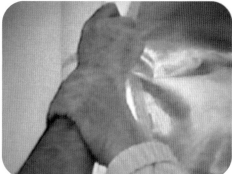

alternative, stating flatly: "Governments make the nation work by recognizing that we are fundamentally a community of communities."

Clark didn't really spell out what he meant by community of communities in policy terms, that day or any other. That wasn't the point. Clark's speech was a manifesto for the construction of a coalition of regions pitted against the very idea of a national vision. Clark was turning away from the national Conservatism of Macdonald and Diefenbaker towards the approaches of Tupper and Borden, who had sought to use the country's divergent power-blocs as stepping-stones to power. "Community of communities" was Clark's way of telling PQ supporters that he didn't support Trudeau's threatening their provincial French-language law, Bill 101, and of encouraging westerners to rise up against Trudeau's insistence that air traffic control be conducted by bilingual personnel. Phrased in the neo-conservative language of smaller government and spoken with a western populist twang, "community of communities" sounded very much like a rational, small-is-beautiful approach to running Canada.

It was certainly good politics. The community of communities Clark would build may perhaps be best understood as an electoral constituency of constituencies: western populists, Bay Street capitalists, perhaps one day Grande Allée nationalists. Clark had developed his "deliberate approach" to winning elections, minus a unifying vision, into a philosophy of government.

By the mid-point in late April, the campaign had taken no clear shape and it was difficult for any ordinary voter to tell who was winning. An April 23 CBC poll showed the Tories ahead of the Grits by only 2 per cent, 40 to 38, much the same as they were at the outset. A follow-up poll taken two weeks later, just before the debates that opened phase three, gave statistically equivalent results. Behind

the scenes, however, Martin Goldfarb's private polls indicated that the Liberals' strategy of playing to Trudeau's leadership strength was actually working, bringing soft, usually Liberal voters back into the fold. Tory pollster Allan Gregg noted a similar rise. Voters were starting to think seriously about whether to make Joe Clark prime minister and were having trouble reconciling themselves to the idea.

The Liberals may have been staging a comeback, but they needed to go a lot further – and fast. Even a popular vote tie spelled Conservative victory, given the number of Liberal points that were "wasted" on super-majorities in Quebec. The public polls gave no particular impression of momentum. The

NAME: Martin Goldfarb

PARTY: Liberal

ROLE: Trudeau's pollster. Toronto market-research whiz imports and improves latest US polling science.

Liberals needed to generate some oomph in the campaign's final phase, commencing around the fast-approaching debate.

The Grits planned a barrage of events to close out phase two and provide the boost for the campaign's final ten days: on May 9 an evening mega-rally at – where else? – Maple Leaf Gardens; on May 10 a major speech in Montreal; and on Friday, May 11, an outdoor lunchtime rally in downtown Toronto. The climax would come on Sunday night, May 13, in Canada's second televised leaders' debate.

By 1979 the Big Toronto Trudeau Rally had become a fixture of Liberal campaigns. On May 9, seventeen thousand sweating Liberals packed the hockey shrine, settled into their seats, and waited for the show to begin. Beneath an immense suspended rack of lights, a massive stage occupied one end of the hall's floor. The Liberal organizers had pulled out all the stops and pressed the city's political buttons with a touch unsubtle enough to get the message of momentum out across the vast country. One warm-up group, the hard-rocking Downchild Blues Band, projected the not-so-hidden message that voting Trudeau was the young, hip thing to do; "the sensuous Lisa DalBello" not only hit the ethnic button but sang a winking little ditty called "You Do It So Well," to remind the "women's vote" of this prime minister's unique appeal. Sylvia Tyson and the Good Brothers added some rural twang for the country music crowd in the out-lying farmland north of Steeles Avenue. After two hours of warm-up, and the introduction of the entire Liberal candidate roster in Metro's thirty-five ridings, the crowd, decked out with balloons, placards, noisemakers, T-shirts, and dumb political hats, were ready for the man. "Fellow Liberals," said the Ontario campaign chairman, Senator Royce Frith, "the prime minister of Canada, Pierre Elliott Trudeau." The lights fell. A spot-lit Trudeau, in a tan summer suit and a wide, striped tie, advance men out in front and behind, came striding swiftly down an aisle running the arena's length, shaking a hand here, nodding there, before at last bounding onto the stage.

Standing before the massive crowd, with his candidates ranged behind him and a giant Canadian flag rearing up as a backdrop, Trudeau launched into his twenty-five-minute address. Much of it was standard campaign fare: "We are engaged in a great battle," "we are winning it in Toronto" – red meat for the converted. The main message came after about twenty minutes, when Trudeau dolloped out his Gainesburger for the night. "We are asking," Trudeau thundered, "for a mandate from the Canadian people in every part of Canada to take action to meet with the premiers one

more time to seek consensus of the premiers to bring the constitution back with an amend-ing formula … And failing that, we will bring the constitution back and consult the Canadian people in a referendum, and that's the way we will do it." He termed the country's inability to amend its own Constitution without Britain's consent Canada's "shame." He repeated with a new urgency his pledge that the Constitution would include a bill of rights to protect all Canadians, "no matter where they are, no matter what colour, race or creed."

Some Gainesburger. More like a twenty-kilo bag of Alpo. Trudeau was proposing direct unilateral federal action, against provincial wishes if necessary, to patriate the Constitution with a charter. It was a his-toric promise, connecting directly to some of the country's most basic questions. For mid-twentieth-century policy-makers, conserv-ative and liberal, the core of the national agenda was to set atop the country's founda-

Trudeau enters Maple Leaf Gardens on May 9, 1979. Tearing Toronto away from its Tory roots was a key achievement of the Pearson–Trudeau era. Rallies like this one celebrated the Liberals' metro-politan dominance and sought to perpetuate it.

THE LAST DAYS OF DISCO

TRUDEAU ON THE CAMPAIGN TRAIL

A LIBERAL CANADA

Trudeau's '79 campaign was a farewell tour –
and it felt like one. As usual, it projected the
party's studiedly modern values, as at this rally
(*top centre*) in Vancouver, with its untraditional
banner, podium-free stage, and Danish-
designed end table. The new face of Canada
was projected as well, such as this multicultural
crowd in Toronto (*centre right*). But any hopes
of smooth sailing for Trudeau (*bottom right*, in
Halifax harbour) foundered when the campaign
encountered real people (*bottom left*, on
Halifax docks) and their quotidian grievances
(*top left*, in Victoria). Canada was changing,
and shaking off Trudeau in the process.

TRUDEAU:
FOR
STRONG
GOVERNMENT

PIERRE:
you light up
my life!

tions three more mighty building blocks: first, a welfare state to contain the class conflicts arising from industrial transformation; second, the final keystones of political independence from Britain; and third, a common national identity to transcend the ancient divides of race and language. The welfare state had been set in place by the end of Pearson's rule. Independence was harder. The Constitution could still be amended only with the consent of the British parliament, and several attempts to "repatriate" it had failed for lack of unanimity among the provinces.

The call for the third keystone, a single identity, had been sounded clearly by Diefenbaker, whose unhyphenated pan-Canadianism was made concrete by acts such as the extension of full voting rights to Status Indians in 1960 and his Bill of Rights of the same year. Yet the writ of Diefenbaker's bill ran only in the federal jurisdiction. (As one legalist wag had put it, "The Bill of Rights is great, as long as you didn't live in one of the provinces.") Diefenbaker's rights-based citizenship was an appropriate response to the rapidly changing facts of Canadian life itself. The national identity of Canadians no longer lay in village and parish. Indeed, as interprovincial migration increased, it no longer necessarily lay in the home region. For the rootless newcomers in the great cities – be they Canadian-born or landed immigrant – their relationship with Canada was direct, unmediated by tribe, language, or region.

Trudeau understood and supported the core agenda of social justice, independence, and human rights. His 1968 campaign for the Liberal leadership and the subsequent election campaign as prime minister brought together his passion for the welfare state and for human rights in the idea of the Just Society. "The Just Society will be one in which personal and political freedom will be more securely ensured than it has ever been in the past …

The Just Society will be one in which those regions and groups which have not fully shared in the country's affluence will be given a better opportunity … The Just Society will be a united Canada where equality of opportunity is ensured and individuals are permitted to fulfil themselves in the fashion they judge best." The Constitution, with its Charter, was the last, best hope of the Just Society; in Trudeau's words, it "sought to strengthen the country's unity by basing the sovereignty of the Canadian people on a set of values common to all." Yet Trudeau's hopes for forging a common, rights-based citizenship for French and English Canadians – an alternative to the separatists' narrow, ethnic nationalism – were caught in the broader constitutional impasse. Now, on the brink of losing office, the prime minister was hoping against hope that his profound conviction of the rightness of his dream and his bold call to roll right over any recalcitrant provinces if they would not climb aboard might re-energize his faltering comeback and give his dream a new lease on life.

Trudeau wasn't really a great orator – certainly no Laurier or Diefenbaker. If anything, his speeches were reminiscent of Meighen's, exercises in precise, deadly logic and mockery of his opponents. What lifted the crowds was Trudeau's intense charisma, the now-shy, now macho postures he could strike effortlessly and in a graceful succession. His best moments didn't, in fact, involve words at all, but were instead visual tableaux: the athlete making a half-gainer in the Florida pool in 1968, the family man swinging his son, Sacha, while walking through Vancouver airport in 1976, the gunslinger icon now at the centre of this 1979 campaign. His speeches were more hit-and-miss. When the charisma was turned on, the words lifted themselves off the page and carried the crowd with them. In the self-penned speech's first half, the crowd had responded with what the *Toronto Star* attested were "huge standing ovations." But on an off-night when the physical magic wasn't present, all that remained was the cold logic, as if a metaphor for the missing magic that had gone out of the Trudeau experiment. So it was on May 9 at Maple Leaf Gardens; energy fled the hall as the constitutional details rolled on. These Liberals knew what sold and what didn't; they did the door-to-door canvassing, answered the phones, and held the coffee parties. The address concluded with less applause than when it began. It was more warmly received in Montreal the next day, but when Trudeau returned to Toronto on May 11, there was no feeling of momentum. Elegy was in the air that day, even as Trudeau's voice echoed beneath a fifteen-storey Canadian flag hung from the black towers of the Toronto-Dominion Centre. Office workers munched on their lunches and clapped, but it all felt a bit forced. On May 12 the *Globe and Mail* once again parodied Trudeau's unity obsession, mock-reporting that "all Toronto is in a constitutional frenzy … Down Yonge Street came a crowd of 100,000 shouting: 'Two, four, six, eight. Help the PM patriate.' … I feared there would be violence … when four amending-formula demonstrations converged at the Royal York Hotel." Trudeau's attempt to boost his campaign from the plateau on which it was stuck was failing, leaving Sunday's debate as his last possible chance to achieve lift off.

In 1979 Trudeau's team figured that any debate would help drive the election onto the question of who was the stronger leader. For their part, Clark's crew believed that their boy would exceed public expectations of his performance. Broadbent, the least known of the three leaders, likewise hoped to do better than expected. Going into the Ottawa studios of the CTV network on Sunday night, the odds were stacked against the prime minister. Absent a defining moment or a knockout blow,

debates tend to be scored on the basis of expectations, and everyone knew that Trudeau was a terrific debater badly in need of a big win. This set up an expectation that was impossible to meet, let alone exceed. If he fell anywhere short of destroying Clark, he'd be seen as having failed. Clark, in contrast, needed only to perform better than the loser most people thought he was, "going the distance," to quote the then-recent hit movie *Rocky*, with the heavyweight rhetoric champ. Only if Trudeau forced a knockout blow or Clark tripped over his shoelaces could the Liberals hope to parlay their edge on the leadership question into the momentum they needed to catch the Tories.

The parties had agreed on a ninety-minute format, divided into three thirty-minute bouts. The coin-toss set the stage for a sequence that worked elegantly towards a fitting climax: Clark versus Broadbent; Broadbent versus Trudeau; then Trudeau and Clark squaring off. In the first segment, Broadbent came away a clear and surprising winner, convincingly attacking the Tory leader on his nose-stretching economic program. "We haven't tried," declared Broadbent, "in my view, to trick the people of Canada and say, on the one hand, 'we will increase the deficit now,' but at the same time … say you would have a balanced budget." In the second round, Broadbent and Trudeau went at each other with the common-room rigour of the ex-professors they both were. Broadbent looked a bit nervous but fought well. Trudeau came across as diffident, even bored, occasionally easing back and relaxing on his stool while in combat.

When the crucial bout at last began, CTV's Bruce Phillips put leadership front and centre, citing public concerns that Clark was "weak and vacillating" and Trudeau "dictatorial." Trudeau responded first, rattling off a smoothly devastating recitation of Clark's wobbly skating on the prime minister's favourite issue. "Mr. Clark said in October that if Quebeckers voted 60 per cent in a referendum on sovereignty-association, and the question was reasonably clear, he would sit down and negotiate. And by December he was saying that he wouldn't negotiate – he would just talk. And in January he said he wouldn't do either and by March he was saying he wouldn't sit down and talk if they voted clearly to get out of Canada ... In all these examples you seem to be changing your mind all the time. If there's a bit of pressure, you change your position." When Trudeau finally stopped cuffing him, Clark weakly joked, "I was afraid I'd have to go through this half-hour without ever having to raise my voice," then quickly and prissily added, "and of course I'd never do that in anger." It looked as though the contender was on the ropes, weakly protesting his drubbing to a bored referee.

But soon Clark found his courage, drilling back at Trudeau in a staccato monotone that finally rang with anger. "If there has been one fundamental political disease in the last eleven years, it is the sense that the government is going one way and the people are going another way – that there has been government by an isolated elite. That has been aggravated very materially by the weakening in the power of Parliament ... Over the years there has been an appropriation of power to Ottawa, to the Office of the Prime Minister, that I think should not be there." It was as though the ghost of Diefenbaker had blown in from the West of Clark's boyhood to hover over him in his hour of trial, excoriating yet another arrogant Liberal for trampling "the rights of the people in parliament."

In the end Trudeau's mocking, world-weary intelligence was only pricked by Clark's indignation. During the debate's dying moments the prime minister jabbed and poked the Tory leader mercilessly, torturing him on

TELEPOLITICS 101

Even before the cameras roll for Canada's
second televised leaders' debate, the hardworking Joe Clark does what he's been
told to do: look relaxed, confident, prime
ministerial. NDP leader Ed Broadbent plays
along, carefully studying his notes for his
big-league debut. Contemptuous of this
contrived spectacle, Trudeau makes no
effort to conceal his boredom.

the weaknesses of his constitutional position and his inability to command the support of his fellow Tory premiers. Harried to the edge of a knock-out, Clark was almost literally saved by the bell.

Trudeau had clearly mauled Clark, but he had failed to inspire viewers with his own qualities or to destroy Clark. The media and the post-debate polls agreed that the Liberal champion had not scored the decisive blow he needed, that Broadbent had won it on points, and that Clark had finished a poor third. Agda Davies, an undecided voter interviewed by the *Globe and Mail* for reaction to the debate, said that "Trudeau was clever, [but] he was always defending himself ... Clark struck me as being a non-person." Yet Clark's main message – that Trudeau wasn't concerned about Canadians – was borne out by the prime minister's generally disengaged performance. Even a tired Trudeau was still clearly the more commanding performer, but he looked as though he didn't care any more.

Not a lot of people sat through the debate broadcast, certainly not enough for anyone to say that the country formed a complete judgment of the performance. It was enough, though, for voters to understand that Trudeau hadn't really done Clark in. What mattered was that Clark had survived, winning a kind of technical victory that presaged an indecisive, technical win on May 22. The confrontation seemed to have a minimal impact on the polls. The final published poll, released in week eight, showed the PCs with 41 per cent, the Liberals at 40 per cent, and the NDP at 16 per cent. Despite the closeness of the numbers, and the Liberals' success in tying the PCs in Toronto, the poll found that the Tories were ahead in every region except Quebec. That put the PCs well ahead in the anticipated seat count. Trudeau was still the overwhelming choice as most competent leader, but leadership ability wasn't the main issue – one in five voters said they were switching their

Gritterdammerung. May 22, 1979, felt like the end of the road for the Liberals, a watershed as profound as 1957. From far left to above right: Clark's victory speech fills the big screen at the Liberal wake in a ballroom of the Château Laurier in Ottawa; Keith and Dorothy Davey and protégé Gordon Ashworth watch glumly; Jim Coutts *(left)* grits his teeth and bears it; Trudeau, dapper in defeat as in victory, goes gently into that not-so-good night.

votes from last time because "it's time for a change" or they "dislike Trudeau." As the day of decision approached, it was clear that the Tory strategy had prevailed. Clark and his team had successfully turned Trudeau's strength against him, winning by putting the prime minister's "negatives" at the centre of the campaign.

Tuesday, May 22, found Pierre Trudeau awaiting the end in Ottawa, while Joe Clark had returned to his hometown of High River. Across Canada, starting at 10 a.m. in Newfoundland, 11.5 million people voted, a heavy turnout, featuring an unusually high number of new voters at 15 per cent (a testament to the surge of immigration to Canada that would become a hallmark of the Trudeau years). By 9 p.m. Eastern, the Ontario results were in and the election was called: PC minority.

Trudeau, watching the returns at 24 Sussex with Coutts and several other aides and friends, was urged by some to hang on and not concede

until the last votes were counted. Perhaps he could hold onto power with NDP support. After all, he was far ahead in the popular vote (and would finish the night with 40 per cent, to the PCs' 36 per cent). But when the BC numbers came in shortly after midnight, Ottawa time, they showed that Clark had won almost 70 per cent of the coastal province's seats, pushing the final total to PC, 136; Liberal, 114; NDP, 26; and Quebec's Ralliement des Créditistes, 6. It was finished.

At midnight Trudeau headed over to the gloomy Liberal campaign reception at the Château Laurier. In his concession, he spoke of "sham, drudgery and broken dreams." Instead of rousing his troops to pick up and fight a new day, the best he could muster was a watery promise that "we'll see victory in the not-too-distant future." It seemed like the end of the line for Canadian Liberalism. The leader's speech suggested an early exit for him at least. All those accumulated economic woes, all those extinguished hopes for Canada and for individual Canadians, all that failed promise since Expo 67 seemed to come home that night. An era had closed.

A thousand miles to the west in High River, Joe Clark accepted the cheers of the hometown crowd. He had done the impossible, coming from nowhere in 1976 to take down a living political legend in just three years. It was a triumph for the Little Operator That Could over the man who had defined the politics of national vision for a generation of Canadians. Trudeau had sought vainly to bridge the chasms that separated the country's regions through his vision of an equal citizenship under a charter of rights and freedoms. Clark had accepted the political divisions of the country, concentrated all his resources on the regions where he could win, and worked them to his advantage, accumulating breakthrough elements of Ontario support on the back of the PCs' western base. He'd reached those voters through effective policy positioning in the pre-writ marathon and by staying on message during eight weeks of campaign performance.

As Allan Gregg explains it now, "like-profiled Liberals who gravitated to the Tories" provided the PCs' Ontario margin. Decoded from strategist-speak, he means that voters in a variety of demographic groups who had always supported the Liberals decided to give the PCs a try. "The ridings we picked up in '79 weren't much different economically or socially from the ones we'd always held. The only difference was that people in the new ridings we won had traditionally thought of themselves as 'insiders' and therefore Liberals." In the 1979 election, "the bank manager switched sides." In places such as Mississauga and London these "insiders," who usually voted Liberal, joined with generally Tory-voting "outsiders" in smaller-centre ridings such as Peterborough and Barrie. Clark and his team offered econom-

ically disappointed Canadians a promise to better their lot. These voters turned away from Trudeau and his constitutional priorities and went with the team that shared their concerns.

The Tory brain trust had pulled off an impressive feat. In an age of leadership-dominated politics, it had managed the election of a man with a very weak leadership profile by turning Trudeau's leadership strengths against him. To be fair, Trudeau had cooperated in his own demise. It is far from certain that Clark would have beaten Trudeau if the prime minister had bothered to make nice about the economy, and it is not at all clear that the PCs could have bested another Liberal leader if Trudeau had returned from Jamaica in January 1979 with his resignation in hand. The election was a close one: a match-up of flawed performers and uninspiring messages that drifted along to a somewhat inconclusive finish.

Yet, somehow, the Tories let their half-measure victory delude them. This misunderstanding can be forgiven. A kind of closing-time music floated across the country that night. All the pundits agreed that the Western world was "going conservative" and that liberalism was in retreat. Margaret Thatcher had just come to power in Britain, while Jimmy Carter's administration was sinking visibly in the United States. Within days, Clark announced his intention to "govern as though I have a majority."

Clark understood that he had taken only the first step. If he wanted to govern on a broader base and for more far-ranging purposes, he would need to include Quebec. He imagined he would repeat Diefenbaker's two-step to majority power by governing with his Anglos-only minority, then inviting Quebec to come in for its share. He believed his community of communities approach, soft-pedalled during the campaign, could appeal to moderate nationalist francophone Quebeckers as much as

PLAYBOOK V

This one is a variant on the third basic play in my imaginary political playbook, the Populist Rush, invented by Diefenbaker in 1957–58. Clark played the populist as best he could. Step one was to harness the West's growing hostility toward Ottawa. Step two was to tap into the sense in Ontario and Atlantic Canada that the elitist Trudeau was out of touch and didn't care about the average guy's everyday concerns. Clark's English-only Populist Rush – essentially a repeat of Diefenbaker's 1957 strategy – likewise produced a minority government. Only if a leader could execute step three and get Quebec to join the rush (Dief in 1958) could the play yield a majority win.

POWER SHIFT

TRUDEAU'S BACKROOMERS

Trudeau relied heavily on unelected advisers, including those gathered for this 1974 campaign victory photo. A few notables: Principal Secretary Jim Coutts (front row, second from right); organizational maven Senator Keith Davey (back row, second from right); communications guru Senator Jerry Grafstein (back row, third from right); polling wizard Martin Goldfarb (back row, fourth from right).

CLARK'S FRONT-BENCHERS

In the campaign, Clark vowed to restore the power of elected members. In office he concentrated power in an "inner cabinet" of key ministers, including John Crosbie (front row, left), Flora MacDonald (front row, third from left), Ray Hnatyshyn (back row, second from right), and Sinclair Stevens (back row, fifth from right).

it did to provincial-rights Albertans. He saw a provinces-first coalition emerging, with Albertans and Quebeckers agreeing at least on devolution of power from Ottawa. He believed he could unite the country with his gentler methods. He thought he could fulfil the old western promise of remaking national politics along the principled lines that pitted the populist provinces against the Ottawa elite. Quebec's moderate nationalists would surely come along for that ride, along with the free-market crowd on Bay Street who also wanted a smaller Ottawa.

If successful, Clark would emerge from this realignment as an odd new hybrid of national visionary and regional operator, raising his regionalism to the level of a national vision. He disdained the old dominance of one region (Quebec) by asserting what he believed was the common goal of all regions – to humble an overweening Ottawa. Like St. Laurent or Dief or even Trudeau, he would unify the whole country around his idea – in this case his community of communities – leaving unrepentant Liberals to flail on nostalgically for the Big Ottawa he had dismantled. Clark was reaching, straining mightily, to become a nation-builder.

The sorry tale of Joe Clark's interregnum need not be retold here in detail. Simply put, Clark and his team made one colossal error: they forgot that a minority parliament is, by definition, a pre-writ campaign. The new prime minister repeated the chain of errors that Mike Pearson had made on the opposition benches in January 1958: underestimating the possibility of a snap election and making too many politically risky decisions on the assumption that there would be no need to explain them anytime soon. You can forgive a career diplomat like Pearson for forgetting he was in a pre-writ campaign; but for Joe Clark, a lifelong politico who knew his parliamentary history, there's just no excuse.

Clark began his tenure assuming he could govern securely for eighteen to twenty-four months. This view arose mainly from the obvious disengagement of opposition leader Trudeau, who took a long vacation that summer, then ambled diffidently through the beginning of the fall session. On November 21 Trudeau finally announced he was leaving politics. The Liberals, who had been forming up into leadership camps for six months, began preparing for a late-winter leadership convention. Clark's confidence was further bolstered by the rest of the opposition; it was difficult to imagine twenty-six New Democrats and six Créditistes agreeing on anything, let alone getting together with the Liberals to topple the government.

While the opposition dragged out Trudeau's departure, Clark turned his attention to governing. This task proved unusually difficult, in no small part because of the contradictions that arose from his piece-by-piece coalition-building in preparation for the 1979 campaign. Prime Minister Clark, now-Senator Lowell Murray, and his Chief-of-Staff Bill Neville found themselves trying to reconcile the largesse of mortgage-interest

NAME: Peter Lougheed

PARTY: PC

ROLE: Alberta premier since 1971. Lives off oil and gas revenues. Wants Clark to let Alberta sell oil at high world prices.

deductibility (Hello, Brampton) with the calls for fiscal discipline (Good morning, Bay Street), or seeking to square privatizing the state-owned PetroCanada oil company (Howdy, Calgary) with many of their voters' instinctive nationalism (G'day, Halifax Centre). Other initiatives simply bumped up against a complex world unimaginable in opposition. Clark had to reverse himself twice on an ill-advised plan to move the Canadian Embassy from Tel Aviv to Jerusalem (Shalom, six ridings in Montreal and Toronto).

Energy policy was Clark's worst headache. The government's attempts to negotiate a move towards world prices for domestic oil split his delicate regional coalition, pitting western producer-province MPs against those from energy-consuming provinces in the East.

NAME: Bill Davis

PARTY: PC

ROLE: Ontario premier since 1971. Lives off artificially cheap Alberta oil and gas. Wants Clark to keep the price low.

His attempts to broker a compromise failed to please anyone, leaving Alberta's Peter Lougheed grousing about Clark's sellout of his home province's interests and Ontario's Bill Davis muttering loudly about the failure of Clark to stand up for Ontario's cheaply fuelled way of life. The community of communities looked like a pack of petty principalities picking over petroleum prices.

The latticework coalition began to buckle under the pressure of governing. The old criticisms about Clark's weak leadership abilities took on a new currency. Moreover, as he scurried here and there to shore up this or that element of his coalition, Clark had no chance to send voters a coherent message about what his government stood for. The PCs' December budget – the centrepiece of any government's program – ran off in several directions at once: raising taxes, increasing the deficit, and laying on a number of direct-spending and tax-expenditure goodies. To make matters worse, the budget's most

noticeable item was a sure-fire vote-loser, an eighteen-cent-a-gallon hike in the excise tax on gasoline. The budget package crystallized the government's policy contradictions, its political insensitivity, and its sheer stupidity. John Crosbie, the shoot-from-the-hip finance minister who parodied the budget tradition of wearing brand-new shoes by delivering the document in Newfoundland mukluks, billed it as "short-term pain for long-term gain." He got it half right.

The budget brought pain, all right, as the Tories received a shocking defeat on their budget motion in the House on Thursday, December 13, at the hands of the Liberals and the NDP (the Créditistes abstained). At 10:20 that evening Clark rose to address the House of Commons. "The government has lost a vote which we have no alternative but to regard as a question of confidence. I simply want to advise the House that I will be seeing His Excellency the Governor General tomorrow morning." Members on both sides threw reams of official documents skyward, the traditional symbol of a parliament's end. The next day at 11 a.m., Clark informed the House that the thirty-first parliament was dissolved and that a general election would be held on February 18, 1980. (The lengthy, sixty-five-day writ period – almost ten weeks – was chosen by Clark and Governor General Schreyer as

NAME: John Crosbie

PARTY: PC

ROLE: Minister of finance in 1979. Newfoundlander with attitude. Wants to hike consumer gas tax to pay for new government spending.

the briefest one possible in light of the upcoming holiday season, during which campaigning could not realistically take place.)

THE HIGHER THEY FLY...

Joe Clark's flight to prime ministerial heights was held aloft by a fickle breeze and powered by wings held together with wax. With only a loosely fashioned regional coalition, a weak mandate, a soft image, and an inexperienced team, he neared the sun and the wings melted (like those of the Greek mythological figure Icarus, pictured in this engraving by Diego Tettanelli) and he fell.

The first item of business following the election call fell to the Liberals, leaderless since Trudeau's resignation announcement of November 21. By December 18 he had been persuaded to rescind his resignation, through the appeals of the caucus, the Liberal Party executive, and public opinion. A Goldfarb poll showed the Liberals holding a commanding head start if Trudeau were to stay on. The stage was set for an early rematch, the first since the Diefenbaker–Pearson duel of 1962–63.

Contrary to Clark's hopes, incumbency would be no advantage at all. According to a memorandum written by Allan Gregg that August, only half of those who voted PC had done so out of active support for the party. For the rest, the election was just a protest vote: "The reasons for voting PC were negative six to one over positive," he wrote. With Trudeau's resignation, half the government's base of support had evaporated. Moreover, Goldfarb's numbers showed that, away from the limelight, the image of Trudeau-the-arrogant had faded. The worse Clark looked, the better Trudeau appeared.

By the time of Clark's December election call, his political situation had deteriorated further. A published November Gallup poll had shown the Tories a catastrophic nineteen points behind the Liberals, yet, incredibly, the government had taken no private polling since August. (This astonishing bit of wilful blindness was the result of Clark's conviction that Trudeau would resign soon and that the battered Liberals would leave his minority government to consolidate its victory for at least a couple of years before threatening it.) When the government fell, Gregg immediately took his first sounding and reported the findings to Clark at 24 Sussex Drive on the night of Sunday, December 23. Gregg's Christmas stocking for Clark contained an ugly lump of coal: the Tories were twenty-one points

behind the Liberals. The same gap showed up in Ontario, which had provided the key to victory in the spring election. Gregg's data revealed no weak spot in the oncoming Liberal phalanx.

There was no point in trying to sell the government's record (barely begun), Clark's image (gone from vague to bad), or even new policies (Why didn't you implement them when you were in government?). Gregg recalls: "There was just nothing to work with. I mean, what were we going to say after months of screwing up, 'Just kidding, folks'?" His intensive polling revealed only the thinnest straws at which the Conservatives could grasp. "We must have tested 150 different variables and only two things got any resonance at all: the idea that the government hadn't had a fair chance, and the idea that people still wanted to see those policy changes that could really change the way things were going economically." These thin fibres were baked into a mushy, plaintive Tory slogan: "Real Change Deserves a Fair Chance." Everyone in the Tory campaign knew, however, that positive slogans or policies wouldn't matter much. The only real hope was to go after Trudeau and to resurrect the animosity that had driven the man from office only months before. Once again, the Tories prepared to build a campaign around Trudeau's negative qualities.

The Liberals' strategists, Keith Davey and Jim Coutts, were not going to let the Tories turn the same trick twice. Rather than give the PCs a target, they determined to deprive them of Trudeau for the duration of the 1980 campaign. They followed a maxim of US president Lyndon Johnson: "When your mother-in-law has one eye, and it's in the middle of her forehead, you don't put her in the parlour." One of Canadian history's most charismatic figures was deliberately "low-bridged" – kept offstage and out of sight through a sixty-five-day election campaign. "We hid Trudeau," chuckled Goldfarb twenty years later. "We'd fly him from Charlottetown to the Yukon, back East and then to Vancouver." Whenever the Liberals' Flying Dutchman tour actually touched down for an event, Trudeau would plod through the same prepared speech with little variation from one venue to the next. The Liberals scuttled the other parties' proposals for a televised debate by dragging out negotiations and loading on onerous conditions. In the face of Liberal demands for a whole series of debates on the minutiae of policy issues, and an insistence that NDP leader Broadbent be excluded, the networks lost interest and the debate project collapsed. The Grits declined even to prepare a campaign slogan, for fear it would give Clark something to shoot at.

Trudeau, who had so fiercely insisted on running the campaign his way the previous spring, acquiesced to the low-bridging strategy with surprising ease. Goldfarb said that talking national unity would reduce support in English Canada? Fine, Trudeau would keep the unity talk to a minimum. Verbal duels with hecklers get in the way of the message? No problem, Trudeau would hold his temper. Need to play up the Liberal team? Good, Trudeau would sit patiently, listening to his candidates' speeches, in contrast to the in-and-out appearances of the year before. Trudeau even let the packagers

go to work on his wardrobe. According to Grafstein, Trudeau in 1979 had insisted on wearing the beige corduroy suit that made him "look like some deep-thinking academic who didn't give a damn about his appearance." In 1980 the suit disappeared, replaced by the spoils of a trip to Harry Rosen's conducted under Grafstein's supervision. "At one point, he actually seemed grateful for my advice on ties."

According to some of Trudeau's advisers, his change in attitude stemmed from some

NAME: Jerry Grafstein

PARTY: Liberal

ROLE: Campaign advertising and communications director. Senator. Toronto broadcasting lawyer. Advises Trudeau on clothes, too.

serious soul-searching in the wake of both the election defeat and the final abandonment of any hope of reconciliation with Margaret. "It was as though in the crucible of the autumn and early winter, he had come to accept his limitations and his strengths, had decided what he could reasonably expect from the rest of his life and what kind of compromises he was prepared to make to achieve his goals," wrote Stephen Clarkson and Christina McCall in

SPRUCE UP YOUR MAN

1979
Before Trudeau goes shopping with Jerry Grafstein ...

1980
And after

Vying for dominance in North Vancouver. The leaders' all-important images overshadow the local candidate (above).

Trudeau and Our Times. "Gunslinger turns fugitive," headlined the *Globe and Mail* in January, and "Team approach keeps Trudeau out of limelight." The Liberals even made it known that, if elected, Trudeau would never run again. Occasionally, he fed the speculation, as on January 27 when he referred to himself as "the almost retiring leader" in front of 1,300 Sault Ste. Marie supporters. If absence had made Canadians grow fonder of Pierre Trudeau, absence they would get.

And if familiarity had made Canadians contemptuous of Joe Clark, Trudeau and his party would ensure that voters heard more than they could stand about their bumbling young prime minister. "Our major element

of strategy," wrote Keith Davey in an internal memo, "should be to reinforce the determination of the people to defeat the Clark Government. Therefore our major campaign plan should be to attack the Clark Government and remind Canadians what it is they dislike about it ... People do not like Tories, and they like Joe Clark even less. We must constantly link these Tory programs and policies to Mr. Clark." The Liberals would keep the campaign focused on leadership, but it was Clark's sorry leadership abilities, not their own prickly leader's, that would come under scrutiny. In 1979 the Tories had campaigned on negative leadership; in 1980 it was the Grits' turn.

The 1980 campaign, conceived in chaos and executed on the run, did not follow the three-phase model. With the holiday season under way, the initial quiet period garnered almost no earned media. Similarly, the absence of a leaders' debate robbed the campaign's final phase of focus. This long and shapeless contest lacked the suspense of 1979; the published polls varied little from week to week, recording approximately the same Liberal twenty-point lead in a pre-election Gallup poll on December 4, a CTV poll on January 18, and another Gallup poll a week later. Only towards the campaign's end did the polls move much; by the time the final published ones came out just before election day, the Tories had managed to cut the yawning gap only in half – too little, too late to generate any excitement.

Out of Canadians' faces: Jim Coutts keeps Trudeau in the sky until Campaign '80 is safely over.

In the blizzards of January, Clark tramped through snowdrifts while Trudeau soared above the clouds in his airplane. From the start the Tory prime minister had his hands full explaining the budget, the embassy fiasco, the PetroCanada flip-flop, and, above all, the gas tax hike. "Students rough on Clark over broken promises," wrote the pro-Tory *Globe and Mail*. "Wrong to run on budget," read the *Halifax Chronicle-Herald*. "Clark's tour first to go adrift in winter blast," heckled the *Montreal Gazette*. "TV image problem for Clark," said the *Winnipeg Free Press*. Writing in the hallowed lower left corner of the *Globe*'s op-ed page, reigning heavyweight Geoff Stevens opined, "Needed: assorted miracles to save Tories."

The Tory team members can't be faulted for their election campaign; they never really had much of a chance once the writ was dropped. Perhaps a better way of understanding their performance is to say that they had done such a bad job in the pre-writ campaign – the one they didn't realize was happening until it was already over – that nothing they did once the writ came down could make a real difference. Still, they put on a game effort, holding up their end of the fight despite the certain knowledge of impending defeat and terrible loss of reputation.

As one might expect in a winter campaign – with most Canadians holed up at home in front of the TV – the election's major battles were fought with television ads, commencing in the latter part of January, the sixth week of the ten-week campaign. The Tories sought to reawaken the dynamics of the 1979 campaign by reusing some of the visuals from their previous effort. A hockey goalie from a 1979 spot, wearing a Team Canada jersey, reappeared in a 1980 commercial as a winger stick-handling the puck before being slammed into the boards by mean-looking players in Liberal and NDP shirts. Another ad depicted the Tory government as a constructive bricklayer, whose patiently tuck-pointed creation is suddenly and rudely shoved over by two Liberal and NDP toughs.

In the changed political climate, however, ads that worked in 1979 suddenly were duds – or worse. One spot reprised the 1979 reel of a slowed-down, incoherent Trudeau in the House, with a new message tacked on. This time, many Canadians were offended by this sleazy little piece of editing-room trickery. One Tory candidate went so far as to call the ad "disgusting and corrupt," and it was withdrawn on January 30.

The Liberal ads were less imaginative but much more effective. They spoke directly to those voters, particularly in Ontario, who had traditionally voted Liberal and had taken a chance on the PCs in 1979. The divisive appeal to regional interests was overt, as in one ad that depicted a grinning Clark cozying up to Alberta's Premier Lougheed. The voice-over stated, "Ontarians should pay attention to the budget that demonstrates how easily Joe Clark would give in to Premier Lougheed and Alberta on energy prices…" In another savagely telling spot, Clark's weakness as a party leader was pointed out by quoting Ontario premier Bill Davis giving a lengthy rubbishing of Clark's energy policy. "If the Joe Clark Conservatives let him down," said the voice-over, "think what they're doing to you." The message was only partly that Clark was dangerous to Ontario. It spoke instead to the real issue of leadership: that Clark couldn't even run his own party, let alone the country.

In 1980 the Liberals put forward one positive policy message to balance their attacks on Clark. The message was economic nationalism, with the sensitive issue of energy as its centrepiece. This policy thrust was carefully calculated to play on the party's regional strengths – Quebec, the Atlantic provinces, urban Ontario – while virtually writing off the country west of the Ontario–Manitoba border. The strategy reached its apogee in Halifax on January 25, when Trudeau stood before the Halifax Board of Trade and laid out the most interventionist, nationalistic, anti-American program ever put forward by a Liberal leader. Trudeau promised a "made-in-Canada" oil price to ensure that Canadian fuel was sold for less than world rates. He committed a Liberal government to self-sufficiency in energy, so that future OPEC embargoes wouldn't affect Canada,

"SCREW THE WEST"

Keith Davey's dictum comes to life in this Liberal TV spot that depicts Clark as the stooge of Alberta's Lougheed *(frame one, right)*, which leaves popular Ontario premier Bill Davis *(frame three, left)* angry with Clark. The ad's kicker is a reference to the hugely unpopular gas tax in the 1979 budget *(frame four)*.

even if it meant cutting off the United States in a squeeze. He pledged an expanded role for the state-owned PetroCanada in exploration and distribution, a status that would come at the expense of foreign-owned oil companies. He specified a transfer of the petroleum industry's foreign-owned assets into Canadian hands, from 50 to 75 per cent in ten years. Cheap oil and gas was something everyone could understand, especially those already inclined to vote Liberal in energy-consuming provinces. What is more, the energy plank was only the most prominent in an overall Liberal platform that called for increased economic nationalism.

The shift to a nationalist policy program was a hell of a lot bigger than adopting Jerry Grafstein's taste in ties. How did Trudeau, who in office had disdained Anglo economic nationalism as akin to the ethnocentric nationalism he detested in Quebec politics, come to accept this change? "We came out of the '79 defeat without a national economic agenda," said Goldfarb later, lamenting the Tories' monopoly on the entire economic question in that campaign. In office, the civil service, the lobbyists, or the pro-business wing of the Liberal Party had always torpedoed any economic nationalist policy proposals. But in opposition, the English Canadian wing of the party had largely fallen by default into the hands of nationalists. Chief among these was principal secretary Jim Coutts's emerging "sidekick," special assistant Tom Axworthy, who pushed the nationalist message on his boss. Coutts wasn't much for nationalism or ideology, but he saw the political worth of a nationalistic message for a Liberal Party in opposition. Amid the increasingly nationalist tenor on the opposition benches, the energy issue grew in real-world prominence. The year 1979 had seen another major oil shock in the United States, triggered by the Iranian revolution of Ayatollah Khomeini. Clark's hapless

NAME: Tom Axworthy

PARTY: Liberal

ROLE: Coutts No. 2 in Trudeau's office. Policy guy. Economic nationalist.

conduct of energy pricing negotiations with producer provinces made for good opposition fodder; it also split Tories of the oil-producing West from their allies in the oil-consuming East. It was a simple matter for English Canadian Liberals to piece together economic nationalism and the new prominence of the energy issue. The problem had been selling it to the Quebec wing, suspicious as always of nationalism in any language.

The key guy to get onside was Marc Lalonde, who had been appointed energy critic and was learning his brief while contemplating the anticipated retirement of his friend and leader, Trudeau. But that summer, as Lalonde sifted through the documents left over from government, he grasped the implications of energy policy for the only question he really cared about: winning the upcoming referendum in Quebec. He easily understood the value of promising cheap gas to the federalist cause in Quebec. He could also see that energy issues might frustrate any harmony among Clark, the western premiers, and the hated Lévesque. Mainly, however, Lalonde focused on the money: unless Ottawa grabbed for itself a share of the burgeoning tax revenues flowing from the oil patch, the producer provinces would get it all, making them infinitely more rich and powerful than the feds. As Lalonde later recalled, "The major factor behind … [what was to become the National Energy Program] wasn't Canadianization or getting more from the industry or even self-sufficiency. The determi-

TAKING CHARGE OF ENERGY

Although Trudeau didn't spell out its details until the fall 1980 budget, he laid out the principles of the National Energy Program during the previous winter's campaign. Ottawa would increase domestic ownership of Canada's US-dominated petroleum industry and swell its coffers with new energy taxes, while the energy-producing provinces and US-owned petroleum companies would just have to do with less.

nant factor was the fiscal imbalance between the provinces and the federal government."

During parliament's fall 1979 session, Lalonde and the Liberals had run with the nationalist energy ball, even as Trudeau limped off the field. In December the Liberals had responded immediately to the Crosbie budget's eighteen-cent-a-gallon gas-tax hike with a pledge to repeal it, and then they had defeated the budget itself. Why not roll out a nationalist energy policy in the election? Lalonde and Axworthy argued. Coutts's position had

NAME: Marc Lalonde

PARTY: Liberal

ROLE: Trudeau's energy critic, Quebec lieutenant, chief associate, iron fist. Recent convert to economic nationalism.

changed, however, with the election call and with Trudeau's return. He feared that any interesting new ideas would disrupt his deliberately dull campaign strategy. He preferred to have the leader simply bash the Tories and their budget with such cheesy gags as "It really was a mukluk budget – it was luck for the privileged few and muck for the rest of us." But Lalonde was totally committed to a nationalistic, cash-grabbing, pro-eastern energy policy. If he could just get a speech draft of the policy in front of Trudeau, the leader would doubtless shrug, agree with the trusted Lalonde, and run with it.

Lalonde had the speech written and pencilled its delivery into the leader's tour schedule in Halifax on January 25. The only obstacle was Coutts, who travelled with Trudeau on the plane and would do whatever it took to keep the physical speech text from crossing the tray in front of Trudeau's seat. Sensing danger, Lalonde flew to a campaign stop in Winnipeg

the night before the Halifax event to make sure nothing went awry. When he caught up with the campaign at the hotel, he discovered that someone had cut the energy material out of the next day's text, leaving only the standard stump remarks. Lalonde ordered an all-night editing session from the speechwriters, demanding a final energy text for his personal approval by 4:30 a.m. the day of the announcement. On January 25 the speech went on the plane, Trudeau signed off and delivered it in Halifax, and Lalonde went back to his riding in Montreal. He knew he had levered a historic shift in Liberal economic policy.

The Liberals' energy policy clearly risked alienating the West. Folks in the energy-producing provinces would soon understand that the Liberals wanted money to flow from their provincial governments and the oil companies that employed them to both eastern consumers and the government they controlled in Ottawa. This policy set a much sharper edge on the Liberals' national unity approach than had Trudeau's constitutional musings of 1979. But the Grits didn't care. In 1980 they dropped their unity message and ran on a bald program of redistributing wealth from the West to the East. As Keith Davey subsequently put it, "Screw the West. We'll take the rest." The Liberals figured that any western outrage would be more than offset elsewhere, especially Ontario.

The balance of the nationalist program had already been laid out in a January 12 speech in Toronto, where Trudeau promised tougher foreign investment rules and specific industrial strategies from Ottawa to promote key sectors. The nationalistic policy platform neatly lined up with Trudeau's vision of a strong central government, enriched with energy wealth taxed out of the provinces. It played to his regional strengths and provided a sufficiently clear, positive message to make

PLAYBOOK VI

In order to win the 1980 election, Trudeau had to lean heavily on one of the three basic plays in the Canadian political playbook, the Quebec Bridge. Trudeau's hold on Quebec had tightened throughout his years in power and, as the 1980 referendum approached, became a hammerlock. His variant on the play was reminiscent of Mackenzie King's; he reached out to progressive voters, lower-income households, women, recent immigrants, and youth in Ontario and the Atlantic region. But whereas King had often settled for weak results in Ontario, the West was written off by Trudeau.

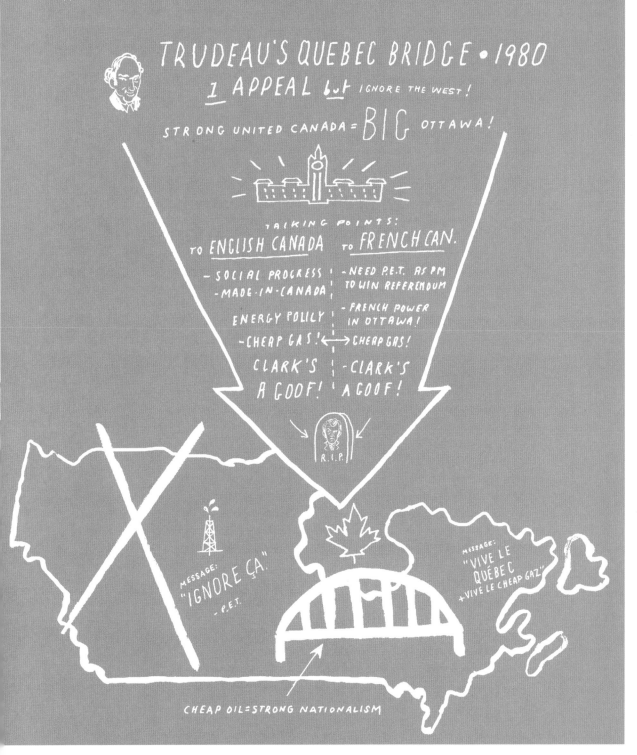

TRUDEAU'S QUEBEC BRIDGE • 1980

<u>1</u> APPEAL but IGNORE THE WEST!

STRONG UNITED CANADA = BIG OTTAWA!

TALKING POINTS:

TO ENGLISH CANADA

- SOCIAL PROGRESS
- MADE·IN·CANADA
ENERGY POLICY
- CHEAP GAS! ⟷

CLARK'S A GOOF!

TO FRENCH CAN.

- NEED P.E.T. AS PM TO WIN REFERENDUM
- FRENCH POWER IN OTTAWA!
CHEAP GAS!
- CLARK'S A GOOF!

R.I.P.

MESSAGE: "IGNORE ÇA." - P.E.T.

MESSAGE: "VIVE LE QUÉBEC + VIVE LE CHEAP GAZ"

CHEAP OIL = STRONG NATIONALISM

up for his near-invisibility on the campaign trail. The program was cynical (at least on Trudeau's part) and divisive, but it was effective. To quote Goldfarb, "Nationalism won that campaign."

Goldfarb is stretching the point. The Liberals probably could have won the 1980 campaign by sticking with Coutts's strategy, which is, in fact, what they did for the most part. The energy speech certainly wasn't followed up with much advertising or energy-themed earned media events. However, it played an important role in signalling to voters that Trudeau was no longer the lofty snob who never talked about those trivial things that real people actually cared about. They cared about gas prices and security of supply, and they cared about the idea of an independent Canada setting its own oil prices and standing up to foreign oil companies. Nationalism on its own didn't win the 1980 campaign, but nationalism plus energy plus Trudeau proved an unbeatable combination.

Another plus to the nationalist Liberal thrust was the thoroughness with which it mowed Ed Broadbent's lawn. That fall, the NDP had anticipated a leftward tilt among Liberals, but was unable to respond before the election sprang upon them. All Broadbent and his team could do was run on his increasing public acceptance and weakly inveigh against the negative campaigning between the two major parties.

On the ground, the miserable election dragged towards its close. A February 4 CTV poll showed that the Liberal lead had shrunk to thirteen points. A week later, on February 9, a final Gallup survey tallied a seventeen-point lead. A final CTV poll put the Liberals at 43 per cent, the PCs at 33 per cent, and the NDP at 22 per cent. They all pointed to the same inevitable Liberal victory. By the tenth week the indignities of performing in a campaign centred so closely on personality seemed to wear on

the leaders themselves. A CBC interviewer in Halifax asked Clark about the image problems associated with the way he walked. With a brittle laugh he replied: "I don't know who taught me to walk. I'll have to go back to my parents or grandparents and say, 'Look at the campaign issue you created in 1980 by the way you taught me to walk.'" Trudeau, on one of his last stops in the perennial battleground of London, Ontario, let slip his disciplined mask of low-bridged cheer. Faced with a heckler, the real Trudeau flashed forth to accuse the man of having a small mind. Remembering himself, he swiftly, ironically recovered: "I hope it will be noted that I didn't say that in an arrogant tone."

The Château Laurier ballroom was hot with excitement, steamed up in the television lights' glare, as the returning prime minister, Pierre Trudeau, tried to quiet the crowd. The Liberal throng was high on an election-night cocktail of alcohol, ambition, and tribal roars of triumph. In contrast, the man who stood beneath the hot lights was cool, in control, the very embodiment of his personal motto: "La raison avant la passion." He smiled: "Well, welcome to the 1980s." It was just after midnight, February 19. The numbers proclaimed a solid Liberal majority: 147 out of 282 seats, based on 44 per cent of the popular vote. Clark's Conservatives had been hammered, dropping 33 seats to 103. The West held firm for the PCs, and the NDP made gains in the Prairies and BC to edge their total up to 32 seats. But Ontario had swung back hard to the Liberals.

From the standpoint of political mechanics, there's no great mystery to what took place in the fight of 1979–80. In 1979 Clark, who was a weak performer but had a strong message, managed to eke out a minority victory over Trudeau, who performed well as a leader but had a weak message that year. Nine months later, Trudeau's strong leadership profile combined with a strong message to clobber Joe Clark, who was weak in both the performance and the message departments. Two mediocre campaigns produced a minority in 1979; in 1980 a really good campaign flattened a really bad campaign to take a majority victory.

At least that's what happened among the approximately 175,000 swing voters in Ontario who determined both outcomes, but how did the rest of the country factor into the calculus? What about those who voted the same way in both elections? The 4.5 million people who voted Liberal in 1979 must have really believed in what they were doing; so must the 3.5 million who voted PC in 1980. These folks, most of them in the regional bastions of Liberal Quebec and the Tory West, were committed to something deeper.

Part of it was the impulse towards electing a favourite son. The 68 per cent of Quebeckers who voted Liberal knew that, with Trudeau at the helm, René Lévesque's forthcoming sovereignty-association referendum would be at the centre of the national agenda. Whether they were Quebec federalists looking for back-up, separatists making sure that Quebec would be looked after if they lost the referendum, or just regular voters thinking about how the country should be run, they voted for Trudeau. The bit about cheap gas didn't hurt either; indeed, it fleshed out the whole pan-Canadian, nationalist, vision thing in a tangible and pleasingly beneficial way.

The same kind of feeling was fairly widespread in Liberal Ontario as well. Ontarians at the time instinctively regarded the federal government as their own; they felt quite comfortable with the Big Ottawa approach. The West did not feel that kind of comfort – at least not the 46 per cent of westerners who voted PC. They can't have been any more impressed by Clark's lead-

ership skills than the next guy. What turned them on was his idea that Ottawa should back off from bilingualism, the Quebec obsession, and the energy prices that took money from the West and gave it to the East – in short, the idea that Ottawa should just be cut down to size.

The western viewpoint had its chance in 1979, but in 1980 the Empire of the St. Lawrence struck back, making this back-and-forth struggle the most exciting battle between regions since the 1920s. The claim was bolstered by the scale of the events set in motion by the power-struggle's resolution. Marc Lalonde later encapsulated the Liberal revanchism felt during the Tory interregnum: "If we ever got another kick at the can, we were really going to kick it." Kick it they did. Trudeau's new, harder-edged approach contributed to the separatist defeat in the referendum, the imposition of the interventionist National Energy Program at the heart of an aggressively nationalist economic agenda, and the repatriation of the Constitution with its Charter of Rights and Freedoms. Throughout the late 1970s, Trudeau had asked who would speak for Canada. The electorate answered: Ottawa would.

At least the electorate of the Liberal heartland said so. Trudeau's willingness to run, win, and govern without western support was remarkable for a man who had come to power as a perfect expression of the visionary tendency in Canadian politics. In embracing the regional coalition politics he had always eschewed, Trudeau had become what he could never have imagined himself as being – a political operator in the Mackenzie King mould. He would play his regional card in Quebec aggressively – as had Laurier and King – although, where these predecessors had largely frozen Ontario out, Trudeau would let westerners do the shivering. And wherever in Canada moderately "progressive" social ideas held sway, there would be Trudeau, like King before him. The national visionary of the Just Society became just another Liberal running the Quebec Bridge play.

With Trudeau's conversion to the old/new politics of region, the era of national vision politics came to a close, marking an evolutionary shift in the structure of national politics and allowing the twin elections to meet a second test of greatness. Trudeau, at the moment of his 1979 defeat, was the last in a line of visionary prime ministers, starting with St. Laurent, who ran without overt regional appeals or approaches. From then on, first Clark, then the resurrected Trudeau, were the first of the new/old breed of prime minister – men like Mulroney and Chrétien who were ready, willing, and able to work the axis of region with a vengeance in the pursuit and maintenance of national power.

In a world filled with referendum-wielding separatists in Quebec and blue-eyed sheiks in the West, there might be room for visions, but only for those mounted on the durable, battle-tested realities of race, language, and region. The two decades since Trudeau's 1980 resurrection have been dominated by the questions posed by his Big Ottawa approach. Ottawa's role in the federation drove the constitutional debates of Meech and Charlottetown; its economic role lay at the centre of the battles over free trade with the United States and then with Mexico. In all these fights, it has been prime ministers who have kept a firm grip on their regional coalitions who have survived politically and pushed their policies through. The twin elections of 1979 and 1980 represent the pivotal point at which Canadians and their political leaders turned away from the politics of what could unite us, back to the politics of our inherent divisions.

But did we really ring down the curtain on the national visionary approach to politics? True, the overdue business of accommodating the new West and the modern Quebec remains an urgent political task for our national government. True, insofar as Canadians in these regions think of themselves as citizens of regions as well as of a country, their reconciliation remains a standing challenge in the building of our nation. True, the obsessions of region, rights, and citizenship have drained precious energy away from the critical race to compete in the remorseless global economy. But, at the same time, Trudeau's pan-Canadian, rights-based citizenship – the fundamental issue of nation building lying at the heart of the 1979–80 fight – has become dear to us, clearly standing alongside the achievements of Laurier's accommodation of Quebec, King's drive towards nationhood, and Mulroney's connecting Canada into the North American economic powerhouse. The election allowed Pierre Trudeau to finish the act of nation building that John Diefenbaker and a generation of intellectuals had started. Trudeau completed the forging of an unhyphenated identity for the new, multicultural, urbanized generations of Canadians that arose in the mid-twentieth century. This was his contribution to our nation-building story, and it happened because enough of us voted for him and his vision in 1979 and 1980. And that is the way a democracy is supposed to work.

Taking aim: on his first day back in power, Trudeau clowns with the media, but his consolidation of power in Ottawa would be no joke. Within eight months, Lévesque's referendum would be defeated and the National Energy Program introduced. In less than two years, the Constitution would be brought home on Ottawa's terms.

TRIPLE PLAY

THE ELECTION OF 1984

WITH VARYING DEGREES OF SUCCESS, Joe Clark and Pierre Trudeau had experimented with blending traditional regional politics with the new style of leadership and vision brought in by Diefenbaker. In 1984 Brian Mulroney brilliantly exploited the opportunities offered by this new hybrid to win the second-largest majority in Canadian history and bring the Liberals to the brink of ruin.

Trudeau's final mandate set the stage for the Tory resurgence with a mix of triumph and tragedy. The triumph of his Big Ottawa vision came with the repatriation of the Constitution and the Charter, but that same vision led to tragedy on the economic front. As a severe global recession ripped the Canadian economy in 1981–82, unemployment insurance and other welfare payments ballooned while Ottawa's revenues plummeted. When world oil prices unexpectedly collapsed, the National Energy Program, designed to fill Ottawa's coffers with western oil money, utterly failed to deliver. The federal deficit soared to $33 billion, crippling for a generation the federal power the prime minister had laboured so tirelessly to build. By the time of his resignation on February 29, 1984, the country was ready for a change.

The agent of that change came in the form of a very different man from Quebec, Brian Mulroney. Unlike Trudeau, he'd been a politician from his late teens. If Trudeau was a man who put intellectual vision before all else, Mulroney was an operator par excellence, knitting together disparate people and interests not on the basis of common visions but on the promise of power. When the

May 1980
QUEBEC VOTES NON
A referendum on Quebec sovereignty is defeated 60 per cent to 40 per cent. (*Above*) *Non* forces at a rally in Montreal.

March 1981
OTTAWA STARTS ENERGY WAR
Trudeau enacts the National Energy Program and stokes western alienation. (*Above*) An Alberta protester manages simultaneously to attack Trudeau, state-owned PetroCanada, and Ottawa power in general.

June 1981
TERRY FOX DIES
On June 28, less than a year after cancer forced him to quit his "Marathon of Hope" near Thunder Bay, Ontario, the one-legged runner from New Westminster, BC, dies.

April 1982
CANADA'S CONSTITUTION COMES HOME
With Queen Elizabeth's signature at a ceremony on Parliament Hill (*above*), the Constitution Act, 1982, becomes the law of the land.

June 1983
CLARK OUSTED AS LEADER
Montrealer Brian Mulroney captures the PC leadership from Joe Clark (*above*) at an Ottawa convention after three years of bitter in-fighting. The final ballot result: Mulroney 1,584; Clark 1,325.

forty-four-year-old backroom player was elected Tory leader on the second try in June 1983, he had already made a lifetime study of the structure and mechanics of the Liberal hold on power.

The ambitious, bilingual Mulroney had ridden the Diefenbaker roller coaster to its ultimate derailment, which left him a very big player in the suddenly very small Quebec Tory Party. Mulroney's ambitions were vast, and when the party's federal leadership came open in 1976, he went for it, finishing third to Joe Clark. Embittered despite his respectable finish, Mulroney had nursed his grudges (and his double scotches) until Clark's bungling in 1980 drove the Tories from their brief moment in government and put the party leadership back into play. Mulroney, who had quit drinking, hit the phones and started organizing to take Clark's place. His message to his fellow Tories was a simple assertion of the Quebec Bridge play: we have to win in Quebec and only I can do it.

Mulroney's grand plan went against the basic Tory strategy that had been in place since Gordon Churchill's memorandum in 1956: concentrate on English Canada, especially the West, hoping that, as with Dief in 1958, Quebec might jump

February 1984
CANADA ACCEPTS CRUISE MISSILES
Just before announcing his retirement, Trudeau allows the first American cruise missiles to be tested over northern Alberta. *(Above)* The PM confronts anti-cruise protesters.

June 1984
TRUDEAU SAYS GOODBYE
Pierre Trudeau bids adieu to a grateful Liberal Party with one of his finest speeches ever.

January 1984
TRUDEAU APPOINTS FIRST WOMAN GOVERNOR GENERAL
Jeanne Sauvé, Liberal MP since 1972 and Speaker since 1980, becomes the country's first female governor general.

June 1984
TURNER WINS LEADERSHIP
Two days later, the Liberal convention elects Torontonian John Turner as leader and, automatically, as prime minister. *(Above)* Turner mobbed on the convention floor.

on their bandwagon once it got rolling. Mulroney argued that Quebec had become not only a necessity for the Tories but a glittering, historic opportunity. Following the 1976 election of René Lévesque's Parti Québécois and the 1980 referendum, politics in the province had been polarized by the separation question. Roughly equal camps of hard-core federalists and *pur et dur* separatists glared at each other, while a critical swing vote supported the Liberals federally and the PQ provincially. The 1980 election had wiped out the Créditistes, leaving rural nationalists with nowhere to go but, perhaps, to the Progressive Conservatives. Moreover, by 1983, Mulroney saw that Trudeau's imminent retirement would loosen many swing voters from the Liberals. The stars were aligned for a once-in-a-lifetime chance to transfer Quebec from the Liberals' orbit to the Conservatives' – not just for one election as in 1911, 1930, or 1958, but for the indefinite future. Mulroney's aim was nothing less than to re-create Macdonald's first coalition, with the Tories instead of the Grits crossing the Quebec Bridge to national power.

When Trudeau finally resigned in late February, his party was at the then-unprecedented low of 23 per cent in the national polls. The now-silver-haired former golden boy, John Turner, was anointed his successor by a jittery convention on June 16. With the polls showing the Grits regaining the lead for the first time in three years, he called an election on July 9 for September 4.

The seven-week 1984 campaign saw Mulroney pull off three winning plays, any one of which would probably have given him victory. He successfully executed Joe Clark's western-based Populist Rush from '79 among English Canadians by lambasting the corrupt, arrogant Liberals. He flawlessly pulled off the Quebec Bridge as he had ordained, by offering Quebec a new constitutional settlement on more favourable terms than Trudeau's. Above all, he managed to replicate Trudeau's devastating leadership advantage of 1980 by nailing Turner in the first back-to-back French and English televised leaders' debates. In the English debate, faced with an assault by Mulroney over a raft of patronage appointments he had made, Turner lamely asserted that he "had no option" but to make the appointments. "You had an option," thundered Mulroney. "You are the prime minister of Canada." This single exchange shoved the Liberals' shaky support into freefall as swing voters, along with many who had been loyal to the Liberals for generations, abandoned the party of Trudeau and Pearson overnight. A month later Mulroney was elected prime minister in a landslide.

The Tories took 50 per cent of the popular vote and 211 of 282 seats on September 4, a share surpassed only by Diefenbaker in 1958 – and with an infinitely more solid grounding in Quebec. The Liberals crumpled to forty seats, obtaining only 28 per cent of the national popular vote. In English Canada they finished behind the NDP, which won thirty seats despite being sidelined in the stampede towards Mulroney.

The 1984 election wasn't a great one – too little nation building and a hopelessly bad Liberal effort took care of that – but it demonstrated more clearly than even 1980 the possibilities inherent in mixing old-style regional politicking with the post-Diefenbaker politics of vision and leadership.

Once in office, however, Brian Mulroney found governing within this hybrid system tougher than winning at it. At the mid-point of his first term it seemed as though Mulroney's mandate for change had been thrown away for the sake of party patronage and regional pork barrelling. To retain the power he treasured, the prime minister had to give Canadians in every part of the country a reason to support him. He needed a vision, and the search for one was to lead him back to a nation-building issue that had lain dormant for three-quarters of a century.

Brian Mulroney leads the Progressive Conservative Party to a smashing victory, winning 211 seats out of a possible 282. John Turner's Liberals win only 40 seats, the smallest caucus in their history, and Ed Broadbent's New Democrats win 30 seats.

Mulroney ran a nearly perfect campaign, while Turner ran a dreadful one. During his brief stint in office, Turner acted too much like a member of the old regime, a Trudeau without the panache. By contrast, Mulroney (here with wife Mila) looked a fresh, even exciting alternative, the true agent of change voters were craving. Even in traditionally Liberal Quebec, voters stampeded to this "new man with a new plan," in Allan Gregg's words. With his massive majority behind him, Mulroney expected to sit back and enjoy the fruits of power. Within months, however, he would be forced by political problems and public policy imperatives to bet his government on an issue that had not been put before the voters in seventy-five years – free trade with the United States.

MANO A MANO

NOV. 21

1988

BRIAN MULRONEY

VS.

JOHN TURNER

and ED BROADBENT

It is 7 P.M. on Tuesday, October 25, 1988. The studio in Ottawa is wired for sound and lit up with ranks of overhead kliegs, spots, and gels. The show onstage will be fed to the three national television networks and beamed out across the country's 5,000-kilometre breadth into the homes of hundreds of thousands of Canadians who have tuned in for this televised English-language leaders' debate. The debate production is a high-tech political marvel, the focal point for the vast array of telecommunications, data analysis, and sophisticated marketing techniques that make up a modern election campaign. But the surest aid for late-twentieth-century voters is the oldest one in their hands: the timeless ability of one human to look another in the eye and judge him or her worthy of trust. By bringing the leaders directly before the voters as never before, the whiz-bang new technologies of politics have reduced the vast and intricate machinery of a national election campaign to the most ancient political transaction, the one-to-one handshake. Mano a mano; hand to hand. A compact between citizen and leader? A gladiatorial prize fight? Whichever it is, the encounter is up close and personal, for the combatants on the studio floor and for the crowd watching at home. It's a long way from the nineteenth-century campaigns with their strawberry socials and *mandements* read from the church pulpit. This is democracy *en direct*, served up LIVE AND RAW – the way YOU, the voter, WANT IT! No elites! No backroom compacts! Just big leaders and big issues – AND THE CHOICE IS YOURS!!

As anyone who lived through the 1988 election knows, the debate that night is remembered for one brief exchange between the Tory prime minister, Brian Mulroney, and the Liberal leader, John Turner, on free trade: a made-for-TV moment that crystallized the entire campaign and suddenly gave the underdog Turner a real shot at winning. That moment brought into sharp focus the fact that a fundamental policy issue was at stake in the election – an

(Opposite) Brian Mulroney revels in the pomp and perks of office, such as introducing his wife, Mila, to this German count at Bonn in 1985. His love of performance was matched by his delight in the strategic aspects of politics – at which he excelled.

agreement to implement at long last free trade with the United States, a deal that carried immense implications for Canada's economy, sovereignty, and future as a nation. After that critical exchange between the two leaders, the once-hopeless Liberals surged to the very threshold of power before slipping back into a respectable second-place finish.

The great free trade election of 1988 wasn't really a single-issue campaign, any more than was, say, the 1896 fight solely about Manitoba schools. Free trade and its companion piece, the decentralizing Meech Lake constitutional accord, together represented a coherent alternative to Trudeau's Big Ottawa vision. And, as always, there were regional and French–English cross-currents at play. The two issues were used to reaffirm a historic coalition of two regions, the West and Quebec, which, under Mulroney, had combined in 1984 to create the only break in Liberal Ontario's four-decade hammerlock on national power that persists to this day. Finally, 1988 zeroed in as well on the party leaders, laying bare their strengths and weaknesses as has no campaign before or since.

So what was Campaign '88? The final triumph of superficial image politics over substantive policy? Not at all. In defining the national campaign as a battle of two men over a single issue, the debate and the campaign in general marked a new prominence in the role given to policy issues in election campaigns. The evolutionary change completed in the 1988 campaign was the near-disappearance of the great parties. These institutions, which a century ago had splendidly and solemnly mediated between the people below and the leaders and their great concerns above, were reduced to a part-time sales force and cheering section. On debate night and for a delicious week thereafter, even the leaders seemed to take a back seat as the public wrestled directly with a momentous issue.

In 1988 the people found themselves with the power to choose. They exercised their power vigorously in a wild campaign where almost one voter in five changed voting intentions once, and one in ten may well have switched sides two times between the election call and election day, November 21, 1988. Never did Canadians more firmly grasp the levers of power than when they watched Brian Mulroney and John Turner go at it, mano a mano, over free trade.

The 1988 pre-writ campaign began in earnest in early October 1987, one year before the election was formally called. On October 2 through October 4, with only brief respite for sleep, top-level Canadian and American teams negotiated and initialled a free trade agreement between the two countries. Free trade was a lot more than a policy issue for Brian Mulroney. It was the key to his political survival.

Mulroney had swept to power in a mighty wave in 1984 by reforging a version of Mackenzie King's Quebec–western alliance and positioning himself as an agent of much-needed change. He certainly seemed different from Trudeau – all big-shouldered suits and new-money, stock-market sheen. In his first years in office, however, he had let the voters down badly. His government was hit with wave after wave of ministerial scandal, which forced eight of his thirty-eight colleagues to resign from cabinet during the first mandate, over abuses ranging from a liaison with a stripper through to serious criminal matters, such as profiteering from a government defence contract. The polls recorded a growing public sense that Mulroney was an old-time fixer – not the patronage-busting paladin he had seemed in 1984 – in short, a fraud.

The new prime minister had been caught in a trap of his own making – and not just the obvious one, by which his reckless promises to Tories of the spoils of office wound up attracting the unscrupulous to Ottawa like flies.

THE TWO FACES OF BRIAN MULRONEY

Politics in the 1980s was about the leader delivering a simple message directly to the voters. Ideally, every aspect of a politician's public (and sometimes private) life would be "on message," that is, helping to illustrate the basic point he or she was trying to get across. When a politician went "off message," it was usually because of circumstances beyond his control.

NAME: Brian Mulroney

PARTY: PC

ROLE: Prime minister since 1984. Heads massive majority government. Adrift in scandal, policy disarray. Needs an issue to focus his government.

Mulroney's fixation on winning power had always come at the expense of thinking deeply about what he would do if he won it.

Now, sitting in the prime minister's chair in 1985, he had no particular goals other than, somehow or other, to clean up the economic mess he had inherited from Trudeau. The hitch was that cleaning up Trudeau's mess was going to take some big moves, risky ones. Here was Brian Mulroney, the political reincarnation of Mackenzie King, suddenly forced to think seriously about where to lead the country.

Fortunately for Mulroney, a vision was waiting for him ready-made. In the depths of 1985 the Ottawa bureaucracy informed the prime minister that free trade with the United States might be an idea whose time at last had come. Mulroney, who had casually spoken against free trade during his successful 1983 leadership campaign, grabbed it with both hands.

There were sound policy reasons for Mulroney's conversion. The prime minister had come to share a widespread view among Canada's business and policy elites that something drastic needed to be done for the Canadian economy, which had just emerged from a vicious recession in 1982–83. However, most politicians – especially those down in the polls – would have taken one look at free trade and its troubled political history and fled from it. Not Mulroney. He instinctively saw that free trade offered him a ticket to political salvation. His intuitive stroke of genius was to understand the opportunity he could seize by embracing this

risky policy, which had destroyed no less a man than Laurier. Here was an issue that played to his party's strength as the agent of economic change, a new course in economic policy with which to regain the initiative and dominate the national agenda. As he would say in an interview a couple of months before the 1988 election call, "If you are asking how you are going to vote tomorrow … [the voter says] I'm going to vote Liberal. The next question: If free trade plays a part in the next election campaign, how are you going to vote? Conservatives first, Liberals second, NDP third."

Mulroney also understood that pushing free trade squarely addressed the all-important question of leadership; by showing guts and foresight in proposing free trade, he could drive up his personal ratings. "Who is most able to govern Canada?" he asked, mimicking the pollster's question. "Mulroney first, Broadbent a poor second, and then Turner, who is so far behind you can't see him. And perhaps the second question," Mulroney sequenced, the way a pollster might to relate free trade with leadership, "'If free trade plays a role in the next election, how will you vote?' Well I am going to vote Conservative first, Liberals second, then new Democrats a poor third. Now think about the question for a second. What the hell do you think is going to be part and parcel of the next election?" Mulroney believed he had found his re-election formula: free trade equals leadership equals Tory victory.

If free trade worked magic as a piece of policy and leadership positioning, it was no less promising when looked at through the lens of region. In the PC Party's western heartland, free trade had been popular since Laurier's day as a counter to the power of central Canadian manufacturing and transport interests. It was also popular in many of the swing ridings of Ontario – the affluent constituencies in Toronto and down the 401 towards London.

WHY DID THE PARTIES CROSS THE ROAD?

AGAINST FREE TRADE

FOR FREE TRADE

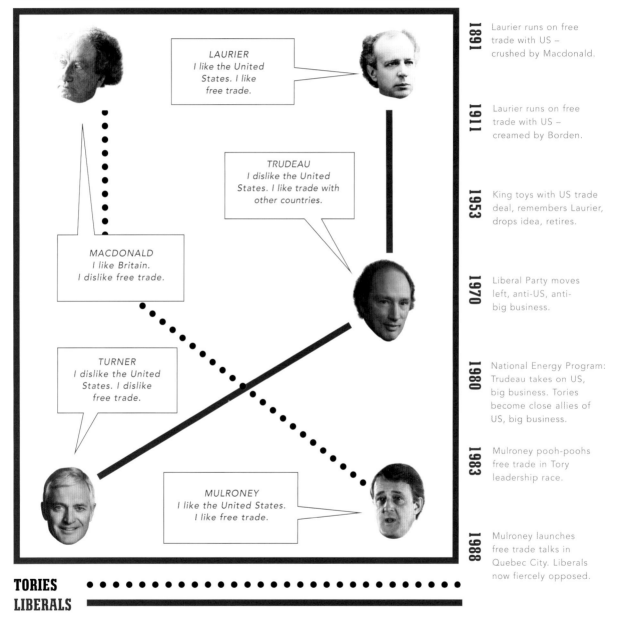

LAURIER
I like the United States. I like free trade.

TRUDEAU
I dislike the United States. I like trade with other countries.

MACDONALD
I like Britain. I dislike free trade.

TURNER
I dislike the United States. I dislike free trade.

MULRONEY
I like the United States. I like free trade.

1891 — Laurier runs on free trade with US – crushed by Macdonald.

1911 — Laurier runs on free trade with US – creamed by Borden.

1953 — King toys with US trade deal, remembers Laurier, drops idea, retires.

1970 — Liberal Party moves left, anti-US, anti-big business.

1980 — National Energy Program: Trudeau takes on US, big business. Tories become close allies of US, big business.

1983 — Mulroney pooh-poohs free trade in Tory leadership race.

1988 — Mulroney launches free trade talks in Quebec City. Liberals now fiercely opposed.

TORIES
LIBERALS

Last and most important for Mulroney, free trade sold well in his native province. Quebec certainly saw itself as a winner in the mid-1980s. Quebeckers believed they had developed a distinct formula for economic success: a combination of mighty state enterprises like Hydro-Québec and the Caisse de Dépôt et Placement along with private companies like the giant Bombardier manufacturing concern or Lavalin engineering. The Quiet Revolution had stormed the private sector, and Quebec Inc. was ready to take on the world.

Much of Mulroney's attraction to free trade was political, but this electoral chicken sprang from a public policy egg that was bigger even than bringing Canada back from the economic mess in which Trudeau had left it. An agreement would force Canada's decreasingly competitive industrial base to face up to US competition. Moreover, new countries, bristling with vigour, were entering the worldwide economy. This emerging phenomenon, called "globalization" by a few academics, made it all the more imperative for Canada to get serious about competing. There was no room in this new world for the anti-market, big government economic approaches of Trudeau's final mandate. "What makes us so special?" Mulroney asked witheringly in a House economic debate in 1985. A free trade agreement would signal that there was no going back into a protectionist bunker; it would commit Canada never to do so again.

The free trade deal initialled in Washington on October 4, 1987, was a massive, complex document: 194 pages covering everything from agriculture policy to subsidy definitions, with a thousand additional pages of tariff schedules. A free trade agreement commits two governments to refrain from using a range of policy tools to penalize the goods imported from the other country. Once that principle is accepted, the rest of the negotiation is spent drafting hundreds of exemptions, areas where the countries can keep on penalizing one another. The most important part is deciding what happens when one side thinks the other is breaking the new rules. It's a bit like writing a marriage contract while simultaneously establishing a family court system to enforce it. It's easy to get confused about what's being traded away here and exempted there, and even easier to get scared. There were no simple answers to some of the most explosive questions on the table between Canada and the United States — for example, on social programs. The teams couldn't agree on how to define a government subsidy, so the agreement was silent about them. What did the agreement's silences mean for social programs? Protection or exposure? What would the consequences be? Who knew? The deal was loaded with such political timebombs.

The Liberal and NDP opposition pounced on the agreement immediately, attacking it on a host of fronts in a campaign that would last right through to election day more than a year later. In a dramatic statement in a House of Commons debate on free trade on October 26, 1987, opposition leader Turner thundered: "We did not negotiate this deal, we are not bound by the deal, we will not live with this deal, and if the deal and the final contract reflects the principles and the general terms of the agreement we have seen, we are going to tear the deal up." Turner was not against free trade as such. "We are not a protectionist party like the NDP," he said in countless speeches and interviews. But the Liberals were deeply opposed to the specific Canada–US Free Trade Agreement (or "CUSTA" in the inelegant bureaucratese of the day) Mulroney and Reagan had cooked up. "I'm convinced that Canadians can be persuaded to look at the contract as a bad contract for Canada, as having been badly negotiated," Turner claimed in an interview with journalist Graham Fraser, "and having not achieved what it was supposed to achieve, and having given away too much." Turner understood that his was a lawyer's argument, too complex for the mass of undecided voters and too limited to generate emotion among them. He realized that, before the election, he needed to pare down the legalities and pump up the emotion: less on the weak dispute settlement mechanism and more on how Canadian culture would be engulfed in a tide of US swill. He needed to sound less like a gowned legalist and more like an old, righteous, hand-on-the-heart legionnaire.

The New Democrats shared none of the Liberals' anxieties over the nuances of free trade. They were heart and soul against it. Ed Broadbent, his caucus, the party rank and file, and his supporters in the electorate all opposed the deal on several levels. As social democrats they were opposed to free trade as such, believing that, once states withdrew from regulating trade, transnational corporations would move into the vacuum and capture for themselves the benefits at the expense of workers. As Canadian social democrats, they saw free trade with the United States as singularly inappropriate, since it would surrender in advance several of Ottawa's weapons in any trade disputes with the giant next door. And they shared with the Liberals a disdain for the particular deal the Tories and the Republicans had signed: it gave the Americans vast potential power to dismantle Canada's social programs, they claimed, and gave back next to nothing in return.

To the average voter, however, the position of the two opposition parties looked virtually indistinguishable on days like October 26, when Turner threatened to "tear up the deal." That morning, as on so many others since the trade negotiations had entered their most intense phase in the spring of 1987, Turner threw rhetorical caution to the wind, essentially abandoning his attempts to distinguish the hated deal from the principle of free trade, which he said he supported. Why had he gone so far?

The answer could be found on the floor of the House of Commons on the same day as the dramatic free trade debate. Around dinner time a majority of MPs in all parties serenely passed the Meech Lake accord to amend the Constitution, sending it off to the Senate by a vote of 242 to 16, giving force of law to Mulroney's signature on the constitutional agreement he had struck with the ten premiers the previous spring. Turner's hard-edged free trade position – in fact, the whole 1988 election – can only be understood by taking Meech into account as well. The deal was constructed to meet five demands made by Quebec's Liberal premier, Robert Bourassa: recognition of the province as a "distinct society"; restriction on the federal government's ability to spend money in areas of provincial jurisdiction; greater power for Quebec over immigration; increased control over federal judicial appointments for the provinces; and increased control over appointments to the Senate. Trudeau's 1982 deal had patriated the Constitution over Quebec's objections, and the province had never signed. For Mulroney, Meech Lake was the fulfilment of his pledge to Quebec from the 1984 campaign (drafted by his old university friend Lucien Bouchard) to negotiate a deal that would make Quebec want to "join the constitutional family" cheerfully, "with honour and enthusiasm."

By simultaneously advancing Meech Lake and free trade, Mulroney was trying to craft a Little Ottawa vision to succeed Trudeau's aggressive conception of the central government's role in both the federation and the economy. The provincialist federalism embodied in Meech Lake was an experiment in re-arranging national sovereignty, as was the Free Trade Agreement. Such experiments were common in the 1980s. While Meech Lake was

NAME: Robert Bourassa

PARTY: Liberal

ROLE: Quebec premier since 1985. Wants constitutional amendments. Will support Tories to get them.

being negotiated, the US government was also experimenting with devolving certain federal spending powers to the states, and Western Europe was embarking on a particularly fruitful period of strengthening its common governmental structure, the European Union.

Like any serious political vision, Mulroney's Little Ottawa tendency galvanized his coalition, bringing together those of a common policy view and uniting the regional elements of his support. Together, these initiatives allowed him to demonstrate a high order of leadership skill. It had the virtue of confounding his main opponent. The NDP weren't all that relevant and couldn't cost the Tories many votes. Consequently, the NDP's simple, coherent critique of the Tory approach – that in both the free trade deal and the Meech Lake Accord Ottawa was blindly handing its political

and economic power over to provincial governments, transnational corporations, and the United States – didn't trouble Mulroney. What excited the prime minister was the divisions the policy caused among his real competition, the Liberals. Many Grits shared the NDP's horror of this decentralizing juggernaut, but many others were more sympathetic – at least in private. Thus the Liberals, battered by their precipitous fall from power in 1984, experienced the combination of free trade and Meech as a wedge that threatened to split the "Natural Governing Party" into pieces.

NAME: Lucien Bouchard

PARTY: PC

ROLE: Mulroney's Quebec point-man. Ambassador to France since 1984. Elected in 1988 by-election.

When John Turner took over as Liberal leader in 1984, he was determined to moderate his party's policies away from Trudeau's Big Ottawa approach to both constitutional and economic affairs. He had served as a minister under Pearson and Trudeau before leaving for

NAME: John Turner

PARTY: Liberal

ROLE: Leader since 1984, defeated in election. Shaky hold on leadership. Must support Meech to maintain toehold in Quebec.

the private sector in 1975, and he pined for the old days when the federal government gave the provinces a little room to breathe and Ottawa worked with big business, not against it. But from the moment Turner left Bay Street to announce his candidacy for the Liberal leadership in April 1984, he found himself in a perpetual struggle with the Trudeau Liberals, who still dominated the party and who had supported his leadership bid only because they thought he could win the election.

When Turner blew the 1984 campaign, only narrowly winning his chosen seat in Vancouver Quadra, the Trudeau crew, led by Marc Lalonde and Keith Davey, decided they would dump the leader at the late November 1986 Liberal Convention and put in his place the Trudeau-era warhorse Jean Chrétien. They had judged Chrétien too "down-market" (in 80s real-estate lingo) when he ran to succeed their hero in 1984, but now, suddenly, he looked mighty fine. Chrétien had cagily resigned his seat in early 1986, partly to be offstage while the unseemly brawl that might give him the leadership played out.

As the convention neared, Turner needed friends, fast. He cobbled together a rambunctious crew of mostly younger Liberals who had impatiently waited their turn at power through the long twilight of the Trudeau era. These

new players — MPs like Sheila Copps and Jean Lapierre — arranged a mass recruitment of new members to vote for Turner at the constituency level. The 1984 leadership convention had been a proving ground for this new style of party politics: sleepy riding associations made up of Pearson-era grandees and ladies auxiliary envelope-stuffers had watched in horror as hundreds of "instant Liberals" — many of them drawn from the ethnocultural communities that had been the silent bedrock of Liberal support through the 1970s — poured out of rented school buses and elected their own as delegates to the leadership convention. Turner and the new-style Liberals triumphed.

NAME: Jean Chrétien

PARTY: Liberal

ROLE: Beaten by Turner in 1984 leadership. Resigns as MP in 1986. Trying to force Turner from office.

Turner used opposition to the anticipated trade deal to rally the troops at the convention against external enemies: Mulroney and the Americans. This tactic cost him the support not only of those personally dearest to him, his Bay Street buddies, but also of those most removed: Quebeckers. So, when the Meech Lake agreement was reached on April 30, 1987, Turner had to choose between supporting the deal to mend his Quebec fences and kissing the last of his support in the province goodbye if he opposed it.

He announced his support for the deal in early May, calling it an acceptable and hon-

(Opposite) Pierre Trudeau's worst nightmare: a nationalistic Quebec premier (Bourassa, *at right*) looking for more powers and a decentralizing prime minister (Mulroney, *at left* with Barbara McDougall) ready to deal.

ourable compromise, well in line with his detailed understanding of the country's constitutional history. But he also knew that position would anger a sizable swath of his English Canadian caucus and that it would put the two factions of his Quebec wing at each other's

NAME: Sheila Copps

PARTY: Liberal

ROLE: MP from Hamilton, Ontario. Turner backer, member of so-called Rat Pack. Pro-Meech, anti-free trade.

throats: the old Trudeauites versus the younger folks linked to Bourassa's provincial Liberal Party who had backed Turner at the convention. On May 8, 1987, Don Johnston, a former Trudeau minister and 1984 leadership candidate, resigned his seat in protest. Coup rumours swirled around the Liberal backrooms.

Meech didn't really play all that big among the public that summer, but within the interlocking Montreal-Ottawa-Toronto political community the buzz was dominated by the Liberals tearing themselves apart over the accord and, to a lesser extent, free trade. It was all Turner could do to sell his party on a compromise: "Yes" to Meech and "No" to free trade. Predictably, in August 1987 a full-scale caucus revolt broke out, with as many as a dozen MPs moving to depose the recently reconfirmed leader. The internal havoc wreaked on the Liberals by Mulroney's twin policy thrusts was demonstrated with brutal clarity in one stormy meeting that month, when Lloyd Axworthy shouted at Raymond Garneau, "Dammit, Raymond, you know the deal. I have to support your damned Meech Lake Accord so you better stick with me against free trade!" The more Turner's pro-Meech position infuri-

ated his English Canadian caucus, the more fiercely Turner pushed his opposition to free trade to mollify them.

Through November 1987, the House of Commons held public hearings on the agreement. These sessions were a big media show, political theatre in which each of the parties threw easy "fat-ball" questions to the witnesses they had recruited. A good example of this puppetry was Lloyd Axworthy's "questioning" of Margaret Atwood when she appeared before the committee. The Liberal external affairs critic, an opponent of globalization in general, asked the Toronto literary doyenne what Canadians thought of the deal. Atwood said that when she asked people what they thought of free trade, some said yes. But she claimed to receive different answers when she asked in the context of what the deal means: "If it means you have to give up your health insurance, unemployment benefits and regional development aid ... if you also have to give up Canada's foreign affairs autonomy and our visibility in arts and entertainment, and if it means the loss of a million jobs with only a vague notion of how they will be replaced, and if it also means we are committed to playing only by the other guy's rules ... and if it means the disintegration of Canada."

NAME: Don Johnston

PARTY: Liberal

ROLE: Montreal Anglo MP. Former Trudeau minister. Anti-Meech, pro-free trade.

The operetta in the committee room on Parliament Hill was part of a much broader, nationwide festival of political theatre known as a consultation process — what bureaucrats call "a consult." Even before the deal was ini-

NAME: Raymond Garneau

PARTY: Liberal

ROLE: Montreal MP. Turner's Quebec lieutenant. Close to Bourassa government. Pro-Meech, pro-free trade.

tialled in October 1987, the government had organized a massive apparatus so that inputs could be solicited, options refined, and recommendations developed. The basic goal of this pre-deal effort was to get the business community and as many other economic policy interest groups as possible onside for an initiative that could make losers out of a lot of them. Once the deal was signed, the bill implementing the agreement began moving through the legislative process.

To some extent, the hearings were just for show, enabling the government to say it had consulted widely. However, as the endless consultation process ground through its parliamentary phase, the ever-intensifying media coverage of the issue began signalling to Canadians that something very big was happening. The consultation process fed on itself. Huge numbers of groups and even individual citizens asked for a chance to appear – not just the usual suspects, lobby groups that come to every parliamentary committee, but common folks as well. This strange phenomenon further intensified media coverage, which in turn drove public concern even higher. Eventually, the logic would inevitably take hold among the people: if free trade was as big and as important as the government, the opposition, and the groups were saying it was, then maybe we should have an election about it. Consultations are for the usual suspects; elections are the way that real people get their say on an issue that really matters.

But as the public appetite for a free trade election grew through the late fall and into the winter, election strategists in all three parties were moving in the opposite direction. Throughout early 1988 the three parties' strategic teams wrestled with the intricate problem of how to win a national election with an unpredictable mega-issue like free trade lumbering around out there. The biggest problem was gauging how big you wanted it to be. When Mulroney had launched the initiative back in 1985, free trade seemed to be the vehicle that could carry his scandal-plagued government back to power. By early 1988 he wasn't so sure. True, his government was back on its feet politically, and the PCs' perennial pollster, Allan Gregg, had reams of data showing that, although all three parties were roughly even in the polls, many indicators beneath the surface were pointing in the right direction. Yet free trade, considered strictly on its merits, might not generate a renewed majority. Something felt wrong with the winning equation, and the prime minister set out to find what it was.

NAME: Lloyd Axworthy

PARTY: Liberal

ROLE: Winnipeg MP. Manitoba power broker when there's power to broker. Anti-Meech, anti-free trade.

Brian Mulroney was many things, but, foremost among them, he was a strategy guy, an accomplished practitioner at every aspect of orchestrating a modern campaign, from polling right through to advertising. To ensure his control of the strategy, and to keep his diverse and frequently fractious group of strategic talents happily in harness, Mulroney set up three different apparatuses: a formal campaign strategy group, including key ministers and organizers; a second network of leading back-room boys, former premiers, and the like; and a Quebec group. The only person with access to all three groups was the prime minister himself, and he tended to stay away from the actual meetings. Once in a while someone would be plucked from a group and brought into direct contact with the prime minister. Allan Gregg was used in this way, as were luminaries such as former Alberta premier Peter Lougheed and old sage Dalton Camp. But the only guy holding all the threads was Mulroney.

As much as any prime minister in our history, Mulroney understood how issues fit into a broader campaign. In the pre-writ period,

it's essential to raise the profile of issues that divide your opponents and appeal to your natural constituents – free trade and Meech Lake were perfect that way. Then, with the campaign about a year away, switch the focus to leadership positioning. When people think about the most important qualities in a leader, they should concentrate on the things this candidate happens to be good at. So, if you were Mulroney at the beginning of 1988 with eight cabinet resignations behind you, you wouldn't want to make "honesty and integrity" the most important leadership quality on voters' minds. More likely, you'd be making sure that "makes tough decisions" or "delivers prosperity" were the things people were looking for when they thought about choosing a prime minister.

PLAY UP FREE TRADE?

Hmm. It's early '88. Gonna call an election this year. This free trade issue is working well for me – shows me as a strong leader, plays to my economic credibility, which gives me a good lead over Turner on "Who's the best leader?" Best of all, it takes the scandal stuff off the front page. But free trade could take over the whole campaign. Should I really bet the farm on a single issue? This is an election, not a referendum, after all.

PLAY DOWN FREE TRADE?

By itself, free trade is too dangerous. I need to use its strengths without assuming too much risk. And that means fitting it into a broader context of leadership, which is what elections today are about. Sooo, I'll pitch free trade as just one of a number of economic issues – along with tax, job creation, etc. – that show how good a leader I am when it comes to delivering jobs and prosperity. It isn't the story; it's a picture in a story about me. Yeah, that's safer.

BRIAN MULRONEY
STRATEGY GUY

Mulroney scanned the situation in early 1988: the polls seemed to indicate that the Liberals' attempts to milk the trade issue were going nowhere. That reaction allowed the prime minister to change course somewhat: free trade could still be a big issue, but not the only one. In January 1988 one of his three strategy groups had reviewed a paper which argued that "the negative appeal against free trade, and in particular that our cultural identity and other distinctive features of Canadian life are endangered, has failed." Into the spring the polling numbers for the Tories continued to improve, confirming their sense that riding the free trade vehicle wasn't really necessary any more. By July 15 a session of the key Cabinet Committee on Priorities and Planning was informed: "The central message of our campaign is that the continuation of Canada's present prosperity depends on the re-election of a PC government … The issue of competent, successful economic management, set in the context of the recent Liberal recession and the present economic expansion, must condition and shape the debate on all other issues of voter concern. It is the issue on which all others turn."

Mulroney didn't write the papers or argue for them at meetings; rather, he arranged things so that the decisions made at the meetings had a way of being what he wanted them to be. (This light-touch style helped keep the Tory caucus together through thick and thin, without any grumbling over the prime minister's leadership ever leaking out.) As the decision to call an election loomed, Mulroney had his game plan in place and the marching orders issued. Ballot box question: "Which leader is most able to govern Canada?" Key criterion for answering the question: economic ability. Illustrations: free trade, job creation, GDP growth. That was in English Canada, of course. In Quebec the question would be: "Qui c'est qui va nous représenter?" Who should represent us?

As a native son – the north shore Irish were so assimilated into francophone Quebec they might as well have come from Normandy – Mulroney had a big advantage. Moreover, given Turner's effective-but-not-perfect French, the Grits' anti–free trade position, and, above all, their only shaky support for Meech Lake, answering the Quebec ballot box question was pretty much a no-brainer.

For the New Democratic Party, the real question was how to use the 1988 campaign to finish off the Liberals, who looked set up for the kill. The 1984 election had brought the party of the left to the very threshold of a historic breakthrough, with just ten seats fewer than the Liberals and actually overtaking them in English Canada. New Democrats saw the destruction of the Liberals as a historic inevitability, the precursor to a "normal," two-party system of conservatives and socialists along the British model. The NDP's ace was Ed Broadbent. After three general elections as leader, his brown-jacketed presence had become a comfortable part of Canada's national political furniture. When the polls showed Broadbent as the most trusted of the three leaders, New Democrats smiled at how well their "Main Street" man's image played against "Bay Street's" Mulroney and Turner. When they showed the party at 28–30 per cent, as they did routinely in the run-up to the election, they smiled even more.

But when New Democrats thought about connecting the looming issue of free trade to their strengths in the leadership area, their foreheads crinkled. Voters were not likely to trust the NDP on economic policy questions; they trusted the Liberals more. Broadbent's two chief strategists, the intense Montrealer chief of staff, George Nakitsas, and the party's easy-going federal secretary, Saskatchewan's Bill Knight, agreed that a free trade–dominated campaign seemed "a sure loser." New Democrats wanted the electorate to divide on the issue of trust,

ED BROADBENT, PART OF THE FURNITURE

Broadbent, the New Democrat helmsman since 1975, had become a familiar and comfortable figure as the 1988 election neared. In terms of personal popularity, his rumpled, avuncular presence routinely out-polled the sleek Mulroney and the tightly wound Turner – between elections. After three campaigns, however, this one would be do-or-die for Broadbent. Poised to eclipse the weakened Liberals, he would follow a two-pronged strategy. In English Canada, he would seek to contrast his trustworthy image against Mulroney's slippery public profile. And in Quebec, for the first time, his party would mount a serious effort, building on its 1987 by-election win south of Montreal (*below*), which yielded the NDP its first-ever Quebec seat. If it worked, Broadbent and the NDP would emerge from Campaign '88 as the official opposition. If it failed, Broadbent knew it would be time to step down.

which would pit the ultra-trustworthy Broadbent against the cynically regarded Mulroney and squeeze Turner out of the play. To force that division, the NDP strategy proposed to use free trade as one of many illustrations of Mulroney's untrustworthiness, along with scandals, tax cuts for the wealthy, and other misdeeds.

NAME: George Nakitsas

PARTY: New Democrat

ROLE: Campaign manager. Montrealer. Determined to engineer party breakthrough in Quebec. Brooding, intense.

The Liberal team also wanted to ease up on the free trade issue. Martin Goldfarb – Trudeau's pollster and now, after some uncertainty in 1986, Turner's – argued alongside his associate, Senator Michael Kirby, for a broader approach. "Free trade should not be the central issue of the campaign … Free trade should be used as a device to demonstrate that Mulroney cannot and should not be trusted." In the run-up to the election, all three parties were strategically comfortable with fighting the campaign on leadership, Mulroney's in particular.

NAME: Michael Kirby

PARTY: Liberal

ROLE: Campaign co-chair (with André Ouellette). Senator. Former constitutional strategist to Trudeau.

All three wanted to use free trade as an illustration of their theme, not as the main message. For the Liberals, the ballot box question would be: "Who should govern?" The key criterion would be trustworthiness. Turner should start pushing the message of trust, not just trade.

With hindsight, it's obvious that, in their fixation on Mulroney's leadership, all three parties' strategists missed the latent importance of the free trade issue. They all made this judgement in the belief that their party would lose if a single-issue campaign broke out, but they couldn't all be right. Perhaps the political pros were somewhat resistant to an election fought on free trade. They knew how a campaign about leadership would work. An issue-dominated election wasn't in their playbook, so they went on planning for the kind of election they knew how to run.

But one leader wasn't always listening to his strategists. Out in the backways of the country, through the spring and summer of 1988, in linoleum-floored church basements and pine-panelled local radio studios, John

NAME: Bill Knight

PARTY: New Democrat

ROLE: Federal secretary (runs the party). Easy-going former chief of staff to Saskatchewan premier Blakeney.

Turner was discovering that what a Goldfarb might call "recontextualizing CUSTA as an illustrator of Mulroney's leadership/credibility factor" didn't work. The only thing that did work for him, the only thing that got crowds looking up from their programs and clapping, then cheering, then standing and hollering "Go, John, Go!" – the only thing that felt like politics oughta feel for Turner – was free trade. "Canadians are not anti-American," he would say, "but we do happen to be pro-Canadian." "This is not a trade deal which merely lowers tariffs," he said. "It goes beyond that. It's the Sale of Canada Act."

Outside Ottawa in the hinterland, Turner was throwing his own intellectual nuances out

SIR JOHN A. TURNER

In 1988 John Turner transforms his complex, lawyerly dissection of the free trade agreement into a passionate defence of Canada's economic nationalist traditions. Ironically, chief among these was the National Policy of Sir John A. Macdonald *(below)*, a protectionist approach the Tory Party had now abandoned.

the window in favour of a big, passionate, roundhouse denunciation – not only of the deal's terms and conditions but also of its whole impetus, its thrust and its impact on the existence of Canada itself. Consciously or not, he'd given up trying to balance opposition to this particular deal with support of free trade in principle. Consultation wasn't good enough, he roared. "The people must decide! Call an election!" Turner began to label the battle over free trade "the fight of my life." It was easy to see why. "This will really be an election that has something to do with history, because we'll be deciding as a people whether to recommit ourselves to Canada, or we'll be deciding to succumb, after one-hundred-and-twenty courageous years of struggling against American continentalism and manifest destiny … the question is whether we have something worth fighting for. I believe we do. And I am going to fight." John Turner was off-message, but he was loving it and it was working.

As the summer 1988 parliamentary recess loomed, Mulroney's plans began to come together. On June 21 his friend and ambassador to France, Lucien Bouchard, was elected to parliament in a by-election to put a scandal-free face on the party in Quebec. The Toronto Summit of G-7 leaders, which took place at the same time, was a success. On June 22 the final House vote on Meech Lake passed overwhelmingly, with a handful of Liberals and New Democrats opposing.

But once the House went into summer recess, Turner decided to take a huge gamble. With the legislation approving the free trade agreement coming before the House at the end of summer, after the recess, Turner on July 20 publicly instructed the Liberal-controlled, unelected Senate to block passage of the bill until after an election. Turner understood the risk – highlighting the trade issue ran counter to his party's new strategy – but he concluded he needed to give it a try in order to prop up his soft image as a leader. His reputation, after all, had been further damaged by another caucus revolt that spring. Turner's gutsy move, taken in part to respond to public concerns that his commitment to fighting free trade might itself be negotiable, was a public success. Despite heavy criticism from Mulroney, who said Turner had "decided to resign his leadership" to the senators, and Broadbent, who charged that Turner was "prepared to abandon democracy," a Reid poll on July 29 showed 65 per cent supported the Liberal leader's move. An impressive 69 per cent agreed that Mulroney should call an election by the end of the year.

In an August 28 TV interview, the prime minister promised that an election would be held that fall. Three days later the legislation implementing the deal cleared the House of Commons and was sent to the Senate, where the Liberal blockade awaited. On September 28 President Reagan signed the US version of the bill. For Brian Mulroney and John Turner, the fight of their lives was about to begin.

Campaign '88 began on Saturday, October 1, with the required visit of the prime minister to Rideau Hall. Exercising his sole prerogative of election timing, Brian Mulroney asked Governor General Jeanne Sauvé (the first woman to hold the job) to dissolve parliament for an election on November 21, seven weeks hence. It would be a full-length campaign, carefully blocked out by Mulroney to place the now *de rigueur* TV debates at the mid-point – once the World Series was over – and leave enough time before election day to recover if they went badly. Election day was chosen so as not to fall on Rosh Hashanah or Yom Kippur, or to conflict with Ontario's municipal elections on November 14.

The timing of the October 24 (French) and 25 (English) debates, agreed upon in the campaign's first week, would coincide with the release of paid advertising on October 23. As a result, the 1988 campaign departed from the three-part campaign structure of earned media only; earned media and bought media; debates and after. Instead, Mulroney divided the campaign into two long frames: a three-week earned-media-only period; then the simultaneous onslaught of advertising and debates commencing a month-long free-for-all of post-debate dynamics, earned media, and intensive advertising.

As the prime minister made his announcement that bright fall morning, he was perfectly on-message, acting out the Tory strategy by personifying sound management in word and deed. "The key question for the electorate," he intoned as he stood in front of stately Rideau Hall, "will be who can best manage change in the years ahead. We intend to run on our record of the past and our plans for the future." When a television reporter asked, "Will it [free trade] be the centrepiece of your campaign?" Mulroney replied, "It will be very much a centrepiece of our political action in the campaign." Not the centrepiece, but a centrepiece; not the campaign, but "our political action in the campaign." The prime minister rattled off a list of other centrepieces: Meech Lake, childcare, the environment. The harvest table fairly groaned with centrepieces. Mulroney then went home to 24 Sussex to prepare for an easy-going, tightly controlled tour of friendly ridings, factory floors, and other velvet-rope venues. They were carefully selected to present to the cameras attractive visuals illustrating the many aspects of "change" and how well Brian Mulroney was "managing" them.

The machine behind Mulroney, headed by Senator Norman Atkins, was in some ways built around Atkins's operational talents and in other ways around Mulroney's strategic skills. Atkins was an organization guy, a former army quartermaster who had come up through Bill Davis's Ontario PC machine and excelled at logistics, supply, and keeping everyone on the team pulling in the same direction. A squad of functionaries worked under him to transmit the PM's strategic thoughts into a dazzling array of events, messages, endorsements, ads, planted stories, poll questions, phone-bank operations, posters, buttons, brochures – you name it, the awe-inspiring, well-financed, shrewdly staffed PC machine could make it happen.

The Liberal campaign organization was nowhere near as impressive. Mulroney's election call found John Turner at the ready, mainstreeting in Toronto's rambunctious, multi-ethnic Kensington Market, a place chosen to project the Liberals' self-image: real people, from "many colours/many cultures," all in a vibrant community. The market's general cheery chaos – a riot of fish smells, chicken slaughter, and bump-and-grind in the pickle line-up – was also an accurate projection of the Liberal Party. It was under-financed, understaffed, undertechnologized – it was underdog to the core. For example, two twenty-five-year-olds were responsible for organizing all the Toronto ridings. Talented though they were, their lofty stature says more about the Liberals' 1988 campaign than it does about them. Because there wasn't time or

MULRONEY'S "COCOON" TOUR

The Tory leader's tour consisted of a string of events that were stagey, plastic, boring – and effective. Print reporters might scribble their outrage at the campaign's empty cynicism, but the TV cameras – for which the tour was designed – got the visuals the nightly newscasts needed.

money for much else, Turner's team, headed by Kirby and Goldfarb along with Quebec MP André Ouellette, was more organization driven than the machine Atkins had built for Mulroney. The heart of the campaign was a grim effort, conducted chiefly by campaign director John Webster, to wrestle form out of chaos in 295 ridings: recruiting candidates, holding nomination meetings, filing papers, organizing rallies, bringing the leader through. Amazingly, the satellite uplinks worked that Sunday morning, allowing the networks to capture Turner's campaign launch live.

The Liberal leader was in fine form. "For two months," he said, "I have been asking the prime minister to let the people decide; today he finally agreed … This election is primarily about two things: an independent and sovereign Canada … and fairness, particularly for low- and middle-income Canadians who have been hit by Tory tax increases over the last four years." Having elbowed aside free trade to share primary status with tax fairness, Turner was now trotting out his own collection of centrepieces: "equality for women," "rights of minorities," "secure pensions," "our priceless environment"… Goldfarb must have been proud of his boy, too, although the Liberals had clearly not resolved their mixed feelings about blending a free trade attack in with other themes. The slogan under which Turner would fight was a clear pitch along the free trade/sale-of-Canada line, a long, thin banner bearing the legend "This Is More Than an Election. This Is Your Future."

An Angus Reid poll published on Wednesday, October 5, showed the Tories at a domineering 45 per cent. At 26 per cent, the Liberals were actually one point behind the NDP. This unprecedented ranking of the parties made for a fascinating opening phase. Instead of the customary phoney war, the first two weeks turned into a Liberal deathwatch. The polling itself was news: never before had the mighty Liberals entered a campaign anywhere near third place. This ranking forced Turner to spend much of his air time on the defensive, trying to answer questions about his dire prospects with attacks on Mulroney.

On the days when the Liberals managed to focus attention on their message, the results were even worse. The day of the Reid poll, a spectacular pratfall came when Turner, flanked by caucus critics and policy advisers, announced an expansive child-care policy in Montreal. Questioned by reporters about some particularly complicated accounting in the program's price tag, it became clear that the Liberal leader did not fully understand how his child-care program would be paid for. His shadow minister, his social policy adviser, and, later, his chief of staff, Peter Connolly, each rode to his rescue, but each failed miserably to clarify the issue. The evening's newscasts gave prominent play to the Keystone Kops–style Liberal mathematicians and the incident reverberated for days, illustrated by visual clips of Turner limping in pain from a flare-up of a chronic medical condition in his back. That Friday night Connolly, sharing a drink with reporters at a Toronto hotel bar, let loose with a screaming tirade, a performance that served only to heighten their conviction that the wheels were coming off the Liberal campaign bus.

As the second week began, an Environics poll echoed Reid's week one tally: PCS 42; NDP 29; Liberals 25. Statistically the numbers were indistinguishable from Reid's, but they created the public impression that the Liberals were falling behind the NDP (which was, in fact, what private Liberal polls showed). The data on leadership were even more crushing: 40 per cent of Canadians would like to see Mulroney as prime minister; Broadbent stood at 29 per cent; and Turner commanded a miserable 15 per cent. At the weekly sum-up

IRISH EYES SMILING
MULRONEY ON THE CAMPAIGN TRAIL

Brian Mulroney may have been its mastermind, but the PC campaign was operated by the "Big Blue Machine," a coterie of Ontario Tories who had perfected an antiseptic but reliable method of keeping incumbents in power. Sometimes the events were a little boring, or broke cardinal rules like the "no stupid hats" dictum flouted at this aerospace factory visit *(left middle)*. But most of the time they provided a controlled, TV-friendly environment in which the prime minister's formidable campaigning skills could shine. With his wife, Mila, present by his side, Mulroney was relaxed, comfortable, and having fun, as in this sendoff at an Ottawa airport *(top left)*. His cool professionalism is on display handling a large scrum *(bottom middle)* and his victory wave is well polished *(below)* as he campaigns for a second straight majority win. And when it came time to lay on the serious messages – as when he alleged John Turner was a liar – he knew how to emote the intensity of his concern *(left)*. Much as he was a gifted talent on the hustings, however, strategy was his ultimate forte. In this photo taken at night in the House of Commons *(bottom left)*, he gives Finance Minister Mike Wilson his latest orders as he keeps the Tory machine humming along towards victory.

meeting that Friday, the Liberal strategic team headed by Michael Kirby drafted a frank memo warning Turner of the gravity of the situation.

The polls led NDP leader Ed Broadbent, campaigning in Hamilton, Ontario, to speculate publicly about the death of Liberalism and the establishment of a two-party system in Canada. These gleeful remarks were thoroughly out of character for the usually disciplined Broadbent – and costly. The gentlemanly leader was revealed to voters as just another ambitious politician. Wavering Liberals everywhere rallied to their tottering standard, and Liberal strategists reported that the NDP's upward climb in the campaign promptly levelled off.

Mulroney always enjoyed Liberal–NDP scraps: he called them "lovers' quarrels." It was certainly easy going for Mulroney in those first two weeks: an endless procession through fundraising breakfasts, chamber of commerce luncheons, and plant openings in which he linked the economic prosperity of the present to the opportunities free trade would open in the future. In 1988 the media hated covering the Mulroney tour. They were herded around like children on a field trip, bored to stupefaction by hours' worth of set-up for six seconds' worth of predictable content, and deprived of their lifeblood: news. In desperation, they probed relentlessly for a crack in the armour of high-production values and scripted messaging that surrounded the prime minister, but to no avail. The PCs were playing it safe and sticking to their plan. If the tour was banal and lacked verve, so what? Parties at 45 per cent don't take chances because they don't need to. Besides, the Tories were following Admiral Nelson's dictum: "When the enemy is committed to a mistake, we must not interrupt him too soon."

Committing to mistakes is exactly what the Liberals now did with a renewed vengeance. Through most of week three, from Friday, October 14, to Wednesday, October 19, an extraordinary set of events unfolded, an episode that would come to be known as "the coup attempt" – which was, depending on how you looked at it, either the most dastardly, uncalled-for, mid-campaign back-stab a party

TURNER'S CHILD-CARE PRATFALL

A camera-friendly announcement in a Montreal daycare centre becomes a catastrophe for the Liberals, as no one on the Grit team can explain precisely how their child-care program will be funded.

But sir, these costing figures just don't add up.

Heh, heh. Pipe down kid. The press is here.

Why are all those TV men laughing?

ever perpetrated on its leader or the most dastardly, mid-campaign back-stab the media ever perpetrated on a party. The facts are spare, but the opportunities for speculation and misinterpretation hung off each part of the episode like ornaments from a Christmas tree.

By week three the Grits' private polls were catastrophic, projecting as few as eight Liberal seats on election day. From Wednesday, October 12, to Friday, October 14, a number of senior Liberal campaign operatives, including Kirby and Ouellette, began individually and in groups to think through the question on the mind of every Liberal in the know: whether things weren't going so badly that Turner might as well step down, Chrétien take over, and the party try to salvage the campaign with him as leader. It was a crazy plan, born of panic. The idea that the public would put its trust in a politician sprung upon them mid-campaign as leader of the opposition was almost as daft as the notion that Chrétien could go from working in a law office to a televised leaders' debate against Mulroney and Broadbent in the space of a week. Yet the idea took on a life of its own, with some players promoting it, some considering it out loud, others keeping their own counsel, and still others rejecting it outright as too stupid, unworkable, and dangerous even to listen to.

On Saturday night, October 15, Turner's debate preparation at Stornaway was interrupted when Peter Connolly arrived to report on the rumblings. Turner, used to this stuff after two public coup attempts, dismissed Connolly: "They're nuts. Tell whoever it is 'no way.'" He wasn't about to give his job to Chrétien, the man he'd beaten in a bitter leadership race. He figured he'd do just fine in the campaign, thank you very much. And, as a veteran of seven elections, Turner had some sense of how ridiculous the whole stunt would seem to the voters.

On Sunday, October 16, and Monday, October 17, senior Liberal MPs joined the *danse macabre*. The politicians were wrestling with the same issue as the strategists and were, moreover, intensely angry over a newspaper story accurately reporting that, without informing them, Turner was considering a headline-grabbing announcement of a new, more pro-choice abortion policy, perhaps during the televised leaders' debates scheduled for the following week. All these phone calls, cloakroom whispers, and coded luncheon chats had to leak out, and, by Monday night, both Mulroney and Broadbent were aware that weird things were going on inside the Liberal campaign. They couldn't believe the madness that had descended on their opponents, but, holding to Nelson's advice, they told no one outside their innermost circles.

By now, however, the media had picked up the scent. On Saturday, October 15, *Le Devoir* ran a story with the subhead-line "coup rumours resurface." The CBC's national news anchor, Peter Mansbridge, and Ottawa bureau chief, Elly Alboim, were already working on a major story about the challenge to Turner from within. The story was ready to air by Tuesday night, but was pulled before broadcast to allow for some loose reporting ends to be tied up. Then the Liberals found out the CBC had a story in the can and started calling to find out what was in it. Realizing that other media would soon break the CBC's own story, the network resolved to broadcast it on Wednesday night's newscast. At 10:08 on the 19th, Canadians who had tuned into *The National* heard that "our chief correspondent, Peter Mansbridge, has the story of a party in crisis."

The CBC had the goods all right, with names, dates, phone calls, and places of every meeting, non-meeting, and huddle that had taken place the previous week. The essence of the story was that "deep into this campaign …

[some of the most senior Liberals] thought about putting pressure on John Turner to quit." The news report went off like a bomb. Competing media quoted every Liberal willing to offer an opinion. Turner and everyone else attacked the story's innuendoes, declining to quarrel with its facts. Assorted second-tier Liberals – candidates and backroom figures – replicated the same process of promotion, reaction, and denial, ultimately settling down just as the inner ring had done the week before. By the weekend, the tide had ebbed, leaving an inky residue of think pieces in the newspapers about what it all meant and who had screwed up worse – the Liberals or the CBC.

From a journalism standpoint it was a loose story, filled with hearsay and reportage about an elusive flow of ideas and possibilities, an amalgam of almost pure abstraction: some Liberals gave some thought to some options. Still, the Liberals in question were senior enough for the story to be newsworthy. Only three things are indisputable: that the Liberals were desperate; that the whole week was severely damaging to public perception of the Grits; and that modern, high-speed campaigning had reached the level at which every Canadian could find out what was going on in the heart of a campaign, sometimes only hours after the latest developments had materialized. It was as though voters could check out the gin bottle stashed in the lower right-hand drawer of Sir John A.'s desk.

By the weekend of October 22–23 the leaders were intensively preparing for the French debate on Monday and its English-language sequel on Tuesday. Mulroney and Broadbent engaged in lengthy preparation sessions with key advisers, Broadbent laying on additional time with his French teacher. Turner, in desperate need both of a big win and a quantum leap in the quality of his television performance, pulled out all the stops.

Friday was devoted to a full-scale simulation of the debate in an Ottawa TV studio, with Turner's key aide Scott Sheppard playing Mulroney and the role of Broadbent played by Hershell Ezrin, chief of staff to Ontario's Liberal premier, David Peterson. Saturday was spent endlessly replaying tapes of the simulation with Henry Comor, a former West End actor and television producer who was training Turner in television presentation techniques. The two men scrolled for hours through facial close-ups revealing annoying tics and wayward eye movements or outbreaks of throat-clearing and hunched-shoulder atrocities. The same routine took place on Sunday in French: former Trudeau minister Francis Fox played Mulroney, former MP Serge Joyal played Broadbent, and advertising executive André Morrow analyzed the tapes with Turner. Both Ouellette and Kirby stayed out of the final debate preparations.

Purists decry this kind of image doctoring, but it's actually quite healthy. Comor's and Morrow's thrust was simple and fundamentally democratic: Turner had to stop creating visual clutter so that viewers could pay attention to what he was saying. Well-cut suits and proper breathing were necessary for Canadians to give their undistracted attention to Turner's arguments about the country's future.

While the leaders were finishing preparations on Sunday night, the campaign was entering its next phase. That night, the Elections Act's ban on paid advertising elapsed, unleashing a wave of party propaganda into the nation's living rooms. The Liberals' principal spot for English Canada was far and away the best of the campaign and the finest piece of political image-making since Macdonald's "Old Leader" poster of 1891. The commercial was set in an imaginary meeting room in which Canadian and US negotiators are bargaining over free trade. The young, very Wall Street US guy says to the aging

BEWARE THE IDES OF OCTOBER

The mid-campaign "coup attempt" to dump Turner for Jean Chrétien was an eruption of desperation fed by panic over horrendous poll results and the endless scheming that had plagued the Liberals since Turner had gained – then lost – the prime ministership in 1984. The poor guy must have felt about as loved as Julius Caesar on the Ides of March.

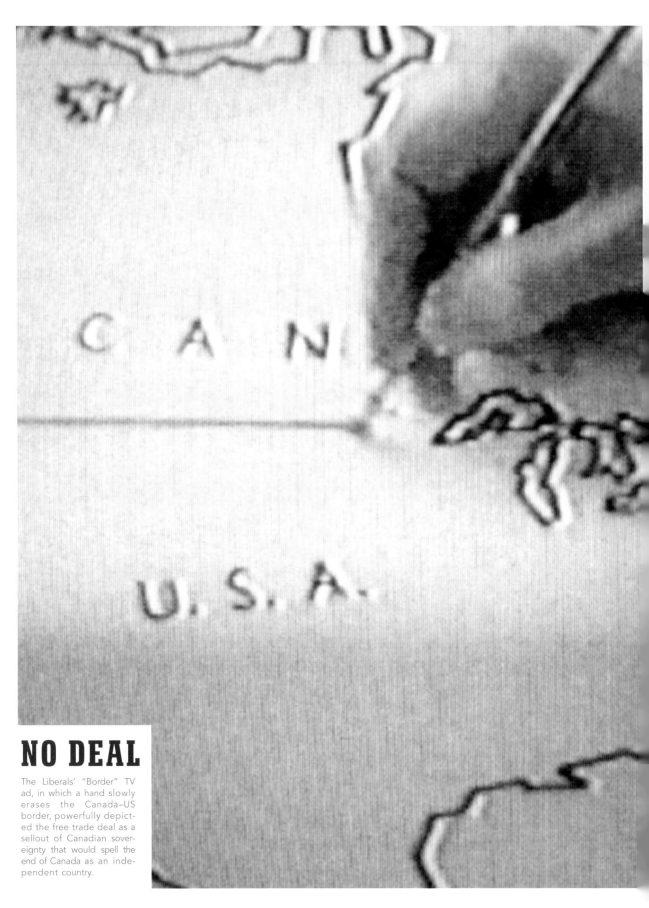

NO DEAL

The Liberals' "Border" TV ad, in which a hand slowly erases the Canada–US border, powerfully depicted the free trade deal as a sellout of Canadian sovereignty that would spell the end of Canada as an independent country.

Canadian mandarin-*manqué*, "There is one line I'd like to change." "Which line is that?" The camera shows a map of North America, with a hand holding a pencil eraser, steadily rubbing out the Canada–us border. "This one here," says Mr. Harvard Yard. The voice-over cuts in: "Just how much are we giving away in the Mulroney free trade deal? Our water? Our health care? Our future? The line has been drawn – Which side do you stand on?"

"Border" (as the commercial was called) may have lacked subtlety, but it was brutally effective. It took a very abstract and complex idea – this free trade thing could threaten sovereignty – and turned it into something very simple: we'll be swallowed by the United States. It depicted that swallowing-up with a light touch that was all the more menacing for its delicacy. There were no marines raising Old Glory over Green Gables, just something precious being quietly erased in some backroom somewhere. The ad's kicker was a reaction shot of the Canadian negotiator: a little half-smile played across his face. With that, it zoomed right past the merits of the deal and into Mulroney's trustworthiness. The spot put on-screen a little drama that had been playing in a lot of minds since Mulroney, President Reagan, and their wives got onstage to sing "When Irish Eyes Are Smiling" in Quebec City in March 1985. Maybe that bastard Mulroney is selling us all up the river! A viewer had about two beats to think that one through before the voice-over rolled in: "Don't let Mulroney deceive you again – this is more than an election; this is your future. On November 21, vote Liberal."

By contrast, the Tory ads were about as exciting and grabby as the rest of their campaign. The one with the heaviest rotation simply threw a bunch of newspaper quotes over stills of Mulroney doing prime minister-ish things: sitting at his desk, chatting with the chancellor of West Germany, giving a speech. The voice-over concluded the laundry list of kudos with: "Prime Minister Mulroney: 'The initiator of [Canada's] great new era.'"

The best NDP spot dealt with the environment. An old man and his grandson ruminated over an environmentally damaged alpine lake. "Can we fix it?" asks the tyke. "First we need a leader who isn't afraid to stand up to the big corporations," says the septuagenarian socialist. "Brian Mulroney promised that, but he let us down, just like the Liberals." The kid throws a stone in the lake. "What are you going to do, Grampa?" "This time, I'm voting for Ed Broadbent." Point made, a little kicker was thrown in: "Can I vote for Ed Broadbent too, Grampa?" It was impossible not to smile at the artistry, but almost equally difficult to keep the spot in mind while the shoot-out between Turner and Mulroney was brewing.

It is difficult to imagine the pressure John Turner carried on his stiffened shoulders as the final hours before the debates ticked away. The Liberal Party of Canada was staring death in the face on his watch, creating the possibility that Turner would go down in Canadian history as the all-time worst leader of a major national party. There was only one slender chance to avert collapse: a smashing, come-from-behind debate victory. The expectations of Turner were so low it really wasn't an impossible mission. As Mulroney himself told a friend, "If this guy shows up and makes a nice presentation, he's going to be canonized." But Turner had to do more than just show up; he needed to hit Mulroney hard. It didn't hurt that, as far as Turner was concerned, Mulroney was a low-down untrustworthy so-and-so who had pole-axed him on the patronage issue in 1984, won the election on his promise to clean things up, then turned around and gone on a troughing binge that would have made King wince. Four years later, far from being afraid of the man who'd flattened him, Turner relished a rematch.

The French debate featured a predictably fine performance from Mulroney, clearly the only one of the leaders who felt at home speaking the language. Mulroney laid it on thick, at one point deploying the magical Québécois phrase "chez nous" three times in a single sentence. But Turner, whose French was more than workable, delivered a strong performance. He focused on the Mulroney government's record of scandal among Quebec ministers. The Liberals in Quebec ran under the slogan *Un gouvernement Libéral, c'est clair et net* (it's open and clean). It may have sounded more like a pitch for window spray, but translating the English slogan – telling Quebeckers that this wasn't just an election, that free trade was at stake – would probably have only increased the Tories' turnout.

Turner supplemented his verbal attacks with a tactic from his trainer Comor – glaring at Mulroney throughout the debate and, when it was his turn to be seated, remaining standing with a somewhat predatory expression. Mulroney found himself turning his eyes downward to avoid Turner's gaze, creating the impression that Turner was confident and powerful, Mulroney weak and defensive. Viewers also got the sense that Turner's confidence stemmed from arguing something he believed in, a fine contrast to the tentativeness shown by the prime minister. Turner gave many Quebeckers their first real introduction to English Canadian economic nationalism, thus presenting the novel image of a wealthy Anglo, Turner, in the role of underdog, for which Quebeckers instinctively cheer. The Quebec media sat up and took notice. At the end of the three-hour marathon, media opinion was split between those who said Mulroney had won and those who argued Turner had so greatly surpassed expectations that he would gain the most from the debate. All agreed that Broadbent had been much weaker than expected, his second-language skills failing him in the crucial test.

Mulroney had been surprised by Turner's strong performance in the French debate, but not enough to change his debate strategy: appear prime ministerial, take it as it comes, win by not losing. As for Broadbent, he began to shift strategy. The key to the English debate for him was both to demonstrate the prime ministerial demeanour to ensure that, in so doing, he was not shunted aside while Turner and Mulroney blasted away at each other. Sensing that the free trade issue might become the focus of a direct personal confrontation among leaders, the NDP team resolved to put a greater focus on the deal than had originally been contemplated – in the debate and in their campaign.

The English debate was formatted in three broad segments: an hour on general issues, an hour on "issues of particular concern to women," and a final hour of general debate. Each of these hours was further divided into three one-on-one match-ups, with one leader sitting out the segment. The marathon structure favoured Mulroney, whose strategy called more for endurance than for spectacular sprints that would use up energy.

When Broadbent led off the leaders' opening statements, he placed front and centre a tight, pithy attack on the free trade agreement. He charged that the agreement would jeopardize Canada's social programs: "Mr. Mulroney's deal threatens our medicare and pension plans. As businessmen are already saying, benefits in Canada must be reduced to meet US standards ..." Broadbent's goal was to draw public concern away from economic issues, about which the NDP had little credibility, and onto the social programs, an area where Canadians trusted the party. The strong opening, however, soon got lost in the shuffle of debate about a variety of issues from taxes to scandals.

Through the debate's first segments, the handlers in Mulroney's trailer and his claque of spin-doctors in the off-stage pressroom were feeling good. Broadbent's slow fade into the background seemed their biggest concern, in that his weak performance would tend to loosen up NDP voters who might then go with the Liberals. But these were minor matters compared with Mulroney's confident, evenly paced defence of the government's record and his well-rounded articulation of the "managing change" theme. Turner had taken a couple of runs at him on trade and scandal, but hadn't managed to entice Mulroney into an all-out confrontation and end it with a knock-out blow.

As the debate's second hour wound down, the mood in the Liberal trailer was anxious. Inside were two aides: tour boss Doug Kirkpatrick was there to keep others from entering and harassing the leader during the breaks; Scott Sheppard stood at the ready with the facts and argumentation he had mastered over three years as Turner's chief House assistant. Both excelled at maintaining a calm atmosphere so that their leader could focus on what mattered, yet, when the boss came in for a break during Mulroney's and Broadbent's segment on women's issues, they felt tense. Turner had assured them that the three-hour debate would offer an opening for the confrontation he sought, but with only a single twenty-minute one-on-one exchange remaining between him and Mulroney, Sheppard and Kirkpatrick were praying that their man would stop waiting for an opening and force one instead. In the trailer's confines, "Turner was like a racehorse," remembered Sheppard years later, "very high energy … The vein on his neck was going." But the Liberal leader wasn't fearful. With minutes to go before entering the final round, Turner sensed the anxiety of his men. He turned from his pacing, grinned, and said "Relax."

It was just before 9 p.m. Turner walked across the parking lot, alone, down the narrow, dry-walled hallways, past the doormen, and out onto the studio floor to face Mulroney. The first question of the round was about free trade. Turner gave his lawyer's argument that the deal had given too much away for too little in return. Mulroney countered with a list of anticipated job-creation benefits. But Turner jabbed back, attacking the deal as undemocratic and going after the prime minister for his refusal to agree to a third debate exclusively about the free trade deal. Somewhat taken aback by Turner's intensity, Mulroney said wearily that he had spent six hours on national television answering Turner's objections and what more was there to say?

This left Turner no choice but to keep charging. He rushed at Mulroney with his ultimate argument: the country's sovereignty, its very existence. "I think the issues happen to be so important … I happen to believe that you have sold us out …"

At this point, Turner stepped out from behind his lectern. This aggressive, menacing move (which he and Comor had worked out on the weekend) was clearly intended to cow Mulroney in the studio. On television it created an even more powerful effect. The cameras, fixed in their angles according to debate rules, no longer showed two men of roughly equal height taking up roughly equal on-screen space. Now, the shot looking over Turner's back at Mulroney was dominated by the spread of the opposition leader's muscular, flexing shoulders and it made the figure of Mulroney seem small, almost cringing by comparison. When the camera reversed angles to Mulroney's point of view, it showed Turner draw up to full height, then step out from behind his lectern. On-screen he towered over Mulroney, his blue eyes flashing like an avenging angel's. By revealing his entire body before the cameras, Turner conveyed the crucial message about trust: I have nothing to hide. "I happen to believe that, once you – "

MANO A MANO

The climactic Mulroney–Turner confrontation took just 2 minutes and 38 seconds at the tail end of the English-language leaders' debate. Not only did it blow the election wide open but did so across both regional and class lines. Nothing like this had ever happened before. The age of mass political participation – individual voters watching unscripted debate and making spontaneous choices – had arrived with a bang.

"Mr. Turner, just one second," Mulroney rejoined. He was giving battle.

"Once any region – "

"You do not have a monopoly on patriotism – "

"Once – "

"And I resent the fact that your implication is that only you are a Canadian."

"I am sorry, I – "

Mulroney saw an opening. Had Turner reached too far in questioning his patriotism? Was he coming on too strong? "I want to tell you that I come from a Canadian family and I love Canada and that is why I did it, and don't you – "

"Once – " Turner fought to break in. "Once any – Once any country yields its economic levers, once a country yields its energy – "

Now the prime minister was on the defensive, denying the opposition leader's staccato attacks. Turner, his shoulder cocked aggressively, his right hand jammed straight down into his pocket, gunned at Mulroney with his left. "Once a country yields its agriculture, once a country opens itself up to a subsidy war with the United States, in terms of definition, then the political ability of this country to sustain the influence of the United States, that is, to remain a competitive nation, that will go on forever – and that is the issue of this election, sir." Inside the trailers, handlers for both men stretched towards the monitors, shaking their fists and cheering their champions on. Across the country, viewers leaned forward in their chairs. Mulroney breathed in, confident that Turner had overreached in attacking his credibility. He let fly at his opponent.

"Mr. Turner, let me tell you something, sir. This country is only about one-hundred-and-twenty years old, but my own father, fifty-five years ago, went himself, as a labourer, with hundreds of other Canadians, and with their own hands, in northeastern Quebec, they built

a little town and schools and churches and they, in their own way, were nation-building; in the same way as the waves of immigrants from the Ukraine and Eastern Europe rolled back the prairies and, in their own way, in their own time, they were nation-building because they loved Canada." (This is great stuff: here's Mulroney, in a defining-moment brawl, still thinking about his regional coalition, Quebec and the West.) "I, today, sir, as a Canadian, believe genuinely in what I am doing. I believe it is right for Canada. I believe that, in my own modest way, I am nation-building because I believe this benefits Canada and I love Canada."

Turner took the counter-attack calmly. "I admire your father for what he did," he said. "My grandfather" – Turner struck back at the same place – "moved to British Columbia. My mother was a miner's daughter there." (Cue violins. A miner's daughter. Top that, buddy!) "We are just as Canadian as you are, Mr. Mulroney …" Now throw the haymaker: "But I will tell you this. You mentioned one-hundred-and-twenty years of history. We built a country east and west and north. We built it on an infrastructure that deliberately resisted the continental pressure of the United States. For one-hundred-and-twenty years we have done it. With one signature of a pen, you have reversed that, thrown us into the north–south influence of the United States, and will reduce us, I am sure, to a colony of the United States, because when the economic levers go, the political independence is sure to follow."

Once again Mulroney sensed overreach in Turner's history homily. Everyone knows it's a trade deal, for god's sake. Just stick your foot out, show that Turner is overreacting and over he'll go. "With a document that is cancellable on six months' notice? Be serious."

"Cancellable?" said Turner, incredulous. "You are talking about our relationship with the United States. Once that –"

"A commercial contract that is cancellable on six months' notice," Mulroney repeated.

"Commercial document? That document relates – it relates to every facet of our lives!"

"That's what it is, a commercial treaty."

Turner backed off, throwing it to the crowd to decide who'd flattened whom. The debate eased into dénouement, winding down at 10 p.m. All attention immediately focused on the decisive exchange: Who had won it? Had Mulroney played Turner, as a matador plays a bull, letting the momentum of the bull's charge expose the vulnerable neck into which the sword is smoothly driven? Or had the bullfighter himself been run down, his artistry flattened by the snorting, rampaging, desperate animal?

The media were reluctant to decide. Wednesday morning's *Globe and Mail* boldly ventured: "Turner, PM turn trade deal into scrap over patriotism." But the television networks knew a ratings-grabber when they saw one. Almost immediately they went to air with clips from the decisive 2:38-minute exchange between Turner and Mulroney. As the clips were rebroadcast, again and again, over the next forty-eight hours, the debate's effective audience magnified geometrically. Instead of six hours of numbing issue jamming by two old white guys, viewers were watching something much more illuminating: a riveting battle between two superb fighters, each at the top of his form. And in that endless review of the key exchange, a simple truth had emerged: in pleading the merely contractual nature of the free trade agreement, Mulroney had backed down from his argument that the deal was a glorious act of nation-building. This retreat carried two immense implications: first, that Mulroney had been bested in a fight with that supposed non-entity Turner; and, second, that the prime minister must have been lying, either when he said the deal was big stuff or when he said it wasn't.

Across the country, Liberals immediately felt the impact of the English debate. On Wednesday night the Gallup organization reported that 71 per cent of English Canadians said Turner had won the debate, compared with 17 per cent who chose Mulroney and 11 per cent who gave the nod to Broadbent. Several polls rolled out, each reporting similar results. By Friday, a published poll showed that 14 per cent of Tory voters and 16 per cent of NDP voters were more likely to vote Liberal as a result of the debate. On Saturday, a Reid survey came out with the Liberals neck and neck with the Tories at 35 per cent. By Sunday, one poll had the Grits out front at 39 per cent, with the PCs at 35 per cent and the NDP at 23 per cent. The essence of the shift was simple: the field of serious candidates had narrowed from three to two – Mulroney and Turner – and the mix of policy issues had dwindled from many to one: free trade. In effect, the pattern of the debate would be the pattern of the campaign's remainder: a one-on-one fight between Turner and Mulroney, with the trade deal as the weapon of choice.

Something huge was happening out there, but theories abounded as to what that thing might be. At one level, Turner had raised grave concerns about a vital issue in a credible manner. This move drew support from those who shared his doubts about the deal (the NDP slide) and loosened up support among Tories and undecided voters whose doubts had been raised as well. Something else had occurred, though. Turner's personal numbers were soaring while Mulroney's were falling fast. Clearly, Turner's image was transformed from a limping skipper of a mutinous, sinking ship to Captain Canada, breasting the political swells from his command post on the poop deck of the doughty HMCS Dominion.

And there was a third, elusive dimension to the shift in public opinion. Tory pollster Allan Gregg had never before seen so massive a tide of change turn upon a single event. His explanation lay in an underlying mood of national anxiety that had been building through the 1980s, even as the economy recovered from its recessionary nightmare. "In 1988," he said, "the feeling out there was, 'Boy, are things ever good, and it's not going to stay this way.'" Turner, he believed, had been able to link that widespread anxiety to the free trade agreement, creating a current of energy that galvanized his support. "The effect of the television debate was that it moved all that unfocused anxiety about the future to the realization that they'd found the Beast — the Beast is free trade. Are you worried about medicare? Hey, remember John Turner saying that, under free trade, they'll check your wallet before they check your pulse? Afraid of running out of clean water? John Turner says we're going to have to sell our water to the Americans … It goes on and on."

When a big organism, such as an election campaign in full tilt, is suddenly faced with the unexpected, several things happen at once. Everyone starts worrying. Everyone starts calling the next guy up the food chain, asking if everything's okay. Everyone who gets one of these calls, then calls the next guy up, until someone finally says something convincing and word trickles back down that everything's under control. Of course, everything isn't under control. Someone up at the top has to figure out what the hell is going on, come up with a plan, then drive the plan and its messages down the line — fast. This process takes time. In 1988 it took the PC campaign a week.

In the aftermath of the debate, the Tory strategists were not certain of the magnitude of the problem. Their man had stayed on-message,

looked prime ministerial, and denied Turner the defining knock-out blow. Perhaps they'd missed the millennial anxiety. Maybe they had trouble believing that Turner could actually have done as well as he did. Perhaps they were reluctant to depart from the best strategy at which their fine minds had arrived pre-campaign. Each meeting through Wednesday and Thursday told a tale of mounting confusion and concern.

But by the time the backroomers' strategy network got together on Friday, October 28, its members no longer needed much convincing. Their campaign was losing altitude like a crippled bird. When Gregg told them, "Guys, we've got some real serious problems here," they were all ears. What Gregg proposed as a counter-attack was simple: rather than deal with vague voter anxieties or seek to separate them from the trade deal, they would leave those fears floating and seek aggressively to isolate Turner from the support he had been gaining as a result of those fears. As Gregg put it, in a phrase that would enter the Canadian political lexicon, "The bridge between the fears of free trade and John Turner is John Turner's credibility. We've got to bomb the bridge."

While Gregg was doing the polling and devising his bridge-bombing idea throughout the week that followed the debate, the show had to go on, with all eyes on the prime minister. One look at the newscasts on Tuesday night and the prime minister could tell that Turner had nailed him. If he now appeared to be treading water, waiting for a strategy, panic would take hold of the campaign. Mulroney excelled at strategy, and now he had to come up with one all by himself. He couldn't wait for Gregg's data or for some committee to draft a memo. It was out on the bus and in the

Citizens Concerned About Free Trade republished this 1888 artifact, a New York newspaper's dream-map of a fully American continent, as evidence that the free trade agreement of 1988 was just another item in a long litany of US plots against Canada.

THE FUTURE GREAT REPUBLIC.

The Annexation of the Dominion of Canada Would Add Twenty seven States and Territories.

THE UNITED STATES MAY LOOK LIKE THIS AFTER THE ANNEXATION OF CANADA

ROAD TO REDEMPTION
JOHN TURNER ON THE CAMPAIGN TRAIL

John Turner's political style seemed stuck in the early 1960s – all backslapping and bum-patting – until the crucible of the 1988 campaign transformed him into a guardian of the little-understood English Canadian soul, which is perfectly captured by this anti-free-trade button *(bottom right)*. All of Turner's contradictions – Bay Street boy versus social justice crusader, managerial pragmatist versus blazing idealist, passionate scrapper versus rigid, uptight suit – were resolved as he rose to the moment he had awaited for decades ... He was free of his demons and flying high, at events like this one in Quebec *(top right)*, on the campaign plane *(bottom, second from right)*, and at three or more speaking engagements per day (such as this one on Montreal's South Shore).

no, eh

airplane on Wednesday, Thursday, and Friday that Brian Mulroney showed what he was made of, taking control of his faltering campaign.

It's easy to imagine his thoughts. Thank God I loaded in that one-month cushion at the back end of this damn thing! Now, what the hell am I gonna say? Can't downplay it, the media have decided it's huge, so there's no appealing that. Stick to the commercial contract line? No, that's really just a form of downplaying. Defend the deal? Gotta do that, but the deal isn't the real issue … leadership? Okay, so Turner made me look like a liar. But, damn it, everyone knows he doesn't really believe that free trade's the end of the country – he's from Bay Street. Hell, everyone knows Turner's a goof who just makes stuff up. Which means he's the liar, not me. If I say that, will people believe it? Sure, I've got more credibility on economic issues than he does. So when he says I'm lying about sovereignty, I'll say he's lying about economics.

Instinctively, in the manner in which someone who just lost an argument tells his friends what he should have said, Mulroney began in the debate's immediate aftermath to replay the crucial exchange with Turner on the hustings. This time, however, he did not seek to downplay the deal as a commercial contract. Instead, he went after the messenger, building on his own sense that Turner had overreached himself in his attacks. He did so on his own, initially without polling data, without a formally adopted shift in strategy, and without endorsers, tour events, advertising, or much of anything. On Thursday morning, October 27, when the majority of the Tory strategy network still believed that everything was fine, Mulroney decided to change his message.

In Toronto, halfway through his noon-time speech to a business group, the prime minister shifted gear from the managing change message. "At worst, the tactics of Mr. Turner and Mr. Broadbent are shameful and dishonest," he said. "At the least, they are an attempt to hide the fact they offer Canadians no realistic alternatives, no plan of their own … Our opponents would have you believe that they have a monopoly on patriotism … I think they have impugned the motives of many Canadians. They have insulted the intelligence of the Canadian voters. And they have resorted to the most shameful kind of scare tactics."

In accusing Turner of lying (he mentioned Broadbent only to prop up the sagging NDP), Mulroney was groping his way towards the same place Gregg wound up. The two talked daily from Wednesday through to the weekend, comparing notes, matching hunches, devising research to confirm or modify Mulroney's gut instincts. Meanwhile, as his sense grew that he was on the right track, Mulroney pushed his new message a little harder each day. It isn't easy to go out on camera and execute a strategy that hasn't been researched or tested and that you yourself have only partially figured out. Not only are you flying blind but you have to look as though you know exactly where you're going or the crew will all bail out. According to campaign chairman Norm Atkins's deputy, Harry Near, Mulroney "literally carried the campaign on his back for four or five days" while the team "retooled." Week four, from debate night on the 25th to the weekend of the 29th–30th, was Brian Mulroney's finest hour.

From the end of week four on, the campaign became a shouting match that boiled down to Turner and Mulroney accusing each other of lying. On this level patch of ground, the Tories' advantage in firepower would soon tell. By the beginning of week five Turner-seeking missiles were rolling off the PCs' assembly line. The first was Finance Minister Michael Wilson, who, on Monday, October 31, blasted the Liberal leader and the NDP. "Taking this lie [that free trade threatened social programs] into our senior citizens' homes is the cruellest form of campaigning I've seen in ten years in politics. When politicians feel that they have to prey upon the fears and emotions of some of the most defenceless people in our society today, I say that is despicable." Joe Clark weighed in, saying, "Now, Mr. Turner says, join his crusade … Is this the type of man you would like to lead a crusade? No wonder half his caucus told him to quit." Lucien Bouchard offered the most interesting attack, relating the free trade deal to his Québécois audience's recollections of the referendum debate eight years before. In both campaigns, "Liberals, Ontarians, intervened heavily to scare a fraction of the Quebec population into preserving the status quo … In 1980, Ontarians came to Quebec to tell us, 'You are ghettoizing yourselves. Don't do that. Open up to the world instead' … Now they want us to stop? That happens every time Quebec is on the verge of a breakthrough … We have become a vibrant, aggressive partner in Confederation. And now, Ontario tells us: 'Hold it. You, in Quebec, just stay at home, and just be an economic ghetto vis-à-vis the United States. We'll do the trading with them and you'll get the equalization payments.'"

Another major event took place in the fifth week. On Tuesday, November 1, an Environics poll was published with the Liberals at 37 per cent, the PCs at 31 per cent, and the NDP at 26 per cent – enough for a Liberal minority. In response, world capital markets dumped Canadian assets by the truckload. The dollar fell half a cent in a single day's trading. The Toronto Stock Exchange began a dive that, by November 7, would take 4 per cent off its 300 index. The market reaction was unprecedented during a campaign, a direct hit on Canadians' pocketbooks tied to political events. Tories cheered the news, knowing it would bolster their case that Liberal political success was harmful to Canada's economic well-being.

Later in week five came an explosion of brochures, advertising supplements, and leaflets from the Tories' mighty print production operation. The splashiest was a tabloid entitled *Ten Big Lies* dissecting the Liberals' case against the free trade agreement with charts, graphs, bulleted facts, and quotations from the deal itself. (The Tory trade lawyer who wrote it, and who had laboured exhaustively on the agreement itself, later spoke with some glee of his role: after being sidelined for weeks, he was suddenly rushed into the campaign's inner circles to save the day.) Then came the complementary private sector onslaught – a massive blitz of propaganda from the business community: company "information sessions," friendly letters about free trade in pay envelopes, local chamber of commerce addresses, full-page ads in community papers – the works. Corporate Canada wanted the deal badly, and rushed to its defence.

Through week five the Liberals worked furiously to press their post-debate advantage. Mostly, they worked the tour, playing up in the media the big crowds and enthusiastic reception that Turner was getting. On November 7, as the campaign's sixth week opened, a Gallup poll appeared, putting the Liberals at a new high-water mark of 43 per cent, with the Tories well back at 31 per cent and the NDP fading fast down to 22 per cent. But the Grits' internal numbers showed a different story: they had peaked and were starting to slip. The November 7 poll was the high-water mark. In fact, it was probably a "rogue poll," the one in twenty that is bound to be off base by more than 4 per cent. When the Tories attacked the poll as inaccurate and the Liberals defended it, both knew it was wrong.

Two weeks after the debate, in the campaign's sixth and seventh weeks, it was clear that the Conservative counter-attack had halted the Liberal advance. Now was the time for the PCs to drive the Grits back to defeat. A new wave of

Tory ads hit the air, the first big one a direct rebuttal to the Liberals' "Border" TV spot. In it, a Canadian hand reaches out and arrests the American hand erasing the border on a map. "John Turner says there's something in the free trade agreement that threatens Canadian sovereignty." The Canadian hand takes the pencil from the American and firmly redraws the border. "That's a lie," says the voice-over, "and this is where we draw the line." The ad wasn't aimed at voters so much as at intimidating the Liberals into pulling "Border." The Liberal ad did come out of the rotation shortly after "Drawing the Line" appeared, although the Liberals never conceded any relationship between the two events.

Another PC ad was even more direct and brutal. It showed grainy, out-of-focus black and white stills of Turner looking dishevelled and like a deer caught in the headlights. Tough anti-Turner editorials were quoted at the bottom of the screen, ending with the *Calgary Herald*'s definitive "John Turner is lying."

Realizing that the free trade issue had taken them as far as it could, the Liberals struggled in week six to execute their original strategy devised in the spring and summer. They sought to widen the mix of issues in play, releasing advertisements about tax proposals and varying Turner's messages. But out on the hustings, the leader was trapped in his own crusade. The crowds came to hear him reprise his debate performance, and he had to give them what they wanted. He found himself sharing the stage with a cast of nationalistic characters usually found in the cheap seats at an NDP rally. Campaign workers recall the look of bemused bewilderment on Turner's face at a rally in the campaign's final phase when they brought a bearded, longhaired folk singer onstage to strum away about "Big John, the people's man" or some such.

In fact, Turner was having a blast and got somewhat carried away with his crusade. In Saint-Jérome, on November 10, he lashed out at "les Boys du Ritz," the businessmen who were blasting at him shoulder to shoulder with Mulroney. Such raw, populist rhetoric sounded bizarre in the mouth of this wealthy Toronto corporate type, creating a dissonance that fuelled the impression that the Liberal leader was willing to go to any lengths to make his case. The Tories were delighted to reinforce this view with a TV spot in which a young female voter said, "I think that he is more interested in saving his job than he is in saving mine."

At the end of the sixth week, the weekend of November 12–13, various polls registered the success of the Tory assault: PCs 39 per cent, Liberals 35 per cent, NDP 24 per cent. Ominously for the Liberals, the poll showed that 40 per cent of Canadians thought that Turner would sign the trade deal anyway if elected. Two voters in five simply didn't believe him any more. The tide was now running fast. The final week, from November 14 to 21, was devoted mainly to a furious scramble by the respective campaigns to inject a few more advertising hits or a visit by the leader into regions and ridings where it might make the difference on election day. Turner went to Montreal and Quebec City on Wednesday and Thursday, where he hoped his class-based pitch might take local Liberal candidates over the top. Mulroney spent Friday in Yarmouth, Nova Scotia. Broadbent went to Edmonton, where it was hoped that the city's traditional working-class base (which gives it the nickname "Red-monton") would vote New Democrat, unable to stomach voting for the Grits, still hated in Alberta.

With the election in hand, seeking to impart an air of closure, the Tories orchestrated some resounding final chords for the nationwide audience. Interventions came from Washington and London. On November 17 President Reagan called the agreement "an

SHELL-SHOCKED

The Tories "bombed the bridge" of Turner's credibility with brutal negative TV ads like this one, reminding voters that the election would determine who was prime minister, not just the fate of the trade deal.

example of cooperation at its best." The next day Prime Minister Thatcher was quoted in the *Washington Post* saying that, if the agreement failed to pass, it would be "very difficult for any prime minister of Canada to negotiate another international agreement with another country." Predictably, Turner and Broadbent exploded in outrage at the outside interference, but the point had been made.

Election day, November 21, broke clear and cold across the country. The polls opened at 10 a.m. in Newfoundland and remained open until 8 that evening, as voters performed a ritual essentially unchanged since the introduction of the secret ballot in the 1878 election. Those whose names were on the enumerated voters' lists were checked off, issued a ballot, and retreated behind a small cardboard shield to place an X beside the name of the candidate of their choice. There were few irregularities and, despite the most intense, passionate campaign since 1917, there was, as usual, no election-day violence.

Shortly after 8 p.m. as Mulroney and a group of family and friends applauded in their suite at Baie Comeau's finest hotel, Le Manoir, the networks called a Tory majority. Soon concessionary phone calls came in, first from Broadbent in Oshawa, then from Turner in Vancouver. Yet when the re-elected prime minister entered the Baie Comeau hockey arena to claim his triumph, the hometown crowd was subdued, almost thoughtful, and Mulroney sensed it. The mood fit well with the note of conciliation he wished to strike in the wake of the wild, passionate election that had just been fought. "Because the issues were historic, the campaign was especially challenging. But however impassioned the debate, this campaign has shown that Canadians agree on what it is that we most cherish in our national life … This election, then, has not been about those values, but about the means to give them greater

effect. So now, it is a time for healing in this land. For in the end, irrespective of our party preference, we are all Canadians, we all love our country, and we all put the national interest first." So there, Turner!

The final results were PCS 169, Liberals 83, and New Democrats 43. Turnout was high, at 76 per cent. Mulroney's 1984 coalition had survived. Quebec voted 53 per cent for the PCS, giving them 63 of 75 seats. The Prairies also held rock solid, electing 36 Tories to the NDP's 13 and the Grits' 5. The fledgling Reform Party was swamped as Alberta conservatives rallied to the free trade standard. The Tories sustained substantial losses, however, in British Columbia and, especially, Ontario. On the west coast, they took only 12 of 32 seats (the NDP won 19), while, in Ontario, they slid to 46 from 67 four years before – barely shading the Liberals' 43. The NDP gathered 10 seats in the largest province – a loss of 3.

The NDP could be consoled by its impressive seat count – at 43, by far the largest harvest it had ever brought in. But it had fallen well below its own expectations and now saw the Liberals restored to solid official opposition status. The death of the Grits and the rise of a two-party system would have to wait. Within months, Broadbent stepped down.

The Liberals were immensely relieved by the election result, even if it was a disappointment compared with the dizzying prospects that had opened up in the week after the debate. At the Ontario campaign party in North York, for example, half the room was thrilled with the final outcome and half of it dejected, depending on which part of the campaign one remembered better: the post-debate high or the hideous three weeks that had preceded it. Turner would soon retire but he would leave the party in better condition than he found it. He had done so with personal courage and his own passionate patriotism. Even his enemies conceded that.

With Mulroney's second successive majority the post-Trudeau kingdom appeared to be at hand. The electorate of 1988 had abandoned its 1980 experiment with a Big Ottawa approach to economic policy. Moreover, with the Meech Lake accord awaiting only final ratification by the provinces, it seemed that Mulroney's Little Ottawa view was about to triumph on the constitutional side as well. Mulroney had orchestrated this turnabout by harnessing the two mighty forces that had shaken the country from the mid-1960s on: Quebec nationalism and the West's growing power. By abolishing Trudeau's National Energy Program upon taking office, then offering the fulfilment of westerners' historic dream of free trade, the Tory prime minister seemed to have yoked the region's muscle, and its long-held anger, to the PC cause. And, by reaching out to nationalist Quebeckers with Meech Lake, he had, as Graham Fraser pointed out, offered Quebeckers the same formula as had René Lévesque: sovereignty-association. Whereas the PQ stood for political sovereignty and economic association, Mulroney offered, in free trade, economic sovereignty, and, in Meech Lake, political association on looser terms. A reliable Quebec and a steadfast West gave Mulroney an electoral advantage: a head start in more than half the country.

The 1988 election was a struggle only in the other half of the country, Ontario and Atlantic Canada, areas where the free trade issue carried much less regional resonance. In those places, the resonances were located along the axis of ideology. In both regions, Mulroney went up against the ingrained Loyalist traditions and, in Ontario, against the 1960s-style economic nationalism of urban baby-boomers. (Both groups, traditionally either Tory or New Democrat, wound up voting Liberal almost in spite of themselves.) As he had done in 1984, Mulroney split the Liberals' post-Diefenbaker Ontario–Quebec alliance, leaving the party with

a few Trudeauvians in Montreal and in a fight with the NDP for the centre-left in Ontario.

Mulroney's win may have been a regional operator's victory, but it was built on more than a set of assorted bon-bons for one region or the next (Joe Clark in 1979). The free trade issue cut substantially across the normal lines of region to create a national political dynamic worthy of Diefenbaker in 1957–58 or the early Trudeau. The purely regional operators were swamped in this national wave for or against the agreement. In the Alberta riding of Yellowhead, Clark himself was challenged by a former provincial premier's son, Preston Manning, running for the infant Reform Party. The Reformers' campaign manager confirmed the value of free trade as a means of holding Mulroney's coalition together when he lamented after the election, "But all of the issues for which the Reform Party came into existence … were sideswiped by the whole free trade thing … People here wanted free trade, and there was only one party to vote for." In sum, the historical grievances and aspirations of the regions Mulroney counted on were addressed by free trade, while the Liberals won in those parts of the country where regional consciousness was usually less of a factor in voting behaviour.

This regional pattern helps explain the great paradox of the 1988 election: how the people, having responded massively to the attacks on the trade deal and having outvoted the pro-deal government 52 per cent to 43 per cent, then accepted the election's result as a mandate for Mulroney to implement the deal. At no other point in the nation's history had the electoral process produced a mandate so dramatically at odds with the will of a clear majority on a vital and widely understood issue. The first-past-the-post mechanism and the fact of two opposition parties had translated the deal's concentrated support in Quebec and the West into the basis of a national majority, while leaving the more

PLAYBOOK VII

Mulroney was the first prime minister to successfully combine two of the three basic plays in Canada's political playbook. In both of his majority victories, he took the best aspects of the Quebec Bridge and blended them with a textbook Populist Rush. If you look carefully, you can see the traces of both Diefenbaker's and Mackenzie King's strategies in this complex, highly effective play. Outside Ontario, the free trade agreement had a populist tinge to it, offering relief in particular for the traditional discontents of the West against the dominant Toronto/Ottawa economic power structure. And in Quebec, Mulroney cornered the market on representing the province's interests on the national stage.

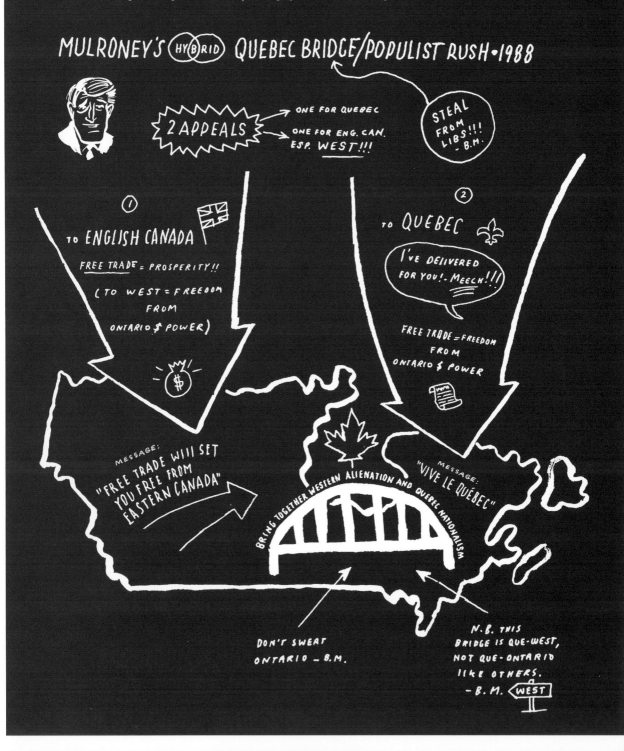

numerous but diffuse opponents of the deal out. In a raw electoral confrontation, the axis of region had won out over the axis of ideas.

After the election, Canada faced a potential constitutional crisis. In some countries, such a blatant systemic distortion of a popular majority on a major issue would have provoked at least a round of electoral reform, if not a constitutional meltdown. In Canada, the potential crisis was largely averted when Turner and Broadbent accepted the results of the election as a mandate for the trade deal to go through. They did so because to argue otherwise would be to call into doubt the legitimacy of the parliamentary system – and from the position of men who had just lost a fair fight. At the same time, those regions that had most powerfully supported the deal – Quebec and the West – would likely have erupted if their victory and their deal had been snatched away from them by Ontario and the Atlantic.

The Canadian people went along with them. Their reasons for accepting the election's paradoxical outcome probably had more to do with battle fatigue than anything else. The empowered voters of 1988 had taken the free trade agreement to the front of the agenda, but were then content to let the electoral system, and its political actors, bring matters to a conclusion. The Liberal slogan, "This Is More Than an Election. This Is Your Future," asked voters to set aside their usual approach to elections and to vote on the free trade issue. Inverted, however, the slogan would read: "This is more than your future. This is an election." And that's how the people saw the campaign on voting day, and, in its wake, they were in no mood to upgrade the exercise to a constitutional crisis. Knowingly or not, they chose to accept a healthy splash of the system's region-oriented water in the heady democratic wine of their new and direct involvement in matters of high policy.

And what about free trade itself? Did the public make the right call? What call, in fact, had the public made? A late-campaign poll showed the electorate 51 per cent opposed to the deal, 39 per cent in favour, and 11 per cent undecided, a division that reflected where the votes ended up on election night. Yet, a little over a decade later, the public had changed its mind on the issue. The Liberals had also swung around, from leading the fight against the deal in 1988 to implementing the wider North American Free Trade Agreement (NAFTA) with the United States and Mexico in 1993 and pushing the hemispheric Free Trade Agreement of the Americas in 2001. According to non-partisan polling taken in 1995, support for NAFTA had climbed to 73 per cent. In February 2001 Liberal minister Brian Tobin, one of the deal's leading assailants in 1988, publicly told a smiling Brian Mulroney: "You were right and I was wrong" about free trade. In 1988 Canadians somehow balanced the democratic principle of pure majority rule with representative government, a system in which we elect our parliamentarians to make policy choices on our behalf. There was no clear consensus for or against free trade; rather, the right way to deal with it was to elect a government with the authority to make the final call. Canadians would abide with their system of representative government and make up their own minds in the fullness of time.

A good definition of leading comes from the American economist Lester Thurow: "to represent the future to the present." In 1988 widespread public support for globalization and free trade was still a dozen years ahead. Mulroney and his party showed commendable leadership in anticipating the eventual acceptance of the wisdom of their policy. Canadians showed similar wisdom by putting leadership first, then placing their trust in the leader who would best bring the future to them.

Maybe we got it right after all.

AFTERWORD

THE THREE ELECTIONS SINCE 1988 have produced a curious political stalemate. In 1993 a massive nation-wide democratic upsurge against the detested Mulroney government reduced the Tory Party to just two seats in the House. Yet the result of citizens flexing their democratic muscles has been a seemingly permanent Liberal government under Jean Chrétien and a perplexing political paradox: a democratically empowered modern electorate that has voted itself a virtual one-party system.

This fourth era of Liberal dominance is founded on the wreck of Mulroney's old coalition. In seat-rich Ontario, vote-splitting on the right and the collapse of the NDP vote have given the Grits almost every riding in three successive elections, something no party had ever before achieved in even one campaign. Yet, nationwide, the secret of Liberal power has been the exploitation not so much of vote-splitting among right-wingers over ideology as among Tories along regional lines. Formerly Tory elements in the West and Quebec flocked, in 1993 and thereafter, to the regional parties of Reform/Canadian Alliance and the Bloc Québécois. Simply put, Chrétien has stayed on top by working to his electoral advantage the deep regional divisions left by Mulroney and by avoiding the politics of national vision that most politicians since Diefenbaker have aspired to. Seen this way, our federal politics since 1988 has completed its retreat from national vision back towards the eternal verities of region.

The other major shift in 1990s politics has been the discovery by pollsters of the relationship between people's values and their voting behaviour. Voters, the pollsters show, gravitate towards the leaders who best embody the values they care about – community, enterprise, tolerance, or family. This latest nugget of polling science does a lot to explain exactly how the post-Diefenbaker politics of leadership has evolved, but it has had an unfortunate side effect. If national leaders can win votes simply by being something, why should they bother doing anything of importance? Meanwhile, beyond this self-referential world where politicians sculpt themselves ever more artfully to mirror the electorate, the real issues pile up.

These issues will only be resolved by women and men of vision who are not content simply to reflect what we are, but who can lead us towards what we must become. The values that inform their visions will matter, and they will tailor their visions to accommodate the stubborn – yet also wonderfully creative – diversity that Canada's history and geography have placed at the heart of our life as a country. But if the politics of vision is to return, it will do so because the people want it to.

As I walked over the old political battlefields of the five great elections chronicled in this book, I was struck less by the cleverness of the generals than by the wisdom of the foot soldiers, the ordinary people. In 1896 Canadian voters chose racial accommodation over tribalism, albeit indirectly. In 1926, through the admittedly tortuous means of King's manoeuvring, they chose nationhood over colonial status. In 1957 they unseated a dangerously technocratic government that had begun to threaten the basic norms of Canadian democracy. In 1980 they chose Big Ottawa over the community of communities and got the Charter of Rights and Freedoms in the bargain. In 1988 they elected a government committed to embracing the opportunities of globalization. They turned us outward towards a greater world.

Time and again, in the most important fights of our lives, Canadians have made the right call. They will do so again.

ACKNOWLEDGEMENTS

THIS BOOK WAS CONCEIVED in 1999, shortly after my wife, Jill, became pregnant with our first child. At the time, a dear friend told me that pregnancy in the family can be an "intensely creative period" for the husband as well. Taking his wisdom to heart, I thought writing a book about my favourite subject would be a pleasant way to pass the time as our fun-filled pre-kid lives curdled into torpid domesticity. So I started writing *Fights of Our Lives*.

Three years later, readers can enjoy the finished product, but dozens of people have suffered through seeing this book come into being on the instalment plan. Sara Borins of Otherwise Editions immediately grasped the kind of book I wanted to make and rigorously followed that vision through to publication. I don't know what Sara's role is called in publishing, but in politics the job is called "campaign manager." Her contributions have been manifold: project management; conception, organization, and execution of the book's visual program, including photography, illustration, and design; editorial coordination; business strategy, including marketing; and overall team leadership. My gratitude to her is immense and lasting. Editor Rick Archbold, a *miglior fabro* if ever there was one, gracefully and tirelessly turned my ideas – conceived in a typical consultant's PowerPoint style – into Word and narrative flow. He took on a simple assignment and not only accepted with grace and humour each expansion of the project but also spurred the process with his deep commitment to producing the best book possible. Phyllis Bruce of HarperCollins Canada put the full range of her considerable resources behind this project – an outstanding act of faith in a first-time author from a very senior player in the publishing business. My agent David Johnston of Livingston Cooke Curtis Brown guided me through the process with good humour and cheer, as did my counsel, John Duncan.

Karen Press and the staff at Otherwise admirably and patiently performed innumerable tasks in the areas of visual research, text research, and production through countless layouts and drafts. Nicholas Blechman in New York lavished his talents on designing and illustrating the book. Others too numerous to mention made available their memorabilia collections, folk tales, and insights, in the process allowing this book to become the trove of political memory I hoped it would be.

A few deserve particular recognition. Rick Anderson, Catherine Annau and Dominic Patten, Andrée Appleton and Alex Leman, Mark and Karen Belanger, Charles Bird, Diane Brady, Michele Caderio, Alister Campbell, Jean Daigneault, Daniel Despins, Sister Mary Ann Donovan, Dan Dunsky, Ron Dunsky and Nancy Minty, David Eddie, Ivan Fecan, Kaz Flinn, David Frum, Claude Galipeau, Arthur Gelgoot, Martin Goldfarb, Alex Graham, Ed Greenspon, Allan Gregg, Don Guy, Alison Gzowski, the Handelman family, John Ibbitson, Mary Margaret Jones, Seymour Kanowitch, Charles King and Kelly Mounce, Warren Kinsella, Michael Levine, Karl Littler, Richard Mahoney, Mike Marzolini, John Matheson, Craig McFadyen, Tim Murphy, Harry Near, Leslie Noble, Dick O'Hagan, Terrie O'Leary, Steve Paikin, Patricia Pearson, Doug Pepper, Scott Reid, Paul Rhodes, Doug Richardson, Eugene Siklos, Jeffrey Simpson, Caspar Sinnige, the Honourable David Smith, PC, MP, Tom Sommerville, Rob Steiner, Steven Theobold, Paul Wells, Ken Whyte, and Bruce Young provided me with insight, wisdom, memory or encouragement. Some gave all four in great measure.

Many teachers – the late Neil McLean, Michael Gendron, and Stuart Bull in particular – brought me to love history, especially Canada's.

Stephen Johnson and my strategic avatar, David Herle, read and subjected to rigorous intellectual scrutiny the book's early drafts. Richard Gwyn, Senator Michael Kirby, Desmond Morton, Hugh Segal, and Andrew Coyne read and commented on later drafts.

My profound thanks go as well to the politicians and strategists who have allowed me to learn on the job the political craft that I have tried to describe in these pages. They are legion, but, in particular, the Honourable John Roberts, PC, MP, Gordon Floyd, Ross McGregor, Greg Sorbara, MPP, Alvin Curling, MPP, Carol Beckmann, Kathryn Robinson, John and Beth Webster, Patrick Gossage, Scott Sheppard, the Rt. Honourable John Turner, PC, MP, Mike Robinson, the Honourable David Peterson, PC, MPP, Lyn McLeod, MPP, Bob Richardson, Torrance Wylie, Barry Campbell, MP, Carolyn Bennett, MP, Tony Ianno, MP, Joe Volpe, MP, the Honourable Jim Peterson, PC, MP, and Heather Peterson, Dalton McGuinty, MPP, Michael Bryant, MPP, and the Honourable Paul Martin, PC, MP, have honoured me with the opportunity to help them serve.

My business partners literally suffered through years of lost productivity as I laboured on this book. Their support and understanding is gratefully acknowledged.

Much as my political and business "families" were instrumental in bringing this book about, the greatest burden was borne by my real family, and to them goes my deepest thanks. My father Dennis Duffy (a genuine, card-carrying, and distinguished scholar) provided me with much wise advice, and also assumed the gruesome job of fact-checking the text as work-therapy in the face of a devastating personal loss. The book's errors and misinterpretations are, of course, my own, and not those of anyone indicated above.

My late mother Mary Ann showered me with encouragement, especially in her last weeks, sweetly reminding me as always of the ultimate purposes of politics and life itself. Above all, Jill and Martine, my beloved wife and daughter, allowed this book to occupy a very large space in a life already crammed with birth, death, and other challenges. Their unstinting support and self-sacrifice made *Fights of Our Lives* – indeed, most of the fulfilment in my life – possible.

I wrote this book so that one day I can show Martine why it is that Daddy has such strange friends and keeps such odd hours. In this sense, as in so many others, this book belongs to my family.

John Duffy
Toronto, spring 2002

PHOTO SOURCES

The following agency and archive names have been abbreviated:

AO Archives of Ontario; BG Bill Greenberg / BPS Merchandise (private collection); BCA British Columbia Archives; CBC Canadian Broadcasting Corporation; CIN Canadian Illustrated News; CMCP Canadian Museum of Contemporary Photography; CP Canadian Press Picture Archive; CTA City of Toronto Archives; CVA City of Vancouver Archives; DCA Diefenbaker Centre Archives; EBP Election Broadcasting Project at York University; GMA Glenbow Museum Archives; MMM Musée McCord Museum; NAC National Archives of Canada; NFB National Film Board of Canada; NLC National Library of Canada; PC Private Collection; PAM Provincial Archives of Manitoba; SHSB Société historique de Saint-Boniface; TRL Toronto Reference Library; VPL Vancouver Public Library; WCPI Western Canada Pictorial Index.

Original illustrations throughout by Christoph Niemann.

All photos clockwise from top left.

COVER, FRONTMATTER, AND BACKMATTER
Cover CTA SC 244-581, AO, TRL, NAC, NAC; p.2 NAC PA-13269; p.5 NAC PA-60819; p.6 Gazette/NAC PA-145477; back cover PMA, WCPI A1304-39050, Toronto Sun, NAC PA-206450, Photo by Boris Spremo CM.

FROM CREATION TO CRISIS
p.17 NAC PA-210064; p.18 Nova Scotia Archives N-4149, NAC PA-210098, E.S. Glover/NAC C-107375; p.19 NAC PA-121571, MMM/Notman VIEW-5939, VPL, NAC PA-26522; p.21 NLC/CIN 31 January, 1874; p.22 Bell Canada, GMA NA-13-2, NLC/CIN 14 September, 1878; p.23 NAC C-095470, NAC PA-210075, NAC PA-210063; p.24 NAC MG29/B1 vol.102/file 33, NAC PA-210074, NAC PA-21022, NAC PA-31845; p.25 NAC PA-43133, NAC PA-25601, NAC, SHSB 9021, N3028; p.27 NAC C-6536.

TO THE BRINK
p.31 Foote/NAC C-34457; p.32 PC; p.33 CTA SC 244, Item 581; p.34 CTA SC 244, item 668; p.35 PAM 2376; p.38 MMM/Notman MP-0000.25.932, TRL; p.40 NAC C-1879, NAC PA-210116, NAC PA-210123, NAC PA-210120, NAC PA-210117; p.42 Whyte Museum V116-PA3, PAM N14998; p.43 NAC PA-27943; p.44 Lake of the Woods Museum 967.15.45; NAC C-463; p.46 NAC; p.48 NAC PA-066544, NAC C-43450, SHSB 9021; p.49 NAC PA-210094; p.50 NAC, NAC PA-33933; p.51 NAC C-698; p.52 BCA D-04931, NAC PA-38662, GMA NA-789-104, NAC C-8708; p.53 NAC PA-66544, NAC PA-800199, NAC PA-137941, NAC PA-210070; p.54 MMM/Notman N-0000.134.14; p.56 NAC C-690; p.57 NAC PA-27159; p.58 National Gallery of Art, Washington; p.59 NAC PA-13027, NAC C-1860; p.60 NAC; p.61 Musée Cantonal des Beaux-Arts Lausanne, NAC PA-18766; p.62 NAC C-21313; p.64 Toronto Public Library Osborne Collection, Cranston Military Prints, MMM/Notman MP-0000.25.932; p.68 NLC; p.69 PAM; p.70 CTA SC 244-587; p.72 NAC PA-028631; p.73 AO C 279-0-0-0-75 2896; p.75 TRL; p.76 NAC C-35359, PC; p.79 AO F10-2-3-16; p.80 TRL; p.82 PC; p.83 NAC; p.86 NAC C-1986.

ON BORROWED TIME
p.90 NAC C-37613, CVA Port P.990 N651, NAC C-10464, NAC PA-210094; p.91 Provincial Archives of Newfoundland and Labrador NA 1974, GMA NA-663-1, CVA 2-99, CTA SC 244-46; p.93 NAC C-5093, Ontario Hydro Archives HP 1075, GMA PA-404-1, NAC C-27358; p.95 NAC, NAC, NAC; p.97 NAC; p.98 TRL, NLC, CVA Gr.War. P.18; p.99 PMA Events 173/3 N9905, CTA SC244-736, CTA SC 244-1782, NAC C-2279; p.101 NAC; p.102 NAC PA-139684, NAC-2745, CTA 244-526, CTA-James 2345; p.103 NAC-C46315, PC, NAC PA-127295; p.105 NAC.

KINGDOM COME
p.109 NAC PA-210343; p.110 Collection Orion, NAC C-26782, Minnesota Historical Society; p.111; PAM N-1610, Moose Jaw Public Library Archives 73-96; p.112 PAM N-1982, CTA 2017A, CTA SC-244-579, NAC PA-54398; p.113 NAC PA-210352, NAC PA-43102; p.114 NAC PA-139601, CTA 643, NAC C-25281; p.115 NAC PA-210354, NAC C-46312; p116 NAC C-28570; p.118 NAC PA-1111; p.119 PAM/Foote N1759; p.120 NAC C-29632; p.121 NAC; p.122 Le Soleil; p.124 NAC PA-26987; p.125 NAC PA C-9796; p.126 NAC C-34443; p.127 GMA ND-3-3147; p.128 NAC C-62100; p.129 (from start) PAM N-1759, NAC C-34443; NAC C-21247, NFB, NAC C-9055, NAC PA-210345, GMA ND-3-3360; p.132 CTA SC 244-1761; p.133 NAC PA-26987; p.135 NAC W.L. Mackenzie King Papers/Vol. 149/p.109527; p.136 NAC PA-210106; p.137 NAC C-038952, NAC C-047344; p.138 NFB; p.141 NAC/C.W. Jefferys, NAC C-24698, AO S-2123, MMM/Notman MP-0000.25.932; p.145 WCPI A1304-39050; p.146 NAC PA-138868, NAC C-13269; p.147 AO 3117-2, NAC PA-210345, NAC C-24698; p.148 GMA NA-789-95; p.151 PAM N7539; p.152 NAC C-44301; p.157 NAC PA210347.

THE KINGDOM AT HAND
p.160 NAC C-147643, PAM Events 278/10 N9126, Provincial Archives of Alberta A-3742, CTA 244-8054; p.161 NAC, NAC C-55451, NAC-124370, GMA NA-2888-7; p.163 NAC C-148557; p.164 NAC PA-119013, NAC C-65503, NAC-PA 116363; p.165 NAC PA-148207, NAC PA-103542, TRL; p.166 NAC C-87471, NAC PA-210282, NAC PA-162243, NAC; p.167 NAC C-148563, GMA NA-3770-6, York University/Toronto Telegram Collection Y.U. 1686; p.169 NAC C-068676; p.170 NAC PA-210239, PC, NAC PA-123988, NAC PA-128804; p.171 Gazette/NAC PA-77934, NAC PA-210299, DCA JGD-389, CMCP.

FOLLOW JOHN
p.175 DCA JGD-369: p.176 CTA SC 244-2198; p.177 New York Public Library Stuart Collection, NAC PA-110822, Gazette/NAC PA-108300; p.178 NAC PA-210246; p.180 NAC PA-210242; p.181 NAC PA-210264, NAC PA-210263; p.182 NAC PA-206474, Quebec Archives E6 S7 P90-59, Chris Lund/NFB/NAC PA-152023, AO 4471 F2229-308-0-1118-B449; p.183 NAC C-20021; p.184 Bill Reidford/Globe and Mail; p.185 PC; p.186 NAC PA-123523; p.187 City of Ottawa Archives AN 47308-18; p.188 DCA POS 026; p.189 TRL; p.190 NAC PA-206475; p.191 Canada Wide; p.192 PC; p.193 NAC PA-121703; p.195 DCA POS 026; p.198 CVA 2-34, GMA NA-2497-13, NAC PA-210074; p.199 Radio Times Hulton Picture Library, NAC PA-111420; p.200 NAC PA-210301, DCA POS 073, BG; p.201 DCA JGD-389; p.203 NAC PA-210243; p.204 NAC PA-210261; p.205 NAC PA-210240, NAC PA-210295, NAC PA-210258; NAC PA-210300; p.208 NAC PA-211208, NAC PA-211217; p.209 NAC PA-211203, NAC PA-211216, NAC PA-211217, NAC PA-211214; p.210 BG; p.211 Toronto Sun Syndicated Services; p.212 DCA; p.213 NAC; p.214 NAC PA-125801; p.217 DCA JGD 2054 XB; p.218 NAC PA-210251; p.219 NAC PA-211460; p.221 DCA POS 048; p.222 NAC C-19526; p.223 Pendulum of Power by J. Murray Beck (Prentice-Hall); p.224 NAC; p.225 NAC PA-211207; p.228 NAC PA-169758; p.231 NAC PA-211206.

BEYOND REGION
p.234 AO-4473 F 229-308-0-1728, Guy Borrmans, Ted Grant/NAC PA-206762, Ted Grant/CMCP 63-9342C, NAC C-148541; p.235 NAC PA-210077, NAC, Government of Canada Department of Communications, BG; p.237 NAC PA-121563; p.238 Sam Tata, NAC PA-211211, Ted Grant, NAC PA-206473; p.239 PA-117107, George S. Zimbel, NAC-PA-211463; p.241 NAC C-121325; p.243 NAC; p.244 Michael Lambeth, NAC PA-206463, NAC PA-206338; p.245 NAC PA-193986, NAC, NAC; p.246 NAC, CP (Ryan Remiorz), NAC; p.247 Photo by Boris Spremo CM, Daniel Kieffer/Groupe Zone, CP.

HE STOOPS TO CONQUER
p.251 NAC PA-205518; p.253 CMCP/Pierre Gaudard; p.254 CP; p.255 NAC PA-206450; p.256 NAC, NAC; p.257 Ted Grant/NAC; p.259 AO 5343 C 193-3-1177-84084-24A; p.260 NAC, Ted Grant; p.261 CP (Roger Arar); p.262 NAC; p.263 Michael Bedford Studio, NAC; p.264, NAC, NAC; p.265 PC; p.266 PC; p.267 David Montgomery/Weekend magazine; p.270 NAC, NAC, NAC; p.271 NAC, NAC; p.273 Catherine Dean/EBP; p.274 Office of Martin Goldfarb; p.275 William Stratus; p.276 NAC, NAC; p.277 NAC, NAC, NAC; p.280 NAC; p.282 NAC, NAC; p.283 NAC, NAC; p.286 NAC PA-115167, NAC; p.288 NAC PA-206596; p.289 NAC, NAC; p.290 Il Volo in Italia/Rom o.J. S.291; p.292 Office of Jerry Grafstein, NAC, NAC; p.293 NAC; p.294 NAC; p.295 Catherine Dean/EBP; p.296 The Rainmaker by Keith Davey (Stoddart Publishing); p.297 NAC; p.298 NAC; p.301 Photo by Boris Spremo, CM.

TRIPLE PLAY
p.306 NAC, CP, Toronto Star, NAC, William Stratus; p.307 R. Cooper/NAC PA-152417, NAC, NAC, NAC; p.309 BG.

MANO A MANO
p.313 David Burnett/Contact Press/Picturequest; p.315 CP (Fred Chartrand), NAC; p.316 NAC; p.317 MMM/Notman MP-0000.25.932, NAC PA-43133, BG, BG, BG; p.320 NAC PA 206592, The Montreal Gazette, © Raffi Kirdi/Ponopresse; p.321 NAC, NAC PA-201061; p.322 Office of Sheila Copps, Up the Hill by Don Johnston (Optimum Publishing International); p.323 Industrielle Alliance, CP (Efram Lijatsky); p.324 NAC; p.326 © Robert Giroux/Ponopresse; p.327 Canadian Steel Trade and Employment Congress, CP (Mike Pinder), Office of Michael Kirby; p.328 The Gazette, NAC; p.330 Ponopresse; p.332 CP (Ron Poling), NAC, NAC, NAC, NAC; p.333 NAC; p.334 © Robert Giroux/Ponopresse; p.337 ©Bettman/Corbis/Magma; p.338 Catherine Dean/EBP; p.342 Catherine Dean/CBC; p.343 Catherine Dean/CBC; p.347 Citizens Concerned About Free Trade; p.348 CP; p.349 Photo by Boris Spremo CM, BG, Photo by Boris Spremo CM; p.353 Catherine Dean/EBP.

LITERARY SOURCES

GENERAL

Beck, M. *Pendulum of Power.* Scarborough: Prentice-Hall of Canada, c1968.

Bliss, M. *Right Honourable Men.* Toronto: HarperCollins Canada, 1994.

Bothwell, R., I. Drummond, and J. English. *Canada Since 1945: Power, Politics and Provincialism.* Toronto, University of Toronto Press, 1981.

Carty, R.K. "Three Canadian Party Systems," in R.K. Carty (ed.), *Canadian Political Party Systems.* Peterborough: Broadview Press, 1992.

Careless, J.M.S. *Canada: A Story of Challenge.* Toronto: MacMillan, 1970.

Horowitz, G. "Conservatism, Liberalism and Socialism in Canada: An Interpretation," in Hugh Thorburn (ed.), *Party Politics in Canada.* Scarborough: Prentice-Hall of Canada, 1991.

Hutchison, B. *Mr. Prime Minister: 1867 – 1964.* Don Mills: Longmans Canada, 1964.

Kerr, D. and Holdsworth, D. (eds.). *Historical Atlas of Canada* (3 vols.). Toronto: University of Toronto Press, 1990.

Johnston, R. et al. "The Electoral Basis of the Canadian Party Systems," in Carty, R.K. (ed.), *Canadian Political Party Systems.* Peterborough: Broadview Press, 1992.

Meisel, J. "The Decline of Party in Canada," in Hugh Thorburn (ed.), *Party Politics in Canada.* Scarborough: Prentice-Hall of Canada, 1991.

Morton, W.L. "The Progressive Tradition in Canadian Politics," in Hugh Thorburn (ed.), *Party Politics in Canada.* Scarborough: Prentice-Hall of Canada, 1991.

Smith, D. "Party Government in Canada," in R.K. Carty (ed.), *Canadian Political Party Systems.* Peterborough: Broadview Press, 1992.

Wade, M. *The French Canadians: 1760 – 1967* (2 vols.). Toronto: Macmillan, 1968.

WEB

First among Equals: Canada's Prime Ministers. On the National Library of Canada's website (www.nlc-bnc.ca).

History of the Federal Electoral Ridings since 1867, and numerous associated pages forming a comprehensive set of searchable databases on the website of the Library of Parliament's Information and Documentation Branch: http://www.parl.gc.ca/information.

Political Database of the Americas (2000) Canada: Electoral Results. [Internet]. Georgetown University and the Organization of American States. In: http://www.georgetown.edu/pdba/Elecdata/Canada.

Newspapers

Extensive Research was conducted from the archives of the following newspapers: *Halifax Chronicle-Herald, La Presse, Toronto Globe, Globe and Mail, Winnipeg Free Press,* the *Victoria Times-Colonist.*

FROM CREATION TO CRISIS

Creighton, D. *John A. Macdonald: the Young Politician, the Old Chieftain.* Toronto: University of Toronto Press, 1998.

TO THE BRINK

Crunican, P. *Priests and Politicians: Manitoba Schools and the Election of 1896.* Toronto: University of Toronto Press, 1974.

LaPierre, L. *Sir Wilfrid Laurier and the Romance of Canada.* Toronto: Stoddart, 1996.

Longley, J.W. *Sir Charles Tupper.* London; Toronto: Oxford University Press, 1928.

Schull, J. *Laurier: The First Canadian.* Toronto: Macmillan of Canada, 1987.

Skelton, O.D. *Life and Letters of Sir Wilfrid Laurier.* Toronto: McClelland & Stewart, 1921.

ON BORROWED TIME

Ames, H.B. "Electoral Management," in R.K. Carty (ed.), *Canadian Political Party Systems.* Peterborough: Broadview Press, 1992.

Brown, R.C. *Robert Laird Borden: A Biography.* Toronto: Macmillan of Canada, 1975.

English. "The End of the Great Party Era," in R.K. Carty (ed.), *Canadian Political Party Systems.* Peterborough: Broadview Press, 1992.

KINGDOM COME

Dawson, R. M. and Neatby, B. *William Lyon Mackenzie King: A Political Biography* (3 vols.). Toronto: University of Toronto Press, 1958.

Graham, R. *Arthur Meighen, A Biography* (3 vols.). Toronto: Clarke, Irwin, 1960-1965.

Hutchison, B. *The Incredible Canadian: A Candid Portrait of Mackenzie King: His Works, His Times, and His Nation.* Don Mills, Ont.: Longmans Canada, 1952.

Stacey, C. P. *A Very Double Life: the Private World of Mackenzie King.* Halifax: Goodread Biographies, 1976.

Wardhaugh, R. *Mackenzie King and the Prairie West.* Toronto: University of Toronto Press, 2000.

Williams, J. *Byng of Vimy: General and Governor General.* Toronto: University of Toronto Press, 1983.

THE KINGDOM AT HAND

Granatstein, J. *The Politics of Survival: The Conservative Party of Canada, 1939 – 1945.* Toronto: University of Toronto Press, 1967.

Whittaker, R. *The Governing Party: Organizing and Financing the Liberal Party of Canada, 1930 – 1958.* Toronto: University of Toronto Press, 1977.

FOLLOW JOHN

Camp, D. *Gentlemen, Players and Politicians.* Toronto: McClelland & Stewart, 1970.

Diefenbaker, J. *One Canada: Memoirs of the Right Honourable John G. Diefenbaker.* Scarborough: Macmillan-NAL, 1978.

English, J. *Shadow of Heaven: The Life of Lester Pearson.* Toronto: Lester & Orpen Dennys, 1989, and *The Worldly Years: The Life of Lester Pearson.* Toronto: Knopf Canada, 1992.

Lewis, D. *The Good Fight: Political Memoirs, 1909 – 1958.* Toronto: Macmillan of Canada, 1981.

Martin, P. *A Very Public Life* (3 vols.). Ottawa: Deneau, 1983.

Meisel, J. *The Canadian General Election of 1957.* Toronto: University of Toronto Press, 1962.

Newman, P. *Renegade in Power: The Diefenbaker Years.* Toronto: McClelland & Stewart, 1963.

Pearson, L. *Mike: The Memoirs of the Right Honourable Lester B. Pearson.* (3 vols.) Toronto: University of Toronto Press, 1972-1975.

Regenstreif, P. *The Diefenbaker Interlude.* Don Mills: Longmans, 1965.

Smith, D. *Rogue Tory: The Life and Legend of John G. Diefenbaker.* Toronto: Macfarlane Walter & Ross, 1995.

Stursberg, P. *Diefenbaker: Leadership Gained: 1957-1962.* Toronto: University of Toronto Press, 1975.

Thomson, D. *Louis St. Laurent, Canadian.* New York: St. Martin's Press, 1968.

BEYOND REGION

Gwyn, R. *The Shape of Scandal: A Study of a Government in Crisis.* Toronto: Clarke, Irwin, 1965.

Newman, P. *The Distemper of Our Times: Canadian Politics in Transition 1963-1968.* Toronto: McClelland & Stewart, 1969.

Radwanski, George. *Trudeau.* Toronto: Macmillan of Canada, 1978.

Sullivan, Martin. *Mandate '68.* Toronto: Doubleday, 1968.

HE STOOPS TO CONQUER

Brimelow, P. *The Patriot Game: Canada and the Canadian Question Revisited.* Toronto: Key Porter, 1986.

Camp, Dalton. *Points of Departure.* Ottawa: Deneau and Greenberg, 1979.

Clarkson, S. and C. McCall. *Trudeau and Our Times.* (2 vols.) Toronto: McClelland & Stewart, 1990 –1994.

Cohen, A., and J. Granatstein. (eds.) *Trudeau's Shadow: The Life and Legacy of Pierre Elliott Trudeau.* Toronto: Vintage Canada, 1999.

Gwyn, R. *The Northern Magus: Pierre Trudeau and Canadians.* Toronto: McClelland & Stewart, 1980.

Graham, R. *One-Eyed Kings: Promise and Illusion in Canadian Politics.* Toronto: Collins, 1986.

McCall-Newman, C. *Grits: An Intimate Portrait of the Liberal Party.* Toronto: Macmillan, 1982.

Simpson, J. *Discipline of Power: The Conservative Interlude and the Liberal Restoration.* Toronto: Personal Library, 1980.

Trudeau, P. *The Essential Trudeau.* Toronto: McClelland & Stewart, 1998.

Trudeau, P. *Federalism and the French Canadians.* Toronto: Macmillan, 1968.

Vastel, Michel. *The Outsider: The Life of Pierre Elliott Trudeau.* Toronto: Macmillan of Canada, 1990.

TRIPLE PLAY

Gratton, M. *"So, What Are the Boys Saying?": An Inside Look at Brian Mulroney in Power.* Toronto: McGraw-Hill Ryerson, 1987.

Sawatsky, J. *The Insiders: Government, Business, and the Lobbyists.* Toronto: McClelland & Stewart, 1987.

Sawatsky, J. *Mulroney: The Politics of Ambition.* Toronto: Macfarlane Walter & Ross, 1991.

Weston, Greg. *Reign of Error: The Inside Story of John Turner's Troubled Leadership.* Toronto: McGraw-Hill Ryerson, 1988.

MANO A MANO

Crosbie, J. *No Holds Barred: My Life in Politics.* Toronto: McClelland & Stewart, 1997.

Fraser, G. *Playing for Keeps: The Making of the Prime Minister, 1988.* Toronto: McClelland & Stewart, 1989.

Lee, R. M. *One Hundred Monkeys: The Triumph of Popular Wisdom in Canadian Politics.* Toronto: Macfarlane Walter & Ross, 1989.

Fights of Our Lives was produced by Otherwise Editions
under the *editorial and art direction* of Sara Borins

Editor Rick Archbold
Assistant editor Karen Press
Design and typesetting Knickerbocker Design
Production Implosion Post Media
Photo research Sara Borins with Karen Press, Tonia Addison, Sophie Hackett, Catherine Dean
Original illustrations Christoph Niemann
Copyeditor Rosemary Shipton
Proofreaders Karen Alliston and Tasneem Jamal
Index Christopher Blackburn
Warm-up caption research Philip Preville

Otherwise Editions offers special thanks to Michael Angel, Megan Barnes, Daniel Borins,
Christine Bourolias, Phyllis Bruce, Jean-Marc Carisse, Citizens Concerned About Free Trade,
Shannon Conway, Jennifer Devine, Greig Dymond, Anna Erwin-Iles, Rick Feldman, Bill
Greenberg, Vivian Hanwell, Todd Harris, Jennifer Heyns, Jonathan Howells, Emily Govier
Honderich, Eleanor Ireland, David Kent, Mark Kubas, Adam Levin, Michael Levine, Maya
Mavjee, Leslie McGrath, David Millar, Desmond Morton, Rob Paul, Naomi Pauls, Chris
Pommer, Michel Ponomareff, Janelle Reynolds, Alex Sadvari, Amanda Sebris, Leanne Shapton,
David Sherman, Boris Spremo, Dianna Symonds, and Iris Tupholme.

Knickerbocker offers special thanks to R.O. Blechman, Cup and Saucer, Greg Grabowy, André
Lee, Christoph Niemann, and Lauren Panepinto.